gotta
tell
you"

Lee Iacocca. Photo courtesy of Tony Spina.

"I gotta tell you"

SPEECHES OF LEE IACOCCA

Edited by Matthew W. Seeger
with a foreword by Lee Iacocca

Wayne State University Press   Detroit

Copyright © 1994 by Wayne State University Press, Detroit, Michigan 48202.
All rights are reserved. No part of this book may be reproduced without
formal permission. Manufactured in the United States of America.
99 98 97 96 95 94   5 4 3 2 1

Library of Congress Cataloging-in-Publication Data

Iacocca, Lee A.
   I gotta tell you : speeches of Lee Iacocca / edited by Matthew W. Seeger ; with a
foreword by Lee A. Iacocca.
      p. cm.
   Includes bibliographical references and index.
   ISBN 0-8143-2522-X (alk. paper). — ISBN 0-8143-2546-7 (pbk. : alk. paper)
   1. Iacocca, Lee A.   2. Industrial management—United States.
3. Automobile industry and trade—United States—Management.
I. Seeger, Matthew W. (Matthew Wayne), 1957- . II. Title.
HD9710.U52I22   1994
658.4'52—dc20   94-19337

Designer: Mary Primeau

Grateful acknowledgment is made to the Chrysler Corporation for permission to re-
print the speeches delivered by Lee Iacocca that appear in this volume.

Contents

II. Speeches to External Constituencies

III. Speeches Concerning Social Values and Issues

Contents

Acknowledgments

Any edited book is dependent on the cooperation, support, and assistance of a number of people. This book was particularily dependent on the cooperation and support of people at the Chrysler Corporation and Wayne State University. Chief among those is Mike Morrison, executive director of communication at Chrysler. He assisted in selecting appropriate speeches, provided critical insight into the various speaking contexts, and lent his considerable insight into corporate communication to this project. Mr. Iacocca's interest and cooperation with this project were also instrumental. His willingness not only to make these important documents available but also to prepare the foreword to this book is indicative of his commitment to excellence in corporate communication and his willingness to share his experiences. Thanks to Barbara Spicer for her research assistance and to Tim Borchers for his very keen eye. Jack Kay and David Magidson provided support and encouragement. Arthur Evans and the staff at Wayne State University Press provided excellent editorial support, and Wayne State University Graduate School provided financial support.

Finally, I would like to thank Beth, Maggie, and Henry for their patience and support. I dedicate my portion of this work to them.

Matthew Seeger

Foreword
Lee Iacocca

Like just about everybody else, I grew up scared to death at the thought of standing in front of a group of people and giving a speech. It still terrifies me. When I landed my first important job at Ford, they sent me to a Dale Carnegie course. The idea was to make me more comfortable in front of an audience, and it worked. The fear didn't go away, but I learned how to control it. Fear takes a lot of energy, I discovered, and channeling all that energy into the speech itself is the best way to make it work *for* you instead of *against* you.

I don't know how many speeches I gave in my forty-six years in the auto industry, but it was easily more than a thousand. By actual count, I gave 663 during my fourteen years at Chrysler. Some were to small groups of employees, dealers, or suppliers. Others were to large audiences of several thousand. One was to five hundred thousand people in Central Park during the big Liberty Weekend celebration in 1986. I spoke in the Superdome in New Orleans and in the Great Hall of the People of Beijing. And I spoke to an eighth-grade graduation class in a small park across from their school in Lowell, Massachusetts. I spoke in the main ballroom of the Waldorf-Astoria so many times that the waiters used to lip-sync my best lines.

Communication has been my most valuable management tool. Some business leaders succeed because they are technical or financial geniuses. I realized early that I was pretty good at using the spoken word to move an organization in the direction I wanted, and I used that tool every day. I realized that if people understand what you want them to do, and it makes sense, they'll do it.

11

But effective communication has to do more than just deliver information. It has to motivate. In every speech I give, the objective is to motivate. You can deliver information in a letter or tack it on a bulletin board. But motivation takes human contact, and a speech is the best vehicle for one person to motivate many.

During most of my time at Chrysler, I was a contrarian. I gave speech after speech saying that the "Roaring Eighties" were going to collapse in a heap someday, that the huge public debt we were running up would cripple our kids, that gas should be taxed to conserve energy and encourage people to buy smaller cars, and that throwing open our market to people who were shutting us out of their markets was sapping America's industrial competitiveness. I deliberately set out to make audiences uncomfortable. I wanted them to think. I wanted to motivate them to challenge much of the conventional wisdom of the time.

A good speech, like a good novel, is constructed around conflict. If all is right with the world, there's no need for a speech. Usually, the conflict is between something that's comfortable but wrong and something that's disturbing but true. The best speeches are those in which you tell people things they don't want to hear in order to get them to believe things they don't want to believe so they'll be motivated to do things they don't want to do.

When I told the American Bar Association in 1987 that lawyers were inflicting grievous harm on the country and they should be more responsible in using our courts to distribute justice instead of redistributing wealth, I didn't know whether they would applaud or pelt me with tomatoes. Fortunately, they applauded, and did it on their feet. The truth may sometimes hurt, but there's always a market for it if it's sold right.

A speech is a sales opportunity. I had a reputation all during my career for being a good salesman. And any good salesman knows that you have to do more than just interest the customer in your product, you have to get the order. That's true whether the product is a car or a public policy that needs to be changed. In almost all of my speeches at Chrysler, I wound up by asking for the order. I threw my arguments right into the front row and asked the audience what they were willing to do to help solve the problems I was talking about. There has to be a call to action. You can't let the audience off the hook. They have to leave the auditorium wanting to do something.

Running Chrysler was a full-time job. I didn't enjoy flying around the country giving speeches on top of my other responsibilities. But I did enjoy the satisfaction I got when people would come up to me afterward or write me a letter and say that I'd helped change their minds on some of the burning issues of the day.

Oratory used to be what television and newspapers are today—the principal means of mass communication. Today, speeches have not only been replaced by the mass media, but too often they are written and delivered mainly to accommodate those media, with sound bites for TV or pithy quotes that look good in print. Too often, especially with political speeches, the speaker plays to the cameras in the back of the room or the reporters taking notes over in the corner. The audience is reduced to a prop.

That's unfortunate. And it may explain why there are so many bad speeches given every day.

I'm flattered that several hundred people would take an hour or so out of their lives to come and hear what I have to say. I get their full attention, and they get mine. In a previous life, I may have been an actor, because I feel the same sense of obligation to an audience that a good performer does.

I've been asked many times what makes a good speech. Good writing, practice, something worthwhile to say—all of them are important. But I think if a speaker begins with that deep sense of obligation to the audience, everything else falls into place.

Lee Iacocca as Business Statesman

Matthew W. Seeger

Rarely has a business executive captured the attention of society in as influential a way as Lee A. Iacocca. Much of this attention can be attributed to the success of Iacocca the business person. A significant portion of his notoriety also must be attributed to Iacocca the communicator. During his tenure as chief executive officer at the Chrysler Corporation, Iacocca was an avid and inordinately successful communicator with internal audiences including employees and dealers and a vocal advocate for the American automobile industry with external audiences. He also has served as spokesperson for more general business issues and concerns. Iacocca gave more than six hundred formal speeches as CEO of Chrysler, and he continues to speak out on important issues since his retirement, including the Clinton administration's campaign to ratify the North American Free Trade Agreement. His success as a communicator has helped to redefine the model of the proactive business leader.

Iacocca's attention to issues of competitiveness, trade, and jobs has resonated with large and diverse audiences. Following the resurrection of Chrysler in the early 1980s, he became the voice of his industry, arguing for social and political reforms and governmental regulations that directly benefit Chrysler and the entire domestic car industry. He was offered a vacant U.S. Senate seat in Pennsylvania, and he is frequently mentioned as a possible presidential candidate. His speaking schedule took him all over the world. He spoke to the National Press Club, Chrysler employees, the American

15

Chamber of Commerce in Japan, newspaper editors and publishers, members of Congress, Chinese business leaders, the National Governors Conference, the League of Women Voters, the Detroit Economic Club, automobile trade associations, and stockholders and dealers. His writings include editorials, a syndicated newspaper column, and his best-selling books *Iacocca: An Autobiography* in 1984 and *Talking Straight* in 1988.

Throughout his writing and speaking, Iacocca has offered a pragmatic approach to America's business, economic, and social problems. Specifically, he has argued consistently for a new federal industrial policy based on the government-union-management cooperation that saved Chrysler. The Iacocca message also draws heavily on powerful themes of patriotism, liberty, family, cooperative free enterprise, preserving jobs, and the American Dream. In his straight-talking and direct style, Iacocca also has consistently identified Japanese business practices, the trade deficit, and fair trade as America's major economic obstacles.

In successfully addressing nontraditional topics and audiences, Iacocca changed the model of proactive corporate leadership from that of a business speaker toward the notion of business statesman and ambassador. Iacocca represents a new kind of corporate spokesperson who discusses the organization's role and responsibility in society in broad terms while at the same time defending, justifying, and legitimizing the organization's actions. Public address, in Iacocca's view, is a critical part of the management process. The message of the business statesman is not limited to the domain of business but branches out to address a wide range of social issues. Iacocca's messages, articulated in a number of public speeches before diverse and often nontraditional audiences, represent an important body of work worthy of critical and scholarly attention.

IACOCCA AS BUSINESS COMMUNICATOR

Business communication in the form of executive speaking is seen most often as a necessary yet usually ritualized, poorly executed, and essentially sterile activity. Business leaders usually rise to the tops of their organizations based on their technical expertise, financial savvy, or managerial abilities rather than their rhetorical skills. Conventional wisdom suggests that the typical business speech is mundane, colorless, and generally lacking in any compelling style. Business speakers most often read a prepared manuscript with little enthusiasm, animation, or flair. The business speech itself is frequently culled from corporate manuals, policy statements, and other speeches, assembled by a committee and drained of all personality by countless reviews, revisions, and approvals. Executives, too busy with the day-to-day demands of running a company, delegate the task of speech writing to support staff. Facts in the form of statistics usually comprise the primary supporting materials. Audiences are typically composed of employees, stockholders, or industry groups, who share the speaker's overall outlook. For internal audiences, speeches are characteristically limited to the informative function and avoid any attempt to persuade or entertain. For external audiences, and even many internal audiences, the speech that reveals the least is often judged as the most successful by legal staffs and public relations professionals who seek to avoid any controversy or risk. Traditional wisdom even suggests that business leaders should maintain a sense of personal anonymity and remain well hidden behind the corporate veil. Most executives leave the difficult issues and hard audiences to public relations professionals. The high levels of social and political influence attributed to business leaders typically occur behind the scenes rather than through participation in public debates and discussions of social problems and issues.

Much of this conventional wisdom regarding business communication and business speaking began to crumble in 1978 when Lee Iacocca started speaking out first about the difficulties facing the Chrysler Corporation and later about a host of business, economic, political, and social problems. Several factors distinguish Iacocca's public communication from that of other prominent business speakers.

First, Iacocca's style is direct, to the point, and highly credible. With a "call it as it is" approach to issues, Iacocca's often blunt discussion of business and social problems appeals to both blue- and white-collar workers. The practical business person's approach to social problems and issues is particularly attractive to audiences frustrated with government's inability to solve complex problems. Business speakers also have more latitude to address controversial issues than elected officials. Iacocca acknowledged that much of his credibility is simply because "People are hungry for somebody to tell the truth" (Iacocca and Novak 277). Moreover, Iacocca's unparalleled record of success as a leader, manager, and problem solver is clearly evident in the form of a healthy and viable Chrysler Corporation. Even in those instances when he adopts the unabashed tenor of a salesperson, Iacocca offers a believable message.

Second, Iacocca uses the notoriety garnered from the unprecedented turnaround at Chrysler to address larger audiences and more general issues. In many ways, he symbolizes Chrysler's resurrection which, in turn, is symbolic of America's larger economic struggle. In Iacocca's discourse, the Chrysler story is a microcosm of America's problems as well as a source of practical and tested solutions. Audiences, hungry for success stories in an economy dominated by reports of hostile takeovers, savings and loan scandals, insider trading, and ballooning federal and trade deficits, crave the Chrysler story.

And the Chrysler story, built around a heroic struggle against overwhelming odds culminating in stunning success, is powerful and compelling.

Third, unlike many business leaders, Iacocca takes a public stand regarding a wide range of complex and sensitive economic and social issues, including education reform, the trade deficit, the federal budget deficit, business competitiveness, and, most recently, the North American Free Trade Agreement. Conventional wisdom suggests that business leaders avoid controversial issues, for fear of alienating potential customers and investors. Iacocca rejects the notion that business people should stick only to business issues and has added his voice to a variety of important public debates.

Fourth, unlike most business speakers, Iacocca appeals to fundamental values. In Iacocca's message, business is much more than making a profit. Business is also related to deeply held values and beliefs concerning jobs, sacrifice, cooperation, and the uniqueness of the American experience. In appealing to basic values, Iacocca created speeches that were more powerful and persuasive than typical business addresses. His value appeals are often framed in the rich imagery and symbolism typically associated with ceremonial or epideictic addresses.

Finally, Iacocca's skill as a public communicator sets him apart from most other business speakers. He speaks with authority, flair, and an animated delivery, frequently embellishing the prepared manuscript with off-the-cuff remarks and reactions. This spontaneity contributes to his believability. He appears confident and relaxed and is able to establish a sense of personal rapport with an audience, often referring directly to members of the audience in his speeches. Most important, perhaps, is that Iacocca is sensitive to the needs, interests, and concerns of his audiences and understands the process of communication and his responsibilities as a communicator.

THE CHRYSLER SAGA

In the mid-1970s, the Chrysler Corporation, third in the domestic auto industry, was being ravaged by competition from low-priced, fuel-efficient, and high-quality imports. With a badly outdated product line, poor quality, and gas-hungry products, Chrysler was struggling to compete (Moritz and Seaman). Chrysler management, overwhelmed by problems, moved quickly to bring in the articulate and well-respected Lee A. Iacocca, recently fired from Ford, for a last-ditch effort to save the company. The dual headlines in the November 2, 1978, *Detroit Free Press* read: "Chrysler Losses Worst Ever" and "Lee Iacocca Joins Chrysler."

When the Arab oil embargo of 1978 hit the domestic automobile industry only a few months later, Chrysler was, for all intents and purposes, in its final death throes, barely able to meet its multimillion-dollar payroll and struggling to keep creditors at bay while continuing to run up record losses. Members of the financial community predicted that it would be only a matter of time before the company opted for receivership.

Iacocca quickly recognized that the only viable option for Chrysler's survival—a package of federal guaranteed loans—required an active coalition of support from workers, management, creditors, suppliers, government, and customers. This unique coalition of support was created, bolstered, and justified by compelling and persuasive arguments offered by the new CEO. Iacocca argued that Chrysler was victimized by an irrational federal industrial policy of trade, investment, and competitiveness. His ideas struck a strong chord throughout industrial Middle America.

In creating this coalition of support, Iacocca had to overcome traditional free-market wisdom, grounded in classical Adam Smith economics, and recreate, at least symbolically, his corporation. The fundamental concepts of free-market economics dictated that a corporation like Chrysler close its doors, that Chrysler workers lose their jobs and local communities forfeit their tax base. Free-market principles of private enterprise were firmly rooted in the almost sacred notion that economic competitiveness alone determined survival. Government intervention, the purists argued, would upset the entire system of private capitalism and establish a dangerous precedent. Chrysler soon would be followed by a long line of poorly managed organizations seeking similar federal bailouts. As economist Alan Greenspan observed, "Propping up failing companies with government loans delays the shift of resources into more productive ventures" ("Was the Bailout a Blunder?" 54). Senator William Proxmire argued, "We will have better business management in the long run if we allow the tough, cold cruel system of free enterprise to work" ("Was the Bailout a Blunder?" 54). Iacocca rejected these critics as ideologues and instead emphasized the practical benefits of supporting Chrysler, including the salvation of thousands of American manufacturing jobs and maintaining the local, state, and federal tax base. He argued that Chrysler's inability to compete was the result of hostile federal policies and predatory trade practices by the Japanese.

Second, Iacocca was forced to demonstrate that various groups, including workers, creditors, governments, and suppliers, had a vested interest in the salvation of Chrysler Corporation. He did so by emphasizing that these groups had a stake in Chrysler's survival and that the impending bankruptcy was so unpalatable to an already shaky economy that it was not a realistic option. Reich and Donahue, in their study of the economic impact of the Chrysler guarantee loans, suggest that the new Chrysler Corporation that arose from this effort was an extended network of claims and obligations. Iacocca made the stakes clear for various groups, who, in turn, actively supported the company. When Iacocca addressed Congress about the loans, he began by noting, "I do not speak alone here today. I speak for the hundreds of thousands of people whose livelihood depends on Chrysler remaining in business" (Iacocca and Novak 215).

In addition, Iacocca needed to recreate Chrysler symbolically for its most important constituency: the car-buying public. He did so by personally representing the company in television commercials and providing personal assurances about Chrysler products. In these commercials, Iacocca was aggressive, direct, and tough, traits that soon were associated with Chrysler. This personification of a large corporation was unique and enhanced the sense of identification consumers felt with the struggling Chrysler and its visible leader. The acting-out of Chrysler's struggle on television also increased its dramatic appeal. As Reich and Donahue note, Iacocca's commercials were designed "not so much to sell Chrysler cars, as the company itself" (215). Consumers bought Chrysler products in part because they were compelled to participate in the Chrysler drama and wanted to help Iacocca succeed.

Much has been written about the resurrection of Chrysler in an effort to assess what factors accounted for this unprecedented recovery. Several observers have suggested that the economy rebounded at a fortuitous time for Chrysler. Others have argued that the federal loans and Chrysler turnaround were a victory for the interests of big business. Chrysler, they argue, was simply too big to die ("Was the Bailout a Blunder?" 54). Some communication critics have argued that Chrysler survived because it was able to atone publicly for the guilt associated with the bailout (Foss). Most observers, including Iacocca, point to this extended network of claims and obligations, including union, management, government, and consumers, as the primary reason Chrysler survived. Chrysler translated this network into an active coalition of economic and political support.

Following Chrysler's almost miraculous return to profitability, Iacocca became a highly sought-after speaker and successful author, not only because of his experience at Chrysler but also for his perspective on the industry, on business problems in general, and on general social problems, values, and issues. He was the modern archetype of the American folk hero, a scrappy underdog, the son of immigrant parents who through hard work, vision, personal risk, and sacrifice had brought a huge American company back from the brink of bankruptcy (Dionisopoulos). The faltering American economy had created hardship for many, and Iacocca came to symbolize this larger struggle. He was tapped by President Reagan to head the Statue of Liberty and Ellis Island renovation, a project Iacocca considered sacred. His first book, *Iacocca: An Autobiography,* was almost instantly an international bestseller and even sold very well in Japan. He accompanied President Bush on a much-publicized trip to Japan to help open Japanese markets for American goods. Later, after Iacocca's retirement from Chrysler, President Clinton asked for his help in selling the North American Free Trade Agreement, a job he tackled with his usual gusto.

Few public figures, even those very few who rise to the heads of large and profitable corporations, ever reach this level of prominence. Business leaders who make an impact on the basis of their ability to publicly frame and articulate compelling views of critical social and economic issues are even rarer. With his success as a public communicator, Iacocca has provided a new model for business communication which reaches beyond the sterile and ritualized business speech and beyond the traditional topics and audiences such a figure usually addresses.

IACOCCA'S SPEECHES

Although the Chrysler success gave Iacocca the businessman the unique opportunity to address wider audiences and issues, Iacocca's success in these situations must be attributed in large measure to his speaking style. During high school, Iacocca participated in extemporaneous speaking and academic debate, which he said taught him "how to think on my feet" (Iacocca and Novak 16). Early in his career at Ford, Iacocca attended Dale Carnegie seminars, to which he also attributes much of his public speaking success. The impromptu speaking exercises helped reduce his speech anxiety (Iacocca and Novak 54). In writing about speaking style, Iacocca often makes reference to the fundamental importance of public address for any business leader. In particular, he refers to the critical role of public speaking in persuading and motivating. His writings about communication also suggest a command of the fundamental principles of public address, including careful organization, preparation, audience analysis, use of direct language, and the need to be personable. The performance nature of public communication and the need to entertain, critical parts of the Iacocca speaking style, are carefully designed into his messages. Most important perhaps, is that Iacocca seems to have an intuitive grasp of the role of communication in effective leadership. In recounting the loss of a student council election, he once wrote, "I had not yet learned what I know now—that the ability to communicate is everything" (Iacocca and Novak 18).

This volume examines the public discourse of Lee Iacocca from several divergent perspectives. Iacocca's discourse is representative of many of the public speaking situations corporate and industry leaders typically face. His addresses to employees, shareholders, and dealers and his messages during crisis are, in many ways, typical of the communicative responsibilities of most CEOs. At the same time, however, it must be recognized that Iacocca's skill as a communicator and many of the audiences he had an opportunity to address are almost entirely unique. His addresses about the Statue of Liberty and many of his addresses to international audiences have much more in common with presidential rhetoric than with traditional business communication. In these cases, Iacocca was speaking as a national statesman who could shed light on American values and the nature of the American Dream. In order to capture the diversity of Iacocca's public addresses, while attending to the most influential and memorable, speeches in this volume have been selected and organized in terms of both the audiences and the issues he addressed.

The first section focuses on Iacocca's addresses to internal audiences and constituencies. These are in many ways typical business speeches. This section contains addresses to employees and dealers, including those who joined Chrysler after its acquisition of American Motors Corporation. Also in this section are addresses given during annual corporate meetings. Two of these shareholder addresses, Iacocca's first when the company was facing the strong possibility of bankruptcy and his last as CEO after almost fourteen years at Chrysler, are presented.

The second section focuses on addresses to external audiences. Iacocca's crisis communication is examined, including press conferences about the indictment of Chrysler executives for odometer tampering and his remarks on the closing of the former American Motors Corporation plant in Kenosha, Wisconsin. Iacocca also gave several speeches to external audiences in which he examined the problems and the future of the automobile industry. In two of these speeches, Iacocca served as an ambassador to international audiences. Among those issues Iacocca addressed most often and directly are trade with Japan and the continuing problem of the American trade deficit. In these often controversial speeches, Iacocca was most clearly involved in the process of corporate advocacy, arguing for specific changes in federal policy that would help his company and his industry. Finally, among those addresses in which he represented business and industry to nonbusiness audiences are speeches in which he discussed the general problems faced by American business. In these speeches, Iacocca typically focused on broad issues of economic competitiveness and the development of favorable business environments.

The third section turns to those speeches of special occasion, when Iacocca spoke as a celebrity and statesman. This section includes his commencement speeches at the University of Southern California and Michigan State University. Iacocca also has given special attention to issues of educational reform, and two of those speeches are presented. Finally, this section includes two of the speeches Iacocca gave when he served as chair of the Statue of Liberty-Ellis Island Centennial Commission. These speeches are rich in imagery, solidly grounded in Iacocca's interpretation of the American Dream, and they draw heavily on the symbolism of the Chrysler saga.

The essays included in this book provide critical and historical contexts for Iacocca's speeches. Several recurrent themes about the constraints and characteristics of corporate rhetoric and about the specific speeches of Lee Iacocca are evident. First, several of the essays point out the important role of genre in understanding Iacocca's addresses. A rhetorical genre is a particular type of speech that conforms to particular audience expectations and conventions (Ware and Linkugel). Shareholder addresses, for example, may be understood as a class of speeches with specific goals given on a recurring occasion to a particular type of audience. Similarly, commencement addresses are expected to celebrate the graduates' success and provide some advice about their movement out into the world. Iacocca's success as a communicator may be attributed in part to his ability to speak to the constraints of the genre while at the same time making these generic addresses fresh.

Second, several of the writers who examine Iacocca's speeches point out that much of his speaking is corporate advocacy. Iacocca spoke from a particular position as CEO of Chrysler and as an industry leader. This position carries with it the responsibility of advocating policies that would benefit his company and industry. Iacocca's rhetoric may be distinguished from that of many other corporate speakers on this basis. He used public address to call for changes in the political and economic environment that would help Chrysler. While politicians are expected to publicly advocate specific legislation, industry leaders do not typically involve themselves publicly in such debates. In serving as an advocate, however, Iacocca did not simply react to problems but sought to manage public issues by contributing his point of view to the debate.

A third theme noted by critics examining these speeches concerns Iacocca's use of supporting materials and appeals. Iacocca draws heavily on the field of arguments based in logic, rationality, and bottom-line facts typically associated with business discourse. He balances his speeches, however, by also drawing on the field of symbols, values, and dreams in constructing balanced motivational appeals. Business speeches are not typically grounded in fundamental values such as liberty, freedom, and the American Dream.

Fourth, the issue of credibility is a recurring point of attack in any careful examination of Iacocca's discourse. Iacocca is spontaneous and believable. For an American public used to empty platitudes and puffery from business spokespersons, Iacocca is refreshing. He revived his corporation, paid back the federal loans, and kept his word. In typical straightforward fashion, he told his television audience, "If you find a better car, buy it!" Given the long history of deep distrust of big American businesses, Iacocca's credibility is particularly noteworthy. It is one of the most important factors setting him apart from other business celebrities.

Finally, there is the question of the Iacocca image. A number of observers and critics have suggested that Iacocca is "larger than life," that he has taken on symbolic meaning beyond the scope of the immediate situation and message (Dionisopoulos). Iacocca has come to symbolize a number of larger issues and values associated with business, including fair trade, American entrepreneurism, and success. Iacocca also symbolizes fundamental American values such as hard work, cooperation, and the need to continue to fight against overwhelming odds. And he symbolizes the powerful value of economic success. The media contributed to this symbolization of Iacocca by first depicting Chrysler's efforts as "hopeless" and then depicting the Chrysler recovery as "miraculous." Iacocca was portrayed by the media as the primary agent of the miracle (Dionisopoulos 238). The rich imagery and symbolism of the Statue of Liberty-Ellis Island renovation further embellished Iacocca the symbol. He became not only the agent of Chrysler's salvation but a "reflection of [American] cultural values and the promise of our greatness" (Dionisopoulos 238). This symbolic image is a powerful asset which enriches both his credibility and the meaning of his message.

CONCLUSION

Lee A. Iacocca and the resurrection of Chrysler will continue to hold much fascination for students of business, economics, management, and leadership for some time to come. It is not possible to understand Iacocca the business leader without examining Iacocca the business statesman. Iacocca made the Chrysler story meaningful to employees, shareholders, dealers, customers, and the general public.

While Iacocca has demonstrated overwhelming success as a corporate communicator and business statesman, he is not without some very vocal critics. He has been labeled racist for his persistent attacks on Japanese trade practices. His calls for a national industrial policy have been labeled self-serving, protectionist, anticonsumer, and anti-free enterprise. Others have referred to him as an apologist for the shoddy managerial practices of American business and industry. Iacocca, however, seems to accept the fact that in any society built on open discussion and debate, such criticism goes with the territory. If anything, the criticism has enriched the public dialogue about the evolving roles and responsibilities of American business and industry.

WORKS CITED

Dionisopoulos, George N. "A Case Study in Print Media and Heroic Myth: Lee Ia- cocca 1978-1985." *Southern Speech Communication Journal* 53 (1988): 227–43.

Foss, Sonja K. "Retooling an Image: Chrysler Corporation's Rhetoric of Redemp- tion." *Western Journal of Speech Communication* 48 (1984): 75–91.

Iacocca, Lee A. and William Novak. *Iacocca: An Autobiography.* New York: Ban- tam, 1984.

Moritz, Michael, and Barrett Seaman. *Going for Broke: Lee Iacocca's Battle to Save Chrysler.* Garden City, N.Y.: Anchor, 1984.

Reich, William, and William Donahue. *New Deals: The Chrysler Revival and the American System.* New York: Times Books, 1985.

Ware, B. L., and Linkugel, Wil. "They Spoke in Defense of Themselves: On Ge- neric Criticism of Apologia." *Quarterly Journal of Speech* 54 (1973): 273–283.

"Was the Bailout a Blunder?" *Time* 21 March 1983: 54.

I

Speeches to Internal Constituencies

1. Lee Iacocca as Internal Issues Manager in Speeches to Employees and Dealers

Carl Botan

As the 1970s closed, the auto industry was in full recession. That recession did not have the depth of the Great Depression, but it did have its own unique character. One of the things that made this recession different from previous ones was greatly increased market competition from Japanese auto-makers, with import penetration of the U.S. auto market reaching 26.5 percent by April 1980 ("Wrapup 1980" 9). Such competition raised the strong possibility that this recession might not end with things returning to normal among the Big Three, as they had after so many other recessions. Many people were speculating that there might not even be a Big Three after the recession, with most of the speculation focusing on the weakest of the three—Chrysler.

Lee Iacocca is best known for piloting the Chrysler Corporation through this brush with bankruptcy, although he has accomplished many other things. Possibly no other example of saving a major corporation has been so widely followed as the Chrysler comeback, and it is quite possible that no other corporate leader has been so widely credited with a great business success. His tenure at Chrysler transformed Iacocca into a national, even international, figure (Andersen 30) one who has been referred to as a folk hero (Reibstein and Washington 31), and advocated as a candidate for the presidency ("Wrapup 1987" 10).

Chrysler's brush with death left all its stakeholders, particularly employees and dealers, indelibly marked. In speeches delivered in later years, such as the 1984, 1987, 1988, and 1992 speeches discussed in this chapter, the memories of that great struggle and the price paid to win it were still major

29

themes. A unique relationship between management and labor had been formed, and with it came high expectations for internal communication, as evidenced by the UAW's Douglas Fraser serving on the Chrysler Board of Directors—in a largely communication-centered role. While the first responsibility of any corporate communicator is to communicate with internal audiences, the Chrysler situation put special demands on Iacocca's skills as an internal communicator.

IACOCCA'S INDUSTRIAL RELATIONS ROLE

Iacocca's role in American industrial relations history is unique. Few industrial leaders have attained such high stature in the eyes of their own employees, and fewer still have achieved this during a period of economic decline and cutbacks in their companies. The strategies and values that Iacocca used to pilot the Chrysler Corporation through a massive downsizing and near bankruptcy, while maintaining both the support of his internal audiences and a working, if sometimes guarded, relationship with the UAW, have impressed most observers.

Iacocca sees himself as a communicator and a leader, rather than as a technician or a financial expert. With this self-perception, it is not surprising to find that Iacocca sees his own function as identifying issues and using communication to get others to join in attacking them. Iacocca defines himself and his speeches as primarily concerned with what has come to be known as issues management. This chapter analyzes four of Iacocca's speeches to internal audiences in which he sought to manage major issues.

Two points condition this analysis of Iacocca's role, the first methodological and the second a matter of perspective. Methodologically, the speeches of famous persons often have been used as windows that open directly onto the speaker's motivation and strategy and indirectly onto the speaker's assessments of the values and fears motivating the audience. Such an approach has the advantage of using primary sources to focus the analysis on the speaker's own words rather than on the researcher's data collection techniques. Such an approach is limited, however, by its reliance only on the speaker's words in formal settings. In a large and complex organization such as Chrysler, communication is meaningfully interpreted only within a larger context. Additionally, a CEO of a complex organization has many other channels for defining and enforcing values and strategies. These channels are largely invisible, particularly to an external audience. A methodology that focuses on formal speeches accepts such potential limitations as the price for gaining the advantages of a window onto the speaker's thoughts and what the speaker assumes to be the values and motivations of the audience.

Second, the credit given to Iacocca for his leading role in saving Chrysler is entirely appropriate. The importance assigned to the loan guarantees from the federal government is also appropriate. Chrysler was also saved in large part by the tremendous sacrifices of its employees, a fact acknowledged often by Iacocca. Tens of thousands of Chrysler employees worked for years under concession contracts. These employees also accepted more layoffs and altered work rules than their fellow autoworkers, thus making additional contributions to Chrysler's economic survival. For many, there was a good return on this investment when their jobs were saved and their economic future assured. For others, jobs were lost. In this analysis, I draw on the perspectives of the UAW audience and my experience as one of Iacocca's troops during a time of threatened bankruptcy, concessions, and downsizing.[1]

Highly successful CEOs are, quite naturally, larger-than-life figures to assembly-line workers. But even here, Iacocca was a unique case: Iacocca's leadership was felt, and/or commented on, almost daily up and down the line. He was a presence for rank-and-file assembly-line workers in a way that was qualitatively different from his predecessors or the leaders of the other auto companies. Of course, not everyone agreed with him. Iacocca, however, personified leadership and company policy, in effect making leadership concrete, in a work environment in which the work group foreman, general foreman, and industrial engineer are usually all the leadership you see or care about. In fact, there was some level of identification with Iacocca because he had been fired from Ford, many thought unjustly, by Henry Ford II.

Many UAW members, and even many UAW leaders, spoke of Iacocca during the crisis as the best possible person to be protecting all their jobs. It was not uncommon to hear other union members' comments suggesting that Iacocca would make a good candidate for governor of Michigan or even president of the United States. The latter suggestion became somewhat of a cause célèbre a few years later.

All of this resulted in our listening a little more than usual when Iacocca spoke—the greatest asset an internal communicator can have. (Ironically, this is the same asset Iacocca was afraid he was losing in the 1992 speech discussed below.) The same issues of credibility were probably present for Chrysler-Plymouth dealers who also had suffered severely during Chrysler's near-death experience. Iacocca had been a palpable force in their survival as he took to the airwaves in Chrysler commercials to sell cars personally.

THE ISSUES MANAGEMENT APPROACH

This approach has sometimes been referred to as strategic communication, external communication, public relations, public affairs, government relations, and various other names. Jones and Chase, discussed two key ideas in issues management. The first involves trends that are the detectable changes that precede issues. Issues themselves are continuing trends, events, or conditions that affect an organization's performance and are ready for decision (Culbertson, Jeffers, Stone, and Terrell). The second key idea was a category system for discussing the change strategies used by issues managers.

For Jones and Chase, "discernible trends always precede emerging issues" (3). The process of watching for trends in what is going on around us is also known as environmental scanning. Iacocca's record, the success of the Mustang and the minivan, the prediction of Chrysler's turnaround, the acquisition of AMC, and numerous other instances documented throughout this book, suggest that among his primary skills was a unique ability to scan the environment, to discern trends, and to lay strategic plans to manage the issues identified from those trends. In short, one of Iacocca's primary strengths was an ability to manage issues.

Jones and Chase defined three catagories of possible strategic responses to issues. The first, and simplest, response strategy is reactive. This strategy, because it does not feature environmental scanning for trends, often involves reacting to issues for which careful plans have not been laid. As a result, it seeks to continue past behavior and postpone making any real changes in the organization, and it "can be summed up when management says, 'Let's stonewall this issue'" (16). The second kind of response strategy is adaptive, in which the organization seeks to make "an adjustment . . . that makes it more fit for existence under the conditions of its environment" (6). This strategy features environmental scanning for trends because "it relies on planning as a tool to anticipate change and to offer an accommodation" (16). The third kind of response strategy is dynamic, in which issue managers "consider the past and look forward to future events or conditions" (6). Here the response focuses on understanding current trends, and the issues that will result from them, well enough to plan future courses of action that will make the organization a participant in determining how the issues evolve. In 1985, Crable and Vibbert extended the original Jones and Chase category system to include what they called catalytic responses in which "the organization does not wait for things to happen around it . . . instead . . . [it] aims at promoting or making things happen; it 'urges' organizations to take the offensive and engage in affirmative action" (9). Crable and Vibbert said that the catalytic strategy "begins earlier in the issues management process" (9) than even the dynamic strategy.

As the speeches in this book make clear, Iacocca, while sometimes having to react to issues, specialized in creating adaptive strategies whenever possible. Iacocca's consistent use of speaking opportunities to build support for overriding public policy goals, such as trade restrictions on Japanese imports, suggests that his preferred strategy for managing issues may be similar to Crable and Vibbert's catalytic model.

The remainder of this chapter applies a trends-issues-strategy analysis to four of Iacocca's internal speeches. The use of this issues management model, will allow positioning of each speech within the trends it grew out of while at the same time facilitating issue and strategy identification.

REMARKS TO CHRYSLER-PLYMOUTH
AND DODGE DEALERS

Trends. Iacocca and the Chrysler-Plymouth dealers were in a festive mood in 1984. Dealers are independent business people, and so are not internal in the same sense as Chrysler management or hourly employees. Nonetheless, the relationship between dealer and manufacturer is one of mutual interdependence. Chrysler depended on dealers to sell and service its products, while dealers required strong products and support from the company. Chrysler dealers had suffered during the near bankruptcy, and many had not survived. The mood in 1984, however, was confident because of what Iacocca characterized as "rock-sound success," as demonstrated by all-time record earnings of $706 million in the first quarter, more profit than in any twelve-month period in the sixty-year history of Chrysler ("Detroit Rolls in the Dough" 9). This was followed by an even bigger second quarter, with $803 million dollars in earnings. Chrysler, however, still had to operate on the tightest margins in the Big Three. GM and Ford had not matched Chrysler's percentage improvement and did not have the euphoria of Chrysler's turnaround to build on; nevertheless, they reported profits for the same period of $897 million and approximately $1.6 billion, respectively. Ford's share of the domestic market had also increased 2.6 percent over the same period.

The brush with corporate extinction was still fresh in everyone's minds. This is what Iacocca referred to when he said early in the speech, "This is a family reunion . . . of a family that's been through some rough times and has stuck together through it all." The celebratory and self-congratulatory aspects of the 1984 dealers announcement show were in direct response and contrast to the recent experience of everyone in the room.

Issue. Iacocca identified "three tough issues" that Chrysler would have to "manage [our way] around": interest rates, labor negotiations, and Japanese imports. But these were really just examples of the larger issue facing the company. Chrysler needed to agree on a strategic plan to avoid facing bankruptcy again in the next down cycle in the auto industry. Specifically, Iacocca wanted to combat any tendency toward complacency and make sure there was no letdown after the recent victory over bankruptcy. For example, he said: "You remember what interest rates did to us a few years ago? The prime rate was moving every week—mostly up. Well, with the deficits now projected at $200 billion per year for the next five years, interest rates sure aren't coming down."

Strategy. Although there were adaptive aspects to these speeches, the strategy Iacocca used was largely dynamic because it focused on potential future problems if current trends were not responded to effectively. There were three elements to this strategy.

First, Iacocca announced plans to invest close to $10 billion over five years, launch several new models, and build on recent improvements in productivity. As a second strategy, Iacocca called on the assembled dealers to make a shared commitment to help cement relations with customers through better treatment. One of the main trends Iacocca was attacking was the pricing policy of some dealers. The new minivans, a success story to rival the legendary Mustang, were selling faster than they could be built. Some dealers had taken advantage of the opportunity to charge more than the sticker price for them. Iacocca appealed to pride by saying, "when you get above sticker, you haven't made much of a sale, have you? All you've done is fill an order," and to guilt when he said, "All you're doing is charging whatever the marketplace will allow. Well, on that theory, I could have raised the Voyager price a couple of grand and pocketed it myself." The third strategy was to position others, such as the government and competitors, as the primary agent of future problems because they refused to accept Iacocca's positions, particularly on import restraints. For example, he sarcastically said, "Never mind that Japanese cars have an unfair advantage of $1,600 per car," and "Never mind that another million American jobs are up for grabs."

REMARKS TO AMERICAN MOTORS
CORPORATION DEALERS

Trends. The heady days of turnaround and record profits had faded by 1987, and Chrysler's market share stood at 11.5 percent of the U.S. car and truck market (Hampton and Rossant 23). In 1987, Chrysler was looking for strategies to reverse several lean years. One such strategy was to take over the long-struggling American Motors. AMC was associated with two pieces of Americana: the Rambler and Jeep nameplates. Jeep was known both nationally and internationally and was very successful, accounting for more than 4 percent of U.S. truck sales even while AMCs car sales had slipped to less than 1 percent of the 1986 market (Hampton and Rossant 23). Acquiring the Jeep nameplate was expected to make a major contribution to Chrysler, leading to as much as a 2-point increase in market share (Hampton and Rossant 32). AMC was a candidate for such a move because it had lost $91.3 million in 1986, and its parent, Renault of France, expected to lose $707 million in 1987 (Lowell 34). Jeep was the plum, but other parts of AMC, including dealers, could not be entirely sure of their future in the merger.

AMC and Chrysler had been working cooperatively since the large-bodied Chrysler M-cars had begun production at AMC's Kenosha, Wisconsin, plant in February (Hampton and Rossant 33) and discussions had started about assembling the small Omni/Horizon cars there as well (Lowell 34). As the merger of Chrysler and AMC was announced, speculation increased about which parts of AMC would become expendable, because car lines overlapped. In addition, AMC's four assembly plants, when added to Chrysler's nine, were a clear case of overcapacity (Lowell 34). Concern was great among AMC dealers, according to Lowell, who warned that "bitterness is commonplace among those who have labored hard for the taken-over company, and that likely will be an even bigger problem than usual for Chrysler at AMC" (35). Problems were anticipated because "analysts say it will take about two years for Chrysler to assimilate AMC. But long before that, Iacocca is likely to wield the cost-cutting knife he used to save Chrysler" (Hampton and Rossant 33). Nevertheless, many AMC dealers were happy with the prospect of merger because they believed Iacocca could save AMC just as he had saved Chrysler (Cain and Kerwin 7).

Issue. AMC dealers were a new internal audience in the summer of 1987. Dealers have huge investments in their businesses and have built them in part on the basis of brand identity and loyalty. Brand identity for AMC dealers was particularly focused on the Jeep nameplate, which Iacocca called "the best-known auto nameplate in the world." The acquisition of AMC generated some uncertainty about the future for dealers who could greatly diminish the worth of Chrysler's investment in AMC if they were alienated. Had the AMC dealers lost faith in their new supplier, what had been viewed as a smart business move by Chrysler could have turned into a major financial fiasco very quickly.

The issue facing Iacocca, therefore, was how to create a new relationship with the AMC dealers that would instill confidence in an internal public he needed, even though both he and they knew that he would soon have to make some of the same kinds of cutbacks at AMC that had been used to save Chrysler a few years before.

Strategy. Chrysler's management now controlled the fate of AMC dealers. So it fell to Iacocca to combine the adaptive and dynamic models, as he often did, to manage the issue of relations with the AMC dealers. He sought both to adapt to the existing situation and to lay a foundation for managing future relations. Iacocca used two strategies. The first, showing commonality with the audience, was largely metaphoric, returning to the family metaphor he had used with Chrysler dealers in 1984 and including a "comrades in arms/ unified in adversity" metaphor. The second strategy, assuring AMC dealers that Chrysler really needed and valued them and their car line, took the form of announcing future plans for AMC cars and a new car line called Eagle.

Iacocca opened his speech with a family metaphor when he said, "Well, the deal is officially done . . . Chrysler and AMC are now one . . . and I can finally say to all of you: Welcome to the Chrysler family!" He returned to this metaphor later in the speech but first moved to a "comrade in arms/unified in adversity" metaphor by saying "we're the same kind of people. We've been through the same kind of trials by fire. . . . Something happens when you've been through all that we have. . . . When you take the Chrysler experience, and then add the AMC experience to it. . . . well, I'll tell you honestly, I wouldn't want to compete against us!"

Explaining that AMC products and dealers really did fit into the future plans of Chrysler's management was addressed when Iacocca said, "now, with some of the strengths that AMC brings to the effort, we're going to get there [being the best] a little faster." In particular, it was Jeep's strength in four-wheel-drive vehicles that Iacocca embraced: "When you put the talents and resources of *both* Chrysler and AMC behind it, the sky's the limit!" Possibly even more important to the dealers, however, was the announcement of a new nameplate: Eagle. This was to be a new line of cars that brought hope of a brighter future for AMC dealers.

REMARKS AT CHRYSLER CORPORATE COMMUNICATORS CONFERENCE

Trends. The trends faced by Chrysler and Iacocca had not changed appreciably in a year. Chrysler continued its aggressive acquisitions, adding to its existing Diamond Star-Mitsubishi venture and its ownership of AMC by acquiring high-prestige Italian nameplates. Chrysler already owned part of Maserati, and in 1987 it bought Lamborghini outright. Rumors suggested a possible merger with Fiat, which included the Fiat, Alfa Romeo, Lancia, Ferrari, and Autobianchi nameplates and was the seventh largest auto company in the world, with 1.7 million units sold in 1987. Chrysler was ranked twelfth in the world and was only slightly smaller, with 1.2 million units sold.

By August 1988, the new Chrysler New Yorker had garnered 35 percent of its sales by winning over previous GM buyers, although it still only amounted to 50,000 sales ("Mouse That Squeaked" 19). European sales were going well, with 35,000 sales by November. Not surprisingly, one of Chrysler's biggest sellers was the Jeep Cherokee heading toward a 200,000 sales year ("Jeep Cherokee" 19) confirming the wisdom of the AMC acquisition. But Chrysler, although showing very strong profits, continued to operate on tight margins.

Issue. With new partners, new models, new plants, and new nameplates, it was no wonder that as Iacocca put it, "In a nutshell, our employees said they don't understand where the company is headed . . . that we seem to change directions at the flick of a switch." Iacocca was sensing a communication problem growing at Chrysler. Specifically, he was concerned that his messages were beginning to fall on deaf ears. He felt that "it was easy [ten years earlier] because everybody was nervous about losing their job. When you're scared, you try to get your hands on any bit of information, and you pull together any way you can." Now, however, "it's a different story. We're not hanging on a cliff." This was a problem because Iacocca had been trying for years to communicate the need for better quality and customer service to increase sales and customer loyalty by becoming "the best car company in the world." An important link was the Car Buyer's Bill of Rights, an attempt to articulate clearly the things Chrysler should do for its customers. This bill of rights was to be "the root of our operating philosophy for a long, long time," but Iacocca was convinced that it was not understood or embraced by Chrysler employees.

Strategy. Iacocca was essentially using corporate communicators as a channel to send a message to all the internal publics of Chrysler. He adopted a primarily adaptive strategy. The strategy was not a reactive attempt to stonewall the situation because Iacocca candidly admitted, "I have a problem, don't I? . . . I'm out of touch." He sought to adapt to this situation by asking "Jerry Greenwald and his people to come up with programs that open up the Chrysler channels" of communication. He sought to adapt the internal communication at Chrysler, putting a new focus on finding "ways for you to get messages moving into Highland Park." To overcome any lack of confidence or coordination that would result from employees not being clear about the corporation's strategic direction, Iacocca also took the opportunity to articulate what he called a "Communication Countdown," a list of six overall corporate goals, including improved communication, that were also primarily adaptive.

REMARKS AT A SENIOR MANAGEMENT MEETING

Trends. The years leading up to 1992 had not been entirely kind, either to Iacocca or to Chrysler, with profits declining for several years (Taylor, 70). In

37

reporting on Chrysler's situation in 1992, Reibstein and Washington wrote that "over time, as Chrysler's health has gone into a tailspin, Iacocca has taken on some warts" (30). Further, "The company of venerable nameplates like Dodge and Plymouth is peddling an aging line of cars, its sales are dwindling and its cash reserve is dropping. Counting cars alone, Chrysler lost its No. 3 ranking to Honda. It is expected to report a loss of around $1 billion for this year. . . . The comeback king [Iacocca], the critics now say, had no follow-through" (Reibstein and Washington 30).

Some sources even questioned Chrysler's ability to survive as an independent car company (Reibstein and Washington; Taylor 70). There was also some speculation about unrest in the leadership ranks at Chrysler and Iacocca's reluctance to retire (Taylor; Woodruff 31).

But by late 1992, there was a vast silver lining in the clouds surrounding Chrysler as Iacocca, having announced his retirement as CEO, prepared to address a meeting of his senior managers. On Wall Street, Chrysler's stock had gone up an astonishing 80 percent during 1992. Chrysler had found a well-qualified replacement to fill the soon-to-be vacant CEO suite. Several new and highly regarded models were coming out, including the much touted LH cars (Woodruff 25). Jeeps and minivans were still highly successful, and Chrysler had a new state-of-the-art facility in Auburn Hills, Michigan (Reibstein and Washington 30; Taylor 65). Chrysler was poised for a renaissance on a scale not seen since the early 1980s. Iacocca himself said, "We're going to see a lot of black ink. . . . Has the tide turned? Yeah! This is a confluence of events the likes of which I've never seen" (Taylor "Iacocca: Lee's Parting Shots" 56).

Issue. The issues Iacocca sought to manage on this occasion were his own imminent retirement and ensuing legacy as well as Chrysler's future. Much of Iacocca's last year at Chrysler had been an effort to "ensure Chrysler's survival and his own place in history" (Reibstein and Washington 30). In these speeches, he was genuinely concerned with both.

Strategy. Iacocca was attempting to manage the issue of his postretirement reputation and Chrysler's health by addressing those members of the management team who would direct the company's day-to-day operations. He delivered a heartfelt farewell in which he observed that many of his unpopular actions had been necessary and said Chrysler's future could best be ensured by continuing many of the policies he had established. In that he was seeking to influence future interpretations of his career and future conditions at Chrysler, Iacocca's strategy was primarily dynamic. He sought to respond to criticisms, some already voiced and some that would not be spoken until long after his retirement.

In this speech, Iacocca cast many of his unpopular actions and decisions while leading Chrysler as either necessary or mistakes that came out of good intentions. For example, about the decision to extend his retirement date for three years, he said, "I couldn't leave three years ago . . . because we had problems. . . . I was in the corner office, so I had to accept the responsibility." But Iacocca, regretted "having had to close thirty-two plants . . . not having the time to make some of the changes we had to do more slowly and with less pain . . . not [being] able to convince Washington to make some of the public policy changes that would have . . . eased some of that pain." Iacocca sought to ensure that those who followed him heard and understood his perspective on these unpopular decisions.

Iacocca also sought to clarify expectations about Chrysler's impending renaissance. He warned that "we're a cyclical industry . . . the auto cycle is finally heading north. Now is the time to realize that it will go south again." He also offered the advice that "you, the management of this company . . . manage it like it's 1979 or 1989 again." In short, Iacocca wanted the company he had put so much into to survive and flourish, and he sought to pass his wisdom on to the next generation. Finally, Iacocca sought to express his feeling about the company and thank his coworkers who had been through so much with him.

CONCLUSION

The trends and issues Iacocca responded to in these four speeches ranged from celebration to takeover to farewell. They came in the middle of economic conditions ranging from record profits to declining market share. Because each speech was a strategic response to specific trends and the issues that resulted from them, each speech is unique. In addition, these speeches represent only a tiny percentage of the 663 speeches Iacocca gave while representing Chrysler. Nevertheless, three tentative generalizations can be drawn about Iacocca's approach to internal issues management from these speeches.

First, like everyone else connected with Chrysler during the brush with bankruptcy, Iacocca was indelibly marked by the experience. It continued to influence his actions and message until he left Chrysler. For example, in his farewell speech, he observed that "closing a plant is the hardest thing a CEO ever has to do." Iacocca's speeches built on this experience and repeatedly appealed to internal audiences to share his vision of a Chrysler family and to follow the lessons of Chrysler's survival. He sought consensus on what they had achieved together in overcoming the threat of bankruptcy and on the goal "to be the best."

Second, Iacocca understood that internal issues managers must respond to a situation within the limitations imposed by that situation. As a result, there is never a completely free choice of strategy. Within these bounds, however, Iacocca showed a clear preference for dynamic strategies that consider the past but also "look forward to future events or conditions" (Jones and Chase 6). Although the speech to the Chrysler-Plymouth and Dodge dealers in 1984, to the AMC dealers in 1987, and to the senior managers in 1992 all contained large elements of the adaptive approach, Iacocca took a primarily dynamic stance in these speeches. The one speech that was primarily adaptive, to the corporate communicators in 1988, was so because of the issue being confronted, and even it included clearly dynamic elements.

Finally, Iacocca's addresses to internal audiences show unique sensitivity to both these audiences and to the communication process. Most speeches to internal audiences follow a reactive strategy. After all, the audience is captive and must in some sense simply accept what the CEO says. Iacocca, however, chose dynamic strategies. Rather than simply report on trends and issues, Iacocca sought to interpret them for his internal audiences. And in these speeches, he addressed his internal audiences with the same level of skill, thoughtfulness, and respect evidenced in addresses to shareholders, political bodies, industry groups, or other external audiences.

NOTES

1. I was a member of Iacocca's internal audience when I worked on the Chrysler assembly line. I was one of the thousands who worked under concession contracts to help save Chrysler. I was laid off on July 3, 1979. My Chrysler career started at the old Lynch Road assembly plant on the east side of Detroit, where I helped build such cars as the Plymouth Duster by operating a spot-welder in Department 9110 and driving a forklift. I was an active member of Local 51 of the United Auto Workers. After the second or third layoff at Lynch Road, I was transferred a few miles north to the Dodge Truck Plant on Mound Road. I was a member of UAW Local 140 and was active in the local union, serving as a "blue button" or line steward, among other things. I consciously draw on this perspective as one of Iacocca's troops in this analysis. I also attempt to convey some of the feeling of the times and to report on some of the responses and feelings among the legions of Chrysler foot soldiers who sacrificed to save the company.

WORKS CITED

Andersen, Kurt. "A Spunky Tycoon Turned Superstar." *Time,* 1 April 1985: 30.

Cain, Carol, and Katie Kerwin. "Dealers are Elated." *Detroit News,* 10 March 1987: 7A.

Crable, Richard E., and Steven L. Vibbert. "Managing Issues and Influencing Public Policy." *Public Relations Review* 11 (1985): 3–16.

Culbertson, Hugh M., Dennis W. Jeffers, Donna B. Stone, and Martin Terrell. *Social, Political and Economic Contexts in Public Relations: Theory and Cases.* Hillsdale, N.J.: Lawrence Erlbaum, 1993.

"Detroit Rolls in the Dough." *Ward's Automotive World,* May 1984: 9.

Hampton, William J., and John Rossant. "Now, for Chrysler's Next Trick." *Business Week,* 23 March 1987: 23, 32–33.

"Jeep Cherokee Is Chrysler's Best Seller." *Ward's Automotive World,* Oct. 1988: 19.

Jones, Barrie L., and W. Howard Chase. "Managing Public Policy Issues." *Public Relations Review* 7 (1979): 3–23.

Lowell, Jon. "AMC Deal Shocks Execs with Decisiveness." *Ward's Automotive World,* April 1987: 34–35.

"Mouse That Squeaked: Chrysler Takes on GM." *Ward's Automotive World,* Oct. 1988: 19.

Reibstein, Larry, and F. Washington. "Lee's Last Stand." *Newsweek,* 6 Jan. 1992: 30–32.

Taylor, Alexander L. "Iacocca's Last Stand at Chrysler," *Fortune,* 20 April 1992: 63–65, 70, 72–73.

———. "Iacocca: Lee's Parting Shots." *Fortune* 7 Sept. 1992: 56–58.

Woodruff, David. "Life After Lee at Chrysler." *Business Week,* 30 March 1992: 24–26.

"Wrapup 1980." *Ward's Automotive World,* June 1980: 9.

"Wrapup 1987." *Ward's Automotive World,* March 1987: 10.

REMARKS AT THE
CHRYSLER-PLYMOUTH AND DODGE
DEALER ANNOUNCEMENT SHOWS

New Orleans, Louisiana, August 20 and 22, 1984

The biggest speech each year for Iacocca at Chrysler was the one he gave to the dealers assembled to see the new vehicles for the coming year. In 1984, the dealers met in the Superdome in New Orleans. The World's Fair was going on. Chrysler had paid off its federally guaranteed loans a year earlier and was on its way to its most profitable year ever. It had just launched a new advertising program—"To Be The Best." The mood was festive. There was a pattern to Iacocca's speeches to the dealers: He reminded them of what Chrysler was doing for them, and then he asked for something in return.

Good evening, ladies and gentlemen.

Have you noticed? Every year the room seems to get a little bigger. I thought last year it was big, but I didn't know this year I'd be playing the Superdome—as a warm-up for the great Kenny Rogers, yet!

Just a couple of years ago, I'd have settled for a tent. (Or anything out of the rain.) And I'd have been happy with an audience of maybe fifty dealers . . . or fifty of anybody.*

We must be doing something right.

We're having the best year in Chrysler's history. We're here tonight to celebrate . . . and we've got a right to!

This is a family reunion . . . of a family that's been through some rough times and has stuck together through it all. And one of the things you do at a family reunion is look at a few of the old snapshots and reminisce a little before you get on with the party. So, I got the album out to see what I said to you the last couple of years.

Three years ago, at the 1982 announcement show, I told you that we had turned the corner . . . and that we were on the verge of reaping some of the

---

*These speeches are reproduced from the original manuscripts with the intent of remaining as consistent with the manuscripts as possible. They include various marks, ellipses, dashes, and material set off in parentheses, to indicate emphasis, pauses, and changes in inflection. Ellipses in this case do not indicate material omitted.

rewards. Chrysler had just reported a profit, its first in three years . . . $12 million worth. And I said "That $12 million profit number ought to be permanently retired, and enshrined forever in the corporate hall of fame."

At the 1983 announcement show, I told you we'd gotten some cash together . . . (about $1 billion worth) . . . and had just finished two back-to-back profitable quarters for the first time in five and a half years.

And last year, we celebrated our independence. I said to you that the week I had just been through was the best week of four long years at Chrysler, and it had made the whole miserable time worth it. I had checked on the check to the government . . . all $900 million of it . . . and it had cleared! I had been to St. Louis, and driven the first Chrysler Laser off the line . . . and it had *started*!

And I had been to Windsor, and checked on the progress there on building the new minivans—and they looked great. In fact, I said to you . . . I *guaranteed* to you . . . that they would be the hottest thing this industry had seen in the last ten years. And I thanked you for the tremendous role you had played in the Chrysler turnaround, and for sticking with us when it would have been so much easier to get out, or just roll over and die . . . like the *Wall Street Journal* said we should.

I concluded last year's talk by saying, "Just stand back a step and think about it this way: Very few people in their lifetimes will ever get to see the kind of victory we've won . . . to live through the worst of times—and in the end make things come out right!"

Well, together, we've done it, and we all should be proud —very proud . . . and I am proud of every single one of you in this room.

By the way, I also made a personal request of you last year. I asked for your help with the Statue of Liberty campaign . . . something you all know means a lot to me . . . and it obviously means a lot to you, too. Because—last week you hit your goal of $5.5 million dollars. And you did it two years ahead of schedule!

I'm proud of every schoolkid in the country who sends me nickels and dimes to save the lady in the harbor. We have $1.2 million of those already. But I have got to tell you . . . from deep down . . . nothing makes me prouder than the support of the Chrysler family. Again, thanks to every one of you.

Well, it'd be pretty tough to top last year's announcement show for *emotion*. But I can equal it, or top it, this year in terms of *pride*. If last year's meeting was a celebration of independence, then this year's is a celebration of honest, solid, rock-sound *success*. And the feeling, this year, is just as good, if not better.

The two proudest moments of the year for me personally came on April 18, when I announced our first-quarter earnings . . . $706 million, an all-time record; and on July 19, when I announced our second quarter earnings . . .

$803 million, a *new* all-time record! I'd sure like to keep *doing* that . . . I certainly don't want to retire *those* numbers, ever. It sort of gets addictive, and it also keeps getting harder and harder to improve on.

You're not doing too badly, either. You made $466 million through June. (Split almost exactly between Chrysler-Plymouth and the Dodge dealers.) That's more than you made all last year—and last year was a record. You're making $450 net profit on every car and truck you sell . . . four years ago you were making exactly eleven dollars! Your return on investment is averaging a phenomenal 54 percent . . . and your net worth has improved almost a half a billion in the first six months of this year.

So we both have reason to celebrate . . . and we should. But let's not get too euphoric. Everybody's happy now, but we've still got some tough issues to face. Some of the problems we can fix on our own, and together we will. But some of them we can't fix by ourselves, so we'll have to learn to manage our way around them. Of course, I'm referring to the dark clouds on the horizon: interest rates, labor negotiations, and Japanese imports.

You remember what interest rates did to us a few years ago? The prime rate was moving every week—mostly up. Well, with the deficits now projected at $200 billion per year for the next five years, interest rates sure aren't going to come down.

But unlike three years ago, we've now got Chrysler Financial back in good shape, and if the rates skyrocket again, we'll be a lot more help to you than we were last time.

We can't do much about the deficits and their effect on interest rates, so we're developing programs to be competitive on our own.

Japanese imports have just passed the 2 million mark, and this administration is almost apologizing for the restraints. In fact, they are making noises that come next March the restraints will come off altogether.

Never mind that the United States trade deficit this year will pass $125 billion—double last year's all-time record.

Never mind that Japanese cars have an unfair advantage of $1,600 per car due to currency and tax differences.

Never mind that another million American jobs are up for grabs.

I've had a lot to say about this issue over the past two years, and I've gotten nowhere. So we're hedging our bet here, too. We've just negotiated a new agreement with Mitsubishi through 1995 . . . and now we're discussing a possible venture in Korea. As an American, I don't like doing that very much, but we're going to protect Chrysler, and we're going to protect you. We're also going to build a P-car to protect you in the low end of the market. If we have to go offshore to build parts of it, we will. If that's what GM and the federal government force us to do—we have no choice.

A few years ago one of the darkest clouds on the horizon was the price of gasoline. That one seems to have disappeared. But even if gas prices should turn up again, this time we're really ready. We've got the best fuel economy of the Big Three—by far . . . in fact, we're the *only* ones who are meeting the *law!*

Then comes the uncertainty of the labor negotiations and the high expectations of the workers. Last year we negotiated a fair contract—it cost us $1.2 billion—so we're set for the next fourteen months. But, of course, what GM and Ford do next month will have an effect on us next year. So we're more than just innocent bystanders. Let's hope they don't give the farm away, and affect our ability to compete down the road.

On all these issues, we're taking a strong stand and we've done our best to get the government and others to listen to reason. A couple of months ago, I talked to the League of Women Voters . . . and I made a proposal. I offered to freeze small car prices and freeze the offshore sourcing of jobs. I also offered to exercise restraint in executive pay. But I said the other auto companies would have to go along. And I said the UAW would have to bring something to the party too . . . like tying wages to productivity and quality, and attacking health-care costs. And I said the government would have to do its job and address the unfair trade advantages of the Japanese.

I thought it made a lot of sense. We'd help preserve jobs, and the consumer would get a break. Owen Bieber said he'd give it a try if everybody else would. Even the administration nibbled at it a little—I got invited to the White House twice to discuss it. But nothing came of it, and the silence from Ford and GM has been deafening.

Now, take heart, at least it's an election year, and that's the time to get the politicians to go on record on these issues . . . and then hold their feet to the fire. I'm still trying to do that . . . and I hope you will too. Remember—where it affects your *business,* and your *future,* and your *kids' future,* don't be timid in asking the guys or gals running for office what the *hell* they stand for!

Enough of these great national issues that we don't have any direct control over. Let me move to those issues that are *absolutely* under our control.

If the cars don't work right or the customer isn't satisfied . . . those are things *we* control . . . and we better *never* lose sight of that.

If the government doesn't have a plan to handle its problems . . . that's too bad. But we can't afford *not* to have one. So we've got a new five-year business plan, just approved by our board . . . that will spend almost $10 billion to simply make Chrysler . . . not the biggest—but the *best* car company in the world. It's the best five-year business plan I've ever seen, and I've been doing them for thirty-nine years.

Let me tell you how we put it together. I've been giving a lot of talks lately on the subject: "What kind of country do we want *America* to be?" I've been doing that to get people thinking about the kinds of problems the country faces.

I think it is time to ask *ourselves* the same question. So I got everybody together and asked "What kind of *company* do we want *Chrysler* to be?" *And our answer was simple: to be the best!*

What does it take to be the best in this business? Really just two things—quality products and satisfied customers. The products are *my* job . . . the satisfied customers are *yours.*

We decided right off to put our money where our mouth is. So we committed to invest $9.5 billion over the next five years to give you the best-quality products at competitive prices.

We're fortunate, because for the first time in a long time we've got the money to do that. We're flush right now . . . and the next twelve months are going to be good ones. So, this is the time to make a commitment to the future . . . and we have.

In the product area, the same people who brought you the K-cars . . . and convertibles . . . and the minivans . . . have some new dandies planned for you—H-cars this fall, (that's the LeBaron GTS and Dodge Lancer) and starting in 1986, a whole new car or truck line every six months right through 1988!

In engineering, the same people who wrote the best recall record in the industry . . . at a time when their resources were stretched thin . . . who gave you *good* turbochargers, that worked . . . who gave you the best fuel economy average in the industry . . . have committed to give you the most technologically advanced cars in the world.

In manufacturing, the people who stretched capacity—without losing quality—to give you the cars you needed, have *committed* to productivity and quality improvements that will take the Japanese head-on.

Just three years ago, those same people were building 10.6 cars per employee per year—now they are building 19.0 —now that's productivity!

Even sales and marketing didn't do too badly. Marketing did some good advertising, and the sales group handled the volume that we poured out, and distributed it fairly effectively. (Except for minivans—it's always tough to distribute a shortage!) And they rebuilt a dealer organization in the south and in the west. So our people are doing their part . . . and they're committed to doing even better.

Let me ask you, though: what are you investing in the future? What is your *commitment?* You guys are pretty flush, too. You're making more money than you ever thought you'd see. What are you going to do with it?

I remember, back in the early 1950s I was a young district sales manager in Pennsylvania, responsible for just eighteen dealers. Cars were still in short supply after the war, and the dealers had a couple of barn-burner years (like we're having now) . . . and they made a bundle. They thought it would go on forever, so a lot of them went out and bought themselves yachts, and racehorses, and an apartment building here or there. They didn't put much back into the business.

Then things went back to normal (meaning the dealers had to compete and start selling and taking care of people!) and most of them got in deep trouble. They hadn't planned ahead. They didn't have their priorities straight. They didn't make a commitment to their business.

Well, history has a funny way of repeating itself . . . especially in this business. So, let me ask you: *'confidentially,'* boys, *what are you going to do with all the money?*

Guess what? I've got a couple of ideas for you!

First,—the best statement you can make about your quality is your warranty. That tells the customer that you've got confidence in the product. And we already have the best warranty in the business. Nobody can match us today. And we're going to do more! The 5-year/50,000-mile warranty is a big selling point already . . . but we're going to improve on it. We're going to take part of that $9.5 billion and tell the customer we're not only the best . . . but we're getting *better.* So, that takes us to Dealer Commitment Number One: *service.*

Whether the car's under warranty or not . . . service is one of those problems you can do something about. And it *is* a problem. We're slipping here. Customer satisfaction rose steadily for two years . . . until this year . . . and now it's dropped right back to where it was two years ago. Poor service is the customer's biggest gripe. We aren't even doing the job we should *prepping* the car and *delivering* it right. Our research shows that 13 percent of your customers were *less* than satisfied with the way the car was prepped and delivered. That's 169,000 unhappy customers right there!

But that's a problem you can *fix.* When a guy comes in and drops ten or twelve grand for a car, you ought to be sure he leaves with a big smile on his face. Prep the car right. Fill up the tank—you can afford it! Shine his shoes if you have to. But send him out happy!

Let me talk to you big dealers for a minute. Your service complaints are way above the smaller dealers—up to 20 percent higher. Now, we've concluded we don't need many more dealers. At about four thousand, we're just about full up.) That means as we grow you've got a shot at even bigger volumes. That means bigger service responsibilities. Maybe that's the place to start when you decide how much money you're going to put back in the business.

The last time I looked, we weren't building a perfect car. Nobody ever does. But we're going to spend a lot of money to make them better. You've got to hold up your end. You've got to give the customer the service he wants and demands.

I don't have to tell you that the products are bringing more customers into your stores than you've seen in a lot of years. We've given you the cars and vans that people want. We read the market right, and we built the right products. And we're going to continue to do that.

So, you've got customers again. And not the random tire kickers who stopped by a few years ago just for a free cup of coffee . . . but quality buyers. You're getting more women buyers than GM or Ford . . . more single buyers . . . more affluent buyers. Compared to the other two, your customers are younger . . . more of them have been to college . . . more of them have white-collar jobs . . . and more of them live in the suburbs.

(What a switch from four years ago, when we were the blue-collar company building only stodgy old four-doors.)

And how about this? Our research shows that about 30 percent of the people who bought minivans had *never* been in a Chrysler Corporation dealership in their lives!

We're bringing in a new breed of buyer—and we're going to continue to give you the products to attract them. What are you going to do to *keep* them? That's a problem . . . and another one you can do something about.

Let me be frank with you—judging from my mail, the prices some of you are getting are driving a lot of them right back out the door. Okay . . . you've got some products that are in hot demand, and you're making up for the lean years. I'm not going to lecture you for that. All I'm asking is for you to look ahead a couple of years . . . when you're going to want these folks to come in again.

Sure—the minivans are red-hot—a lot of people want them, and we can't build enough of them. You're getting above sticker price on them . . . they're the easiest things in the world to peddle, right now. Well, boys, when you get above sticker, you haven't made much of a *sale,* have you?—all you've done is fill an *order.* Not much effort in that, is there? In fact, a lot of you have told me all you're doing is charging whatever the marketplace will allow. Well, on that theory, I could have raised the Voyager price a couple of grand and pocketed it myself—if only to pay for the $300 million investment for a second minivan plant.

You can't do business that way—you better get ready for the future . . . because our annual rate of 225,000 minivans goes to 270,000 just a month from now. And then a year from now . . . you'll be getting them at a rate of over 400,000 per year, so you *better* learn how to *sell* them.

I told you earlier that we have a plan . . . to be the best. But our plan won't be any good unless you have one, too.

I'm asking you tonight (I always ask for something at these meetings . . . you know that) . . . I'm asking you to put a plan together.

Lock yourselves in a room with your best people and don't come out until you decide what it is you want to be. Then figure out what you have to do to get there. Write it down . . . on paper. Read it . . . a couple of times a week. Make your people read it, too. Carry it around in your wallet.

And in that plan put down what you're going to do to keep the customer happy . . . and keep him coming back. Put down how you're going to improve service. Put down how much of your big profits you're going to put back in the business. Think five years ahead, and then put down all the things you have to do to stay as healthy and as happy as you are right now.

Don't forget your facilities when you write that plan down. What can you do to make them more productive . . . better places to work in . . . better places to visit? As we bring in all these new products, we're tearing the plants up at the same time . . . to get productivity and quality. In other words . . . to *compete.*

And don't forget sales and service training, and diagnostic equipment. That's all part of productivity and quality, too.

And why, oh why, can't you follow up on every customer thirty days after he's taken delivery—just to ask him how he and his friends like his car? He'll love you for it, and you might get a couple of leads to boot!

You know, when it comes to having a plan and making it work I've always admired the people at Sears. They're one hundred years old this year; they used to manufacture a lot of things. They don't do that anymore—now all they do is sell and finance and service customers. They were the first ones, back in the last century, who said, "Satisfaction guaranteed or your money back." And they've stuck to it. I asked them once how they did that. They told me they'd found that 98 percent of the people were honest, and maybe 2 percent might take advantage of them. And since they didn't know who the 2 percent were, they just took care of *everybody!* You see, they've got confidence in *themselves,* and in their *customers.* That's what makes them the best at what they do.

I'm asking you tonight to make a plan to help us be the best at what *we* do. And I'm going to ask you for something else.

You saw the new television commercial today . . . the one where I say that we're gonna be the *best.* Well, I'm making one helluva promise . . . and I'm making it for *you.* You're the only ones that can make me honest; if people trust me when I say that, then in the end they have to trust *you!*

I've been making a lot of promises since I came to Chrysler. First, I went on TV and told everybody we were going to make it. Remember? And a lot of people didn't believe me. But we *did* make it.

Then, as our products got better, I said, "I'm not asking you to buy on faith. I'm asking you to *compare.*" Then I really turned up the volume and said, "If you can find a better car, buy it!" Once I even told people if they didn't like the car . . . bring it back within thirty days and I'll give you your money back!

I know you probably wish I'd stop making promises . . . but now I'm making the ultimate promise. I'm saying we're going to be the *best—period.*

So come on, boys . . . don't leave me out there all by myself. If you don't make the same commitment I've made—you're going to hang me out to dry.

And you wouldn't do that to me, would you?

Remember what I said in that commercial:

Quality. Hard work. Commitment.

They are the stuff we're made of.

Without them there is no future.

I have one and only one ambition for Chrysler.

To be the best.

What else is there?

Thank you.

VIDEOTAPED MESSAGE TO AMERICAN MOTORS CORPORATION DEALERS

Highland Park, Michigan, July 24, 1987

American Motors Corporation dealers were scared when AMC was acquired by Chrysler in 1987. As independent business people, they had invested heavily in their dealerships. They needed reassurance that unique products were going to continue to flow to them from the new, merged operations of Chrysler and AMC. Iacocca tried to put their minds at rest as soon as the papers were signed. And to do that, he announced a new automotive brand: Eagle.

Well, the deal is officially done . . . Chrysler and AMC are now one . . . and I can finally say to all of you—*welcome* to the Chrysler family! For the past three years at Chrysler, we've had signs on the walls and tag lines on our ads (and I think there are even some T-shirts out there)—that all say, "To Be the Best." That's what we're shooting for. And now, with some of the strengths that AMC brings to the effort, we're going to get there a little *faster.*

Because starting right now, we're "*Teaming Up . . . To Be the Best!*"

I'm looking forward to seeing all of you in October at the dealer introduction show in Detroit, but I couldn't wait until then to welcome you. And I couldn't wait until then to tell you why I think this new team is headed for big things.

In the old country, no matchmaker ever arranged a better marriage than this one. It just plain *makes sense,* and for *both sides.*

For one thing, we're the same kind of people. We've been through the same kind of trials by fire, and we've survived them. We've rebuilt a couple of auto companies that a lot of people said couldn't be saved. We turned a lot of red ink to black. And probably most important of all—we've earned the confidence and the trust of the public again.

Something happens to you when you've been through all that we have: You get a whole lot *smarter* and a whole lot *tougher.* When you take the Chrysler experience, and then add the AMC experience to it . . . well, I'll tell you honestly, *I* wouldn't want to compete against us!

Nobody else in our industry has been through what we have. That's why we're the same kind of people . . . and that's why this deal makes so much sense, and why it will work.

And like any good deal, both sides come with strengths the other one needs. AMC brings—to name just one—a reputation for world leadership in four-wheel-drive technology. And Chrysler brings the resources to take that leadership a couple of steps further.

Jeep is already the best-known auto nameplate in the world. When you put the talents and resources of *both* Chrysler and AMC behind it, the sky's the limit!

And speaking of the sky, there's something about to take off, and it's something else that can't wait until October.

That's the new *logo.*

Chrysler . . . Jeep . . . and *Eagle.* That's the new team.

It's a new team, but there's really only one new player.

Chrysler and Jeep have already written a few chapters in the history book of this industry. And now that they're teaming up, they'll write a few more.

Eagle is the new kid on the block. We've all got a few big challenges in the months ahead of us, but none of them is more important than making the Eagle name as familiar and as respected as Chrysler and Jeep.

It's going to take more than a new sign, of course, to breathe life into Eagle, and to develop a personality for the brand that's *unique* . . . and *exciting* . . . and *upscale.*

You start with the right *products,* of course—with the Eagle Medallion . . . and the Eagle Premier, coming in a few months . . . and then its sporty two-door companion, coming next year. And there'll be other Eagles coming soon, all cut from the same mold.

To get Eagle soaring, you have to back it up with a warranty second to none. And we're going to do that. Every Eagle will carry the 7-year or 70,000-mile powertrain warranty—the same as every Chrysler, Plymouth, or Dodge.

Nobody outside the family backs their cars better than we'll back Eagle . . . and that's a fact we can all take pride in.

It's *our* first contribution to the pot, if you will . . . our ante. And I've got to ask you for yours. You know what I mean, because in the real world the guys on Madison Avenue or in the engineering labs won't single-handedly create the Eagle image—*you will,* by the way you treat the customers and service the cars.

We'll *back* the product—and we'll back *you*—but you're the point men. Help us launch this new brand *right.* Very few ever even get the opportunity.

So the Eagle takes off in a few months, and how high it flies depends on all of us. Now, in closing, let me tell you that the coming months are going to be *exciting,* but they're also going to be difficult. It is no small task trying to integrate two big companies, a couple hundred thousand employees, and about 5,400 dealers.

We're probably going to make a few mistakes. Bear with us. Because when it's all over, we're going to have a company and a dealer body that may never be the *biggest,* but it will be *the best!*

The only question is when . . . how soon?

By teaming up . . . we're going to get there sooner than you think.

Good luck—and thank you. We'll stay in touch.

REMARKS AT THE CORPORATE
COMMUNICATORS CONFERENCE
Windsor, Ontario Canada, November 1, 1988

The editors of Chrysler's plant newspapers are not professional writers. Most are hourly workers who have volunteered to perform this communication function. The company's policy has been to give employees as much ownership as possible of the internal communication process. Iacocca talked to all the plant editors in 1988, and of course he asked for something.

This is one group I've especially wanted a shot at talking to, because a long time ago I learned who the most powerful people in the world are: *editors*. And I don't just mean the editors of the *New York Times* and the *Washington Post*. I mean you people!

In fact, on Friday I was visiting Lehigh University, my alma mater, and I was reminded how I first learned that lesson.

I was interviewed by a bright kid from their student newspaper, the *Brown and White*. Well, I told this kid that I used to work for the paper, too . . . forty-five years ago, if you can believe that! I wasn't good enough to be the editor-in-chief, but I was the layout or makeup editor.

And as the lay-out editor, I learned pretty quickly who has clout in the world. Most people don't have time to read stories, but they do read headlines, which I used to write.

I also learned how you can turn something that's real important to somebody else into a real nothing. You just bury it on page 9.

And I learned—and this was the biggest lesson of all—how easy it is to get even with people you're mad at. You just run unflattering pictures of them. That happens to me all the time!

Well, I know you people are putting out some great work—and it's not just in your photo selection. I've seen some of your newsletters, and I've heard about the fact sheets, and weekly department meetings, and town hall sessions.

In fact, I'm going to pass out some awards later on.

No matter how good the writing and editing is, though, I think in your business you need something more. You need credibility. You need your readers to say, "Hey, this isn't propaganda the guy's putting out. This is good stuff we need to know about."

By the way, it's always amazed me how easy it is to lose credibility-one bad screw-up will usually do it—and how tough it is to earn it back.

That's why I have to hand it to you people. When we did a survey this year, we found your publications are the second most important source of information at Chrysler, right behind supervisors. That tells me you're close to your audience, you know what they want, and they think you're credible. So, congratulations.

You know, when I first came to Chrysler, it will be ten years tomorrow, by the way, I was surprised—pleasantly surprised —at how well we did at communicating with our employees. And how well we did at building teams. I think communication and teamwork were the best things we had going for us. In fact, they were the *only* things we had going for us!

But it was easy back then because everybody was nervous about losing their job. When you're scared, you try to get your hands on any bit of information, and you pull together any way you can. We could say just about anything in Highland Park, and everybody was automatically all tuned in.

In fact, when historians write the history of Chrysler fifty years from now, I suspect our comeback still will be the part they play up the most.

But right now, it's a different story. We're not hanging on a cliff, so Chrysler people are a lot more independent—especially when it comes to news. They still want news, but they pick and choose what *they* want to hear.

I don't have to tell you that, though. You see it every day.

Everyday you watch coworkers pass the bulletin board on the way to the water fountain, but they're not always standing in line to read what you've just put up, are they? Or you can break your neck to meet your Thursday night news deadline, but don't count on people rushing to pick up the paper on the way in Friday morning.

I worry about these things. Here you're trying to put out a message, and the message isn't going anywhere because people on the line aren't interested.

And I *really* worry when the message is one *I* want out. The new Car Buyer's Bill of Rights is a good example. It will be the root of our operating philosophy for a long, long time. We're spending millions to get the message out to the public.

I want Chrysler people to know the rights so well they can recite them in their sleep. Because when I signed off on the campaign, I wasn't just signing for myself. I was signing for everybody! Everybody has to know how we're going to satisfy the customer, if we're going to keep my commitment.

By now you've run articles on the Bill of Rights, at least I hope you have. You've posted it in the halls.

So, let me ask: Do you know anybody who can tick off *all* the rights? Or three out of six? Or even *one* out of six?

You get my drift, don't you? People pick out only what *they* want to listen to.

They'll listen if you talk pay raises. They'll listen if you talk benefits. They'll listen if you talk job security. They'll hear you loud and clear if you talk anything that hits their personal hot button.

But when it comes to mission statements, and goals, and operating philosophies, they're not listening all that well. At least, not like they listened during our dark days.

I'll tell you, you don't see that in Japan. I was in Tokyo last month. I've been there a half a dozen times, and what always impresses me is how the Japanese have their act together. They're marching to the same drummer, and that's why when the plant manager at Toyota says he needs to cut costs, he gets eighteen thousand suggestions—*per month!*

If you want to run a business that can compete with Japan, I don't know how the hell you do it, unless everybody on your team's paying attention.

So that's my gripe—not enough listening.

But guess what? I'm not the only one with that gripe.

You know, we did that comprehensive employee attitude survey. Fourteen thousand people gave us a report card and they said: Management communicates down ... but it doesn't *listen* on the way up!

We didn't flunk anything, but we did get a few bad grades in some pretty important subjects.

In a nutshell, our employees said they don't understand where the company is headed ... that we seem to change directions at the flick of a switch ... and that there's too much competition between departments.

They also said that the people in charge (that's me) are out of touch ... and that we don't (I don't) understand what's going on. Other than that, they like me!

Well, communicators, I have a problem, don't I?

From where I sit, I say the guys at the plants aren't listening. And from where they sit, they say I'm not listening.

And you know who's smack in the middle of all this? And who's going to help us solve our little problem, don't you? *You people!*

Communication has to go in both directions. Some of it has to start at the top and go down. But more of it has to come back up, too. It's a two-way street, and I think what we need right now is a traffic light.

So I want you to leave here tomorrow, go back to your plant, and tell your boss that you have a new mandate. You got this mandate directly from me, so if he has any questions, have him call me.

The mandate has two parts. First part: Let's find ways for you to get messages moving into Highland Park. That's gonna be tough, especially to get it all the way to me. It seems there's always a couple roadblocks before news makes it to my desk, particularly if it's bad news.

They tell me at Indy Foundry you have something called NETMA, which stands for Nobody Ever Tells Me Anything. I guess you've got it for the whole plant there. I'll tell you, I could use a NETMA network just for me!

NETMA's a neat idea, because if somebody has a problem or question, they can ask the plant manager and he gets them an answer. And if he thinks it's something a lot of other people should know, too, he shares the information. He writes an article in the newsletter, or tells everybody about it at a town hall meeting.

It all boils down to *information sharing.* You don't need a fancy computer network to do it. You don't need fax machines or electronic mail. You just have to stand up sometimes, maybe even pound on the desk, and get the guy an answer. And if that answer will help somebody else, share it.

I'm convinced the only way to get feedback *up* the street is more one-on-one communication . . . more *informal* channels. Even if people don't always read the bulletin board or pick up the newsletter, they still talk to you, at least I hope they do.

When Chrysler was smaller, it was easier to do one-on-ones because bosses had fewer people reporting to them. If a guy had a problem, he'd just go talk to the boss. And if he was a good boss, he probably was the guy's mentor, too, so the guy could learn from him.

Of course, now everybody's so damn busy and has so many people under them, who has time to talk? You're lucky if the boss remembers your name, hell, he doesn't want to hear about your problems!

So you lose out . . . the boss loses out . . . and I lose out. I'm not getting feedback. I'm out of touch.

Well, if you're going to be the traffic light, I want to make life as easy as I can for you. And I want to make life as easy as I can for all the people *you* have to listen to. So, we've got to do this right.

That's why I've asked Jerry Greenwald and his people to come up with programs that open up the Chrysler channels.

You're going to see more bureaucracy busting, for one. No more truckloads of documents coming out of Detroit to tell you how to do your job in Kokomo. You make your own decisions.

You're also going to see more openness on issues . . . more access to top management . . . more communications on our plans. That's what you're going to get from us.

What we want from you are programs at each plant that let the plant management get feedback. Maybe it's more personal communication. Maybe it's more time-out meetings. Maybe it's more suggestion boxes—I don't know. You're the experts . . . it's up to you . . . whatever makes sense for your environment.

Then I want you to let us in Highland Park know what your troops are saying. You don't have to give us written reports, or every single hard fact and figure.

Just pick up the phone every now and then, and call us. We're partners here, and we want to know what's up on your end. In other words, what's hot out there.

So, that's how I'm going to try to listen to you better. But listening is a two-way street, and we think everybody at the plant needs to listen better, too.

I wish we had satellites in the sky and TVs in every aisle to stay in touch. We do have an outside press corps that follows Detroit—which is why Chrysler employees know a lot more about Chrysler than guys at GE know about GE. But what they print isn't always too accurate. So, we need our own internal system.

That's where you come in. This is the second part of today's mandate. (By the way, if you haven't been taking notes, you better get the pencil and paper out. Because I came with a long list of things I'd like you to do.)

On the employee attitude survey, one of the most common complaints was our people don't know where we're headed . . . they don't know what we're up to.

Well, after today, I don't want to hear that complaint ever again. So, I've come up with a list of six corporate directions I hope you can communicate.

If we call this meeting "Counting on Communication" (at least that's what the banner says), well, I have a name for my list. "Communication Countdown."

I want you to go back tomorrow, and pin Communication Countdown up on your wall. Every day you come into work for the next year, I want you to take a look at the list. And I want you to ask yourselves, "What can I do today, to get these points across?"

You're the communication pros. You decide how to do it . . . articles . . . bulletin boards . . . banners . . . department meetings. Whatever works for your plant. I'm just here to give you my two cents' worth on what the points are, and then I'm going to get the hell out of your way.

So here's the list:

Number One: Chrysler is dedicated to succeeding in the car and truck business. Cars and trucks are our primary business, and we're not abandoning it for one minute.

We've diversified a little with Chrysler Financial and Chrysler Technologies, and that will help us if there's a recession.

But cars are what we'll be doing for the rest of our lives.

Number Two: Chrysler will be the quality leader. We've already passed GM and Ford on customer satisfaction—now I want to pass Ford in quality by 1990 (only fourteen months from now), and we can do it if everybody in the system puts their mind to it.

Last week, the Spirit and Acclaim was our best launch *ever*. And their record's only going to last seventen days, because a week from Thursday, I get to cut the ribbon on our new Diamond Star plant and the new Laser sports car, and there we're already at Japanese quality levels.

I know you people have been knee-deep in covering quality issues. That kind of communication has let people know we mean business on quality, but we can't let up now.

Take one day's look at my mailbag, and you'll see why. I get letters from customers who still think we're building dogs.

And the customer is the only real judge on quality—not me, not you. So we have our work cut out for us, and I need you to repeat that message.

Number Three: Get new customers (and don't forget to retain the old ones). This is life and death for us. You either attract new blood into the showrooms, or the only story anyone writes will be Chrysler's obituary.

That's why we have 7/70 . . . and Crystal Key Warranty. . . and the Car Buyer's Bill of Rights . . . and we're going head-to-head with GM right now, testing money-back guarantees. And that's why we bought AMC last year . . . and started Jeep-Eagle . . . and are bringing out six brand new models in '89.

Anything we can do to increase showroom traffic, we do.

It's been working, by the way . . . 87 percent of Premier buyers are new to Chrysler . . . 35 percent of New Yorker buyers trade in GM products . . . and over the last four years, our loyalty ratings are up. So let's get that message out, okay?

Number Four: We're going international. We have no choice. It's a global business, and we need to find international ties. We need partners—for their ideas, and for their money.

That's why we signed up to sell Alfa Romeos with Fiat last month. We're partners with the Japanese at Diamond Star, we couldn't have done the plant by ourselves, believe me. We own Lamborghini. We have ties with Maserati. And in China we have teams at Beijing Jeep and First Auto Works in Manchuria.

By the way, if you ever have a chance to visit that plant in Manchuria, it's a real eye-opener, but I wouldn't recommend vacationing there!

We're getting a piece of the action on all these deals, but I'll tell you what the real international prize is. It's our export program. That's *our* baby.

We moved into Europe this year, and do you know some Germans are trading in classy Mercedes and BMWs for our LeBarons? So far sales are way beyond expectations—about 35,000 this year and about 60,000 in 1989!

And I never thought I'd live to see this, but we're even moving into Japan! I'm not crazy enough to say we'll sell a plant out there, but I bet we can sell at least a thousand cars our first year. Big deal, huh?

The key point here is that exporting cars means we're importing jobs—finally. Now 13 percent of production at Brampton and Toledo is for building vehicles headed out of the country, and that's one helluva story.

Number Five: We're committed to being truly competitive. I've said it a hundred times, but I'll say it again: The only job security at Chrysler is to be competitive. Period.

If the guy likes your design . . . if he opens the door and the fit's good . . . if he sits in the seat and it's comfortable . . . if he takes a test drive and the shift's smooth . . . and if he looks at the price and you're giving him value . . . bingo! You have a sale.

But if any of those things don't measure up, Honda or Toyota will get the sale because you can bet they build good cars and your customer will check them out before he lays out ten or fifteen grand.

Okay, so what do we have on the list so far? Chrysler is in the car and truck business. We're going to be the quality leader. We're going to get new customers. We're going international. And we're going to be truly competitive.

Well, that brings me up to the last point, and this one puts it all together. *Number Six: We're dedicating ourselves to improving our communications network.*

Any competitor can match you on technology. They can buy the robots . . . and the lasers . . . and the computers . . . just like we can.

But where they can't match you is with your people. We have to be smart enough to know that it's people who make the difference. People will make or break us.

So—and I'm going to end on this—we better be willing to listen and to learn from our people. Which means we better learn to communicate better.

You have all kinds of seminars to go to today and tomorrow. I hear there's even one on listening, and I'd sure recommend that one.

Just learn all you can . . . and improve your skills . . . then always remember our mission . . . communicate clearly in both directions.

Good luck, and have a great conference.

REMARKS AT A SENIOR MANAGEMENT MEETING

Auburn Hills, Michigan, November 18, 1992

Iacocca's farewell to his troops was emotional for him, and for them. The top two thousand managers in the company assembled in the new Chrysler Technology Center in Auburn Hills, Michigan. As usual, he had some advice. Then he said thanks, and good-bye.

Thanks, and good afternoon to all of you. And thanks for coming out. Sorry so many of you have to stand. Maybe we should have built this main dining room a little bigger! But we couldn't afford it!

I spent the morning at Warren Truck plant and I had a memorable experience. We honored Vangie Jones—fifty years and never missed *one day* or was late for work! Now that's a *role model*! He said he likes his work and the people he works with. So he's happy!

I asked for this meeting today. If you came thinking I had some big announcement to make, or even to talk business, then I got you here under false pretenses.

This is personal.

I asked you here because, as you all know, I'm getting to be a short-timer. I've worked in the auto industry forty-six years . . . two months . . . three weeks . . . and three days. And in another six weeks and one day, it's time for me to get out of here.

I've got a lot of things to do before I clean out the office, but nothing more important than what I want to do today.

And that's simply to say *thanks* . . . thanks to every one of you.

That's the *only* reason I wanted to meet with you today—just to say thanks. For almost two months now, I've been thanking everybody else—the shareholders in May, the dealers in August, the bankers, financial analysts, suppliers, the press, the employees at Warren Truck and here at the Tech Center all day today, and I finally got around to management roll—fourteen hundred of you!

People keep asking me how I feel about retiring. Well, I feel good, and I also feel bad.

I feel good, first of all, because Chrysler is in great shape. I couldn't leave three years ago when my tour of duty was up because we had problems. Some of them were created by forces over which we had no control. Some of them we created ourselves.

But I was in the corner office, so I had to accept the responsibility for getting the place back in shape to compete. Fortunately, we had a terrific top management team in place to help do that. And, even more important, we had *you* and all the other employees of Chrysler buying into what had to be done.

They're starting to talk now about the *second* Chrysler turnaround. I took most of the flak personally for all the problems we faced a few years ago, and now I'll probably get more than my share of the credit for the company overcoming those problems.

That's just the way those things go.

But *I know*, and I hope that every one of *you know*, where the real credit belongs. And that, of course, is *to you*.

If I'd left three years ago, I'd have had to walk away from a job that wasn't finished. I'm not built that way. And now, thanks to all of you, I can walk away proud of what I'm leaving behind.

I was at the press introduction of the LH models a few weeks ago in Los Angeles. When you're from Detroit, and you build cars, you don't expect to get much hospitality in Los Angeles.

Well, it was my *last* product launch . . . my *last* press conference . . . and when I asked for the very *last* question, a reporter stood up and said:

"Mr. Iacocca, you're wrong, you didn't hit a home run your last time at bat" (referring to my last TV commercial).

He paused a little, and he said, *"You hit a grand slam!"*

He said: "You have LH . . . and Viper . . . and Grand Cherokee . . . and the minivans. It's a grand slam."

Well, Chrysler people, *I* didn't do that—*we* did that. And we did it *together*! We hit the grand slam. Hell, we won the world series.

We've come up with vehicles that car buyers (even in California) talk about . . . dream about . . . and can't wait to buy. We really did it—and I thank you for that from the bottom of my heart.

Now, *regrets*, yeah, I have a few.

I regret having had to close thirty-two plants on my watch. Closing a plant is the hardest thing a CEO ever has to do. It hurts, and hurts deeply.

I regret not having the time to make some of the changes we had to do more slowly and with less pain. But we didn't have that luxury.

I regret that we were not able to convince Washington to make some of the public policy changes that would have given us that time, and eased some of that pain.

I wish that we had improved our quality faster and closed in on the Japanese faster than we did.

I wish I could take back a model or two. They weren't all hits.

I wish I'd never heard of odometers.

I wish I'd stop getting letters from customers with complaints about the way they're being treated by dealers—especially the women.

Those are the regrets.

There are a lot of *other* things we did that our critics *told* us we'd regret, but the critics were wrong.

I don't regret the billion dollars we invested in this place, for example, even though we had to mortgage the whole amount at what turned out to be junk bond rates.

I don't regret spending another billion to build the new Jefferson plant. I sure don't regret buying American Motors Corporation.

We took some big risks. And they were worth it.

Since I've been counting down the days, a couple of people on my staff have been making lists. They tell me that since I came to Chrysler, we've built (and sold) 25 million vehicles. We've purchased (this number is unbelievable) a quarter of a trillion dollars' worth of supplies ($250 billion, I think). And, counting today, I've given 663 speeches, 61 commercials, and about 50 town hall meetings.

So, I'm a little tired. I think my job is done. I'm looking forward to spending time in Boston with my grandkids . . . in Aspen and Palm Springs . . . and maybe even a little in Italy.

But I want to leave you with a little advice. I'd say *free* advice, but it comes from *experience,* and that experience was anything but free. In fact, it was expensive as hell.

And the advice is this: Don't read the press clippings you see out there today!

Back in 1983 and '84, the company was in many ways like it is today. We'd just been through hell. The smart money had bet that we'd be dead by then, but we weren't. In fact, we were heroes.

Well, we've been through hell again and we're heroes again. The papers just a year ago said that we were a bunch of stumble bums who didn't know our left from our right. Now they're raving about our new products and the fact that we're the only people in town making money, maybe in the world (including Toyota).

I think that back in '83 and '84, we started to believe all the great stuff we were reading—about Chrysler, about the industry, and about the country. Everything was terrific and would only get better. Reaganomics was in overdrive. We literally were making more money than we knew what to do with.

But we got carried away. We forgot that we're a cyclical industry in a cyclical economy. I've been in this business for the better part of five decades, and we have *always* forgotten the cycles and the bad times just as soon as the dough started rolling in again.

The press will always write stories about us. They have to. They can't call their publishers and say, "Sorry, there's no news today." And what they write will always be good or bad, never neutral—neutral isn't news; it just doesn't sell.

They're usually just as wrong when they praise us as they are when they give us hell, but we only tell them they're wrong when they give us hell. We tend to drink in the praise and pretend we deserve every bit of it.

And that's when it gets dangerous. That's when you need to appoint a designated driver. Maybe a whole team of them.

It looks like the auto cycle is finally heading north. Now is the time to realize that it will go south again, sooner or later. It really will!

The economy is also finally starting to recover. Now is the time to remember that another recession is just a few years down the road.

The competition is frankly weaker now than it has been in years. The Japanese have problems at home and problems here. And they're holding lifeboat drills over at General Motors. We're the ones with all the new products this year, so we're getting all the attention.

Now is the time to understand that the Japanese will be back, tougher than ever. And General Motors will reinvent itself just like we did, and come back as the 800-pound gorilla of the Big Three. (Well, maybe 500-pound gorilla!)

We're making money. As I said, we may well be the *only* company—foreign or domestic—making money in the auto business. In North America, at least.

And now is the time to realize that all that money is spoken for. Part of it is needed to pay for the *last* recession, and part of it for the *next* recession. We've got a huge unfunded pension liability and an even bigger product plan to pay for.

We don't have any loose change around here, and there won't be any in the years ahead, in spite of the strong profit numbers we hope to report.

So my advice to you, the management of this company, is to manage it like it's 1979 or 1989 again, when things were looking bleak. Forget that it's 1992 and things are starting to look pretty good.

Manage it with a certain sense of *creative desperation*. You've had more than three years of practice at that, and you're getting damn good at it. Keep it up.

Keep looking for ways to take costs out and get quality up. Keep acting like every decision, no matter how small, has a major impact on the *vitality* of the company, and it will!

But don't believe the press clippings, okay? Remember, they're written by the same people who predicted we wouldn't even be here today.

Well, with that bit of advice, I'm going to wind this up and open the bar. We've got a senior management meeting next month, but that's all business. I wanted to talk to all of you without the usual charts and slides. As I said, today is *personal*. And I want to keep it short and sweet, if only because so many of you are standing!

I just want to wind up with one last request. It's an important one.

I want all of you to give Bob Eaton the same kind of support you've given me over the years. I envy him and I envy you because, if you take the free advice I just gave you, the best of times are still to come for Chrysler.

And I've got one hope for Bob Eaton.

A few weeks ago, I was on the morning news shows, and all the interviewers asked me what my biggest accomplishment was at Chrysler.

I had to tell them the truth. I said it was simply *survival*. The company *survived.*

My hope is that when they ask Bob Eaton the same question when he retires, he won't have to say "survival." I hope we've put that part of our history behind us.

It's time to move on.

We've got the leadership to do that. We've got the *tools,* like this great facility. And we've got the momentum.

It's a new and better era for Chrysler. Please make the most of it!

So, finally, once again, thanks from me to all of you. It's been a terrific ride.

You know, I came here fourteen years ago only because I'd been fired . . . because I loved this business . . . and because it was the only place in town hiring CEOs that week.

It was the darkest part of my life. And I didn't know what I was getting into.

The *low* points were even lower than I'd ever thought possible. But then, the high points were higher than any one man ever deserved.

All in all, it has been one hell of a ride!

In fact, if I had known that it was going to be this exciting at Chrysler, I would have pissed off Henry Ford a lot sooner than I did!

Thanks for making that ride possible.

Let's go get a drink!

2. Speeches of Challenge and Celebration: Lee Iacocca's 1980 and 1992 Shareholder Addresses

Gaut Ragsdale

It has been referred to as an annual headache, a circus, and a zoo (Saxon 391). Thousands are conducted each year, and often it is the only time of the year when a corporation's chief executive officer interacts without the assistance of aides and talks directly with shareholders (Barnard 15). The event is the corporate annual meeting. Some have become legendary such as the 1971 General Motors meeting which lasted over six hours and considered numerous shareholder resolutions proposed by Ralph Nader's consumer action group (Kuzela 43). Other meetings do indeed have a circus quality, such as the 1988 K-mart meeting which was disrupted by the arrival of celebrity protesters Muhammad Ali and Evel Knievel (Kerwin 1C). Most meetings are simply routine annual events that receive little attention.

One observer of shareholder meetings has written that "chief executives are often considered only as good as their performance at the last annual meeting" (Flax 125). Lee Iacocca performed as CEO at thirteen shareholder meetings from 1980 to 1992. This chapter considers Iacocca's first and last shareholder addresses (1980, 1992), beginning with a discussion of the purpose of a corporate annual meeting followed by a brief commentary on the two speeches. The next section discusses core business values found in these speeches and Iacocca's credibility as a speaker. The final section speculates on Iacocca's worldview and its influence on his speaking style at annual meetings.

THE ANNUAL SHAREHOLDER MEETING

Most of the more than fifteen thousand publicly held corporations in this country conduct annual shareholder meetings (Barnard 15). These meetings are held in response to state statutes and stock exchange listing requirements (Knowlton 137). The key legal requirement for these meetings is to elect a board of directors. Annual meetings usually occur three or four months after the end of the previous fiscal year. Many are held in April and May following a December 31 end of fiscal year for corporations; the two Iacocca speeches treated in this chapter were delivered on May 13, 1980, and May 14, 1992. Because these meetings are annual events, they often become rituals for corporations. In addition to the election of directors, a typical meeting agenda consists of: the address of the CEO followed by a question-and-answer period, the consideration of management and shareholder resolutions, and a brief review of the accounting practices employed by the corporation.

Shareholder meetings possess value beyond the execution of legal requirements; they also embody and manifest core principles of the ideal of shareholder democracy. This ideal legitimizes the function of private capitalism in this society. Central to this ideal is the contention that shareholders are the owners of public corporations. It is the responsibility of a corporation's shareholders to elect a board of directors. As elected representatives, board members participate in corporate governance and have a fiduciary responsibility to the shareholders they represent. As a result of this arrangement, private capitalism is granted the right to function in American society.

The annual meeting also serves a planning function in that it forces an organization to collect, interpret, and present data about past operating results, and it forces a company to establish plans that will be shared with and evaluated by those attending the event (Flax 125). The meeting also functions to personalize a corporation. It is the one day a year when the senior officers, board members, and selected employees, shareholders, and retirees gather. When this occurs, many key parts of the corporation become personified (Flax 125).

The audience at shareholder meetings is usually comprised of retirees, individual investors, institutional investors, members of the press, and, where appropriate, union representatives. Technically, the annual meeting is really the one time a year when audience members can probe into matters that they feel may affect their investments and interests. This is a vital function of the meeting (Saxon 396).

For bigger, more visible corporations, the traditional "in-house" audience is often increased by the inclusion of members of the national financial press and hecklers—better known as corporate gadflies. When members of the national press are present, the audience has the potential to become a mass audience (Jamieson and Campbell 3). When this occurs, a CEO must be aware of not only the immediate audience but also the mass audience that is likely to hear or see parts of the CEO's speech soon after it is given. For example, Iacocca's 1992 speech was reported on in the next day's *Wall Street Journal* and *New York Times.*

Except for the largest and most visible corporations, annual meetings are usually not well attended. A significant event that affects a corporation—especially a negative one—will boost attendance. For example, Exxon's annual meeting after an Alaskan oil spill caused by one of its tankers was a well-attended and boisterous meeting compared to previous Exxon meetings (Sullivan A3). Also, many annual meetings held after the 508-point drop in the stock market on October 19, 1987, were better attended than most of those held the previous year (Allen 89).

A central part of any shareholder meeting is the CEO's speech. This type of speech is a genre of corporate discourse. Such speeches tend to deal with recurrent themes at set places and times, such as presidential inaugural addresses, where similarities of particular speeches outweigh their differences (Jamieson and Campbell 23). The purpose and legal requirements of a corporate annual meeting having largely structured these events, a CEO's speech follows a standard organizational pattern, including an introduction that orients the rest of the speech and provides some personal information about the CEO, a broad review of the company's financial results for the previous year, a specific breakdown of a company's operating results by major units, a discussion of unusual events affecting the organization during the past year, a focus on plans for the future, and a summary that ends on an optimistic note (Boyd 13).

The CEO has the lead role at the annual meeting and his or her speech is usually the centerpiece of the occasion. It is the CEO's responsibility to see that the legal requirements of the meeting are met, that votes are taken, and that questions are answered. At this corporate ritual, the CEO performs the role of figurehead and is a symbol of the larger entity (Seeger 54). During the speech, it is the CEO's obligation to provide good reasons for actions taken or not taken and to justify plans for future stewardship of the corporation.

IACOCCA'S 1980 AND 1992 SHAREHOLDER SPEECHES

Lee Iacocca addressed Chrysler shareholders for the first time in April 1980. As past president of the Ford Motor Company and widely known as "Mr. Mustang," he enjoyed a reputation as a successful manufacturer and marketer of automobiles (Taylor, Moritz, Witteman, and Seaman 52). The challenge for Iacocca at this time was to validate in the minds of his listeners his selection as the individual who was to rescue Chrysler from impending extinction. In his speech, he discussed the following major topics: the bleak economic environment facing the country, the terms for Chrysler's guaranteed loan from the federal government, and the actions taken by Chrysler to market cars that would return the corporation to profitability.

Iacocca began by claiming the "long-awaited" recession had hit the country's economy with a vengeance. He supported his claim with a string of compelling statistics. This claim and subsequent support represents a favorite pattern of argument used by Iacocca—a propositional pattern or a state-your-case-and-prove-it pattern (Rieke and Sillars 60). This was effective because it provided his audience with an easy organizational pattern to follow. It also had the strategic advantage that if the supporting materials were reasonable, then his listeners were more likely to accept his major claims.

By beginning with a discussion of the poor economy, Iacocca was able to anchor his company in a bleak environment for buying cars. He was also able —via comparison—to reveal that the entire industry, not just Chrysler, was facing a challenging economic environment. This tactic enabled Iacocca to shift the focus from Chrysler and its serious financial problems to the financial problems the entire industry faced. He followed the pattern of CEO speeches of reporting financial results by clumping Chrysler's results with the entire auto industry's results. This tactic has been recommended to CEOs for reporting bad news to shareholders at annual meetings (Knowlton 138).

Iacocca's next point contrasted to the first when he told his audience, "we continue to make great progress in building a new, competitive, financially secure Chrysler Corporation." Given the tremendous loss from the year before and the weak economy, he anticipated counterarguments from members in the audience by saying "That is a strong statement. . . . So let me give you some facts to support it." Using the propositional pattern again, he began by offering a detailed description of the loan guarantee plan, focusing on Chrysler's ability to be an active agent in creating a solution for the carmaker's troubles.

He next reviewed actions taken by the corporation to adapt to the difficult economic environment. After this brief discussion he spoke about Chrysler's new ways of doing business, depicting management as an active agent working to save Chrysler. He employed a propositional pattern again by listing seven actions associated with Chrysler's new ways of doing business. With more than half the speech now complete, he returned to the economy and told the audience that Chrysler and the entire industry faced a difficult future. He reminded the audience of the weak economy by listing many of the same factors mentioned previously but in more general terms this time.

The 1980 speech was concluded with yet another reference to the poor economy and its effect on such a dominant and leading industrial group as the automotive industry. He ends by suggesting that Chrysler could operate in a challenging environment because it was on the right track with a realistic plan. This is a ritual conclusion to an annual speech; it summarized major themes introduced in the body, and it ended on an optimistic note (Boyd 13).

Almost thirteen years later to the day, Iacocca addressed the annual Chrysler meeting for the last time. As a speaker, he had different motives for this meeting. In his first meeting the primary motive was to establish in the minds of his listeners that he was indeed an agent of change and that he could meet the challenge of saving and revitalizing Chrysler. At this final meeting, his primary motive was not only to link himself with past successes but also to underscore his devotion to values long associated with success in American business. In short, it was a speech of celebration, one that celebrated Chrysler, Iacocca, and the values that guided them both. In a sense, as a retiring CEO, Iacocca was preaching at his own funeral. As in most eulogies, he sought to link himself with values and principles that would survive and endure in the organization he was departing as CEO (Sproule 454). He also wanted to establish that those principles he had embraced were worth the devotion of younger Chrysler workers.

Iacocca began by recognizing that this particular annual meeting was different because it was his last before retiring. Early on, he introduced the topic of succession at Chrysler. He praised the Chrysler board for doing a great job on a task that was "agony, sheer agony." He concluded the topic of succession by saying that he envied his successor, Bob Eaton. In early 1992, some speculated that Iacocca was somewhat reluctant to retire. It is understandable why Iacocca wanted to remain CEO. After steering the automaker away from bankruptcy in the early 1980s and managing the concern through a recession in the early 1990s, he probably wanted to chair the company during the introduction of several new Chrysler automobiles and in an economy that was showing signs of improvement.

After discussing the launch of new Chrysler cars and four major changes at Chrysler, he pointed out other accomplishments, including construction of a new assembly plant in Detroit that had received an EPA award. At this point, he also noted the availability of air bags and built-in child seats in many of Chrysler's cars. It is interesting to note that during his presidency of the Ford Motor Company, environmental and safety issues were not high priorities for Ford—or for the public (Halberstam 389). However, in 1992, safety and environment were salient issues for most car buyers, and Iacocca was ready to respond to their desires.

In his long conclusion, Iacocca noted that he had been associated with some remarkable accomplishments, including the introduction of the Mustang and the minivan. Yet he underscored that he hoped his biggest moments would be in the future, because he hoped he had helped to plant enduring

71

values that would create a stable and profitable future for Chrysler. Here he was linking his name and his memory to values long considered to be vital to success in the economic arena; here the speech became a celebration of core values. He then thanked his listeners and compared his career to that of a cowboy. He finished by saying that he had had a satisfying and exciting ride, but, as with the cowboy, his ride must end.

VALUES AND CREDIBILITY

Iacocca's speeches are consistent with the genre of the shareholder speech. In both speeches, he draws heavily on five values that often manifest themselves in business discourse (Rieke and Sillars 191): a future orientation, a success orientation, a cost/benefit orientation, a production/consumption orientation, and a competition orientation. These values function to make a corporate annual address plausible and reasonable to listeners. The future and success values, for example, are readily evident in the 1980 address when Iacocca seeks to persuade audience members that Chrysler had a future and a successful one. Their presence provides shareholder-owners with good reasons to continue their investment in Chrysler and provides potential investors with good reasons to invest. The following statement illustrates these two values in the 1980 speech: "By 1984, all the cars Chrysler builds will have front-wheel drive, and nearly all will have four-cylinder engines. With these changes, we will be right on the money with the small cars the market demands."

These same two values appear in his 1992 remarks: "We dedicated another plant just two weeks ago in Graz, Austria. That's our new minivan plant. . . . It means we're back in Europe with a new plant and a new product, and we're back in Europe for good."

Given Chrysler's brush with bankruptcy in the early 1980s and its financial difficulties in the late 1980s, it is not surprising that both speeches also manifest the business value of cost/benefit. With this value, a speaker stresses that costs are either appropriate or are being reduced, and whatever the costs involved the organization ultimately will reap profits. This cost/benefit value is particularly evident in a statement made at the 1992 meeting: "we cut costs—early and fast! . . . at the rate of a billion dollars a year for three years, with another $1 billion scheduled to come out this year." Again, these values are prevalent in business speeches (Rieke and Sillars 191). They are certainly ones that are found in corporate annual speeches as CEOs attempt to provide good reasons to rationalize past actions and justify future ones. Given that most audience members were "owners" of Chrysler and/or interested in its profitability, Iacocca was reflecting accepted and well-known values that were likely to resonate with a largely sympathetic audience.

While manifesting many rhetorical similarities to a typical corporate annual speech, Iacocca's two speeches also have some rhetorical differences that make them something of a variation on a theme. The differences existed because of the financial exigencies facing Chrysler, Iacocca's credibility, and Iacocca's speaking style. In the late 1970s and early 1980s, many analysts and pundits thought the organization would not survive. Under these circumstances, it was unlikely that someone long associated with Chrysler could be an effective advocate for the company (Serafin 1). Iacocca, however, after his successes at Ford, provided the rapidly faltering automaker with a highly credible voice ("Chrysler's Iacocca" 90). As a crisis manager, he helped to redefine Chrysler's image from a hopelessly doomed auto manufacturer to an underdog that might be saved through heroic efforts. By and large, the press assigned Iacocca to play the role of the hero (Dionisopoulos 235).

In 1980, Iacocca's initial high credibility was critical to Chrysler because arguments are judged in large part on the basis of who provides them (Sprague and Stuart 224). So claims of Chrysler's return to financial solvency in the 1980 address were likely to carry more weight with Iacocca—highly credible source—than with an experienced insider (Serafin 1). During the actual presentation of the 1980 speech, Iacocca lent his credibility to Chrysler's efforts to manufacturer quality and profitable cars. This is most evident when, after describing upcoming models, he told the audience: "I have had a hand in introducing some great small cars in my time, and I can assure you that our new cars for 1981 are as good as or better than any of them."

Four factors are associated with credibility: competence, trust, goodwill, and dynamism (Sprague and Stuart 225-226). In ideal form, a highly competent speaker ranks high on each factor. In the course of daily life, however, a person's credibility is not a straightforward issue (Sproule 140). It is difficult for a person to score high on all four factors if that person has been in a visible position of authority for a long period of time. During a speech, members of the audience that assign—in a matter of degrees—credibility to a speaker.

Because someone in Iacocca's position must always balance competing demands and often make decisions that prove unpopular, it is difficult to maintain high credibility with multiple audiences. At the time of the 1992 annual meeting, perceptions of Iacocca's credibility fit the familiar "good news/bad news" scenario. In terms of good news, he was retiring when several highly praised Chrysler cars were being introduced. During his tenure as CEO, he also had been closely associated with the introduction of the successful minivan. Moreover, he had been highly visible in chairing the restoration project for the Statue of Liberty. He was also associated with Chrysler's early payback of the federal loan guarantee.

In the minds of many listeners, however, Iacocca's accomplishments had to be balanced against bad news. For example, during his tenure as CEO,

Chrysler was fined for not connecting the odometers on cars driven by Chrysler executives (Donlan 24). Also in the late 1980s, Iacocca often was cited in the press as being an overpaid executive. In 1990, a *Business Week* article revealed that "for the third year in a row, Chrysler's Iacocca had the worst record when corporate performance was linked with CEO pay" (Byrne 56). Finally, Iacocca received negative publicity when Chrysler closed its Kenosha plant, formerly an American Motors plant. Many observers viewed the layoffs as a betrayal of Kenosha workers by Iacocca. These observers and the Kenosha workers had interpreted his earlier remarks as a pledge to keep the plant open (Treech and Woodruff 92). Iacocca's credibility in 1992 was still generally high compared to 1980, but as a result of his having chaired the company for thirteen years, the factors comprising his credibility carried different and probably lower rankings than they did in 1980. An *Advertising Age* article in April 1992 revealed that as a national personality, Iacocca's positive rating dropped four points from 1987 to 1991, and his negative ratings over the same time period had risen six points (Connelly S46). These data support the notion that his credibility was still high in 1992 but had dropped somewhat.

Another factor in both presentations is the revelation of Iacocca's worldview. It is a worldview shared by many children of immigrant parents (Halberstam 356). It is a view of the world as large, turbulent, and competitive; with a determined effort, one can be active and act upon this world. In the two shareholder speeches, the world is the auto industry. and the agent is Chrysler. In the 1980 address, Iacocca told the audience that Chrysler could survive and ultimately compete in this world. In 1992, he told his listeners that because Chrysler had taken the correct actions during tough economic times, it would prosper in the years to come. Both speeches manifest his worldview of the agent—whether the individual, the organization, or the society—willing to compete and prevail in a challenging environment. In his other speeches, this same worldview seems to be present. In his commencement speeches, it is the college graduate who is the agent and about to enter a challenging and turbulent world. In the economic speeches, it is an American industry that is the agent that must act in an increasingly competitive world. Iacocca is able to substantiate his worldview through his frequent use of a propositional pattern of argument. In the 1980 address, for example, he told the audience that the country's economy was in recession and that the new Chrysler was preparing to compete in this difficult environment. With each proposition, he provided multiple forms of support. The result was a straightforward, illustrated, and plausible argument pattern that provided his listeners with good reasons to accept his worldview.

Not only does Iacocca support his worldview through the use of a particular argument pattern, but he bolsters this view through his speaking style.

Speaking style is the personal manner of expression that gives impact and movement to ideas (Wilson and Arnold 227). What is most prominent in Iacocca's speaking style is the clarity of his language. Clarity comes about through the use of simple, familiar sentences, effective transitions, and words that are instantly intelligible (Wilson and Arnold 233). These specific characteristics are evident in both shareholder speeches. There is also a force or energy and urgency to Iacocca's speaking style. The following statement from his 1992 address reveals these characteristics: "The one constant comment we get from auto writers and others who've already driven them [new cars] is: 'They're not like any cars Chrysler has ever built.' *And they're not!* They're new—really new—from the ground up—and I don't think there's been more internal enthusiasm for a new product at Chrysler since I set foot in the place."

CONCLUSION

Because he was Lee Iacocca and because Chrysler was responding to financial exigencies, Iacocca's 1980 and 1992 shareholder speeches reflect the genre of the corporate annual address—and they are also particular to Iacocca. In both addresses, he applies his worldview to Chrysler. This worldview is one in which an agent of change acts upon a competitive and turbulent environment.

In 1980, he told his audience that Chrysler would survive and prosper in the larger environment. He sought to validate his selection as CEO and underscore that *he* was the agent of change to meet the supreme challenges facing Chrysler. In 1992, the occasion was a combination of the ritual of an annual meeting and a celebration of Iacocca's retirement. On this occasion, he met the requirements of the speech genre and also celebrated core values that have long been associated with success in business. On both occasions, he bolstered the effectiveness of his speeches by employing clear and forceful language structured by a compelling argument pattern. Finally, neither occasion was a circus or a zoo; each was a performance by CEO Iacocca—an agent of change in a turbulent world.

WORKS CITED

Allen, Pat. "The Making of an Annual Meeting—Management Plans—And Worries." *Savings Institutions* Dec. 1987: 89-7.

Barnard, Jayne W. "Giving Voice to Shareholder Choice." *Business and Society Review* (1990): 15-7.

Boyd, Joshua. "A Generic Description and Analysis of Chief Executive Officers' Reports to Annual Shareholders Meetings." Undergraduate Honors Section, Southern States Communication Association and Central States Communication Association Convention. April 1993.

Byrne, John A. "Pay Stubs of the Rich and Corporate." *Business Week* 7 May 1990: 56–108.

"Chrysler's Iacocca: The Most Bang for the Corporation Buck." *Business Week* 7 May 1984: 90+.

Connelly, Mary. "Encore Possible for Adman Iacocca." *Advertising Age* 30 March 1992: S46.

Dionisopoulos, George. "A Case Study in Print Media and Heroic Myth: Lee Iacocca 1978-1985." *Southern Speech Communication Journal* 53 (1988): 227–243.

Donlan, Thomas G. "Still a Lousy Idea: The Odometer Imbroglio Haunts Chrysler." *Barron's* 6 March 1989: 24–25.

Flax, Steven. "Curing the Annual-Meeting Blues." *Institutional Investor* Feb. 1983: 125+.

Halberstam, David. *The Reckoning*. New York: Avon, 1986.

Jamieson, Kathleen Hall and Karlyn Kohrs Campbell. *The Interplay of Influence*. 2nd ed. Belmont, CA: Wadsworth, 1988.

Kerwin, Kathleen. "Ready for the Grill." *Detroit News* 19 April 1988: 1C.

Knowlton, Christopher. "Ready for Your Annual Meeting?" *Fortune* April 1989: 137+.

Kuzela, Lad. "Cluttering Up the Annual Meeting." *Industry Week* 12 Feb. 1988: 43.

Rieke, Richard D., and Malcolm O. Sillars. 3rd ed. *Argumentation: Critical Decision Making*. New York: HarperCollins, 1993.

Saxon, O. Glenn. "Annual Headache: The Stockholders' Meeting." *Business and Its Publics*. Boston: Harvard Business Review Pubs., 1984. 391–400.

Seeger, Matthew W. "CEO Performances: Lee Iacocca and the Case of Chrysler." *Southern Speech Communication Journal* 52 (1986): 52–68.

Serafin, Raymond. "It's Lee's Last Stand as Chrysler Pitchman." *Advertising Age* 14 Sept. 1992: 1, 74+.

Sprague, Jo, and Douglas Stuart. *The Speaker's Handbook*. 3rd ed. Forth Worth: Harcourt Brace Jovanovich, 1992.

Sproule, J. Michael. *Speechmaking: An Introduction to Rhetorical Competence*. Dubuque, IA: W.C. Brown, 1991.

Sullivan, Allanna. "Exxon's Holders Assail Chairman Raul over Firm's Handling of Alaska Oil Spill." *Wall Street Journal* 19 May 1989: A3+.

Taylor, Alexander, Michael Moritz, Paul Witteman, and Barret Seaman. "Iacocca's Tightrope Act." *Time* 21 March 1983: 54+.

Treech, James B., and David Woodruff. "Crunch Time Again for Chrysler." *Business Week* 25 March 1991: 92–94.

Wilson, John F., and Carroll C. Arnold. *Public Speaking as a Liberal Art*. 5th ed. Boston: Allyn & Bacon, 1983.

REMARKS AT THE ANNUAL SHAREHOLDERS MEETING

Rockford, Illinois, May 13, 1980

This was Iacocca's first shareholders meeting as chairman of Chrysler. He'd been to Washington to lobby for loan guarantees. The economy had gone into recession. Inflation and interest rates were well into double digits. Chrysler had just lost over $448 million in three months. And Iacocca the optimist outlined what Chrysler would do to turn the company around.

I am Lee Iacocca, chairman of the board of the corporation. We are pleased to see so many of our shareholders here today.

This is our second meeting outside Detroit.

When we held our annual meeting last year in Syracuse, New York, we knew this company faced a very difficult two-year period while we restructured our entire product line and while we rebuilt our management team.

In the months following that meeting, we did strengthen our management team. We corrected many past business practices. We made great strides in improving product quality. We kept the development of our future product programs on schedule.

In the fall of last year, when it became clear that events—many of which were beyond our control—would cause us to suffer a severe cash shortfall, we sought temporary assistance from the government to help us through this difficult period.

Congress passed the Chrysler Loan Guarantee Act in December, and that helped assure that we would have the financing available to carry out our rebuilding program.

With the passage of that bill, we all had good reason to feel confident that we were on our way to profitability. We had a good, solid operating and financing plan, we had an exciting future product plan, and we had the support of outside consulting firms who agreed with us that we were back on track, given a relatively stable market for cars and trucks.

In January, that market looked pretty good. We actually exceeded our own internal sales targets in January, and we felt things were coming together. Then, in February and March and April, the long-awaited recession finally struck this whole industry with a vengeance. The monetary screws

77

were turned down tight in Washington, and the strategy worked. Housing starts and automobile and truck sales nearly stopped dead in their tracks.

The prime rate went from 13 percent to about 20 percent. Inflation hit at a rate of 18 percent. Overall unemployment went to 7 percent, and it's still rising—in April, the number of people out of work took its biggest monthly increase since January 1975. Credit for new housing starts and automobiles is all but unavailable. Consumer confidence is at its lowest point in thirty-five years. Gasoline prices are up 18 percent since January.

With all the bad news from the Middle East, people are afraid of still higher prices and the return of long gas lines and spot gasoline shortages. They want only the smallest, most fuel-efficient cars, and they want them now.

At the moment, only the foreign companies have the capacity to meet this extraordinary demand. Noncaptive imports are now taking about 26 percent of the car market so far this year, up over five full points over the first four months of last year. Chrysler's new small cars that can meet this strong demand, Plymouth Reliant and Dodge Aries, are still five months away.

But of all these factors, high interest rates and tight money have been the most important factors leading to the industry's present condition. Our dealers estimate that if adequate financing had been available, our first-quarter sales would have been 25 percent higher than they actually were. But the financing wasn't there.

Because dealers were forced to pay more than 20 percent to finance their stocks at wholesale, they had no choice but to cut back drastically on their inventories. For Chrysler, field stocks of cars and trucks are now down about 98,000 units from this time last year.

The drop in retail sales and the reduction in dealer inventories have had a devastating effect on our factory sales. In the first quarter, our United States and Canadian shipments were down about 167,000 units from the first quarter of last year.

The combination of all these developments is causing one of the worst slumps in the automobile industry's history.

Industry car sales in March were off 19 percent from a year ago.

Industry car sales in April were off 24 percent from a year ago.

For the month of April, the domestic industry traveled at an annual rate of less than 6 million cars a year—that is about the low point the industry hit in the automotive depression of 1974–75.

All the companies feel the pressure of these developments. General Motors earnings were off 88 percent in the first quarter. Ford reported the largest loss for any quarter in its history. And Chrysler lost $448.8 million.

You couldn't make the task facing our company more difficult if you tried.

But I can report to you today that in spite of all the negative developments and all the obstacles that have been placed in our path, we continue to make great progress in building a new, competitive, financially secure Chrysler Corporation.

That is a strong statement—especially in light of these terrible first-quarter results. So let me give you some facts to support it.

To start, we secured the interim financing we needed. Our suppliers deferred payments of more than $175 million.

Peugeot loaned us $100 million.

The State of Michigan loaned us $150 million.

This faith in us and our future made all the difference. It gave us the time we needed to put together the package that would qualify us for loan guarantees.

Since the Loan Guarantee Act was passed last December, we have had teams of specialists in the company working around the clock with our consultants, with the federal government, and with all the members of the Chrysler family to secure the financing and to develop the plans that meet the requirements of the Loan Guarantee Act.

We formally submitted our application to the board on April 26. The board announced its decision last Saturday. The board determined that our operating and financing plans meet the requirements of the act, and that there is reason to assume that after 1983, Chrysler will be able to finance itself without further federal assistance.

The act required that we raise $2 billion of assistance without guarantees. The first requirement was a concession from our unions. The UAW and our other unions did their part. We quickly received concessions of more than $462.5 million. Nonunion people contributed more than $125 million.

I hope that all stockholders will understand and appreciate the dedication of the Chrysler workforce, and the sacrifices they have made.

Time and time again in the past year, the employees of Chrysler Corporation have gone that extra mile to help renew the strength and vitality of this great corporation.

The act required $650 million from our lenders. We now have arrangements in principle with our banks and lenders for assistance totaling $680 million.

The act required $300 million from the disposal of assets. We have plans that could raise about $400 million.

The act required $250 million in assistance from state and local governments.

We have legislation in Delaware for assistance of $5 million.

We have legislation in Indiana for assistance of $32 million.

We have received $150 million from Michigan.

We have a commitment from the City of Detroit for $29 million.

We have a commitment from the federal government of Canada and the Province of Ontario for $210 million.

Those are commitments in hand of more than $400 million.

We also have assistance in process from Illinois, Ohio, Alabama, and New York.

The act required $180 million from suppliers and dealers.

We are offering for sale to suppliers and dealers debentures that should raise over $100 million.

All that adds up to well over $2 billion—far in excess of what the act required, and very close to the specific requirements of the Act for contributions from various parties with a stake in Chrysler's future.

That represents an outstanding accomplishment against extraordinary odds. I would like all shareholders to recognize the tremendous job turned in by the staffs of the company, and the contributions made by all the members of the Chrysler family.

We are working now to finalize all the agreements we have reached, and to complete this work very quickly so we can be in a position to start taking down the loan guarantees by about the end of this month.

While we have been putting this package together, we have also been responding to changes in the market for cars and trucks. As the economy moved deeper into a recession in March and April, and the sale rate of new cars declined, we took action to conserve our capital and contain our losses.

We have made additional reductions in our fixed and variable expenses.

We have curtailed spending on all but the most essential programs.

We have announced staff reductions of another seven thousand people.

We have also modified our future product plans to accelerate the conversion of all our products to front-wheel drive. By 1984, all the cars Chrysler builds will have front-wheel drive, and nearly all will have four-cylinder engines. With these changes, we will be right on the money with the small cars the market demands.

We have not taken any action that will weaken the success of our 1981 models, or the models which will follow, in any way. We intend to remain fully competitive in product, in engineering leadership, and in our ability to serve all the major segments of the future market.

Chrysler has a disciplined management team dedicated to completing our rebuilding program and to meeting that goal.

Your management knows what has to be done to get Chrysler back on track. We have adopted what I call new ways of doing business. Let me mention a few.

We have put in place a new order and scheduling system so we can keep production in phase with the actual demands of the market. No longer will we build large factory inventories, and then sell to our dealers out of those inventories. We now run our plants to firm dealer orders.

We are changing our leasing and fleet arrangements. We will no longer have the expensive used car activities which cost us so dearly last year.

We have taken the painful step of closing down marginal manufacturing operations.

We have adopted aggressive new marketing programs, led by the industry's only money-back guarantee.

We have improved the quality of our products dramatically. For the first time in eight years, research shows that customers rate Chrysler-built cars better than GM and Ford. That's quite a turnaround—and it's a tribute to all the men and women in our manufacturing operation.

We are on schedule—and within budget—with our new products. In just five months, when Plymouth Reliant and Dodge Aries go to market, Chrysler will have the capacity to produce nearly 1 million front-wheel-drive small cars a year.

Our new front-wheel drive cars are just right for today's market—small on the outside, lots of room inside, quiet, easy to handle, and very fuel-efficient.

We know that these cars have to be on time, and that they have to be good. I can assure you there will be no compromises. They will be on time, and they will be good.

We started pilot production of our new passenger cars in March. That gives us the longest pilot production period for any major model program in Chrysler's history—plenty of time to prove out the tooling, train our employees, and fine-tune the manufacturing system.

We are testing our preproduction models at our proving grounds, and on city streets and highways around the country. Before the first car is delivered to the first customer, we will have logged several million miles on these prototype vehicles.

We also started building our new 2.2-liter four-cylinder engine at our plant in Trenton, Michigan. So far, we have turned out more than 2,500 engines.

So far, everyone is delighted with the progress of our launch. The performance of the new cars and their new engines has been outstanding.

I have had a hand in introducing some great small cars in my time, and I can assure you that our new cars for 1981 are as good as or better than any of them.

Now, no one has to point out that we are not out of the woods yet. This continues to be a very difficult period for Chrysler, the automobile industry, and the economy in general. We are in a deep recession, and something needs to be done quickly to get the industry back on its feet.

Tomorrow, I will attend a meeting at the White House to talk about the industry's problems, and what can be done to solve them. We are in a unique position to speak to the subject. During the past eight months, we have pointed out that we are at the cutting edge of everything that ails the economy. Here are the problems that affect us all: overregulation, imports, high fuel prices and panic about availability, the highest interest rates since 1860, and continuing inflation, recession, and growing unemployment.

But of all these problems, there are two which are immediate. We must stop the flood of imports into the country, and we must take action to provide financial help to our dealers who are out on the front lines in this battle of the credit crunch.

For more than a year now, imports have been increasing their share of the market quarter by quarter at the expense of the U.S. manufacturers. Today, more than 260,000 American automotive workers are on the streets, while the imports keep coming at us—shiploads every day.

I have been a free trader all my life, and I don't want to change now.

But matters just cannot go on this way. The country needs to reduce the number of imports to more traditional levels while the industry completes its transition to smaller, fuel-efficient vehicles. In two years' time, we will all be in a position to take on the imports, head-to-head.

But in the intervening period, we need a gentleman's agreement with the Japanese to stop shipments to the U.S. of all vehicles they produce on overtime. This would not cause the layoff of a single Japanese worker; it would not require a tariff; it would not start a trade war. It would reduce exports by about 300,000 to 400,000 units a year simply because Japanese automakers would not be working around the clock and on weekends while Americans remain unemployed.

This action would help protect jobs in both countries, and it would give our industry the time it needs to get itself back on track.

Second, our dealers face a terrible problem because of lack of adequate financing. Automobile dealers are in serious trouble because of their inability to finance inventories of new cars.

They need help—and they need it now. To solve their problem, the Small Business Administration, the Federal Reserve, and the industry should work together to develop some mechanism to provide financing for dealers who are good credit risks. We have testified at Senate hearings on this subject in Washington, and I will bring it up at the automotive summit tomorrow.

The problems the industry faces are unprecedented. We are at a unique point in the country's economic and industrial history, and, as usual, the automobile industry is on the cutting edge of change in our society. But unique situations breed unique opportunities. Chrysler knows the direction it is moving in. We are convinced it is the right one. We have a sound, realistic business plan—a plan that is a direct response to the difficult times the country is living through, a plan that has contingencies built in. It is also a plan which the Loan Guarantee Board has determined is realistic and feasible.

We are following through on that plan, and we are all optimistic that Chrysler Corporation will be a stronger company in the future.

REMARKS AT THE ANNUAL SHAREHOLDERS MEETING

Auburn Hills, Michigan, May 14, 1992

This was Iacocca's last time to preside as chairman. In contrast to his first share-holders meeting in 1980, this time the country was coming out of a recession instead of going into one, and Chrysler was about to launch a new product lineup that would excite car buyers. The meeting took place in Chrysler's new billion-dollar technology center, a facility that embodied all the preparation the company had made for a successful future, and one that Iacocca considered the cornerstone of his legacy at Chrysler.

This is the part of the meeting I like—when all the legalisms and reporting requirements get set aside for a minute and I get to tell you in my own personal way where I think we are and where we're going.

This year it's even more personal, of course, because it's the *last* time I'll be doing this. Next year I'll be down there in the front row with the other board members, just listening.

I was reminded of that last week when I got a nice letter and this lifetime membership card in the Salaried Employees Retirement Club of St. Louis. It meets the second Tuesday of every month at 7:30 in the morning for breakfast—and I'm invited!

I understand some of the group even made it up for this meeting? Thanks . . . I'll try to make it for ham and eggs. (Or oat bran, or whatever retirees eat!) But isn't 7:30 a little early for a *new* retiree? I intend to sleep in for a while.

Actually, I intend to keep busy. There's one important part of my job today that I'm going to keep doing for a while—and that's speaking out on the critical issues that directly impact the future competitiveness of your company.

You see, it takes two things to be competitive in the world today. First, of course, is great product, produced with the highest possible quality at the lowest possible cost. There's no substitute for that. And I'm not worried for a minute about Chrysler being competitive in product. The management team we have in place now will do that job just fine.

It's the other half that worries me—the part of our destiny that's tied directly to the policies coming out of Washington instead of the products coming out of our plants.

Like health policies, for example. Health-care costs are bleeding us white. They have now cracked the $1,000 unit level. That's nearly three times what some of our competitors have to pay! So how can we be competitive?

Like trade policies. We don't have time this morning to get me started on this, but the playing field is still a long way from being level. The Japanese *must* open up their market and they *must* play by the rules in ours! The $40-billion annual trade deficit with Japan has to come down.

Like education—where we have a real mess on our hands. And the answer lies in teaching kids to read, in training the untrained, in upgrading the teaching profession, and in getting parents involved.

And tax policies. It would have been nice to get some investment or R&D tax credits for building the new Chrysler Technology Center—like they do in other countries.

And the perennial problem of too much regulation too fast, resulting in costly unrealistic standards, like mandated 40-m.p.g. average fuel economy, which we don't know how to do.

I'm going to leave the day-to-day car building to these guys up here, but I've been a bulldog on some of these public policy issues for ten years or more, and I'm going to keep it up. Because these aren't just political or environmental issues—they are *life-or-death* issues for us.

But there will be someone else up here next year with the gavel and all these black briefing books. Before I introduce him, though, I want to take a moment to say something about the board of directors of Chrysler—*your* board. They just finished doing the toughest and the most important job any board ever has to tackle, and that's succession. It's agony, sheer agony! And they came through with flying colors.

It was tough because they had an obligation to you to scour the whole world to find the right person for the job. They got plenty of advice, of course —a lot of it very bad advice. They were told to move faster . . . to make a choice and get it settled . . . to rush the decision. And to their credit, they didn't listen to that bad advice. They took their time.

Their job was made all the tougher because we had some truly outstanding candidates inside the company. And some outstanding candidates outside as well.

We all owe this board a debt of gratitude for doing a hard job, and doing it superbly. I think what they did and how they did it will become a model for other companies to follow well into the future.

In the end they chose Bob Eaton. And as I said at the time, not because they saw anything wrong with any of the other candidates, but because they saw something right . . . something *very* right . . . with Bob Eaton.

They found him in Europe, where he'd been running GM's European operations for four years with eminent success. Bob started as an engineer (like

I did), but he's *still* an engineer. He comes with the same philosophy we have, but also with some valuable experiences and great ideas to *add* to our team. His strength is in engineering and manufacturing. And his real passion is world-class quality and reliability in everything we build.

Next year this gavel is his. But right now I'd like for all of us to recognize Bob, and give him a warm Chrysler welcome.

He's a lucky man, because he's got an outstanding team behind him. Starting with Bob Lutz, who's worked his tail off on our new products for the last couple of years. The two Bobs may just be the best one-two team of car guys in this business. And with them is Jerry York, our new chief financial officer, who has run a couple of small companies himself and brings added financial and operating experience to the team.

And they're backed by some of the best specialists in the business—too many to mention! But it's a team with great *talent* and great *depth*!

And I envy all of them because after three or four lean years, Chrysler is entering the most exciting era of new product launches in its history. It actually began with the new Jeep Grand Cherokee this spring. It's already in volume production (we've built 19,000 of them so far), and they're drawing raves for both their quality and design.

We talked to some of our top dealers last week, and they told us the quality of the Grand Cherokee is the *very best* they've ever seen. The launch has been a huge success, and that's important to us because now we have to repeat it every six months for the next three years! That's the challenge—a brand-new vehicle platform twice a year through 1995!

All this has been a long time coming, though. We've been in an auto recession for over three full years. In fact, the last time auto sales *peaked* in this country was in 1986. Now I've been in this business just four years shy of a half a century, and I've never seen two auto recessions as bad as this one and the last one that ended in 1983. But the last one featured an oil shock, dou- ble- digit inflation, and interest rates that were over the moon.

This time the consumer just took a hike! Last year was particularly bad. The Big Three collectively lost $13.8 billion in North American automotive operations, before taxes! That made 1991 by far the worst year in the history of the industry.

It was *not* the worst year ever for Chrysler, however, in spite of losing $795 million. That dubious honor goes back to 1980, during that other bad recession and one the company wasn't as well prepared to weather. But this recession has been unlike any other our economy has been through. It was slow developing and it's been very slow recovering. In fact, I have to laugh when I hear them talk on TV about a double-dip or a triple-dip recession, like we're ordering ice cream cones or something, when, in fact, we haven't officially seen our *first* recovery yet.

But *there are* some good signs. Industry volume *is* picking up . . . a *little.* Last year 12.5 million cars and trucks were sold in the U.S.; so far this year, the annual rate is 12.6 million. With more retail and less fleet!

Our economists tell us there is pent-up demand in the market for about 4 million vehicles. Showroom traffic is up from a year ago. We're beginning to see dealer orders pick up. And our inventory is in such good balance, even a modest upturn will translate into instant production. And that triggers instant revenue because we get paid when we ship a car to a dealer.

Add all that to the rays of hope we've been seeing lately from the economy as a whole, and we have reason to be optimistic. Consumer attitude numbers are *finally* turning positive; for example, household income is up, and consumer debt is down. In fact, auto debt is down $13 billion, and that's the first time it's dropped year-to-year since 1958. So people have the money to spend on new cars.

But the best news of all, of course, is that unemployment inched down for April. People are slowly beginning to go back to work. And nothing helps car sales more than people earning a paycheck again.

But we haven't just been sitting around waiting for the things beyond our control to change. If we had, we wouldn't have made it through the tough times. We did four *major* things to get here.

First, we virtually reinvented the company with the development of our platform teams comprised of every discipline from design to engineering to manufacturing to sales and marketing and service—including all of our suppliers. Essentially we now have four "mini-companies" (minivan, truck and Jeep, big car, and small car) which can do a car or a truck in an unbelievable thirty-six months, and do it with higher quality and lower costs. And they do this by focusing only on adding value for the customer. Anything else is considered waste.

And now they can do it better than ever because of this complex. In fact, this room will soon be home to one thousand men and women of our large-car platform team. They'll work shoulder-to-shoulder, living with a vehicle literally from conception through production, and even after that to be sure the whole ownership experience is right.

Second, we cut costs—early and fast! The way the men and women of Chrysler stepped up to that challenge is nothing less than heroic. They cut costs at the rate of a billion dollars a year for three years, with another $1 billion scheduled to come out this year. That took enormous sacrifice, and it took a lot of innovation and ingenuity because they had to improve quality at the same time.

Third, we sold some of the furniture—$1.74 billion worth to be exact, which is one helluva yard sale. But none of it was critical to our core business. We sold Gulfstream Aerospace for $825 million, incidentally about

$200 million more than we paid for it. We sold shares in Mitsubishi Motors worth $813 million, and did very well on that one, too. And we sold our share of Diamond Star Motors to Mitsubishi for $100 million.

Fourth, we sold new equity in Chrysler for almost $1.3 billion. Plus put another $300 million worth into our pension fund. We did it in two phases. We had a public offering of common stock last fall that had gross proceeds of $408 million. If you'll recall, some of the experts were warning us it might fail. It didn't. It was oversubscribed.

In February, we did a private placement of convertible preferred stock that grossed $863 million—also oversubscribed.

We had no choice but to do the offerings. The credit rating agencies in effect said, "Get more capital into the company or else." But it turned out to be a major success for us. We brought in more cash than we anticipated (a lot more), and we got an important vote of confidence from the big investment houses who know us best. But more important, the dilution of our stock was more than offset by the rise in the stock price. We priced our public offering last October at 10⅛, and our stock closed yesterday at 18¾.

So, to get through the recession, we started by reinventing the company, we cut costs, sold assets, and tapped the equity market. But what's most important is what we *did not* do—we *did not* rob from our product plan. Not one dollar. In fact, we added to it. Which means that we have the same products coming out, and on the same *schedule,* that we would have if the recession had never occurred.

And now we not only still have all those products in the pipeline, but it looks like our timing couldn't be better.

In forty-six years I've learned that success in the auto market ultimately comes down to two things: *product* and *timing.* You need both. Product comes from hard work. Timing is more often than not *dumb luck.* That's what makes it scary. Dumb luck or not—I'll take it!

As it turned out, we *had* to launch *one* of our new products in the depths of the recession. But fortuitously, it was the new minivan!

We launched our *second*-generation minivan even before anyone else had gotten their *first* one right. And just like *our* first one, it's been a home run. It turned out to be recession-proof. While car sales were plunging, our minivan sales kept shooting up. And they kept going up until we are now selling on a regular basis over 50 percent of the total minivan market. At the beginning of last year, we had twelve competing models to contend with, by the way, including Japanese models being illegally dumped on the market. Now we're down to eight competitors because some of the others just gave up and left the market.

Right now, as I said, we're in the midst of launching the new Jeep Grand Cherokee—another second-generation entry into a market we—or, I should say, AMC before the merger—invented. We're building it in our new Jefferson North plant in Detroit, and both the plant and the product appear to be home runs.

We're also continuing the existing Cherokee in Toledo. We've repositioned and repriced it to give us a great one-two product punch that straddles the market in four-door sport-utilities.

Jeep has always been strong overseas, and is getting even stronger, especially in Europe and the Middle East. We're selling 25,000 a year there now. We're also adding right-hand drive for countries where they still insist on driving on the wrong side of the road. And, incidentally, it will knock off one of Japan's phony excuses for keeping us shut out of their market.

We're launching another car this spring, too. And it has probably generated more favorable press than anything the industry has ever turned out. I'm talking about *Viper*. We'll build perhaps 200 of them this year, and about 2,000 to 3,000 a year after that. It's been on virtually every magazine cover in the country. We've got customers who'll kill for one. It's a legend already, and it's barely out the door.

But the most important launch of all is the one coming up in just six weeks, and that's the new LH cars—Chrysler Concorde, Dodge Intrepid, and Eagle Vision. It's our first all-new car platform in a decade, and we think its "cab forward" design is going to set the standard for the whole industry in the '90s.

The one constant comment we get from auto writers and others who've already driven them is: "They're not like any cars Chrysler has ever built." *And they're not!* They're new—really new—from the ground up—and I don't think there's been more internal enthusiasm for a new product at Chrysler since I set foot in the place.

The LH line will be filled out early next year with the 207-inch version—the new Chrysler New Yorker. And this one is a real show-stopper!

Then, in mid-1993, we'll have our new T-300 full-size pickup truck. It will have a V-10 engine available for power, but it will have something really new for pickups: a rugged style more unique than anything you've ever seen! The full-size pickup market is about a million units a year. The Japanese don't compete in it. For a long time, it's belonged to Ford and GM almost exclusively.

Today we're selling about 80,000 full-size pickup trucks. Our production planning volume for the T-300 the first year is almost double that. This is virtually a new market for us, and one we think has tremendous growth potential.

Finally, in early '94 comes our new small car, still code-named the "PL." This one is going to be different, too. Not just in styling and performance, though. We're planning for it to be a *profitable* small car built right here in the U.S.A.

So that's what's coming in just the next two years.

Although our primary focus this past year has been on all these new products, we did a few other notable things worth mentioning.

We dedicated this tech center last fall. It's a big place, so it took us a week to do it. We had everybody join us—starting with our employees and retirees, who ate 63,000 hot dogs as they walked through it over a weekend. We had the governor, and other civic leaders, our suppliers, our vendors, our bankers, our competitors, and educators because this place is *about* education. In other words, we had the whole family in! Now it's *your turn* to see it. And it's about time because, after all, you *own* it. When you take the tour today, you'll not only see the *facility*, but you'll see some of the advanced future products being designed here.

We did a couple of other dedications, as well. I've already mentioned our new Jefferson North Assembly Plant. People don't build new car plants in inner cities these days, *unfortunately*. The Japanese build them in cornfields and hire a bunch of young kids right off the farm who never get sick and won't need a pension for about thirty years. That's the smart *economic* decision to make. I guess.

But we couldn't abandon the city we started in. And we couldn't abandon a loyal workforce with an average experience of twenty-six years.

Peter Ueberroth said last week that the key to revitalizing the inner city of Los Angeles is to put *production* jobs into the area. He's right. That's true of all our cities. More than anything else, except maybe good schools, they need some good, high-paying manufacturing jobs. And that will only come with some good vocational training first.

We dedicated another plant just two weeks ago in Graz, Austria. That's our new minivan plant, a joint venture with Steyr, a leader in all-wheel drive and four-wheel design, to serve the European market, 25,000 to 50,000 unit production. But it means we're back in Europe with a new plant and a new product, and we're back in Europe for good.

Speaking of traveling, I made a little trip to Japan in January with President Bush, in case you missed it. Of course, you had to have been away on a trip to Mars to miss it! But if you did, you probably heard it was a disaster. And, of course, you heard *wrong*. A strong message was sent to the Japanese, and they've responded in a lot of ways, including lowering their export limits to the U.S. We're still far from having fair access to the Japanese market, and far from getting a fair shake in our *own* market, for that matter, but there's a little progress right now. Japanese market share in April was down *four points* over last year!

But many of the most important things that happened around here in the past year didn't make big headlines.

Like the fact that every forty-two minutes during that year an air bag deployed in one of our cars. We've put 2.5 million air bags in our vehicles so far. And 28,000 of them have gone off. And every time one goes off there's a story with high human drama. I get lots of letters about them. Cops say it's a miracle! Nobody should have walked away, but they did. Customers send me pictures of themselves and their cars. There's nothing left of the cars, but the customers are still with us.

We changed the world's thinking about safety when we led the way in air bags. We were the first ones to have them standard in all our American-built cars . . . the first ones to put them in minivans . . . and the first ones to put them in sport-utilities, our new Grand Cherokee. We'll continue that undisputed safety leadership with *dual* driver- and passenger-side air bags standard in all our LHs.

Also during the year, one in every four minivan customers ordered our new integrated child seats. The seats have won awards from the National Highway Traffic Safety Administration, *Popular Science* magazine, and *Travel and Leisure* magazine. They've become so popular that we're also offering them on the LH models. You parents and grandparents know why they're popular—if you've ever had to lug those child seats around—and fasten them!

Chrysler was also recognized as a leader in keeping the *environment* safe as well. The Environmental Protection Agency just gave us its top award on Earth Day for the whole range of innovative pollution-control systems we built into our new Jefferson North plant. We are the only auto company ever to win this award.

And last month at the New York auto show, we introduced our electric minivan, the TEVan. The industry has a long way yet to go before electric cars are truly practical for many people, but we're in the forefront of the effort, just as we are with flexible-fuel vehicles. These are the vehicles that run on gasoline or clean methanol or any combination of the two.

So if you look at what's been accomplished here in the past couple of years—or the past several years—you almost wouldn't know we've been in a deep recession. We're in good shape today because when this industry hit the wall, we had the tenacity to stick with our long-range product plans no matter what.

We knew four years ago that the industry was heading into very rough seas, and we began getting ready. Three years ago, while Washington and most economists were still whistling past the graveyard and saying no recession was imminent, we said it was *already here* and began whacking away at costs.

But we did not stop work on this place. We did not stop work on the Jefferson North plant. And we did not take a dime out of the product plan to get us through.

We stayed the course, and we did it because we wanted to be *exactly* where we are as we sit here today, with exactly the great products that we're beginning to roll out. And we were willing to pay whatever price we had to pay to get here.

In case you've forgotten—that's called long-term thinking.

When we dedicated this facility last fall, I called it a monument to the end of short-term thinking in America. That's because all the while it was going up, we had a hundred other uses for a billion dollars. We had a hundred good reasons to delay it, or to turn it into a shopping mall.

But every one of them were *short-term needs* that would pass in a month or a year. Chrysler needs this place for the next decade, and the next century.

We could have put this off, or delayed any one of the new vehicle platforms under development when the recession hit. It would have made our bottom line look terrific and the management look like heroes. But we didn't touch any of them. Instead, we took the long view. I think that's what you pay us to do. At least I sure *hope* it is.

Now, I'd like to close this part of the meeting today with some personal thoughts since it's the last time I'll have the chance to talk to you.

You know you're getting close to retirement when people keep asking things like "What were your biggest accomplishments . . . or disappointments . . . or the biggest challenges . . . the biggest thrills?" Why is it in our nature to always want to look *back*?

But I'm beginning to realize that if you always have to reach *back* for the answers, then maybe you really haven't accomplished that much after all.

I've had some very big moments in my life. I treasure the memories of the Mustang . . . the Chrysler turnaround . . . the minivan revolution . . . the Statue of Liberty . . . the company's leadership position on safety and now education . . . this building that we're in today!

But the biggest moments of all—the ones I'm already the proudest of right now, and the ones I hope somebody will remember to tie my name to some-day—are the ones *yet to come.*

My greatest satisfaction will be seeing where this company goes from here. It's walking around this building and seeing these young designers and engineers who are so turned on by the cars and trucks that are still locked in their minds or scrambled up in their computers.

If I've earned my pay here, it will be for what *they* are able to accomplish. The same will be true of Bob Eaton and all those who follow him. We're really only *custodians* of the present. But we have a big hand in *creating* the future.

And so it doesn't matter much what you *leave behind,* it's what you had a hand in *starting.*

As they say, it's not the big tree you cut down, it's all the little ones you plant along the way. And finally, it's time to just say "Thank you."

I've been a very lucky man in my life because I've been in a business I've loved, and I've been able to do everything I wanted to do in it. I still love it—it's still exciting.

It's been a helluva ride—in good times and in bad. And I've been privileged to take that ride with some of the finest people in the world.

I've done exactly what I always dreamed of doing. You know, every little kid wants to grow up to be a *cowboy*. Well, I did! I really got to be one.

But there's a line from an old western movie called *Monte Walsh* that seems to fit here. Lee Marvin was Monte, and Jack Palance was his sidekick. They rode together for years. But then the Easterners started buying everything up and building fences. The frontier was going. And the two of them were getting older.

Monte Walsh still loved the life, though, and he just couldn't understand it when his pal one day announced that he was going to quit the range, move to town, and marry the "hardware widow." So Palance explained it to him.

"Monte," he said, "nobody gets to be a cowboy *forever!*"

And that includes me. But it's been a great trip. Sometimes it was a rough trip and the roller coaster got a little too steep, but it was pure *excitement*. And I've got *you* to thank for it.

You . . . the *shareholders* of Chrysler. You . . . the members of the *Chrysler board* . . . and you, the *management* and the *employees* and the *retirees* of Chrysler.

To every one of you . . . thanks a lot!

So, God speed. Good luck. I've loved every minute of it! I'm going to miss all of you.

Yes, all of you.

Thanks again.

Good-bye.

II
———
Speeches to External Constituencies

3. Speaking in Defense of Chrysler: Lee Iacocca's Crisis Communication

Timothy L. Sellnow

"I also learned that people can act very serenely in a crisis. They accept their fate. They know it's going to be a tough grind, but they grit their teeth and go with it."

—Lee Iacocca

Lee Iacocca's prepared remarks in the wake of federal indictments against two Chrysler executives for odometer tampering and accusations of reneging on what workers in Kenosha, Wisconsin, considered a binding oral contract are forms of crisis communication. An organizational crisis is a situation that runs the risk of escalating in intensity, falling under close media or government scrutiny, interfering with the normal operations of business, jeopardizing the positive public image enjoyed by a company or its officers, and damaging a company's bottom line (Fink 15-16). The odometer and Kenosha situations focused intense media scrutiny on Iacocca and Chrysler, creating the potential for dashing the corporation's hard-earned image as a trustworthy, no-nonsense organization that pledged to put the customers' needs first. Consequently, failure to respond effectively to either crisis could have caused serious long-term damage to the corporation's bottom line. The characteristics of crisis situations, however, make such a response onerous. For example, crises include elements of threat and surprise, while demanding some sort of reaction in a short time (Seeger 147). As such, organizations must respond quickly to a situation they could not fully anticipate and which imperils the organization's image, profitability, or both. This chapter first provides an explanation of what constitutes an effective response to an organizational crisis. Next, the contexts of the odometer and Kenosha crises are summarized to highlight the specific challenges present in each situation. Then Iacocca's speeches are examined according to these criteria. Finally, some conclusions regarding the effectiveness of Iacocca's crisis messages are offered.

Public messages delivered by an organization's leadership are vital for maintaining or regaining public trust (Seeger). Maintaining a sense of legitimacy in the eyes of the public is "in part rhetorical and involves offering adequate justifications within a consensus producing dialogue concerning the value of the institution and its activities" (Seeger 148). In composing crisis messages, organizational leaders have three general alternatives. They can ignore or downgrade the crisis, they can respond with routine procedures, or they can develop solutions targeted specifically at resolving the crisis. While routine procedures, such as blaming and firing individuals, *can* salvage an organization's credibility, original solutions that signal change within an organization often "enhance a perception of preventive, long-term change and renewed social legitimacy" (Sellnow and Seeger 17). For Iacocca's remarks to be successful in sustaining Chrysler's revered image in the long term, he needed to signal a willingness to develop and adopt unique solutions to each crisis.

Several authors contend that organizations may actually benefit from crisis. Marconi claims that organizations should capitalize on the profuse media coverage sparked by a crisis to draw attention to the organizations' commitment to public service (194). Similarly, Crable and Vibbert argue that organizations can and should participate proactively in the formation of policies that affect them, rather than simply responding or reacting. To do so, they advise organizations to engage in corporate or issue advocacy so that when issues peak in the public agenda, the organization is prepared to argue for policy decisions that are conducive to their goals (3–15).

In short, public communication is essential for regaining or maintaining public trust in the wake of an organizational crisis. Effective crisis messages tend to move beyond routine procedures and toward explaining preventive long-term solutions that indemnify victims. Moreover, organizations can turn the notoriety of a crisis in a positive direction if their response advocates a reasonable policy decision that benefits both the organization in particular and the industry in general. These observations provide a general framework for analyzing the following examples of Iacocca's crisis rhetoric.

THE ODOMETER-TAMPERING INDICTMENTS

On June 24, 1987, Chrysler executives Frank O'Reilly and Allen Scudder were indicted on federal charges of conspiracy to commit odometer fraud. An investigation into part of Chrysler's quality assurance program began "after Missouri state highway patrolmen stopped Chrysler executives for speeding and were frequently told by the drivers that they hadn't realized they were exceeding the speed limit because their odometers were disconnected" (Peterson 1A, 4A). The indictment claimed that Chrysler executives drove cars with the odometers disconnected for one day to five weeks, and that Chrysler replaced odometers showing as much as one hundred miles with new ones. Chrysler was also accused of repairing cars that were damaged in accidents and then selling them as new. Two dramatic examples involved the repair and sale (as new) of one car that was badly damaged in what was described as a rollover accident and a pickup that was damaged while in the parking lot of a lounge. In all, Chrysler was said to have sold sixty thousand previously driven cars as new during 1985 and 1986. The maximum fine facing Chrysler for these charges was $120 million. A company statement, issued shortly after the indictments became public, claimed that Chrysler's actions had been misinterpreted: "The U.S. attorney's office is attacking a legitimate quality assurance program, beneficial to consumers, by attempting to apply to the quality testing of new vehicles a federal statute designed to preclude the rolling back of odometers on used cars" (Peterson 1A). The company statement also challenged many of the accusations included in the indictment. Spokespersons from General Motors Corporation and Ford Motor Company denied that their testing procedures involved disconnecting odometers.

Scudder and O'Reilly pleaded innocent to all charges on June 26, 1987, as national attention spread quickly (Gruley, "2 Chrysler Execs" 14C). When Scudder and O'Reilly entered their plea, consumer activist Ralph Nader insisted publicly that Chrysler should compensate the sixty thousand owners of the disputed vehicles. Baron Bates, Chrysler's vice president for public relations, acknowledged the seriousness of the negative publicity when he said, "If the people feel we are doing something wrong, we have a problem and we're very concerned" (Miller, "Nader Denounces" 1A). Bates, however, did pledge Chrysler's support for the executives named in the federal indictment, saying, "We're behind these executives 100 percent and [Chrysler is] paying their legal fees" (Miller, "Nader Denounces" 4A). When asked about Iacocca's position on the odometer indictment, Bates reminded reporters that "the practice of disconnecting odometers predates Iacocca's arrival at Chrysler in 1978," and he insisted that the Chrysler chairman wanted to "'get out front' with the company's story" (Miller, "Nader Denounces" 4A). In a press conference on July 1, 1987, Iacocca did just that.

99

THE ODOMETER SPEECH

In his first book, Iacocca compared his straightforward style with that of his father: "He got right down to the heart of the matter, and I guess I'm the same way" (Iacocca and Novak 11). True to his word, Iacocca bluntly admitted that Chrysler's policy of testing cars with the odometers disengaged was "dumb." Worse, he contended, was the fact that "a few" cars were "damaged in testing badly enough that they probably should not have been sold as new." This action, Iacocca admitted, "went beyond dumb and reached all the way to *stupid*." In his introduction, Iacocca emphasized that his key concern was not with the quality assurance program. In fact, he suggested that if customers would have known their cars were tested by "a qualified Chrysler representative as a quality check," they would have been grateful. The concern he established as paramount was customer faith. In so doing, Iacocca removed the debate from a technical or legal context and placed it in the jurisdiction of the magistrates he said matter most: the customers. This decision was prudent when considering the fact that customers who had purchased the vehicles in question faced no danger. Iacocca's only reference to the legality of the situation served to dismiss it: "We'll deal with those legal charges in court and at the proper time." The fact that the indictments had caused some to question their faith in Chrysler, however, was something that Iacocca wisely would not tolerate.

Because the odometer situation ran the risk of escalating in intensity, Iacocca was challenged to take action that would quickly defuse customer concern. To do so, he took what could be viewed as an obvious and routine step: the practice of testing cars with odometers disconnected was eliminated. Iacocca's statement, "I'm damned sorry it happened, and you can bet that it won't ever happen again," leaves no room for doubt. Absent in Iacocca's remarks, however, is the assignment of blame to any individual or individuals who were responsible for the program. In *Talking Straight,* Iacocca explained his reaction to the odometer flap: "I was mad—but only at myself. The boss is always supposed to be on top of his team" (Iacocca and Kleinfield 128). The act of purging from an organization those who can be traced to the inception of a crisis is a routine solution that is ubiquitous in these situations. Yet Iacocca never shied from the personal criticism, despite the fact that the testing program predated his arrival at Chrysler and that he was not aware of the practice before the indictments. Had Iacocca distanced himself from the executives indicted for odometer fraud, he may have been able to portray the incident as an aberration limited in scope. While this argument could have turned attention toward these individuals and away from Chrysler, it would have left customers wondering how Chrysler could have let this happen. Instead, Iacocca followed his own management philosophy: "If you own up to your mistakes, you don't suffer as much" (Iacocca and Kleinfield 134).

In owning up to these mistakes, Iacocca offered a generous compensation program for affected customers. This program clearly constitutes an original solution. Iacocca pledged to go beyond a simple apology to regain the faith of Chrysler customers. To do so, he said he would go "overboard." Iacocca's promises to replace any damaged vehicle sold as new, no questions asked; to add two years or 20,000 miles and more comprehensive coverage to the warranties of cars that were in the testing program; and to provide free inspection and repair for affected customers were unprecedented and, by his own admission, constituted "overkill" (Iacocca and Kleinfield 131). Still, Iacocca's dramatic statement, "This is not a product recall. Hell, the only thing we're recalling here is our integrity," reminded listeners that he did not feel the automobiles in the testing program were in any way inferior. In so doing, he kept the focus of his response on rebuilding faith rather than replacing shoddy work. The benefits of this generosity were apparent. As noted earlier, original solutions tend to enhance the public's perception of the organization in the long term. Iacocca himself marveled at the public response to the compensation program he offered Chrysler customers. A Chrysler survey indicated that those with negative feelings about the incident stood at 55 percent before the speech. A similar survey after the speech indicated that 67 percent approved of the company's response. Iacocca said of this swing in opinion, "The survey people were astounded at how fast this flip-flop took place simply because I'd stood up and declared 'I screwed up'" (Iacocca and Kleinfield 132).

The remainder of the speech was devoted to clarifying Chrysler's side of the odometer story. This clarification focused primarily on the press. In his autobiographies, Iacocca candidly admitted that he took pains to maintain a positive relationship with the press. He claimed that dealing with the press, and others for that matter, when facing problems is "a lot easier if you've already got some rapport with the people who can help you solve them" (Iacocca and Kleinfield 79). Iacocca summarized his philosophy for dealing with the press as follows: "You're truthful. You're available. You background reporters when they're in a jam. And guess what? You come out okay" (Iacocca and Kleinfield 163). Perhaps because of his persistent effort to deal positively with the press, Iacocca was able to level some rather harsh criticism toward "some" reporters whose coverage of the odometer crisis, according to Iacocca, "contained inaccuracies and distortions that have blown it all out of proportion." By calling the media's coverage of the situation into question, Iacocca enabled himself to step beyond the indictments and discuss a larger policy issue: fairness in the media. At no point in the speech is this more poignant than when he turns the questions of trust and customer loyalty from Chrysler to some members of the media: "We're bending over backward to be fair to *our* customers. But those people are also *your* customers—your readers and viewers—so I hope you'll be fair to them, too." Iacocca offers compelling support for his accusations of inaccurate coverage by insisting that only a small fraction of the cars were ever damaged and that stories of excessive mileage and extreme damage were fictitious. By couching his efforts to clarify what had actually taken place at Chrysler in terms of fairness and accuracy of the media, Iacocca was able to get Chrysler's version of the story out to the public without denying that mistakes were made. Had the speech contained as much content aimed at dismissing or minimizing the mistakes or violations and emphasized the inaccurate coverage, Iacocca's response would have taken the more routine form of denial or avoidance.

In terms of the criteria established at the beginning of this chapter, Iacocca's response to the odometer indictments constitutes an exemplary speech. He moved quickly from routine procedures of accepting or establishing blame into a detailed description of a solution designed to address this crisis specifically. An editorial in the *Detroit News* argued that this case required publicity rather than prosecution and that the claims in Iacocca's speech went "a long way toward removing the cloud over Chrysler's credibility" (Sorge, "Stupid, Yes" 6A). During the weeks following the speech, media coverage of the indictments quickly dwindled. Six months after Iacocca's remarks, Chrysler entered a plea of nolo contendere, meaning it would neither contest nor admit the criminal charges. In a press release statement, the automaker agreed to pay $16 million to settle the charges, saying, "Testing of cars with odometers disconnected was stupid. It makes no sense to go to trial to defend that practice" ("Chrysler Settles" 1C).

THE KENOSHA SITUATION

In January 1987, Wisconsin Governor Tommy Thompson appeared optimistic that the American Motors Corporation and Chrysler Corporation were willing to spend "hundreds of millions of dollars" to renovate, rather than close, the Kenosha factory—then the oldest operating vehicle assembly plant in the country (Sorge, "Kenosha Eyed" 1C). By late February 1987, however, the entire deal was said to rest in the hands of the United Auto Workers negotiators. AMC demanded a series of concessions that local union leaders labeled "unrealistic" (Miller, "AMC Sets Contract" 1C). By March 1, 1987, talks had collapsed, and optimism for keeping the Kenosha plant open faded. Enthusiasm was roused once more on March 10, 1987, when Chrysler announced that it had proposed to buy AMC. The merger, labeled a "smart move" by analysts, also meant more Chrysler subcontracting work for Kenosha (Gruley, "$1 Billion Bid" 1A). UAW Jeep unit chairman Dan Twiss viewed the merger with tempered enthusiasm, saying, "Too many things can happen between now and January" (Nehman 7A). With approval of the complex merger process on March 21, 1987, came concern that the consolidation would mean the elimination of jobs. Yet the Kenosha workers continued to view the merger as a breath of new life. When in October, 1987, Chrysler eliminated a shift at Kenosha, the jobs of fourteen hundred workers were threatened. However, one thousand of those workers were transferred to a new line of production at the plant, and Iacocca said Chrysler "hoped to avoid job cuts at Kenosha by building 'a lot more cars' there" (Sorge, "Chrysler to Lay Off" 2E).

At the end of October 1987, slower than anticipated sales of Chrysler vehicles created a sense of urgency as the corporation worked to cut overhead to absorb AMC. Downsizing included forty-five hundred salaried workers. Most were engineers and technicians associated with the former AMC (Miller and Sorge 1A). In November, the closing of a Chrysler assembly plant in St. Louis and a major reduction at a Newark, Delaware, plant signaled that Chrysler was having problems "extending beyond its attempts to deal with the acquisition of American Motors Corp." (Miller, "AMC Sets Contract" 1C).

By January 1988, the pessimistic view espoused by UAW leader Dan Twiss at the Chrysler-AMC merger appeared prophetic for the Kenosha plant. Citing problems with the labor agreement, flexibility, and efficiency, Richard E. Dauch, Chrysler's top manufacturing executive, confirmed that the Kenosha plant was a candidate for termination, saying, "We have too much capacity" and that any closing would be made based solely on "business considerations" (Sorge, "Better Listen" 1D). By the end of January, Chrysler announced plans to move its major production in the Kenosha plant to Detroit, putting the eighty-six-year-old plant "at the top of its plant-closing list" ("Omni-Horizons Moved" 2D). On January 28, 1988, Chrysler announced that it would close all but its engine plant in Kenosha, idling fifty-five hundred employees. Chrysler Motors Corporation Chairman Gerald Greenwald blamed the closing on the industrial policies of the Reagan administration, saying, "International currency adjustments have not checked the flow of products from Japanese companies and the American auto companies face intense pressure to keep only the most modern facilities open" (Miller, "5,500 Lose Jobs" 1A). Owen Bieber, UAW President, called the closing "a shock and a terrible tragedy" but agreed with Greenwald, saying, "The root of the problem is the relentless advance of foreign-made vehicles and vehicles assembled here by foreign-based companies" (Miller, "5,500 Lose Jobs" 1A, 12A).

Within days of the announcement to close Kenosha, Chrysler's image and Iacocca's reputation were questioned by Kenosha residents and sympathizers. Donald Holland, Kenosha's city administrator, summarized the mood of the city when he said, "We were happy when Chrysler bought AMC. As it stands now, we would have been better off if they had left us alone" (Sorge, "Era Comes" 1F). Holland accused Iacocca and Greenwald of reneging on a five-year agreement to build cars in Kenosha saying, "We feel they were not truthful when they made that commitment" (Sorge, "Era Comes" 1F). In early February 1988, UAW officials argued that they, too, were told the plant would remain open for five years, and requested that Chrysler rethink its plans. Iacocca responded by saying, "If the comment was made that we hoped it could be five years, the world changed. . . . We screwed up" (Sorge, "UAW Ask Chrysler" 5F). Claiming Chrysler made a binding oral contract to assemble cars in Kenosha for five years, Wisconsin Governor Thompson threatened to sue the corporation (Sorge and Higgins 14F). This was the setting when, on February 16, 1988, Iacocca journeyed to Milwaukee to address the Kenosha controversy.

THE KENOSHA SPEECH

In dealing with the Kenosha situation, Iacocca was true to the management philosophy he espoused in both of his books. In those texts, he claimed that the key quality in a good manager is "decisiveness" (Iacocca and Novak 50), and that as a manager "you simply cannot bow to pressure if you think you've made the right decision—or you'll be too paralyzed to act" (Iacocca and Novak 120). When Chrysler sales dropped late in 1987, the corporation's leadership knew it could no longer afford to keep the Kenosha plant operating. The closing was portrayed by Chrysler as an unfortunate but absolutely necessary business decision. Still, as Schultz and Seeger explain, "The expectations Chrysler created made the Kenosha plant closing a unique case resulting in special obligations" (57). Consequently, for Iacocca's speech to be successful, he had to offer some essence of an original solution to address the unparalleled aspects of the Kenosha situation.

Iacocca wisely established the business logic behind Chrysler's decision at the outset of the speech when he said closing the plant was "a crummy call that we had no choice but to make," because "Time, and the marketplace, just caught up with an 86-year-old plant." The emotional fervor surrounding the closing had resulted in accusations that Chrysler had never had the best interests of the Kenosha plant in mind. Iacocca insisted that he and the rest of the corporation's leadership had simply overestimated what could be done with the Kenosha facilities. He was brutally honest in admitting so: "We made a mistake with Kenosha, and I'm here to admit it. We are guilty as hell of being cockeyed optimists. And we're paying the price for it now."

While he did not seek to avoid blame for misleading the people of Kenosha, Iacocca quickly expanded his remarks to denounce the trade policies of the Reagan administration. By listing thirteen automotive plants owned by three different corporations in eleven cities that were about to close or had closed recently at a cost of 42,450 jobs, he identified a trend reaching far beyond Kenosha or Chrysler. The unique circumstances of the Kenosha closing brought intense media scrutiny to Chrysler, and Iacocca sagely exploited the coverage to advocate his position on free trade. He cogently summarized his position in the speech when he said, "If you want to beat up on me, okay, but you'd better go to Washington if you want to fix it." In his second autobiography, Iacocca detailed the argument he began in Kenosha: "We are trying to help one small community, but the bigger problem is that the federal government doesn't seem too troubled by what this represents. Lost jobs are the end result of unfair trade practices, which is a chapter in itself. We desperately need a national plan to assist people who suddenly find themselves without work. We can't just say, 'Oh, we'll train them to flip hamburgers' " (Iacocca and Kleinfield 112). The absence of government leadership in the area of trade does not excuse the fact that Chrysler created unrealistic expectations for the Kenosha workers. However, the decision to close the plant was made in the context of what Iacocca contended was unfair foreign competition in auto sales. Expanding his argument to include elements of foreign trade policy was both reasonable and, in a crisis situation, advisable.

Based on letters from Kenosha residents, Iacocca summarized the primary fears resulting from the closing in two questions: "Will I be able to keep the family under a roof?" and "What about my kids' education?" He hoped the answer to these questions would come in the form of a "Chrysler-Kenosha Trust" to provide housing and education assistance. This effort clearly constitutes an original solution. Calling the Kenosha situation "truly unique," Iacocca exclaimed he would do what "makes sense, to those who are losing their jobs." By pledging the net profit on car and truck sales for all of 1988 in the state of Wisconsin, Iacocca sought to provide a basis for a short-term retrenchment and a long-term recovery for the Kenosha workers and their families. Again, however, he expands the context to include both Chrysler dealerships in Wisconsin and the city and state government saying, "Chrysler can't do it alone—*no* company can—but *together,* maybe we can do something meaningful—even historic." When considering his initial contention that Chrysler was not solely responsible for the problem, his conclusion that the solution must be shared with others appears reasonable. Iacocca never seeks to avoid blame, but he consistently amplifies the orientation of the crisis to directly or indirectly identify others whose policies either helped to cause or should, in his opinion, be altered to help provide a solution to the crisis.

105

Despite his unprecedented offer to fund the majority of a trust for the Kenosha workers, the intensity of the situation lingered. At the close of his speech, Iacocca indicated he hoped the trust would unite state, local, and corporate leadership so "we can turn off the rhetoric and start helping Kenosha look to the future." His speech in the odometer situation had done just that. People were concerned that they had purchased cars that were used or damaged, and so he gave them tremendous warranties and, in some cases, new cars. Customer ire faded quickly. In Kenosha, the people had lost their jobs, and it was simply not feasible for Chrysler to rehire them in another capacity. In *Talking Straight,* Iacocca recalls that much of his Kenosha message "fell on deaf ears. What they wanted was jobs" (Iacocca and Kleinfield 112). Despite Iacocca's explanation that the Kenosha plant was no longer efficient enough to be competitive, Kenosha workers accused him of closing their plant so he could keep a plant in Detroit open (Higgins, "Chrysler to Aid" 3A). A month after the speech, Kenosha employees rented a billboard on a highway near Detroit saying, "Iacocca Keep Your Word to Kenosha" (Sorge, "Kenosha Workers Send" 3F). In the end, the closing date for Kenosha was moved back slightly, and Chrysler agreed to repay the $60 million in concessions Kenosha workers had initially given AMC (Sedgwick and Fogel 1A). In the wake of the Kenosha crisis, some began to question whether Iacocca's image had been blemished. When asked directly about his public image after the Kenosha closing, Iacocca replied in his typical plainspoken style, "Whatever it is, it is. I never worry about it" (Higgins, "Chrysler Corp. Feels the Heat" 1F).

CONCLUSIONS

Iacocca's remarks in response to the odometer and Kenosha situations are examples of effective crisis rhetoric. In the odometer situation, Iacocca addressed the accusations in a straightforward manner, admitting guilt and offering restitution for all customers affected. His pledge to discontinue the program was given merit by the fact that Iacocca himself labeled the practice dumb and, in some cases, stupid. He offered Chrysler customers an honest assessment and an original solution that was arguably more than fair. Iacocca's willingness to take on what he admitted was a minority in the press allowed him to dedicate more than a third of the speech to clarifying and diminishing the accusations against Chrysler. By admitting up front that the corporation had made a serious error and by placing this segment of the speech in the context of coverage, he was able to avoid any appearance of a guilty party trying to slide out from the consequences of an action.

The Kenosha situation provided a drastically different situation for Iacocca. No plant closing is easy, but the situation in Kenosha was made more difficult by the fact that Chrysler had raised expectations it could not fulfill. The Kenosha workers were irate and Iacocca understood that. In *Talking Straight,* he said of Kenosha, "Business has a responsibility not to go broke, and so, reluctantly, we decided we had to close it down" (Iacocca and Kleinfield 112). In predictable Iacocca fashion, he made a difficult decision and stood by it publicly. In his Kenosha remarks, Iacocca accepted blame for raising expectations too high, but, more importantly, he used the situation to advocate an improved trade policy that he contended would help not only Chrysler employees but the entire American auto industry. Eliminating jobs will always bring negative publicity, but Iacocca's efforts to portray Chrysler as a victim rather than a villain placed his corporation in a proactive rather than reactive position. Iacocca's pledge to work with state and local officials in Wisconsin to create a trust for the Kenosha employees displayed a level of sensitivity that is uncommon, if not unprecedented, in a plant closing. Portraying the trust fund as an effort to satisfy the immediate needs of the workers while preparing them for the long term constituted an original solution.

Iacocca's remarks and his plan for the future of the Kenosha workers and their families did not have the kind of immediate impact that was evident in the odometer situation. Kenosha workers continued to complain publicly, and Wisconsin's governor persisted with his threat of a lawsuit. Still, the intensity of the situation, on a national scale, leveled off after the initial press reaction to Iacocca's speech. In short, the Kenosha situation did not escalate in intensity following Iacocca's remarks and pledges to the workers. Iacocca addressed the crisis head-on and held his ground. The plant was eventually closed, and both Chrysler and Iacocca survived the subsequent storm.

Iacocca's tough, direct style is especially appropriate in crisis situations. His unflappable demeanor and willingness to take heat in controversial situations are characteristics that are enviable for any speaker who must face the controversy of a crisis. The content of his messages also reflected effective crisis communication. In both speeches, he assessed the situation, admitted blame where he felt his corporation was at fault, and devised original plans to resolve the situations. Iacocca's credibility naturally enabled him to discuss policy issues related to the media and foreign trade. In short, Iacocca capitalized on his image and style to deliver well-developed and comprehensive messages in response to two very difficult situations that threatened to tarnish both his and his corporation's public image.

WORKS CITED

"Chrysler Settles Odometer Case." *Detroit News* 15 Dec. 1987: 1C.

Crable, Richard E. and Steven L. Vibbert. "Managing Issues and Influencing Public Policy." *Public Relations Review* 11 (1985): 3–15.

Fink, Steven. *Crisis Management: Planning for the Inevitable.* New York: AMOCOM, 1986.

Gruley, Bryan. "$1 Billion Bid for AMC is a Smart Move, Analysts Say." *Detroit News,* 10 March 1987: 1A, 6A.

———. "2 Chrysler Execs Plead Innocent to Odometer Fraud." *Detroit News,* 27 June 1987: 14C.

Higgins, James V. "Chrysler Corp. Feels the Heat." *Detroit News,* 1 May 1988: 3F.

———. "Chrysler to Aid Kenosha Workers Who Lose Jobs." *Detroit News,* 17 Feb. 1988: 3A.

Iacocca, Lee A. and Sonny Kleinfield. *Talking Straight.* New York: Bantam, 1988.

———, and William Novak. *Iacocca: An Autobiography.* New York: Bantam, 1984.

Marconi, Joe. *Crisis Marketing: When Bad Things Happen to Good Companies.* Chicago: Probus Publishing, 1992.

Miller, Edward. "5,500 Lose Jobs in Chrysler Closing." *Detroit News,* 28 Jan. 1988: 1A, 12A.

———. "AMC Sets Contract Deadline." *Detroit News,* 24 Feb. 1987: 1C, 8C.

———. "Nader Denounces Odometer Tampering." *Detroit News,* 26 June 1987: 1A, 4A.

Miller, Edward and Marjorie Sorge. "Chrysler, AMC Workers Feel Ax." *Detroit News,* 31 Oct. 1987: 1A, 8A.

Nehman, John F. "UAW Leaders Voice Relief." *Detroit News,* 10 March 1987: 7A.

"Omni-Horizons Moved to Detroit." *Detroit News,* 26 Jan. 1988: 2D.

Peterson, John E. "U.S. Charges Chrysler, 2 Execs." *Detroit News,* 25 June 1987: 1A, 4A.

Schultz, Pamela D. and Matthew Seeger. "Corporate Centered Apologia: Iacocca in Defense of Chrysler." *Speaker and Gavel* 28 (1991): 50–60.

Sedgwick, David and Helen Fogel. "Kenosha Deal May Give Workers Up To $10,000 Each." *Detroit News,* 3 May 1988: 1A, 9A.

Seeger, Matthew W. "The Challenger Tragedy and Search for Legitimacy." *Communication Studies* 37 (1987): 147–157.

Sellnow, Timothy and Matthew Seeger. "Crisis Messages: Wall Street and the Reagan Administration After Black Monday." *Speaker and Gavel* 26 (1989): 9–18.

Sorge, Marjorie. "'Better Listen to the Bell.'" Detroit News 18 Jan. 1987: 1D.

———. "Chrysler to Lay Off 400 in Kenosha." *Detroit News,* 30 Oct. 1987: 2E.

———. "Era Comes to an End at Kenosha." *Detroit News,* 28 Jan. 1988: 1F, 3F.

———. "Kenosha Eyed for New Jeeps." *Detroit News,* 7 Jan. 1987: 1C, 6C.

———. "Kenosha Workers Send Chrysler a Big Message." *Detroit News,* 10 March 1988: 1F.

———. "Stupid, Yes; Criminal, No." *Detroit News,* 7 July 1987: 6A.

———. "UAW Asks Chrysler to Keep Kenosha." *Detroit News,* 5 Feb. 1988: 1E.

Sorge, Marjorie and James Higgins. "Wisconsin Readies Kenosha Lawsuit." *Detroit News,* 10 Feb. 1988: 14F.

REMARKS AT A PRESS CONFERENCE CONCERNING ODOMETERS

Highland Park, Michigan, July 1, 1987

Chrysler had been indicted for testing a small number of cars with the odometers disconnected. It was a legal problem, but it was a much bigger public relations problem. Iacocca held a press conference in which he was so candid that the issue died quickly, and both his credibility and Chrysler's actually increased as a result. He challenged the press to be as responsible to their readers as he was being toward Chrysler's customers—and they were.

Good afternoon to all of you. I should start by saying that I've had better weeks. I feel a little *older* than I did a week ago—by at least a couple of years in the last thirty days. In the past month, I paced the field at the Indy 500 and the Monte Carlo Grand Prix—but back home I'd say the field got out ahead of me. But after forty-one years in this business, you learn to take the bitter with the sweet.

As you all know, last week Chrysler was charged with violating the law because of the way we used to conduct our overnight testing program up until last October. We'll deal with those legal charges in court and at the proper time.

But we've got a much more immediate problem, and that problem we're going to handle *today*!

Our big concern is for our *customers*, the people who had enough faith in Chrysler to buy a vehicle from us. These charges, and the press reports about them, are causing some of those customers to question that faith, and we simply cannot tolerate that. If we did something to cause them confusion and concern about the quality of the vehicle they bought, then we're going to fix that right now!

And, by the way, we *did* do something to have them question their faith in us—*two* things, in fact.

The first was *dumb*. We test-drove a small percentage of our cars with the odometers disengaged and didn't tell the customers.

The second went beyond dumb and reached all the way to *stupid*. A few—and I mean a *few*—cars were damaged in testing badly enough that they probably should not have been sold as new.

109

Those are mistakes that we will never make again. *Period*!

The only law we broke was the law of common sense. All of us at Chrysler have broken our backs to get this company where it is today. And no matter how hard we worked, we would have died in our tracks without the confidence of our *customers*. We asked them to trust us, and they did. And now they've been given a reason to question that trust.

That's unforgivable, and we've got nobody but ourselves to blame.

But let me set the record straight before I tell you what we are going to do for those customers.

The overnight testing program that we use is part of our quality assurance program. Its *only purpose* is to help us provide the customer with the best-quality vehicle that we can. Everybody in the industry has a similar program. And, by the way, their cars get sold as *new*, too, regardless of the mileage on the odometer, so some of the headlines have been a little unfair.

Going back through my forty-one years in this industry, a lot of test cars have been driven with the odometers unhooked. Naively or not, we always considered those tests a part of the manufacturing process. Some of the others say they started testing with the odometers engaged a while back, but unfortunately we continued the old practice until last October.

On average, we figure the cars were tested for about forty miles. If we had put them in the showroom with forty miles on the odometer and explained that those miles were driven by a qualified Chrysler representative as a quality check, our customers would not only have *understood*, they would probably have been *grateful*.

Some of the high-priced guys like Porsche actually test-drive every single car they sell, and sometimes for a lot more miles than we do. The only difference is that they say the odometers are hooked up.

By the way, the test mileage is *not* excessive. It's home and back, normally. If a guy lives out in the country the mileage might be a little higher. Sixty-five miles is our limit. In the past, when the odometers were not connected, we now know that some abuses took place.

We are *proud* of the lengths we go to in order to assure quality. We are *not* proud of doing something that has now created the *appearance* in our customers' minds that we weren't treating them squarely.

That was the dumb part.

The stupid part was fixing and selling a few cars that were damaged in testing, and that maybe shouldn't have been sold. *Everybody* fixes *minor* damage, of course. Nobody scraps a $15,000 car for a $15 ding. Neither during the production cycle or when a car is being driven as part of a quality check.

How many cars? Our records show seventy-two cars that were damaged in the testing. We only sold as new forty of those. The other thirty-two were scrapped or sold used at an auction. Of those forty, the worst case we can find is one requiring $950 worth of repairs, and they go all the way down to $91. Most were closer to the $91 than the $950, by the way. No excuses, though—if we sold just *one* car that we shouldn't have, that's too many. But these numbers hardly establish a pattern of abuse. We don't run a bump-and-paint shop around here!

And the horror stories ain't all that horrible if you look at all the facts. Let me take just one, the now-famous hydro-planing Turismo that everybody in the world already knows about.

The guy testing the car was on his way home in a heavy rainstorm, hit a large puddle of standing water in the highway, and slid into a ditch at a very slow rate of speed. The car ended up on its side. It did *not* flip over.

The only damage from the accident was a dented quarter panel. The driver damaged some trim getting out of the car. And a tire and rim were slightly damaged when the car was righted.

The next day, the dent and the trim were fixed, and the wheel was replaced. Total cost: $950. You all know that you can practically do that much damage today backing into your mailbox!

The guy in the accident then took the car again and tested it thoroughly before it was shipped. And I'd say he was particularly well qualified to pass on it, because do you know who the guy was? A senior quality engineer with nineteen years' experience!

Now again, no excuses. Maybe the car shouldn't have been sold as new even if there was nothing wrong with it. For sure, this particular customer should have been told it was damaged and repaired—that's where we let that customer down. I'm damned sorry it happened, and you can bet that it won't ever happen again. And that's a promise.

Believe it or not, we're a helluva lot harder on ourselves than any federal prosecutor or anybody else. If we've had even *one* case where we sold a car that we shouldn't have, then we violated the trust of *every* customer. At least that's the way I choose to see it.

I think we have let some of them down with our testing program, and we're going to make it right. In fact, we're going a little *overboard* maybe, because when people trust you and you give them reason to question that trust, a simple apology isn't enough.

Here's what we are going to do.

For starters, we're offering to replace any vehicle that we know was damaged in our testing program. Not just the ones that should not have been sold —but *all* of them. It doesn't matter how slight the damage, or that it was completely repaired before the vehicle was sold. Those customers get a brand-new car or truck if they want one—no questions asked!

For those whose cars were tested without the odometers connected, we're going to do three things.

First, as a goodwill gesture, we're voluntarily extending their warranty coverage to 7 years or 70,000 miles. It was 5/50 when they bought the vehicles—the best warranty in the industry at the time to begin with. So we're adding 20,000 miles and 2 full years to their coverage.

Second, we're beefing up that coverage by including all the major systems normally not covered by the powertrain 7/70 such as brakes, suspension, electrical, steering, and air conditioning.

And third, just to put their minds at rest, we're telling them to bring the car in when they get the two new warranties for a free inspection. If we find any product deficiency, we'll fix it free of charge.

Now, be sure you understand this: We didn't do anything to *hurt* their warranty protection in the first place. We're just trying to show our good faith to our customers, and to reassure them of the quality of their vehicles. So we're going to back them even *better* and *longer*.

This is not a product recall. Hell, the only thing we're recalling here is our integrity.

So that's what *we're* doing for our customers. I'd like *you* to do something for them, too.

I started out by saying that I've had a bad week. Well, a few of you have had a bad week, too. Some, not *all*, of the coverage of this thing has contained inaccuracies and distortions that have blown it all out of proportion.

I don't mind the cartoons of good old Lee the used car salesman—hell, I laughed at them myself. Well, I cried a little, too. I'll take those shots—fair or unfair.

But I do mind—one helluva lot—the stories that have caused our *customers* more concern than they need to have. Some now think that all we do around here is go joyriding in the cars every night and then roll back the odometers in the morning.

We don't do that, *never* did that, and *you* know it.

We're bending over backward to be fair to *our* customers. But those people are also *your* customers—your readers and viewers—so I hope you'll be fair to them too.

This thing is crying out for a little *perspective*.

We're talking about 2 percent of our cars being tested.

We're talking about an average of forty miles.

We're talking about a tiny fraction of them being damaged, and mostly very minor damage.

And we're talking about an even *tinier* fraction of them being sold when maybe they shouldn't have been.

Did we screw up? You bet. We're human. Sometimes people do dumb things. But all this nonsense about "Where's the pride"—well, we never *lost* it. Because we're *proud* of the huge quality improvements we've made at Chrysler—17 percent last year alone. We're *proud* that our quality allowed us to offer our 5/50 warranty a full five years ahead of anybody else. And we're *proud* that we still back our quality better than anyone else with our 7/70.

Finally, after all we've been through here at Chrysler, we sure as hell aren't going to compromise everything we've accomplished by *intentionally* and systematically mistreating the customer in the way the stories in the past week have portrayed.

You know us better than that. At least I *hope* you do. And I sure have to hope that our *customers* do.

REMARKS AT A PRESS CONFERENCE CONCERNING THE KENOSHA PLANT CLOSING

Milwaukee, Wisconsin, February 16, 1988

Even before Chrysler bought American Motors Corporation in the fall of 1987, it had been building cars in AMC's huge, old Kenosha assembly plant. When the merger took place, the workers in that plant and the people of Kenosha felt secure that Chrysler would keep the plant open. That, in fact, was Chrysler's hope. But by early 1988, the market ended that hope. The plant had to go. And the city felt betrayed. Iacocca went to nearby Milwaukee and held a press conference to outline how the company would help the city deal with the situation.

Good afternoon. Someone just told me that one of your TV stations is interrupting a soap opera to cover this live—as if I didn't have enough problems—irate housewives are going to write in complaining. Based on some of the things I've read and heard in the last two weeks, there are probably a lot of you who doubted I'd ever show up here in person.

Well, I'm here. It may have taken me too long, but there were good reasons for that: I didn't have a message to deliver and I didn't have a plan to present. But we've talked to a lot of people—and heard from the people of Kenosha—and we've put a plan together. That's why I'm here today.

Let me say at the outset that I've seen Chrysler raked over the coals for two weeks, and I think some of it has been unfair. Unfair—but understandable.

In the heat that always follows a plant closing, emotions naturally run high. And I'm an expert on that: I've had to close a lot of plants. It's a lousy time to try and communicate because people are angry, and nobody listens well when they're angry.

Let me start by reminding you that we've said from the outset that we'd not only meet our normal obligations to our workers and the community, we'd go beyond them. We intend to do that, and I'm here today to tell you—and the people in Kenosha—just how we'll do that.

But first, let me repeat that the decision to close the Kenosha stamping and assembly plants later this year was a crummy call that we had no choice but to make. We've been all through that. We didn't renege on anything . . . and we didn't break our word to anybody. Time, and the marketplace, just caught up with an eighty-six-year old plant.

When you have to make a decision like we did, you're the villain. There's no getting around it. It comes with the territory these days. Most people don't see it yet, but we're really not *villains* at Chrysler, we're *victims*—not quite as much as those people losing their jobs, but victims nevertheless.

We're *all* victims—all of us in this country—of years of unfair trade policies that have flooded our market with foreign products, closed our factories, and put our people on the street. This isn't a Chrysler problem, or a Kenosha problem—it's an *American* problem.

But it never hits home, does it, until it's *your* job . . . or the guy's next door . . . or the guy who sits in front of you in church. Until then, it's just a bunch of employment figures or trade numbers in small print at the bottom of the business page.

Well, it hit home in Kenosha a couple of weeks ago. For that community, it felt like the world fell in. But it's not just in Kenosha. Right now, even as we stand here, the same thing is going on in:

Norwood, Ohio . . . 4,000 jobs.

Hamilton, Ohio . . . 2,500 jobs.

St. Louis, Missouri . . . 2,200 jobs.

Leeds, Missouri . . . 1,700 jobs.

Framingham, Massachusetts . . . 3,700 jobs.

Westmoreland, Pennsylvania . . . 2,500 jobs.

Willow Springs, Illinois . . . 2,900 jobs.

Pontiac, Michigan . . . 3,500 jobs.

Flint, Michigan (*two* plants in Flint) . . . 6,650 jobs.

Detroit, Michigan (*two more* plants in Detroit) . . . 7,300 jobs.

And now Kenosha. Eleven cities . . . thirteen automotive plants . . . closed or closing . . . 42,450 jobs!

Eleven General Motors plants, one Volkswagen plant, and the last one—*ours*. (Even if it was only ours for a short time.)

And these are just the *large* plants . . . the big stamping and assembly plants. You wouldn't have time for me to read a list of all the smaller components plants (and *their* cities) that are closing, too.

Worst of all—Kenosha isn't the last. There will be more cities, and more plants, and more jobs, because the American auto industry has too much capacity, and it's being crowded out by the imports and new foreign factories going up here.

But let me add that Kenosha was destined to close. Regardless of who owned it—American Motors Corporation . . . Renault . . . Chrysler . . . or somebody else. It can't compete anymore; the plant, not the people. It's just happened sooner than we expected.

115

That's the stark naked reality of the thing. I'm just the messenger bringing the bad news. If you want to beat up on me, okay, but you'd better go to Washington if you want to *fix* it. I've been just about the loudest critic around of our country's trade policies, and so far they haven't listened to me.

Nevertheless, the people in Kenosha are *our* people . . . and the community has relied for a long time on a plant that is now *ours*, so we've got a special obligation to help them out.

We made a mistake with Kenosha, and I'm here to admit it. We are guilty as hell of being cockeyed optimists. And we're paying the price for it now.

A year ago, we moved our two oldest car lines into the oldest car factory in the country, knowing full well that time would run out for that plant. Moving our cars there extended its life. (And, remember, we didn't even *own* it at the time.)

But we honestly hoped that we could build cars in Kenosha for three to five years. It was our *plan*. Otherwise, we sure wouldn't have invested $200 million of our money to change it over to Chrysler production. (As I said two weeks ago in New York, blame us for being dumb managers for spending $200 million to put two old cars in an eighty-six-year-old plant, but please don't call *me* a liar when I've gotta close it sooner than I thought.)

We felt good at the time about keeping fifty-five hundred people on the job. But what we did—unintentionally—was create expectations that couldn't be fulfilled. That, in retrospect, turns out to have been a mistake.

Now, I understood the strong reaction when the inevitable happened. Because I've been through this before, as I said. I know that the loss of fifty-five hundred jobs is a blow to any community. But I thought maybe we'd get at least *some* credit for extending the life of the plant and putting a $171-million payroll into the community while it was open. We had this quaint idea that keeping 5,500 people on the job was a good thing, even though everybody knew the plant's days were numbered.

But now I see that our life support was a mistake, and the expectations we created have just added to the pain. That makes Kenosha unique—that, and the size of the plant in relation to the size of the community. You know, there are a lot of people who felt we should do nothing special here, for fear we'd set a *precedent*. That we'd incur obligations at all the *other* locations where we—and others—are forced to shut down.

Well, this is not a precedent for anything—*we* know—and *you* know—that the situation here is *truly unique* . . . and because of that, and because the people come first, we've spent a couple of weeks trying to figure out just what we *could* do that would fit this special situation. And we got the answer from the people of Kenosha *themselves*.

I've received a lot of mail from Kenosha, as you can imagine. Some of it you can't print. Most of the letters, though, just have a lot of pain, and a lot of worry in them. I wish I didn't have to read them all—but I do.

This one is from John Hosmanek. He's the superintendent of schools. He says 1,905 families with a total of 2,358 kids in his schools are going to be hurt.

He says, "We accept the fact that our circumstances, though unfortunate, are not the result of some malevolence by Chrysler Corporation, but rather the economic imbalances which have developed internationally." I appreciate that! The super is perceptive! But then he goes on to ask if there is anything we can do to be sure the kids' education doesn't suffer because their parents are out of work.

I noticed in one of the news stories that the parochial school people have the same concern.

Then there are a lot of letters like these. They're wondering how they'll make the house payments when the paychecks stop—or who'll pay the rent. Long, touching, handwritten—with family pictures attached.

Well, those are the first two things that hit people right after they get a pink slip. "Will I be able to keep the family under a roof?" And "What about my kids' education?" Instinctive family reactions!

Those are the big problems that the people in Kenosha have told *us* about. And we're going to do something about them. Starting now. And that's the program I want to outline today.

We're going to create a "Chrysler-Kenosha Trust" to provide housing and education assistance, and whatever else makes sense, to those who are losing their jobs. It'll take at least *some* of the big worries off their shoulders while they get adjusted.

For the entire 1988 calendar year, we will contribute every dime of Chrysler's net profit on every single car and truck that we sell in the entire state of Wisconsin to that trust.

Last year, our net profit averaged $506 per vehicle, so that's the number we'll use. Based upon last year's sales of slightly over 40,000 units, that will amount to about $20 million.

Now, I've told Governor Thompson and Congressman Aspin and Owen Bieber about the program, and I've invited them to help us structure this trust. We'll ask them to each nominate a trustee. We'll ask for other nominees from the city, the county, and our dealers. And we'll name one. The trustees will decide the best way to use the money. We think housing and education are the big concerns right now, but we'll let them set the priorities and handle the details.

Of course, we still have to sit down with state and local officials and work out other kinds of assistance. And we still have to sit down with the union. This program doesn't replace whatever else we might do.

By the way, our records show that our Wisconsin dealers sold 2,600 cars and trucks in January, so we'll shortly be depositing a check for $1,315,600, that's *2,600* units times $506 a unit, in a bank *here* in the name of the trust. We'll do that every month—we won't sit on the cash—and it'll draw interest for the benefit of the fund.

And incidentally, if anybody thinks this is a rebate program, or something to sell some cars . . . forget it. It's our full bottom-line profit. The more our dealers sell, the better for the trust.

We've thought long and hard about this trust program, and frankly we know that there's been so much anger here that just about anything we do may be suspect. But we'll take that chance. I hope the fact that we won't take a penny of profit from our sales in the whole *state* of Wisconsin for a whole year will say something. We hope it's seen as our attempt to remain a responsible corporate citizen of Wisconsin.

You know, if you just read the headlines lately you might get the impression that Chrysler is pulling out of Wisconsin. We aren't. We're losing fifty-five hundred people. That's unfortunate . . . tragic, really. But we'll still have one thousand in our engine plant. Our dealerships employ about thirty-six hundred people. We also paid $288 million to our 392 suppliers here in Wisconsin last year, and they, of course, provide thousands of other jobs in the state.

Now, when something like this happens, the problems are too big for one company to handle. *Everybody* has to help out. That's why we've asked our *dealers* to contribute to the fund. That's why I'm inviting the *state* to contribute to it . . . and the *city* to contribute to it . . . and *civic organizations* to contribute to it . . . and local *business* to contribute to it. In any manner or form they choose. Because Chrysler can't do it alone—*no* company can—but *together*, maybe we can do something meaningful—even historic.

Now, I know that this program won't *end the pain*, but I sure hope it will *start the healing*. Maybe if we can get people working together to help the Kenosha employees—the company, government, community groups—we can turn off the rhetoric and start helping Kenosha look to the future.

4. Lee Iacocca as Debater and Storyteller: Speeches Concerning the Problems and Future of the Automobile Industry

Jack Kay

Many scholars have studied the success story of Lee Iacocca. Not surprisingly, there are as many explanations for this folk hero's success as there are popular and scholarly works about him. Seeger, for example, attributed Iacocca's accomplishments to the particular situation, Iacocca's ability to utilize potent organizational symbols, and his communicative style and approach. Foss focused on the drama surrounding the Chrysler guaranteed loans and the manner in which the company responded to the drama by accepting and atoning for the public guilt represented by the "bailout." Dionisopoulos, also utilizing a dramatistic perspective, demonstrated "how the media engendered a sense of collective cultural identification with Lee Iacocca and prompted his proclamation as the first contemporary cultural hero drawn from the ranks of businessmen" (239).

This chapter offers yet another reading of Iacocca's success. Many of the explanations extant in the literature focus on the situation, Iacocca as communicator, Iacocca as corporate leader, or Iacocca as the embodiment of contemporary American values. Each of these explanations rings true. This chapter suggests a broader approach which reconciles and synthesizes the alternative explanations. I argue that a major ingredient in Iacocca's success is his advocacy style—a style that merges the demands of a rational debate model with the expectations of a model in which symbolism dominates decision making and persuasion. In short, Iacocca's speeches bridge the world of reason and the world of symbols (Combs and Mansfield xv-xvi).

This chapter examines four speeches delivered by Iacocca in which problems and the future of the automobile industry are addressed. These four speeches are remarkable specimens of advocacy which demonstrate how arguments are molded into issues, following the format of the stock issues approach in academic debate. In these speeches, Iacocca reached out to larger audiences by retelling the story of Chrysler's success. Consequently, he broadened the appeal of his message. Iacocca observed that in speaking to internal audiences, he seeks to be "as direct and straightforward as possible" (Iacocca and Kleinfield 55). For external audiences, however, careful adaptation, entertainment, and symbolism are more important (Iacocca and Novak 54–60).

As in academic debate, Iacocca examined each stock issue at a literal level and provided the necessary proofs to advance his proposition. The speeches thus serve as exemplars for students of rational decision making and debate, showing how rationality should undergird calls for change. Unlike academic debate, however, Iacocca simultaneously advanced each stock issue at a symbolic-iconic level. Chrysler's repayment of its federal loan thus operates at the literal level by showing that Chrysler met its obligation and at the symbolic-iconic level depicting the organization as one that, in Iacocca's words, borrows money "the old-fashioned way: We pay it back!" The speeches serve as exemplars for corporate persuasion, demonstrating the necessity of merging symbolic and iconic strategies in public policy advocacy. Using a debate-public policy–decision-making approach to analyze these speeches is particularly appropriate given that Iacocca's expertise and stature placed him in the position of public policy advocacy.

STOCK ISSUES: THE LITERAL DIMENSION

Iacocca enjoyed training as a high school debater so there should be little surprise that his speeches adhere to some of the traditions and practices found in academic debate (for an account of Iacocca's debating and public speaking experience, see Iacocca and Novak 16; Wyden 42–43). Regarding his high school debating experience in the Orotan Debating Society, Iacocca wrote: "At first I was scared to death. I had butterflies in my stomach—and to this day I still get a little nervous before giving a speech. But the experience of being on the debating team was crucial. You can have brilliant ideas, but if you can't get them across, your brains won't get you anywhere. When you're fourteen years old, nothing polishes your skills like arguing both sides of 'Should capital punishment be abolished?' That was the hot issue in 1938— and I must have spoken for each side of the debate at least twenty-five times." (Iacocca and Novak 16).

The traditional approach to argument is represented by the stock-issues model used in interscholastic debate (see, for example, Dieter; Hultzen; Mc-Burney and Mills; Ziegelmueller, Kay, and Dause). The term *stock issues* is familiar to virtually every high school and college debater. One of the first concepts novice debaters learn is that winning a proposition that advocates a change in existing policy requires the affirmative side to demonstrate that a problem exists (ill), identify the cause of the problem or why the present system cannot solve the problem (blame), show that they have a plan that is capable of solving the problem (cure), and prove that the benefits of the plan outweigh any costs or disadvantages the plan might cause (cost). The stock issues of ill, blame, cure, and cost are cast into questions that provide debaters with a hunting ground for arguments and issues. According to Ziegelmueller, Kay, and Dause, the stock issue of ill asks, "Are there significant harms or ills or needs within the present system?" (40). Blame asks, "Is the present system inherently responsible for the existence of the ills?" (41). Cure asks, "Will the affirmative proposal remove the ills of the present system?" (43). Cost raises the question, "Do the advantages of the affirmative proposal outweigh the disadvantages?" (45). Those advocating change must prove that each question is answered with a yes; those opposing change need merely show that one of the questions must be answered no, or that the advocate of change has not met their burden of proof in establishing a yes answer to any one of the questions.

Numerous studies have examined the parallel between the stock-issues model in academic debate and the practice of argumentation in such settings as the U.S. Congress, the United Nations Security Council, political debates, and other deliberative assemblies (Kay; Brock, Chesebro, Cragan, and Klumpp). Although some distinctions and caveats are noted, much similarity exists between academic debate and "real world" practice. Stock issues, however, have not been widely used in the analysis of corporate speech making.

Although Iacocca's speeches concerning the problems and the future of the automobile industry all contain multiple propositions, a dominant, audience-specific proposition emerges in each. Speaking to the National Press Club in July 1983, Iacocca celebrated the early repayment of a federally guaranteed loan and used the occasion to solicit support for an industrial policy of management-labor-government partnership. Using the Chrysler experience as proof, Iacocca pointed to the devastation that would have resulted from the unemployment and welfare of a half-million people had the partnership not occurred. Blame was quickly assigned to ideologues in the government and the press who place principles above results in their fight against government interference and to an irrational industrial policy that failed to ensure fair competition. The cure was found in a partnership in which government, labor, management, and banks come together to create an industrial policy. The risks associated with the plan were dismissed as not unique and easily outweighed by the devastation arising from an irrational industrial policy. The stock issues advanced in the speech may be summarized as follows.

Proposition. The United States should implement an industrial policy based on the management-labor-government partnership used in the Chrysler recovery.

Ill. Unemployment and welfare will increase without a change in industrial policy.

Blame. The current, ad hoc industrial policy is not rational and fails to guarantee fair and hard competition.

Cure. Implement an industrial policy (a policy to stay competitive in world markets) that features a management-labor-government partnership and equality of sacrifice as demonstrated by Chrysler's recovery.

Cost. The benefits of corporate survival, including the purchases of goods and services as well as taxes generated, outweigh all possible disadvantages. The guaranteed loans are in no way unique since the federal government already has $500 billion worth of such loans.

Advocating a similar but more specific change in government policy, Iacocca enlisted the support of the press in his remarks to the American Society of Newspaper Editors in April 1986, urging federal action to minimize economic distortions. The specific targets included interest rates, energy prices, and unfair trading practices. Iacocca quickly reminded editors of the havoc resulting from wildly fluctuating energy prices and interest rates. He blamed the federal government for not taking appropriate action. He again used the Chrysler recovery experience to demonstrate the workability of his proposed plan. Finally, he demonstrated how ideological objections were outweighed by the pragmatic benefits guaranteed by the proposal. The stock issues and proposition emphasized in this speech were as follows.

Proposition. The federal government should better manage those forces responsible for significant economic distortions.

Ill. Economic well-being is in jeopardy as a result of potential major fluctuations in energy prices, interest rates, and trading practices.

Blame. The federal government fails to take action that would diminish major fluctuations.

Cure. The federal government should better manage economic fluctuations by implementing such measures as an energy tax and ensuring fair trading practices.

Cost. The practical results outweigh any objections from the ideology of government noninterference.

The remaining two speeches focused less on proposed federal action shifting attention to the global demands facing automobile industries worldwide.

Speaking in 1987 to the German Motor Press Club, Iacocca did a brief commercial for his cars and then used the occasion to establish that global interdependence must dictate future actions of the automobile industry.

Proposition. Globalism is required for the auto industry to flourish.

Ill. The problems facing the U.S. auto industry foreshadow the problems that will face the auto industries of other nations (loss of market share, failure to keep up with technology, failure to keep up with customer concerns, etc.).

Blame. Other countries are overdependent on the U.S. market.

Cure. Pursue globalism in which everyone can have a part of the market (market fragmentation), the recognition of interdependence in the sense that we are the suppliers and customers of each other, and treating the customer better.

Cost. Not doing so results in economic destruction, outweighing all costs to the proposition.

Iacocca, in his 1988 address to Chinese business leaders, provided advice on advancing the Chinese automobile industry through a joint venture with Chrysler, outlined as follows.

Proposition. China should follow Chrysler's "long march" in developing its auto industry.

Ill. New entrants in the global auto industry face dangers that result in failure or losing control of their own economy.

Blame. Multiple forces work to prevent development, including forces from outside that will seek to exploit the development and forces from within that will stifle entrepreneurship.

Cure. Follow the Chrysler lead, but devise a strategy that meets the unique needs of China.

Cost. Not doing so will keep China in the past and limit its power as a world leader. As long as China's self-interests are placed first, disadvantages will not result.

In the addresses to the German Auto Press and the Chinese entrepreneurs, Iacocca extrapolated from Chrysler's case to larger international conditions. In these speeches, Chrysler's experience was used to clarify both the ill and the cure.

THE ILL ISSUE

Iacocca's knowledge of successful sales strategy came through in his development of the ill issue. The successful salesperson recognizes that dwelling on the negative sours most deals. The successful politician—even the challenger—avoids being overly negative in depicting the present scene. After all, the worse the problem is, the more unbelievable it is that the politician can provide an effective solution. In each speech, Iacocca devoted limited attention to the ill issue. He provided his audience with an indication of the problem's magnitude but stopped short of helping his audience to visualize fully the problem and its complete ramifications. In calling for a national industrial policy, for example, Iacocca easily could have detailed the personal hardships and tragedies associated with millions of Americans being out of work. Instead, he simply pointed to Chrysler's experience and the large number of people who would have suffered without the cooperative agreement among government, labor, and management. Iacocca relied on his own credibility to sell the claim that if government failed to deal with an undervalued yen and an unfair Japanese tax policy, "there won't be any industry left in this country to work on."

A similar strategy is followed in Iacocca's remarks to the Chinese business leaders. Critical to the thesis of the speech was the presentation of Chrysler's "long march." Pointing to his own experience and credibility, Iacocca quickly established the ill and moved on to the brighter future. Referring to his firing from Ford and the fact that Chrysler "was dying" when he took over, Iacocca stated, "It was the lowest point in my life . . . and it was the lowest point in the history of Chrysler." He likened the situation to war: "It was the kind of decision you make in a war—to save the army, you have to sacrifice many of your people. We had to retreat, consolidate our forces, and regain our strength."

THE BLAME ISSUE

Successful public speakers and debaters recognize that the blame issue is often the most difficult to establish. At the persuasive level, the issue must be presented so as not to alienate the decision makers who are likely the cause of the problem or the barrier to its solution. At the argumentative level, this issue is often the most complex, with multiple factors responsible for the ill. To identify blame successfully requires the advocate to understand the essence of the present system—the inherent components and relationships that comprise the existing order. Each of the four speeches analyzed in this chapter demonstrate Iacocca's keen understanding of the complexity of the extant system and the ease with which he conveyed that complexity to an informed audience. Too often the public speaker who deals with economic policy issues uses the excuse of time to gloss over the complexities of the subjects. Such is not the case with these speeches.

The blame issue was effectively articulated in all four speeches, with particularly masterful presentation in Iacocca's remarks to the American Society of Newspaper Editors. Referring to the backward movement on fuel economy standards, Iacocca blamed government for caving in to Ford and General Motors. "I raised hell about it," Iacocca said. "We told them that Chrysler—poor little, old Chrysler that everybody was praying over just a few years ago—meets the law." The system's inherent flaw came through loudly in Iacocca's statement: "You know what they said instead? They said Chrysler only meets the law because it built more fuel-efficient cars and fewer gas hogs. Well, hell yes we did. That was the *law*. And it *made sense*. And we *obeyed* it. What's wrong with that? I still can't believe you're a sucker in this country for obeying the law." Blame thus went beyond Ford and General Motors, beyond government, to the essential nature of the present system. It was, to paraphrase Iacocca, a system that did not provide a level playing field.

Iacocca's speaking schedule frequently put him in front of audiences whose members shared the blame for problems confronting the auto industry. Iacocca never avoided finger pointing, but he used personal and collective blame as a way of ensuring a fair hearing for his ideas. In his remarks to the German Motor Press Club, Iacocca blamed many factors for the Big Three losing one-third of its domestic market to foreign carmakers: "And it's always smart to blame *yourself* first. The Big Three didn't keep up in quality, in fuel efficiency, in technology, or in performance. . . . To put it simply, we were in terrible shape to compete."

THE CURE ISSUE

Two aspects of Iacocca's handling of the cure issue stand out as remarkable: the emphasis he placed on this issue and the detailed proof he provided to show that his proposed solutions would work. One of the common criticisms of political and corporate speakers is that their addresses often lack substance, favoring ceremony over seriousness. Iacocca certainly did feature ceremony and puffery in his speeches, frequently securing guffaws from his audience as he quipped about such possibilities as he and Dr. Ruth Westheimer sharing the slate as Democratic Party presidential and vice-presidential nominees. However, the humorous content of Iacocca's speeches never overpowered the serious solutions he posited.

Iacocca clearly understood and implemented in his speech making the salesperson's motto "Show 'em it works." Of the four stock issues, cure received the greatest attention in each of these four speeches. Iacocca understood that the cure issue overshadowed all other issues. To the German Motor Press Club, Iacocca stated: "Well, it doesn't matter who is to blame for this huge trade imbalance, but I think any reasonable man or woman understands that it cannot go on." In reference to Chrysler's comeback, an event renamed "an equality of sacrifice," Iacocca, speaking to the National Press

Club, pointed to Washington's major problem, an ideology that ignores results: "The ideologues in Washington, and there are many, couldn't accept that something truly worked. It's that simple—if it clashes with their principles, they don't care to look at it even if it works. In other words, results are meaningless."

Iacocca offered detailed plans and workable proofs in the four speeches on problems and the future of the automobile industry. Compared to many other public speeches on national and international policy issues, Iacocca's contain far more specifics in proposing solutions. Speaking to Chinese business leaders, Iacocca provided four specific guidelines that should be used to develop the Chinese automobile industry, devoting considerable attention to developing each point. Proof that these principles would result in success came in the form of "Chrysler's 'long march,'" which Iacocca argued was a fitting parallel for understanding the Chinese automobile industry. Early in the speech, Iacocca established the proof value of this comparison: "In fact, in Changchun, I felt like I was returning to my roots. First Auto Works there reminds me of the first auto plant I worked in forty-three years ago—the Rouge plant near Detroit."

THE COST ISSUE

The effective debater is selective, knowing which arguments will be salient to audience members. He or she anticipates and even preempts key objections to the proposed change. Iacocca devoted limited but sufficient attention to the cost issue in the four speeches examined in this chapter, usually concentrating on how the potential disadvantage to his plan was either not unique or could be turned around into an advantage.

A key objection to the Chrysler federally guaranteed loans involved fears by conservatives that the action established a dangerous precedent. This same reasoning was used to argue against any industrial policy. Iacocca responded to these objections by charging that the precedence argument was not unique. In his remarks to the National Press Club, Iacocca countered: "Let's take the federal loan guarantees, for example. When we charged up Capitol Hill to get ours—$1.5 billion—of which we used $1.2 billion—we found out there were already $409 billion—that's right, count them, $409 billion—in federal loans and loan guarantees on the books." Iacocca personalized the situation by reminding listeners that their sons and daughters were benefiting from federally guaranteed college loans.

A second strategy used by Iacocca to deal with objections involved turning the tables or, in debate terminology, the "turnaround." Again referring to the federally guaranteed loans, Iacocca told his American Society of Newspaper Editors audience, "here we are today at the scene of the crime. It was right here in Washington, just six years ago, that I almost single-handedly destroyed the free enterprise system." Iacocca then established how the system actually had been saved from the ravages of added unemployment and welfare. Turning the tables on those who questioned his motives, Iacocca cast his detractors as un-American: "I'm concerned about those issues because I'm a selfish, money-grubbing capitalist and I want my company to stay healthy. But I'm also an *American*, and I talk about those issues because I want my *country* to stay healthy, too." He even turned the tables on ideological objectors to government intervention by focusing on the dogmatism of their views. At the National Press Club, referring to ideologues in government and in the press who "say results don't really matter when it conflicts with their principles," Iacocca lashed out: "What they are saying is they are not interested in hearing about anything that doesn't jibe with their theories. But we didn't have time for theoretical economics."

STOCK ISSUES: THE SYMBOLIC-ICONIC DIMENSION

Iacocca's speeches transcended the literal and logical dimension to offer listeners insight into American values and the American Dream. This is particularly important when considering that two of these speeches were addressed to international audiences. Iacocca was not only a spokesperson for his company and the domestic auto industry but an ambassador for American values. Woven into each of the four speeches on problems and the future of the automobile industry was a symbolic and iconic construction of such concepts as freedom, independence, sacrifice, cooperation, teamwork, and winning. Iacocca became a contemporary Revolutionary War speaker, using rhetoric to define and reconstitute the American ideology. Ritter and Andrews, in their analysis of the colonial rhetoric leading up to and following the American Revolution, noted, "the epedeictic orator constructed and transmitted cultural myths, enhanced by his listeners' high regard for oratory as an intellectual activity. . . . [T]he patriot orators followed a strategy from which emerged some fundamental ideas. Woven together into a unified perception, these ideas helped to make sense out of the rush of events. The ideology, then, was forged through and by a rhetorical process that defined and ordered values, interpreted events to conform to that value pattern, and led ultimately to the formation of a unique perception—an American viewpoint" (2–3).

The symbolic-iconic dimension recognizes that humans are storytelling beings who rely on symbols, metaphors, and icons to construct and make sense of their world. Symbols consist of the language system used to communicate, including verbal and nonverbal signs. Language is viewed not merely as a signifier of objects but also as a way of constructing reality and empowering human beings by allowing their voices to be heard. Metaphors are the substance of reasoning that takes us from known to unknown by analogy or comparison. In Iacocca's speeches, for example, Chrysler, its near bankruptcy and miraculous recovery, is the story and the metaphor for all those who are victimized or potentially victimized. The Chrysler story offers the listener new solutions for old problems. Icons are culturally established and recognized items imbued with particular values. The Statue of Liberty, for example, is to both national and international audiences an icon symbolizing welcome and freedom.

The symbolic-iconic dimension is detailed in the notion of the narrative paradigm (Fisher, *Human Communication as Narration*). Key differences between the symbolic world of storytelling and the rational world of debate include viewing human beings as storytellers rather than as rational beings; using "good reasons" rather than rational evidence as the way to make decisions; giving priority to coherent stories (narrative fidelity) rather than to logically connected arguments and the degree to which stories ring true (narrative probability) rather than the logical adequacy of arguments. Within narrative, the world is viewed as a series of competing stories "which must be chosen among to live the good life in a process of continual recreation," rather than as a set of logical puzzles to be resolved through the proper application of argumentation constructs (Fisher "Narration" 7–8).

The call for freedom and independence is sounded loudly in all four of Iacocca's speeches addressing problems and the future of the automobile industry. When speaking to U.S. reporters and publishers, Iacocca emphasized those values and icons that have become known as the American Dream. In addressing the German press and Chinese business leaders, he exhorted the more general and universal values of freedom, independence, and self-determination. Metaphorically and symbolically, Iacocca's speeches contained a series of coherent stories that enabled listeners to believe that independence, freedom, and the American Dream could be achieved once again. The stories rang true. They were told by someone who had great credibility not only because he believed in the stories but because he lived them.

The symbolic ill described by Iacocca was great. It was not only Chrysler that was in trouble. The entire system was threatened with a loss of freedom. Chrysler was the underdog—a poor, little company that was *hurt a little* by its own mistakes but *victimized a lot* by forces beyond its control. Chrysler represented all those who were victims or potential victims, including the European car companies facing unfavorable business conditions and the infant Chinese auto industry facing the threat of large and powerful multinational firms. Both risked losing their freedom and independence. Iacocca explained to the American Society of Newspaper Editors, that he understood what it was like to lose freedom: "But we also lost a big part of our *independence*, and our *freedom*. We were wards of the state for three years, with people looking over our shoulders every day." He continued: "you don't appreciate the value of independence until you lose it. . . . The Chrysler experience and my work with the Statue of Liberty have made me appreciate what a lot of us take for granted in this country." Washington, through ideology, inaction, and ineptitude, was to blame. Salvation and solution came not from interventionist government action, which conservatives could label and dismiss as socialist, but from a newfound "equality of sacrifice" that partnered management and worker, banker and borrower, Democrat and Republican, and even union and company. Only this equality of sacrifice enabled the system to work and the American Dream to be achieved. The Statue of Liberty served as an icon in which the principles of the American Dream were stored and displayed for both national and international audiences. Just as the Lady of the Harbor was worn and weather-beaten before her refurbishing, so, too, is the struggle to achieve the American Dream. Iacocca responded to the self-asked question, "Did you *learn* anything from all this?": "You bet we did! We learned that people working together can make anything happen!"

CONCLUSIONS

Debaters and corporate leaders have much to learn from Iacocca and his speeches advocating public policy change. "You can have brilliant ideas, but if you can't get them across, your brains won't get you anywhere" (Iacocca and Novak 16). This lesson Iacocca learned as a fourteen-year-old student on the debate team served him well as an advocate for public policy change involving the automobile industry. Iacocca had brilliant ideas—ideas that easily withstood the tests of logic, evidence, and rationality. Iacocca provided his listeners with the needed details and the requisite proofs. Yet Iacocca's speeches demonstrate recognition that quality argument in and of itself, albeit necessary, is often insufficient in persuading audiences—especially the diverse audiences Iacocca confronted because of his stature and success in the industry. To lend a broad perspective on the industry, more universal metaphors and symbols are required. Iacocca encapsulated his arguments in stories that he had the credibility to tell, that rang true, that were coherent, and above all, that captured the essence of American values.

Iacocca was indeed an expert advocate for solutions to the woes confronting the auto industry. Yet he was more than an expert advocate. He transcended the immediate situation and became an important ambassador for the American Dream. Whether speaking at home or abroad, to peers or just plain folks, Iacocca provided everyone with the hope and belief that they, too, would share in the good life. His success in taking the case of fair trade and rational industrial policies forward is probably best understood in terms of his ability to combine rational argument with compelling stories in creating broad messages with general appeal.

During 1993, Iacocca was asked by President Clinton to help sell the controversial North America Free Trade Agreement to the American people. Iacocca accepted the offer. When asked if he would debate one of the leading opponents of the agreement, H. Ross Perot, Iacocca declined. Based on the skills in using stock issues and stories Iacocca demonstrated here, it seems likely that Perot might have met his match.

WORKS CITED

Brock, Bernard L., James W. Chesebro, John F. Cragan, and James F. Klumpp. *Public Policy Decision-Making and Comparative Advantages Debate*. New York: Harper, 1973.

Combs, James E., and Michael W. Mansfield, eds. *Drama in Life: The Uses of Communication in Society*. New York: Hastings House, 1976.

Dieter, Otto Alvin Loeb. "Stasis." *Speech Monographs* 27 (1950): 345–369.

Dionisopoulos, George N. "A Case Study in Print Media and Heroic Myth: Lee Iacocca 1978–1985." *Southern Speech Communication Journal* 53 (1988): 227–243.

Fisher, Walter R. *Human Communication as Narration: Toward a Philosophy of Reason, Value, and Action*. Columbia, SC: U South Carolina P, 1987.

———. "Narration as a Human Communication Paradigm: The Case of Public Moral Argument." *Communication Monographs* 52 (1985): 347–367.

Foss, Sonja K. "Retooling an Image: Chrysler Corporation's Rhetoric of Redemption." *Western Journal of Speech Communication* 48 (1984): 75–91.

Hultzen, Lee S. "Status in Deliberative Analysis." *The Rhetorical Idiom: Essays in Rhetoric, Oratory, Language, and Drama*. Ed. Donald C. Bryant. Ithaca, NY: Cornell U P, 1958. 97–123.

Iacocca, Lee A. and William Novak. *Iacocca: An Autobiography*. New York: Bantam, 1984.

Iacocca, Lee A. and Sonny Kleinfield. *Talking Straight*. New York: Bantam, 1988.

Kay, Jack. "Argument Between Nations: A Case Study of UN Security Council Debate on KAL 007." Paper presented to the Speech Communication Association Convention. Chicago, Nov. 1984.

McBurney, James H., and Glen E. Mills. *Argumentation and Debate: Techniques of a Free Society*. New York: Macmillan, 1964.

Ritter, Kurt W., and James R. Andrews. *The American Ideology: Reflections of the Revolution in American Rhetoric*. Annandale, VA: Speech Communication Association, 1978.

Seeger, Matthew W. "CEO Performances: Lee Iacocca and the Case of Chrysler." *Southern Speech Communication Journal* 52 (1986): 52–68.

Wyden, Peter. *The Unknown Iacocca.* New York: Morrow, 1987.

Ziegelmueller, George W., Jack Kay, and Charles A. Dause. *Argumentation: Inquiry and Advocacy.* Englewood Cliffs NJ: Prentice, 1990.

REMARKS AT THE NATIONAL PRESS CLUB
Washington, D.C., July 13, 1983

Iacocca went to Washington to announce that Chrysler was paying off its federally guaranteed loans seven years early. He took the occasion to use the Chrysler experience as an example of an industrial policy that worked. In many speeches and articles thereafter, he pointed to the management-labor-government partnership that got Chrysler through its crisis as a model for dealing with other national economic issues.

Thank you, distinguished guests, ladies and gentlemen.

This is the political season, or so I've heard, which means it's the season for people to come to this podium to make promises and ask for your support.

I did that two years ago—two years ago next week, as a matter of fact, at this Press Club. And for the last four years, I have been on the stump asking the support of just about anyone who would listen to me.

But today, we are going to turn it around. We are here to celebrate a little and say thank you.

When I was here two years ago, it was a historic occasion for us at Chrysler. We had actually turned a modest profit, $10 million in the preceding quarter—our first profit in three years. It was no big deal, but it was a beginning: a glimmer that *maybe* we could make it, that maybe Chrysler had a future after all.

And you might recall we showed you the first of some exciting new products: the industry's first production convertible—one of the reasons I could stand up here and tell you we were in the ballgame to stay. You might be interested in knowing senators Ted Kennedy and John Glenn and Congressman Jim Coyne all immediately bought one, establishing it quickly as the first bipartisan convertible!

Since then our momentum has picked up month after month. In this business good news always starts with good products, and on that point our record is solid.

We converted our cars to front-wheel drive, about doubled the miles per gallon from 14 to 28, and improved the quality so much we could afford to offer the best warranty in the business. So our sales are up, our market share is up, our resale values are up, we are attracting strong new dealers, we are

132

number two in Canada now, and we haven't had a recall worth mentioning in so long it scares me just to talk about it—and that's about as *commercial* as I am going to get today!

Once we started building the best cars in America again, we started making money. We made a profit for all of 1982 followed by a record profit in the first quarter of this year. This spring we even sold 26 million shares of new stock—would you believe at 16⅝—in about three hours. And just three weeks ago we paid off $400 million, or one-third of our government-guaranteed loans—seven years ahead of schedule.

All this makes it possible for us today to talk about our own declaration of independence—*financial* independence. We are about to reestablish Chrysler as a successful private corporation that pays its own way.

So today, I would like to *complete* the circle. I am proud to announce an even greater milestone on Chrysler's comeback. This is a day that makes the last three miserable years all seem worthwhile.

Today I am here to tell you that we are going to pay off the *last* $800 million in government-guaranteed loans, taking the outstanding debt down to— *zero.*

The actual mortgage burning won't take place today because the law requires sixty days for the paperwork and red tape. Otherwise I'd give someone a check right now, right here.

This isn't an everyday occurrence here in Washington, but, as John Houseman might say, We at Chrysler borrow money the *old-fashioned-way: We pay it back!*

And it's the little things that mean a lot. I've got to call Mayor Koch of New York, who bet me that he would pay back the New York City loan before we paid back the Chrysler loan. I wanted to bet cigars, and he said, "I don't smoke." So we made it a bushel of apples, and I checked this morning, and his outstanding balance is 1,335,000,000. And they said they may pay it by '88—give or take a couple of years.

All the loans, all $1.2 billion, are being paid back seven years early. Why? Because this will save Chrysler $56 million in net interest payments each year for the next seven years or a total of $392 million.

And more importantly, because we believe this action should tell the financial community, but especially the American car buyer, that we are here to stay and have the strength to compete with anybody in the world. But probably even more important than that, I think it shows the system can work if everybody pulls together.

Bear in mind the $1.2 billion we are paying off was part of a $1.5 billion loan guarantee. So we only drew down 80 percent of it. And bear in mind that the guarantee was to be paid off by 1990, if ever, so we are paying it back in three years instead of ten years. In addition, we already have paid a little over $67 million to lawyers, bankers, consultants, and the $33 million in fees to the government, merely to administer the act during the past three years. *So*, it didn't come cheap.

I might add here, we still have a couple of tough issues facing us, and that is the subject of warrants and what constitutes a fair and reasonable profit to the government for a three-year guaranteed loan. Since the government's risk is now zero, I am hopeful that we can reach an agreement that is fair to everyone. I ought to say here that we don't object to the government making a fair profit on the deal, and we never have, in spite of what some of you wrote in the paper. I'm just glad our operating results have been good enough so we can give the government a little help with their operating results. God only knows, they need a little bit coming in right now.

But make no mistake about it, as expensive as it was, the government guarantee was the catalyst that made it all happen. It certainly got all the publicity.

What is often forgotten is the $2.2 billion that everybody else put up to keep the company *together*. And, of course, these were the union workers and the white-collar workers who took pay cuts; the states that loaned us money; and the banks; and the suppliers; and the dealers. All the guys who really had something at stake. So, our whole program was based on equality of sacrifice, because everybody offered up something—something important.

And that's why we have invited representatives from each of these groups to be here today as part of this historic event, and that's why I am glad the Press Club took me off the hook and set up the head table.

First, we couldn't have made it without concessions from the members of the United Automobile Workers—then under the leadership of Doug Fraser and now under new UAW President, Owen Bieber. Doug, as you may have heard, is also a member of our board of directors. So Doug and Owen, we thank you.

Next, our salary and management employees saw their numbers *cut in half* (forty thousand to twenty thousand) and those who stayed took cuts in pay and benefits. Jerry Greenwald, our vice chairman, and Hal Sperlich, president of North American Operations, are representing those employees, and I want to say thank you to them too.

Next, our suppliers—all eleven thousand of them. They rolled back prices, they bankrolled us by letting us pay them *very slowly* and even bought $75 million in debentures to provide us with capital. I'd like to thank all of them, and I will through Pete Love, chairman of the board of National Steel, who is representing them here today.

Next, our dealers. They really sacrificed—over twenty-one thousand of them went out of business and the ones who survived lost lots of money for a couple years running. But about four thousand of them are left—*stronger than ever.* And today our two National Dealer Council chairmen are here. Thank you.

Next, and this will be a first for me, I want to say thank you to my friendly bankers. They helped save us during our darkest days, then supported our re-capitalization program earlier this year. Sometimes their rates were a little high, but their faith in us was even higher; and we thank you.

Then there were the state and local governments that helped us with loans and helped support our employees that were laid off. First, the governor of our home state, Governor Blanchard of Michigan, who as a member of Con-gress sponsored the Chrysler legislation in the House. And Governor Pierre du Pont of Delaware, who came through with the very first "no-strings attached" loan. Thank you, governors.

And then there is that unique institution, the Chrysler Guarantee Loan Board. During the Carter years, they wanted to see us every week. In the Rea-gan administration, they never wanted to see us at all; of course, in the early days, we didn't want to see them. Now I'm trying to find them so that I can pay them back. Well anyway, I want to thank the board members who are here today, for their help during these past three years.

Then there is one more *big* group: All those people who had to stand up on the floor, *and vote,* and then convince the voters back home that they had done the right thing. After a year of debate, we won 53 to 44 in the Senate and 271 to 136 in the House (a two-to-one margin)—mainly due to the im-passioned plea made by Speaker Tip O'Neill on the House floor to save six hundred thousand jobs. So I would first like to recognize and thank the *speaker* and other key House members.

In the Senate, we were fortunate to have the bipartisan leadership of Sena-tors Don Riegle of Michigan and Dick Lugar of Indiana. Thank you, sena-tors.

And last, but maybe they should have been first, I want to thank the first 1 million people who bought our first million K-cars—the Reliant and Aries. Sure we needed the cash, but their faith in us meant even more. They were buying a good car from a company that they felt was *not* so good. And that simply told us that a lot of people were rooting for us.

So today is such a great occasion, my inclination is to just stop now and hold a party. But if we did so, we would miss the most important point—for *all* the American people and the government, itself, have the right to ask: Did you *learn* anything from all of this? You bet we did! We learned that people *working together* can make *anything* happen!

There are some ideologues in government and in the press who are still against the whole idea—they say results don't really matter when it conflicts with their principles. They say our case was unique. Well, it was. But not for the reason they think. It was unique because we did it during four years of a hellish depression in the auto industry. Some even say it was a fluke, and shouldn't be a precedent for anything. What they are saying is they are not interested in hearing about anything that doesn't jibe with their theories. But we didn't have time for theoretical economics.

We were really in the pits. So here's a nontheory, which is really just practical business. If you happen to like statistics, here is what has happened since the loan guarantee was passed, as of today. We have purchased $22.5 billion in goods and services from these eleven thousand suppliers. They employ a lot of people, by the way. We paid U.S. employees $9.7 billion in wages. Our employees then turned around and paid the government $1.41 billion in taxes and $360 million into Social Security which really needs it. We paid direct taxes of $668 million, mostly to state and local governments. By the way, we spent about $1.5 million in high-tech equipment—robots and the like. Now, that really beats paying unemployment compensation and welfare benefits.

We just got everyone working together—We cooperated; we fought for each other; we sacrificed equally—in a way maybe it was social democracy at its best. And we had help from *all* levels of government—Capitol Hill, the White House, the State House, and City Hall. And my question is simply this: What is so wrong with that?

What else can we say about it? It was bipartisan in terms of Democrats and Republicans and in terms of labor and management. We all knew there were a lot of jobs at stake. As Tip O'Neill said in the midst of heated debate, "I have always fought hard to save one hundred jobs so it's a little crazy to argue when more than a half a million families are waiting to hear our verdict." And maybe that's the real reason we all went through so much pain together. In human terms, there was a lot riding on us.

So what was it that we created? I'll tell you what it was, and pardon me for using this term with so many Republicans in the room. I guess you would say it was an ad hoc industrial policy. Better still, let's call it a jobs and economic development policy, because the reality is we already have an industrial policy, even though it's a hodgepodge based on congressional actions or administrative orders during the last fifty years. Some of these actions were taken with broad public support, some by narrow interest groups.

Let's take federal loan guarantees, for example.

When we charged up Capitol Hill to get ours—$1.5 billion—of which we used $1.2 billion—we found out there were already $409 billion—that's right, count them, $409 billion—in federal loans and loan guarantees on the books, or should I say off the books. Because this is all off-balance-sheet accounting that never shows in the deficits. By the way, that number has now climbed to over $500 billion, that's half a trillion!

And who has all those loans? Look around the room boys and girls—big business is on the list. And small businesses of every description. And farmers. And college students; probably some of your sons and daughters.

Now add in all the subsidies, tax credits, loopholes, incentives and grants, and regulations, and you can see that U.S. industrial policy is being made every day, in lots of places, by lots of people. So the question isn't: Should we have a national industrial policy? We already have one, make no mistake about it. The question is: Should we have a rational industrial policy? After all, somebody has to coordinate monetary, fiscal, tax, trade, energy, and regulatory policy—or they all go off in different directions.

Take the steel industry, where U.S. Steel is right now setting industrial policy. While protected by trigger prices, it paid $4.3 billion for an oil company, instead of investing in modern basic oxygen furnaces to be competitive.

Then, while leading the lobbying in Washington against imports of cheap, subsidized foreign steel, it cut a deal with British Steel for—guess what?—cheap, government-subsidized foreign slab steel that would double imports from Europe.

It looks like the company is closing down American furnaces and becoming merely a finisher and fabricator. Well, what happens to the smaller steel companies? Will some of them be forced to shut down their furnaces, too—and switch to imports?

Right or wrong, U.S. Steel is setting industrial policy in the steel business for the next fifty years.

And General Motors and Toyota are about to set industrial policy, not to mention antitrust policy. With 25 percent of the world market and 50 percent of the U.S. market, they want to set up shop in an abandoned GM plant in California.

GM will put up $20 million, Toyota will contribute petty cash and get to sell an extra two hundred thousand cars in this country wearing the Chevrolet label. Most of the parts for the new cars will come from Japan, and the Chevette that's assembled in Delaware with 95 percent of its parts made in the U.S., probably will die.

Shouldn't the government at least ask what they are up to? Even the unions are asking the right questions. But in both industries, steel and autos, once you have asked your government for even some *modest* form of protection, the quid pro quo is an obligation to talk about excessive wage demands or exorbitant pricing or investments or tax breaks.

To start with, it seems the use of the Washington buzzword *industrial policy* is all wrong. So maybe we should call it "a policy to stay competitive in world markets" or something, and bring together the steel and automobile companies, their suppliers, labor, and the general public and get an answer to the gut question: Does the United States really need a steel or automobile industry and what form should they take?

If the answer is yes we do, then solutions to the real problems of the industry could include tax credits and guaranteed loans for productivity improvements and modernization for those companies that choose to participate, and then maybe even commit to wages and prices that are indexed to productivity and real GNP growth, not inflation. And all the people involved could work out their plan for getting it done.

That's what we did at Chrysler and it worked. It was equality of sacrifice —and not just a simple bailout.

The ideologues in Washington, and there are many, couldn't accept that something truly worked. It's that simple—if it clashes with their principles, they don't care to look at it even if it works. In other words, results are meaningless.

Well, fine. Some people may hear inner voices that tell them that what Chrysler did is some kind of sin or worse. I say it is simply a great example of how government, labor, and management can work together to save and create something of real value.

I guess my attitude is the same as Abraham Lincoln's when somebody told him U.S. Grant got drunk a lot: "Find out what kind of whiskey he drinks, and send it to my other generals."

I happen to think we can do a better job than we have in deciding what kind of economy we want to have. Maybe even what kind of a country we want to have.

But in the end, the lesson we have really learned is that we have got to compete. There is just no place to hide for business, for labor, or for government.

You know, as Americans, we seem to have a rather peculiar trait: We run better and faster *scared!* Adversity brings us together. When we had to, because there was a gun at our heads, we learned to work together. Now that things are looking better, the key question is: Can we keep on working together to attack the gut problems of this country?

For our union and the workers they represent, that means we have got to continue to get quality and productivity and we just can't handle demands that exceed our ability to produce and be competitive in a world market.

To those of you in government, I say we cannot handle a 20 percent undervalued yen and a legal but unfair Japanese tax policy—that together adds up to a $2,000 per-car advantage. I know some of you in government are working on these problems, and I believe you should, because otherwise there won't be any industry left in this country to work on.

And while you are doing all of that, management sure has no place to hide. We can't go back to the old ways of getting fat and letting all kinds of costs creep back in. Simply stated, only by competing hard and *fair* will we be able to make it.

So, it's not done yet, not by a long shot. This was kind of a pleasant and personally gratifying pit stop along the road but we have a lot of miles to go before we sleep. We have got to straighten out the warrants issue. I don't want to get into that here, but we will do what's fair, and I am sure the government will, too.

The UAW and its members want to share—as they should—in our success, and we expect to sit down with them shortly and talk it out.

And the suppliers, after many lean years, are going to want to dicker a little—they have already started.

I guess that's the price of success. In some ways, it's easier when you are broke; everybody is a little more patient. But it's *fair* this way. You give me a little transfusion when I am bleeding to death and I try to pay you back a little when I get back on my feet. You could say it's the American way!

As long as we learn from the disease and the illness. Well, I *learned*, and I hope all of you did. I *learned* that a little sacrifice shared equally goes a long way.

I *learned* that we *can* compete, even in the darkest days, with anybody.

I *learned* that when adversarial positions melt under pressure, good things happen.

I even *learned* that an ad hoc industrial policy is better than no policy at all, particularly when much of the rest of the world has a policy, good or bad.

Teamwork is an old, sometimes tired cliché *until you win!* Then you marvel at it and say, "Why did I ever try to do it any other way?"

REMARKS TO THE AMERICAN
SOCIETY OF NEWSPAPER EDITORS
Washington, D.C., April 10, 1986

Iacocca understood the power of the press. He also believed that problems existed to be managed. He went before the country's newspaper editors to enlist their help in convincing the government to begin to manage some of the problems that were causing significant distortions in the economy. Although he had the businessman's natural suspicion of government intervention, he also believed that government had an obligation to deal with artificial economic distortions caused by such things the businessman could do nothing about, such as foreign oil cartels and trade barriers.

At the outset, I want to make it perfectly clear that I'm not running for anything—except maybe for my life! Hell, you've even got my title wrong in the program. I'm *not president* of Chrysler. I'm not president of anything. Everybody keeps trying to run me. And I wish you'd all stop it, because you're making my campaign staff nervous as hell! Although Joe Califano did say I have the right stuff to take a shot at it because I can read cue cards without moving my eyes!

By the way, I understand that you had my personal choice for a running mate on your program. It would make a hell of a ticket, wouldn't it? Iacocca and Dr. Ruth Westheimer! I'd run all over the country telling people *what* to do, and she'd follow me telling them *how*!

But it really is a privilege to talk to such a distinguished and influential group all in one room.

For years, I've contended that the two most powerful groups in the country—other than Dan Rather, Tom Brokaw, and Peter Jennings—have been the administrative assistants in the Congress and the country's newspaper editors—you!

You set the agenda of the country; you decide what's page 1, what's page 38, and what's no page at all. Now that's real clout. Just to illustrate how much clout you really have—most of you in the room rejected my syndicated column out of hand.

But I would like to publicly thank the hundred or so of you in this room who keep sending me those monthly checks. Aside from those deadlines—

and I've missed four so far—it's a pretty good business. My penetration of the market is about 35 percent. In the car business I'm doing 12, and I've been at it for forty years. Of course, my newspaper job doesn't have any stiff Japanese competition.

Seriously though, even though this is my first visit with you, I have been talking to your publishers for twenty-three consecutive years. You see, every year we have them out to Detroit and every year I tell them everything that's wrong with the world—and sometimes I even get carried away and tell them what's wrong with their newspapers.

Well, recently they got tired of my stuff and in their most humble manner said that they merely own the newspapers, that they have very little influence, and that all these years I should really have been talking to their editors. Twenty-three straight years—and now they tell me I've been talking to the wrong people.

So, here I am, I've finally made it to the top. And now I'm not too sure what the hell I have to say to you!

But I'll try.

In all the years I've talked to your publishers, I've covered a lot of issues. But if you ask them, you'll find that I never talk about things like Afghanistan, throw weights, or acid rain because I don't know anything about them. I try to tend to my knitting. A few weeks ago I was in Miami, and the reporters asked me what we should do about Nicaragua. (They want to know about Nicaragua, and I'm looking at my watch because I'm due on the "Miami Vice" set at 2:00 P.M. sharp! You can see where my priorities are.)

Then, a week later, I was in Atlanta and they wanted to know how I would handle Qaddafi. I thought, hell, I don't even know how to handle the UAW!

I try to stick to cars—that's my business.

I talk about gasoline prices and interest rates because they have always been the twin engines that *drive* my business. In recent years I've talked exchange rates—even coined an expression called the level playing field—because of the emergence of Japan as an economic superpower. And I talk jobs because I feel a keen responsibility for about six hundred thousand of them.

I'm concerned about those issues because I'm a selfish, money-grubbing capitalist and I want my company to stay healthy. But I'm also an *American*, and I talk about those issues because I want my *country* to stay healthy, too.

And I guess you all know, I've learned how important those issues are *the hard way*.

In fact, here we are today at the scene of the crime. It was right here in Washington, just six years ago, that I almost single-handedly destroyed the free enterprise system. (At least if you listened to all the guys wearing the Adam Smith neckties.)

I didn't understand the big fuss, to tell you the truth. I just wanted the government to cosign a few small bank notes for my company. It was no big deal, all we needed was 1.2 billion bucks to tide us over through the worst economy since the great depression. I knew the government already had over $400 billion in guaranteed loans on the books to farmers and students and small businesses, and lots of others. All I needed was a lousy billion-two, and dumb me! I thought I could handle it with a phone call.

But it wasn't that easy. All of a sudden people were saying that helping Chrysler would be a *bad* example, and that letting us die would be a *good* example because it would prove that the free enterprise system still works!

Now obviously I thought that logic stunk, and fortunately the zealots were outnumbered by people with enough common sense to see that slamming the door on those six hundred thousand jobs would *really* be a *bad* example.

So we got the loan guarantees, and without them Chrysler would have died. Make no mistake about that—we would have closed up right then. But I want to set the record straight while I've got you all here about what happened because I still pick up your papers now and then and see somebody refer to the Chrysler "bailout." And some people still believe that Chrysler actually survived on taxpayer money.

The truth is, we never got a dime of taxpayer money. The government simply *guaranteed* loans made by the banks. And the government had the first call on all our assets, so they never had a dime at risk. And we paid the money back, seven years early, including interest—at the highest rates that anybody alive could remember. Then we had to redeem our stock warrants from the government by bidding for them in an open auction.

Well, when all the dust had settled, the government cleared about $350 million. Some bailout! If Congress could just find a few more Chryslers to save, they could balance the budget.

But I'm a very patriotic guy, and I'm glad we could help out a little.

We got no handouts. We just got a chance to survive. And we paid one helluva big price for it. Not just in terms of that $350 million, or the factories we closed, or the assets we sold, or the people who lost their jobs. Those were painful enough. But we also lost a big part of our *independence*, and our *freedom*. We were wards of the state for three years, with people looking over our shoulders every day.

I can tell you, you don't appreciate the value of independence until you lose it—even a little bit of it. The Chrysler experience and my work with the Statue of Liberty have made me appreciate what a lot of us just take for granted in this country. And anybody who thinks I like *too much* government intervention—and some people do—is *crazy*. I've been there.

We lost our independence, partly at least, because we made some big mistakes at Chrysler. But *mostly* it was because we got clobbered by forces we couldn't control—forces that only people here in Washington could handle.

We got clobbered, for example, by interest rates that went so high they violated the usury laws in many of our states. And by some trading practices that gave our overseas competitors an unfair leg up in our market. And by gas prices that *doubled* overnight right before our eyes.

Now, normal ups and downs we could have handled. I've been dealing with them all my life. But the swings were too violent. So I started speaking out on these issues.

Well, here we are six years later. And some of you are probably thinking, "He sure doesn't have anything to complain about *now*, does he?"

After all, the prime is all the way down to 9 percent. The yen is all the way down to 180 against the dollar. And *gas prices*—hell, regular gas is selling for 67 cents in Detroit, of all places, and headed south.

And the good news doesn't stop there. Next week we're going to report our first-quarter profits, and they're going to be very good. So, I ought to be dancing in the streets, right?

Wrong! I'll tell you something, I'm not dancing. I'm a little *wiser* after what Chrysler went through, and I'm not dancing. I'm *worried*, because I still remember 1978 when everything was rosy and the auto industry set records it hasn't touched since. I'm not dancing, because literally overnight, with some help from OPEC and the Ayatollah—remember him?—the roof came crashing down on our heads.

We're at the top of the roller coaster right now, but we ought to know what's coming. It's my job to ask, "When things are going so well for my company, what happens next?" It's your job to ask, too. It's your job to ask what happens next to the *country*, isn't it?

A lot of people are positively euphoric about energy prices right now. That's the big story this week. Gas was supposed to be above two dollars by now, but it's way under a buck. The old supply-siders are beside themselves, I'll tell you that. We've had five years of insufficient revenues, and deficits that have gone over the moon. The economy just hasn't grown like the cheerleaders said it would.

But suddenly OPEC comes apart like a three-dollar watch, and it's like life support to the supply-siders. They gotta be wondering how they got so lucky.

But I *hope* they're wondering what happens next. I hope *you're* all wondering what happens next. I can tell you, *I am!*

In fact, I think I *know*. We got hooked on cheap energy twice before, and then got kicked in the head. It was a drug habit, pure and simple. Hell, we were mainlining the stuff. And when OPEC shut us down, we panicked and declared a national emergency.

We realized, a little late, that they had us by the throats. We realized these wild swings in energy could cost us a big part of our *independence*, so we did something about it. We started conserving, and we started exploring for new oil. And it *worked*! We've cut our per capita energy consumption by over 20 percent, and that helped us get our independence back.

But I guess it worked too well, because now there's a glut. The oil cartel unraveled, and now some of the same people who rigged oil prices *up* in the '70s are rigging them *down* in the '80s, in order to whip the cartel back into shape. When that happens, *watch out*, because oil prices will go through the roof again. And the hell of it is, we're playing right into their hands. Now that gas is cheap again, we're starting to tear down some of the programs that got us independent.

The best example in *my* industry is the automobile fuel economy law or CAFE. It's been on the books now for eleven years, and it has saved almost a couple billion barrels of oil. In fact, we almost doubled the fuel economy for the average car—think of that.

Well, now that it's worked so well, General Motors and Ford come to Washington and say we should dial the standards back. (It's free market time —the cartel has been broken up.) Gas is so cheap, let's go on a binge. Let's all drive big cars again. And bigger cars, of course, mean bigger profit margins. But I don't think they really brought *that* last point up.

I can't believe it, but the government is actually caving in and changing the law. We're going to go *backwards* on fuel economy, and that's a tombstone for the best energy program we ever had.

I raised hell about it, but it didn't do any good. We told them that Chrysler—poor little, old Chrysler that everybody was praying over just a few years ago—meets the law. We said the other guys could do it, too, if they wanted to. But nobody listened.

You know what they said instead? They said Chrysler only meets the law because it built more fuel-efficient cars and fewer gas hogs. Well, hell yes we did. That was the *law*. And it *made sense*. And we *obeyed* it. What's wrong with that? I still can't believe you're a sucker in this country for obeying the law.

By the way, changing the law saves GM and Ford about $726 million in fines. So, if nothing else, the next time someone brings up the Chrysler *bailout*, tell them about our $350-million contribution to the Treasury. Tell them there was no *Chrysler* bailout, but there sure is one helluva big bailout for *General Motors* and *Ford* going on right now.

And the timing is all wrong. You don't moderate these huge swings in oil prices by throwing out the programs that are working. You keep the pressure on so the pendulum doesn't swing back and knock your head off.

There's something else we can do to protect ourselves, but, I'll tell you, it's the dirtiest word you can whisper in this town. And it's not a four-letter word, it's three—it's T-A-X—tax!

I know, on this subject the president has his Clint Eastwood routine down pat—"Make my day!" But wait a minute! We've got a made-in-heaven opportunity with gas prices dropping like a rock. God and OPEC will never be this good to us again, believe me!

We've got a chance for a two-fer here, just think about it. We can help protect ourselves from getting hooked again on cheap gas, and at the same time we can do something about the biggest national scandal of them all—a national debt that just went over 2 trillion the week before last.

Every penny you put on a gallon of gas at the pump blots up a billion dollars of that red ink. Every dollar you put on a barrel of imported oil gets you about $2 billion.

The simple way would be to tax gas 25 cents at the pump. That's a cool $25 billion in revenue. If you don't like that, try 15 cents at the pump and a $5 import fee if you want to help the guys in Texas a little bit. That's your call. Either way, it's a quick $25 billion. I mean, really, how much more can we tax cigarettes and booze to help Gramm-Rudman along?

And remember, we've got the lowest gas tax in the industrial world. Federal is nine cents, with state and local it's about a quarter. Right now, most countries pay more just in *tax* on gas than our *total pump price*. So we've got a *bargain*. We can *afford* to take advantage of this windfall.

Now, let me be parochial a minute. There's a personal reason why I want to see some stability in energy prices. I gotta plan ahead. It takes about four years to put a new car on the road, from the drawing board to the showroom. So my 1990 cars are all approved and in the works. I hope I've guessed right. If you tell me gas is gonna be 89 cents, I've got no problem. And if you tell me it'll be $2, I've still got no problem. But if you give me a *range* of 89 cents to $2, I've got a big problem.

I just can't handle it. Any good management can handle changes of 10 or even 15 percent year to year. That's what we get paid for. But a *100 percent jump* in gas prices like we went through a few years ago? And a *100 percent jump* in interest rates like we saw? I can't handle swings like that. *Nobody* can! When that happens, church is out, folks.

Let me ask you, could your papers handle a doubling of newsprint overnight? Could you double your ad rates to cover it or double your circulation? Hell no! If that happened, a lot of you in this room would be out looking for work, wouldn't you?

Let me tell you just how fast things can change. I was in Desperate Dallas and Hobbled Houston last month. I hadn't been there in three years, back when their oil was thirty-four dollars a barrel and Chrysler stock was sixteen dollars. Now they're at twelve dollars a barrel and Chrysler's stock is at sixty-one dollars. What a flipflop.

Three years ago the producers of oil were riding high and the users that was us, we were dying. I told them the tables were turned—now they were being killed by all those cheap imports—oil! Not Toyotas. Other than George Bush—everybody in this town just mumbles—"Isn't this free market just beautiful?"

Let me *really* tell you how bad it is down there. Last week one of the oil companies warned the administration that if this twelve dollar oil keeps up and I'm quoting here "We'll be knocking on your doors just like Chrysler did."

Well, I'll bet that got their attention! One thing I know about *this* administration—they sure don't want to see any more Lee Iacoccas in ten-gallon hats coming around. They've had enough of my kind!

You see, they're in a bind here because they still insist they're committed to a totally free market, no matter what happens to oil prices. And low oil prices are propping up Reaganomics, right now. But suddenly they're beginning to see some of the *other* possible consequences of this big windfall:

Like some oil companies *maybe* looking for a Chrysler deal.

Like some banks *maybe* getting in deep trouble.

Like Mexico *maybe* facing default.

Like some friendly governments maybe *tipping* over.

And we even hear a little whimpering about national security if we get too dependent on foreign oil again. Of course, nobody worried about national security when *steel* or *cars* or even *electronics* got hurt.

Maybe they're beginning to see what we learned the hard way at Chrysler: We can't handle these violent feast-or-famine swings. *Chrysler* can't handle them. *You* can't handle them. And I've got news for you, *America* can't handle them.

We go from huge inflation to almost deflation.

We go from big trade surpluses to big trade deficits.

We go from the world's biggest creditor to the world's biggest debtor.

One year we tell the farmers to plant fence-row to fence-row, the next year we pay them not to plant at all.

First we cry that the dollar value is too *high*. Now some people are scared it'll go too *low*.

Sure there are cycles in life—some are predictable. God takes care of those —you know, night follows day, fall follows summer. The ones man takes care of like business cycles, energy cycles, automotive cycles—those we managed to screw up!

Now, we can't repeal these cycles or just get rid of them, but we could take a stab at moderating them or smoothing them out a little. What's wrong with asking the people running the government to help even out these swings. Isn't that one of the things we're paying them to do . . . to *manage* something?

People here in this town better start realizing that buried somewhere in those numbers, between the highs and lows of these swings, are things like 140,000 bankruptcies, 3 million jobs going overseas, and 100,000 fewer farmers, most of whom have lost their land. And that's only between 1983 and 1985—during the so-called recovery! These aren't just bell curves from a textbook, these are real people—human beings trying to eat and buy shoes for their kids and pay off the mortgage.

Think of it, it seems we've all had our turn in the barrel. The steel people had their ox gored in '79, I joined 'em with cars in '80, machine tools was '81, electronics was '83, farmers were '85—oil men in '86. Who's next? I sure hope it's not you people.

So, we *pay* these people to write policies to smooth out some of these things. But, of course, this administration says we don't *need* policies. We've got the good old free market, and the free market will take care of everything.

Well, I know something about the free market. I'm a capitalist down to the bone. But I know that when you let somebody manipulate the free market, all bets are off.

And does anybody in this room seriously believe that a handful of people in the Middle East aren't manipulating the price of oil right now?

Does anybody seriously believe that international trade in cars, and food and almost everything isn't manipulated every day? The Japanese still keep out our *ravioli*, believe it or not, if they're meat-filled. If the ravioli are filled with cheese, it's okay! It's meat they're after, and they don't want us sneaking it in. They don't miss a trick, those guys!

I'm all for the free market, but it won't be free unless you have some policies to keep it free, and unless you're willing to *act* when somebody starts rigging it their own way.

The national policy now seems to be to *avoid* policies. Never intervene. Let nature take its course. Even when we get fair warning. James Schlesinger told Congress a couple of weeks ago, "We're planting the seeds of the next oil crisis." A couple of days later I wake up and see Sheik Yamani (of all people) on TV warning us that we're gonna have gas lines again in a couple of years, if we don't conserve and keep our drilling programs going. Now here are two guys who have very different axes to grind. But we're not listening to either one of them. And if you don't listen, how can you ever take any action?

Once in a while, though, *somebody* does take action! Last fall Secretary Baker intervened. In currencies, not oil! Some of his colleagues must have choked. The high dollar had just gone too far, so he called a knock-heads meeting in New York and the dollar has been dropping ever since. It must have been a real shock to his predecessor who told us for four years that it absolutely couldn't be done.

Well, I give Baker credit. He *acted*, policy or no policy. I wish they'd swallow their sacred ideology and intervene on some of the other wild gyrations we're seeing today. Much as the free traders hate the sound of it, we ought to *keep* intervening in our own self interest until we get some stability and balance.

Why can't they see that two dollar gas is wrong but so is fifty-cent gas and come up with a policy to split the difference somewhere? Interest rates at 20 percent will wipe everybody out. But if they go too low, all the foreign money we've sucked in to finance our deficits will pack up and go home, and then look for the prime to skyrocket again. The yen at 250, is wrong, and below 150, I can't pick the exact number it's probably wrong too. Can't reasonable men and women manage these things? Why do we always seem to be at one extreme or another, and have so much trouble finding the middle?

These things take policies, not a bunch of ideologies. We need a policy on *energy*, and one on *trade*, and one on keeping our industrial *jobs* in America, and one to balance the *budget*. Now every time I say we need some policies or strategies to handle some of these problems, somebody says it smacks of *planning*, so I must be a *statist* or something worse. Some of my big business friends really go off the deep end and call me a *Democrat*. Damn it! That really hurts.

Well, I don't own up to being *either* one of them. I'm just a guy who's been through a particular kind of wringer in the past six or seven years. I watched a great American company almost go under. And I watched it come back. I know *why* it almost died. And I know *how* it survived. And I sure remember what happened to its *independence*.

I keep getting back to independence, because we lost ours for a while. And the day I paid off those loans and got my independence back was the biggest day of my life.

Ever since then, I've been speaking out on national issues louder than ever before. I've done it because I don't want my *country* to ever go through what my *company* went through. And I see it making a lot of the same mistakes we did. I see it risking its independence in a lot of ways.

Oh, the Russians aren't coming. That doesn't worry me. But you can lose your freedom in more ways than that.

You can lose it, for example, when you forget how to *compete*, when you get so big, and so rich, and so arrogant that you're willing to let others take advantage of you because it's beneath you to climb down into the trenches and slug it out.

You can lose it if your principles are so lofty that you won't play the international trade game by the same *street rules* the other guys use.

You can lose your independence if you're willing to let someone *else* produce the steel and the cars and the machine tools while you just play monopoly with real money, and pray all those service jobs will save us. And, all the while, the guys who used to run the factories are out looking for those service jobs, because theirs have migrated to the Far East.

You can lose your independence by refusing to pay your way, and by piling up massive public debts that you just lay off onto your kids.

And, finally, you can sure as *hell* lose it by letting yourself get so hooked on cheap oil that you put yourself at the mercy of the people who happen to be sitting on it. We learned that the hard way in the '70s. Let's not *forget* it in the '80s.

So, independence is everything. But you don't *get* it, and you don't *keep* it without a fight. You don't keep your independence unless you're willing to intervene now and then, and play a little hard ball. If you don't seize the initiative when you get the chance, you're going to pay the price later.

Let them call me what they want: I don't think a little *planning* and a little *action* is always bad. There's nothing wrong with acting in your own self-interest once in a while. Especially in a world where everybody else does it every day. If we don't, how are we ever going to make America competitive again, and how long can we hang on to our economic independence?

And if *those two* objectives aren't worth the trip—and a little effort—we may as well forget the party on the Fourth of July. Because hard work, competition, and independence are what the history of this country is all about.

Well, thanks for having me. I've enjoyed it. I've talked a lot longer than I ever do to your publishers. But at least I finally got to the right people. Didn't I?

Thanks again.

REMARKS TO THE GERMAN
MOTOR PRESS CLUB

Frankfurt, Germany, September 8, 1987

Chrysler had been forced to abandon its European operations during its brush with bankruptcy in the late 1970s. By 1987, the company was ready to export a few units to Europe again. Iacocca announced Chrysler's return to the European market at the Frankfurt Auto Show and took the occasion to explain how the new "global" auto market would take shape.

Well, it's a high honor to speak to this group, but let me be perfectly candid, I feel a little like Daniel going into the lion's den.

I'm here for the auto show, as you know, because Chrysler is going to start selling cars again in Europe this fall. We haven't done that in a long time, and when we were selling cars here before, we had a couple of serious problems. First, our cars didn't have what it took to compete in this market. And second, back home, we were going broke.

Well, now we're coming back, but we're coming back with our eyes wide open. Europe is the most demanding auto market in the world, and we're going to be the *only* American company relying *entirely* on vehicles engineered and built in the United States for our sales here.

Believe me, we're not kidding ourselves—we know what kind of a challenge we have ahead of us. And that's why I appreciate your hospitality even more.

For our first attempt at exporting cars from North America in a long time, nobody can accuse us of picking an easy target. We're picking the *toughest*!

Now—I promise not to get too commercial tonight—but I also believe that we're coming back with some products that will be *right* for this market. I hope you've all had a chance to see them at our stand.

We're proud of those products or we wouldn't have them here. I think they'll represent good value to the consumer. But we don't have any delusions of grandeur. I'm sure that my colleagues here from Daimler-Benz, BMW, or Volkswagen aren't shaking in their boots because Chrysler is coming back to Europe to sell a few cars.

As I told the press this morning, we would be happy if we sold five thousand units by the end of 1988, and ecstatic at ten thousand.

We're moving very slowly. We've put together an outstanding team under Bob Lutz, who knows the European market as well as and maybe better than any other American does. He knows how demanding this market is, and what we have to do to make it here. I will depend on his firm hand to guide us here.

Now, many people are probably asking *why* we are coming back to Europe. Well, we're doing it for one simple reason: If Chrysler is going to continue to compete effectively in our *own* North American market, and other markets around the world, then we have to be able to compete *here*—against the best in the world.

Competition is the best teacher. It makes all of us better at what we do. If Chrysler can compete *here*, then we can compete *anywhere*!

Nine years ago, when I first joined Chrysler, we couldn't compete here, *or* in our own market. I think you all know the story. We came just a breath away from dying at Chrysler. We only survived because thousands of people put aside all their differences and decided to fight to stay alive.

Our unions, our management, our suppliers, our dealers, our banks, and even some of our politicians pulled together to give Chrysler a chance to live. We coined a term—"equality of sacrifice." It meant that everybody had to *bleed* a little. And they did.

I don't ever want to go through those times again. Believe me, once is enough. And I sincerely hope that none of you ever do. But now we all know that it was the best thing that ever happened to Chrysler. It made us a lot tougher, and a lot smarter . . . and a lot *humbler*.

There were many factors involved in what happened to Chrysler—the oil shock, astronomical interest rates, our own mismanagement, and a few others. But the major problem was that we—like the other American companies —had grossly underestimated our foreign competition.

We'd been competing so hard against *each other* in the *American* market for so long, that we didn't realize until too late that we were really competing in a *global* auto market.

That's a mistake that we will *never* make again!

And that's why I say that if we're going to compete in Detroit, Chicago, and Los Angeles, then we better figure out how to compete in Frankfurt, Amsterdam, and Brussels.

Of course, we already have a number of strong international ties at Chrysler. We own a quarter of Mitsubishi Motors . . . We own 15 percent of Maserati with an option on 51 percent in a few years . . . We recently acquired Lamborghini . . . We now have Jeep—probably the best known American nameplate in the world . . . We have two ventures in China—one to manufacture the Jeep, and another to provide engine technology to a Chinese automaker . . . We have operations in Venezuela and Egypt . . . We buy and sell parts all over the world. And our stock is listed on seventeen stock exchanges around the world, including three here in Germany.

So we're a broad international company, and that's not by design as much as it is by *necessity*. Nearly all major corporations are international today. They have to be. I don't care where you call home, you rely on other countries for materials, for capital, and for markets.

The major change for Chrysler this fall is that sometime in the coming weeks a few cars are going to be loaded onto a ship in the United States and be sent here. That will be a rare scene. Hell, that will be almost a *historic* occasion. And as an American, I want to be part of it. You see, for the last decade, there have been a lot of cars *off*loaded in U.S. ports, but very few *on*loaded for export.

And with this year's U.S. automotive trade imbalance with the rest of the world at almost $60 billion—well, every little bit helps!

So, I can hardly wait to do a TV commercial with me standing on the dock, waving good-bye to some cars going out in the other direction for a change. And before I die, maybe I'll even get a chance to wave to a tiny, little boat going to *Japan*!

The United States has been an enormously profitable auto market for almost everybody. The problem is, for the rest of the world it has been *only* a market. Our auto trade has been *one-way*—lots of vehicles coming into the United States, and almost none *going out*.

It was just a few years ago that there weren't many coming in, either. General Motors, Ford, and Chrysler had the whole, big, profitable American market to ourselves. We had it so good, in fact, that we got a little lazy and a little careless.

Today, there are almost forty companies from all over the world selling cars and trucks in America, and more want in all the time—Koreans, Yugoslavians, Malaysians, you name it. Hell, now, even the *Russians* want in! The Big Three have lost about one-third of their domestic market to foreign carmakers. And when you count the parts coming into the United States, and the foreign cars manufactured in the country, foreign companies could have about half of the U.S. market in a few years.

Now, there are a number of reasons why this happened. And it's always smart to blame *yourself* first. The Big Three didn't keep up in quality, in fuel efficiency, in technology, or in performance. And we lost control of our production costs. To put it simply, we were in terrible shape to compete.

And our timing was awful, because just about then we had a whole series of events that made matters even worse: Gasoline prices doubled overnight, and so did interest rates. Then, our government's fiscal policies changed dramatically. We doubled our national debt in just five years, and that drove the value of the dollar so high that our products were priced out of the world market.

And on top of that, the United States has held on to some unrealistic trade policies that give everybody open access to our market, whether or not we get equal access to their markets in return. We draw no distinction between those countries that trade *fairly* with us and those that don't.

That's unfair to our *own* companies, and it's also unfair to those trading partners who play by the rules.

The result of all this has been a cumulative trade deficit for the United States since 1980 of over $700 billion. And here's the real shocker—the number that brings it home to everybody in this room, I hope—$231 billion or *one-third* of that was in automotive trade alone.

Well, it doesn't matter who is to blame for this huge trade imbalance, but I think any reasonable man or woman understands that it cannot go on. Most of us thought that the big currency swing that began two years ago would change things, but it hasn't. At least not yet.

I'm no economist, but I think the fundamental problem is that too many countries have become too dependent on the American market. They're hooked! They simply have no place else to ship their exports. And if the United States stops taking those exports, we could throw the whole world into turmoil—or a deep recession.

Since one-third of the problem is autos alone, then clearly we aren't going to solve the problem until we deal with the imbalance in auto trade. And when I say *we*, I'm not just talking about Americans: I'm talking about Europeans and Asians as well.

It's in *nobody's* interest to see this imbalance continue, because when the bubble bursts, *everybody* is going to get hurt.

The rest of the world has learned what we learned in the United States and what you learned here in Europe: The auto industry is fundamental to any truly industrialized economy. All the developments in high technology, and all the growth in the service businesses, haven't changed that.

It wasn't many years ago that only eight countries dominated the entire global auto market. Today, eighty countries around the world *assemble* cars, and I have to assume that *every* country produces something that goes *into* cars.

One result, of course, is that today we have about 23 percent unused capacity in the industry. We can build about 10 million more cars and trucks than we can sell.

Back in the *old* days, when there were still only a few of us building cars, we could deal with overcapacity by exporting. But today *everybody* builds cars. We live in a *global* industry, and there's no place for a global industry to export to—unless we start shipping cars to the *moon*.

So there are going to be some big changes in our industry. There have to be. The numbers just don't add up. And I'm sure that *all* of us would like to

153

know just what those changes will be. I'd sure like to have a peek at what the industry will look like twenty years from now.

If you think back to twenty years ago, not many people could have predicted where the world auto industry would be *today*. Not many could have seen Japan as the largest producer of autos, for example, or countries like Korea and Taiwan as major players in our industry.

So it's always dangerous to predict the future, and I don't know if my crystal ball is any better than yours, but when I look into it I see at least three major trends that I'm fairly sure of.

One has to do with the *market*. One has to do with the *customer*. And one has to do with the division of labor within this global industry of ours.

If you want to see the future in engineering and technology, you can walk around the auto show here. But if you want to see the world market of the future, come to the United States. Study the market in the United States *today*, and I think you'll see the world market *tomorrow*.

And what I'm talking about is a *fragmented market*. A market full of niches. It's a market that has a specialty vehicle for just about *everybody*.

When I got into this business more than forty years ago, we made mostly family sedans, some station wagons, and a couple of coupes. That's all. And, of course, pickup trucks, but mostly for our farmers.

Today we've got luxury cars that talk to you and do just about everything but shine your shoes for you when you turn the key. We've got full-size, mid-size, compact, and subcompact sedans. And every one of them seems to have some kind of "sport" version. There are even some *real* sports cars, of course. Then there are "sport-utilities." We've even got pick-up trucks now that are "sporty."

We still have station wagons, of course, but with Chrysler's minivan we created a whole new segment somewhere between the station wagon and the van.

Every population group has its own car line, and it identifies them. American yuppies, for example. I don't even know if that translates here, but I'm talking about the young professionals with lots of money and a taste for the good life. The American yuppie has two cars: One is a BMW, and one is a Jeep. I still don't really understand the connection, but at least one of the two is *ours*.

We used to stay away from so-called niche cars because it didn't make sense to tool up just to produce fifty thousand or one hundred thousand units. But today, just about every model is a niche car. The car dealer is like the ice cream store—you'd better have 28 different flavors or the customers stop coming in. They want more than vanilla, chocolate and strawberry to choose from.

I think this market fragmentation, which started in the United States and is still most pronounced in our market, will spread, especially as buyers in other countries get more affluent.

I don't think the buying trends are going to come and go quite as fast as ladies' fashions, but it does put a lot of pressure on us to identify these special market segments quickly, and fill them before the competition.

The second big change that I see is how we're going to have to deal with the customer in the future. We're going to have to treat him or her *better*. And that job is mainly going to have to be done by the dealer.

All of us who manufacture cars—whether here in Germany, in the United States, or in Thailand—will have the same technology—and it will be *outstanding* technology. The competition will be so keen that before too long there just won't be any junk left in the market. The quality advantages that some manufacturers have traditionally had over others will get narrower and narrower, and will eventually almost disappear.

And when that happens, the relationship between the dealer and the customer—how well that dealer *services* that customer—will become a much bigger competitive factor than it is today.

Just two weeks ago, we held our annual Chrysler dealer meetings in Las Vegas. Usually at these meetings, I give a tough speech telling the dealers that they have to treat the customer better. I didn't do that this year. Instead, I simply stood in front of four thousand of them, raised my glass, and saluted them.

That's because an independent and respected U.S. survey just determined that our Chrysler dealers were the best of the Big Three in customer satisfaction. Some *import* dealers were still ahead of us, but we're closing the gap fast.

I told our dealers—and I really believe it—that the next big leap in this industry won't come from the company with the hottest engine, or the best handling, or the slickest styling. We're *all* going to be good. It will come from the company that can develop a clear lead in *customer service*.

I'm not giving away some deep corporate strategy here tonight. I'm just saying to all our dealers, like you're probably saying to yours—"you better treat the customer right."

Now both of those changes—market fragmentation and more attention to the customer—are already well underway. And so is the third, but I've got to admit that I'm a little more *concerned* about this one because there is a lot of danger involved—not just for our *companies* but also for our respective *countries*.

Who's going to build the cars twenty years from now—and *where*? That's really the big question we all face, and our governments face. We've already seen a big shift in the *past* twenty years. What happens in the *next* twenty years?

Well, the pessimist would say that we'll see more of the same . . . that production will continue to chase the lowest wage rates . . . that some governments and companies will cooperate in targeting foreign markets . . . that the *old* industrial countries will become the *consumers* of cars and the *new* industrial countries will be the *producers* of cars . . . and that this will go on until the newly *poor* get mad as hell at the newly *rich*, and close their borders and default on their foreign debts . . . at which time the whole world's economy collapses for good.

For the record, I don't think that's going to happen.

The optimist, and I'd like to call him the *realist*, would see it differently, I think. He'd say that the auto industry is so fundamental to the global economy, and to all the individual countries of the world, that some rationalization has to take place.

Everybody has to have a piece of the pie. And today, fortunately, that's *possible*. It wasn't possible a few years ago when the economics of our industry were different, the pie was much smaller, and all the major producers were more vertically integrated than we are today.

I went to work at Ford when the ships would offload iron ore at one end of the River Rouge plant, and new cars would come out the other end. Nobody can be that self-sufficient anymore.

Today, this has become a highly *interdependent* industry. While we've been trying our best to beat each other's brains out in the marketplace, we've also become each other's *suppliers* and *customers* as well.

I had an idea about ten years ago for something I called "Global Motors." It meant forming a consortium and combining the strengths of certain companies in the United States, here in Europe, and in the Far East. The consortium never happened, but the *idea* took on a life of its own, and it's become a reality.

We're seeing more and more joint ventures, for example, especially to produce those specialty vehicles for that fragmented market I just talked about. I may need a partner to help fill up my plant . . . to share my development costs . . . and justify big investments in new technology. You just cannot go it alone, anymore.

We've got an arrangement like that, by the way, with Mitsubishi. A big factory in the U.S. that will be producing specialty cars for both of us next year—like two hundred thousand of them.

And, with the pressures we all face in costs and quality today, our *suppliers* already *are* really our *partners*. That's just as true if they happen to be located across the street, or in South America.

The *economic* realities of our business mean that the production has to be spread all over the world—among high-wage and low-wage countries . . . the old industrial countries and the new ones.

156

But we also live in a world with *political* realities, don't we? And those realities are just as compelling. The older industrial democracies of Europe and North America cannot politically tolerate the massive loss of automotive production. The industry remains absolutely vital to their economies, and for as far ahead as I can see, there is nothing that will replace it.

So the only real answer to *who* produces the cars twenty years from now is *all* of us. And the answer to *where* is *everywhere*.

Well, that's all the star-gazing I'm going to do tonight. You'll notice that I didn't have much to say specifically about the *European* market. I really came here this week to *learn* more about this market. I walked through the show this afternoon, and I saw what Chrysler is going to be up against in this market. And I'm very impressed with all your cars—and a little awed by some of them.

As I said at the beginning, we're re-entering this market slowly and, I think, realistically. But this is not an *experiment*. We are not just putting our toe in the water to test the temperature. We're making a firm commitment to Chrysler's presence in Europe—and for a *long*, long time! After a nine and one-half year vacation—we expect to return and do it right!

Well, I've enjoyed being with you tonight . . . seeing some old friends and meeting some new ones. And I hope we'll be seeing more of each other in the future. Good luck to all of you. And I hope I haven't held up your dinner too long!

Thank you very much.

157

REMARKS TO CHINESE BUSINESS LEADERS

Beijing, China, October 15, 1988

By the late 1980s, Iacocca was nearly as big a folk hero in China as he was in the United States. His autobiography was a runaway best-seller. For many emerging Chinese capitalists, he was a role model, and Chrysler's resurrection was an inspiration. He was invited to the Great Hall of the People to talk about Chrysler's "long march" and offer some advice on how China might become a bigger factor in the world auto market.

Thank you, Mr. Chairman, and good afternoon ladies and gentlemen. I want to thank the China Enterprise Management Association for inviting me to talk to you today, and the Ministry of Machine Building and Electronics Industries for inviting me to visit China.

I've had a terrific week. I had an opportunity to see our Beijing Jeep joint venture, and to meet our new partners up in Changchun where we'll soon be jointly producing a modern, four-cylinder engine for China. I've also met a number of government leaders, and we've had some frank discussions about how Chrysler can contribute even more to the growth of the Chinese automotive industry.

The business discussions have made me more optimistic than ever about Chrysler's future here, but the unbelievable hospitality I've been shown by the people here has made me realize more than ever that China is a place where we *want* to do business.

This is my first trip to China, and like all first-time visitors I've been walking around like a child in his first week at school. There is so much that is new . . . so much that I don't understand . . . and so many questions to ask.

Some things are familiar, however, even if I've only seen them in picture books or on television . . . the Great Wall . . . the Forbidden City just down the way from here . . . and Tiananmen Square just outside the doors.

This building, of course, is well known to all Americans. I remember watching on television in 1972 when President Nixon met here with the leaders of China. It was as dramatic as the television pictures a few years earlier of the first American walking on the moon. In a way, it was also a whole new world opening up for us to see, because for too long the American and Chinese peoples had lived on different planets.

158

But we don't anymore. I guess you really know the doors are open wide when you see Kentucky Fried Chicken in the middle of Beijing!

Still, for an American, China is a country of huge contrasts. You can see it in the traffic—with automobiles, bicycles, and horse carts sharing the same streets. And you see farmers working their fields like they did a thousand years ago, and further down the road you pass a satellite receiving dish. You see offices where clerks have a computer and an abacus sitting side by side on their desks.

It's always dangerous for a visitor to form impressions after only a week, but I'll tell you mine anyway. I see a China with one foot leaving the past . . . one foot planted in the present . . . and its eyes focused squarely on the future.

I don't just get that impression from sights along the roads, by the way. I also get it from my visits this week to a couple of your automobile factories. At Beijing Jeep and at First Auto Works up in Changchun, I saw the past . . . the present . . . and the future.

In fact, in Changchun, I felt like I was returning to my roots. First Auto Works there reminds me of the first auto plant I worked in forty-three years ago—the Rouge plant near Detroit. Henry Ford built it sixty years ago, and it was the first to take nearly all of the manufacturing processes involved in building a car, and combine them in one factory.

Why did First Auto Works look so familiar? Because in the 1930s the Russians came to Detroit and made the Rouge plant the model for their auto plants. And I'm told that in the 1950s, those Russian plants, in turn, became the models for the Chinese auto industry.

So even though there was a wall between us in those years, and we weren't even talking to each other, the technology jumped the wall. Ideas and innovation cannot be walled *in* . . . or walled *out*.

But that's nothing new, and it works both ways. We in the West have been the beneficiaries of the genius of China for thousands of years: Cars are made of steel, and where was steel first produced? Here in China! Cars run on petroleum, and where was petroleum first used as fuel? Here in China.

The point is, no matter where in this world a new idea is born, sooner or later we all get to share it. And today, it is definitely *sooner* than later.

In the past, some of the really good ideas took a while to get around. For example, the wheelbarrow, invented here in China, took almost twelve hundred years to get to Europe. The blast furnace to make cast iron took almost eighteen hundred years to get from China to Europe. And something as simple as the common match was used here for over two thousand years before it reached the West.

But since I'm of *Italian* heritage, the one I'm most grateful for is *noodles*, which I call *pasta*. That took a couple of thousand years, too, and Marco Polo had to walk all the way here from Italy to learn the secret.

You can't keep good ideas like those secret for long today, because we live in a much, much smaller world, where new ideas are distributed around the globe with the speed of a phone call. And where the technologies that spring from that human ingenuity can be moved with the speed of a jet airplane. *But* the challenge for all of us who live in this smaller world is to see that we all get a chance to share the rewards of these new ideas and new technologies.

And that's what I want to talk about today. I'm speaking from the viewpoint of a man who has spent his entire adult life in the automotive industry. I've seen some huge changes—changes in automobiles themselves, but even bigger changes in the global environment in which those automobiles are produced and sold. And my industry is not unique: the same kind of changes have taken place in every other industry as well.

Let me tell you briefly what my eyes have seen.

When I started in the American auto industry right after World War II, my country was just about the only major country in the world that was not in ruins. My industry was intact. Three companies in the United States built all the cars and trucks the country needed, and also supplied vehicles for export.

Those three companies—General Motors, Ford, and Chrysler—fought each other hard in the American market. The American economy is built on competition, and we in the American auto industry thought we knew more about competing than anybody else. Why not? All the companies were successful, and all of them made a lot of money. We also freely made our technologies and our methods available to anyone who asked for them because we happen to believe that competition is good for everybody.

But, then, in the late '50s the Germans began selling cars in the United States, and we welcomed the competition. In the '60s, the Japanese began selling cars in the United States, and we again welcomed the competition. But by the late '70s, the American companies all found themselves in trouble because we had made the mistake of underestimating our new competition.

That wasn't the only reason for our problems. We hadn't made the investments needed to keep up with the new plants being built in Europe and Japan. We also had to deal with a burdensome bureaucracy and interference from our own government. And we had trade policies and tax laws that put us at a disadvantage.

But the main problem was our own arrogance. We'd been so successful for so long that we got lazy. And we forgot that we did not have a monopoly on new ideas.

By far, Chrysler was in the most trouble of the three American auto companies. It was dying. That's when I joined Chrysler, almost exactly ten years ago. My timing could not have been worse, but I didn't choose it. I had just been fired from Ford after thirty-two years, and I really had no place else to go if I wanted to stay in the only industry that I knew. It was the lowest point in my life . . . and it was the lowest point in the history of Chrysler. I guess you might say we were perfectly matched.

We were not competing . . . not with the other American companies, and not with the foreign companies selling in our market. We had to make some drastic changes—and fast. In order to survive, we had to get rid of operations that could not help us. We had to close twenty of our factories and lay off thousands of workers and managers. It was the kind of decision you make in a war—to save the army, you have to sacrifice many of your people. We had to retreat, consolidate our forces, and regain our strength.

It was Chrysler's "long march."

We had to focus our attention on two or three products that could compete, and not try to build a product for every segment of the market. We could not do everything well, so we concentrated on a few things and tried to do them better than anybody else.

We told our workers that if the company was to survive and they were to keep their jobs, they would have to work harder for less pay. They agreed to do that. We said the same thing to our managers, and they took even bigger pay cuts.

With the workers and the managers behind us, we were able to take a couple of big risks. We literally bet the existence of the company on the success of a new compact car called the K-car, and on a completely new vehicle called the minivan. If either of them had been failures, Chrysler would have gone bankrupt and closed its doors.

But they were successful. And because the company was saved, the sacrifices we made turned out to be temporary. Today, Chrysler is stronger than ever before and has hired back almost all the workers we lost.

We won a big victory. But victories are useless if they don't teach you something. If you don't learn from victory, then you're certain to repeat the battle.

The most important lesson of all for me was a deeper understanding of the global market that we all live in today. I'd spent most of my life competing against General Motors, and never thought I would be competing against Germans, Japanese, Koreans, and everybody else in the world.

I thought that the best engineering in the automobile industry would always come from Detroit. I was wrong. I thought that countries that were generations, even centuries, behind the United States in technological development would never begin to catch up. I was wrong. I thought that entrepreneurship was a distinctively American quality. I was wrong.

And by the way, a lot of other people have been wrong, too. I think the whole idea of a single, worldwide economy was a concept only for scholars just a few years ago. But now almost everybody understands it. Even the workers who build our cars know that they are competing directly against workers in other factories on the other side of the world.

And I think we've all come to understand that this global economy has created an interdependence among us. We rely like never before on each other for the raw materials, the technology, the innovation, and the markets that we all need in order to be successful.

And this dependence isn't always comfortable, is it? Nobody likes to rely on other people. It's risky. You always have to balance your own self-interest with the reality of living in a world economy that you don't have much control over. In the United States right now many people—including me—are worried that we're losing control of our own economy because of the increasing level of foreign investment in our country. I think it's a case of too much, too fast. It is a real danger, but one that we will simply have to learn to manage.

I'm no expert on China—certainly not after a week. But I assume that you, too, are asking yourselves the same questions that we are in the United States: How can we be a part of this new global economy, and prosper within that economy, and not risk losing control of our own destiny? Well, it can be done.

I have a few suggestions—four to be exact.

First, the most important economic asset you may have is your own market. Don't let anybody exploit it unfairly.

Second, decide what goods or services you can produce better than other people and focus your energies there. Don't try to do everything.

Third, devise your own strategy. Don't try to copy anybody else's.

And four, do everything possible to encourage the best entrepreneurs.

I pick those four not because of anything I've learned in China in a week, but because of what I've learned in the United States over the past four decades.

Let me discuss them one by one.

I'm sometimes accused of being a protectionist in America because I don't believe our market should be wide open to foreign products if other countries don't share their markets with us. I happen to believe that trade should be a two-way street. But I don't think that makes me a protectionist. I think that just makes me a realist.

Every country obviously has the right to set the rules in its own market. If those rules are too restrictive, nobody will trade with you, and you are out of the game. That doesn't make any sense. On the other hand, if you don't have any rules, then somebody's going to grab your market, give you nothing in return, and you're also out of the game. That doesn't make any sense, either.

Obviously a balance has to be struck between your own interests and the obligations you have if you're going to play in the world market. I'm not saying that every business deal has to come with a quid pro quo, and it's not realistic to believe that trade accounts can be balanced every year. But it has to be a two-way street.

I don't know of any country that has become a major trading power without first developing its own home market. The home market is the classroom. That's where the lessons are learned. If you can't meet the demands of your own customers, you sure can't satisfy the ones overseas.

I have to use my own industry to illustrate my points because I happen to know it best. China is a potentially lucrative automobile market in the years ahead. (Not overnight, understand, but over time.) Chrysler would like to be part of that industry. We're not doing it only by trying to export cars and trucks to China; we're building Jeep vehicles here in Beijing, and will help build engines in Changchun. We're in partnership with two local companies. We think producing here, and investing here, and helping to localize production here is the best way to give us a long-term position in the Chinese market.

You see, we're making the assumption that China will be wise enough not to lose control of its home market in the years ahead. And we'll be considered part of the Chinese auto industry, not just a foreign company doing business here.

No other industry can do more to help develop a nation's economy than cars and trucks. No other industry can create so many jobs—not just in auto factories themselves, but in all the industries that crop up due to the automobile. That includes everything from road building to tourism.

The industry does, however, require enormous investment. But investment spent to develop a country's own auto industry pays big dividends. It sure beats spending billions buying built-up cars from another country. Better to spend money to buy the *technology* to *build* cars.

But China must devise its own strategy for becoming a part of that industry. And that's my second point. Even after a week, I can see that China must create its own unique plan because China itself is so unique. It has different problems . . . and different opportunities.

It will have to move at its own pace, and set its own priorities.

China is a latecomer to the world automotive industry. That's a problem because others are so far ahead in technology. But with the right strategy, being late can be turned into an advantage.

For one thing, you can skip whole generations of technology. You can jump from the technologies of the '50s to the technologies of the '90s, as long as there is a profitable use for that technology.

You have the advantage of looking at what we've done in the United States, at what's been done in Europe and Japan, and taking only those things that have worked while avoiding some of the mistakes that we have made.

And, believe me, we have made a lot of mistakes.

We overlooked for a long time the importance of conserving energy, for example. We were lucky enough to have cheap gasoline for so long that we didn't even try to develop engines that used less fuel. Until the day when the world price of oil shot up and we were forced to spend billions of dollars to engineer fuel-efficient cars.

We also ignored what the exhaust from those engines could do to the environment. And when we realized that we had to make those engines run with cleaner exhaust emissions, it cost us billions of dollars more.

Then we came under a great deal of pressure from our customers and our government to build cars that were safer, and once again we spent billions to install safety features.

Perhaps those same pressures don't exist to the same degree here today for fuel economy, or pollution control, or safety. But they will. And they exist in every potential export market already. China is lucky because it can learn from all the mistakes that we made. It does not have to repeat them. And it doesn't have to reinvent the technology to meet these needs.

In the near future, the Chinese auto industry will be selling overseas. I want to see Chrysler be part of that, too.

Which brings me to my third point. To be an auto exporter in the future do you actually have to export complete cars and trucks? There are already forty companies around the world doing that. Why not sell the people who assemble the cars the components that go into those vehicles? That may be where the real future lies in the international automotive business.

I've had a chance this week to eat the famous Peking duck, and everywhere you go you see the ducks hanging in the windows. But what are those ducks, really? Aren't they just packages of grain and sorghum? In a sense, a car or truck is really nothing more than a package containing spark plugs and radios and transmissions and the four thousand or so other parts that make up the vehicle.

My company, Chrysler, buys 70 percent of what we put on a car from somebody else. The auto companies themselves don't have the resources or the creativity to engineer and manufacture every part.

And taken as a whole, the companies that supply the parts for cars are bigger than the companies that assemble the cars. They also employ four-and-a-half times the number of people who work for the auto companies. So that's where the jobs are in my industry.

The automotive industry worldwide already turns out about 45 million vehicles a year, and that number will grow as living standards rise and newly industrialized countries take their places in the world economic order. The good thing is that there's room for everybody in this industry.

But the price of entry into the international automotive market is quality. If you don't have the best product in its class, don't try to compete. We learned that at Chrysler, and that's why we retreated and concentrated on a few products that *were* the best in their class. I believe the industry of the future will be made up of thousands of companies, each of them doing one or two things better than anybody else.

They will survive and prosper because they come up with new ideas. That's the fourth point I'd like to make. They'll be entrepreneurs in the classic sense of the word: people who are smart enough to see a need, who are creative enough to figure out how to fill it, and who are willing to take the risks that always come with trying something new.

I happen to believe that creativity is part of being human. It doesn't have anything to do with ideology or culture. The world is full of geniuses. What separates an entrepreneur from a genius, however, is the willingness or the *ability* to take risks. Not stupid risks or careless risks—but the normal risk that says the market may not always buy your brilliant idea. And that happens all the time.

In our own company we try to encourage new ideas, and give our people the freedom they need to explore them. But like any organization, our own bureaucracy sometimes gets in the way. Our people have been complaining to us, and we've listened. We've got a program underway to cut out lots of paperwork and lots of meetings. Simply put—we've got some of the brightest minds in our industry, and we don't want to get in their way.

We're doing that because we realize that to continue to be successful we need those new ideas. We have to encourage people to take sensible risks, and we have to be tolerant of failure because nothing is a better teacher than failure. Our factories and our laboratories are full of the latest computers and robots, but we know that none of these machines can ever duplicate the ingenuity and resourcefulness of the human mind.

And what's true within Chrysler is certainly true throughout the world.

I want to conclude today by telling you where I think this new global economy we all live in is going to take us. First of all, as I said earlier, none of us has any choice but to compete in that economy. We can't wall ourselves off. To be perfectly honest, sometimes I wish that I could return to the way things were in my business forty years ago. It was easier then. But those days will never return. I'm competing today against the best in the world, not just the best in my country, and I have no choice.

That means bigger risks, but in the long term I think it will also mean bigger rewards.

If—and this is really the biggest risk we all face in the decades ahead—if we can all agree on a set of fair trade rules that allow everybody to prosper in this single world market, and nobody to dominate it.

Today, some countries are piling up huge trade surpluses while other countries especially my own, are going deep into debt. That's a pattern that cannot continue. There has to be some reasonable balance or the walls will go back up.

Trade today cannot be a game that produces winners and losers. It is too important to be a game. It has to produce only winners. The old concept of mercantilism has to be buried in the history books. And slowly, it is being buried.

Trade is too important to everyone for it to be just a means for companies to accumulate wealth and countries to accumulate power, like it has been in the past.

It will have to be a series of partnerships and joint ventures through which the investments, the risks, and the rewards are shared—partnerships like the two that Chrysler has here in China.

Now, I'm a realist, and I know that these partnerships are never going to be easy to maintain. We've got a number of joint ventures at Chrysler with foreign partners, both in the United States and abroad. There are sometimes vast differences in everything from labor practices to management control. It's not easy to put two cultures side by side in the same factory.

But that's the wave of the future. And let me tell you what the biggest reward of all will be as these partnerships spring up all over the world: One of these days we'll stop talking about countries "competing" in this global market. The word will lose some of the meaning it has today. Maybe we'll go back to the word that was used in the days of the old Silk Road: "trading."

I said that I'm a realist, but I'm also an idealist, too. And I happen to believe that this global economy of ours will get stronger, and the world will get safer, if we return to the idea of *trading* the resources of this planet among ourselves rather than *competing* for them.

I'm leaving here with a lot of positive impressions of China, but the thing that has impressed me the most has been the *openness* I've found here. That's what makes partnerships work—open and frank discussions. And that's how problems get solved, whether in a company or a country—you get them out in the open so you can do something about them.

The kind of openness I've found just about guarantees that the progress China has seen in recent years will move even faster.

I hope to come back again soon—if not before, certainly for the Asian Games in a couple of years. And I know that I'll see a lot of changes even in that short time.

China's place in the world economy will grow larger and larger, there's no doubt about that. And Chrysler wants to be invited along for the exciting journey ahead.

Thank you very much.

5. The Japanese Trade Imbalance: Lee Iacocca and Corporate Advocacy

Judith Hoover

No single issue characterizes the public communication and the public image of Lee Iacocca more than the trade imbalance with Japan. Since his initial efforts to generate support for the Chrysler guarantee loans, he has consistently identified fair trade as an overriding goal. Indeed, he has managed to frame much of the public discourse about fair trade through his early and persistent attention to the topic. Although a typical CEO might find international relations a difficult topic to tackle, Iacocca has had both the status and the credibility to make this his abiding issue since he began this series of three speeches in 1985 designating the problem of trade with Japan as his central theme.

He spoke first to the American Chamber of Commerce in Tokyo, then to a congressional delegation in Highland Park, Michigan. In January 1992, less than twelve hours after returning from his trip to Japan with a contingent of business leaders accompanying President George Bush's trade mission, he presented the most controversial of these speeches to the Economic Club of Detroit. In addressing these immediate audiences, Iacocca managed to speak to multiple publics made up of members of the American citizenry and the executive and legislative branches, as well as to comparable constituencies in Japan.

These three speeches offer valuable insights for those interested in his persuasive methods, for those concerned with continuity in issue management over a span of time, and perhaps especially for those who have wondered whether charges of "Japan bashing" were true or were merely confusions about the nature of or acceptability of criticism, even strong criticism. In this analysis, I begin with the assumption that all three speeches were persuasive in intent, although they both informed and entertained audiences. The three speeches may be viewed, then, with the following questions in mind: Who made up his target audiences? What was the single compelling question he chose to pose and then to answer? What sorts of evidence and arguments did he present to support that answer? What emotional appeals did he utilize? Did he arrange these materials for maximum effect? How did his audiences respond? Once these questions have been answered, I will look again at the speeches for their implications for both the field of communication in general and the genre of communication known as organizational advocacy, which includes corporate rhetoric, issue management, public relations, and corporate apologia, or defense.

REMARKS TO THE AMERICAN CHAMBER OF COMMERCE IN TOKYO

Although primarily a speech about the trade imbalance, these remarks also may be seen as corporate apologia, or as an effort to explain or justify Chrysler's call for more, rather than fewer, imported cars from Japan as part of a joint venture agreement with Mitsubishi Motors. While Iacocca spoke to 762 Americans working in Japan, he combined praise for individual Japanese and individual Americans with blame for their two governments and their opposing philosophies and ideologies. The Japanese, he noted, were characterized by "strong will, hard work, perseverance, and intelligence," while their counterparts in America possessed "generosity, patience, and friendship." He hoped, he said, that the Japanese would "understand that American political swings can, and often do, go to wild extremes." In speaking so broadly to both Japanese and American publics, Iacocca sought to condemn United States and Japanese trade policies, justify Chrysler's partnership with Mitsubishi Motors, and still retain the goodwill of the Japanese people. If we reduce his purpose to a single compelling question, we can phrase it in this way: How can I explain the magnitude of our trade problems so that the Japanese can understand them from an American perspective?

Rather than creating a simple problem-solution speech, Iacocca used a more complex structure that is explained in almost every public speaking text, and certainly may have found its way into his Dale Carnegie training, a method of arrangement known as Monroe's Motivated Sequence (Monroe and Ehninger). The sequence consists of an attention-gaining device, presentation of a need or problem, satisfaction of the need through a solution, a visualization step that may be negative or positive or a contrast of the two, and a request for action. In his introduction, Iacocca mentioned sales in Japan of 331,000 copies of his autobiography and noted that "if the product is right," Americans could sell it there. He then made light of Chrysler's "half-billion dollars in losses" that had "play[ed] hell" with his "travel schedule" and prevented him from visiting Japan for six years. During those years, people were "worried about all those Japanese cars coming in," and this worry now had brought him to Japan.

Once attention had been gained, Iacocca moved into his explanation of the problems caused by American and Japanese trade policies. His own company, in order to maintain a large enough share of the American market, needed to depend on a partnership with Mitsubishi, since voluntary restraint agreements allowed "an unrestricted flow of Japanese cars into the U.S." The U.S. Senate, on the other hand, had recently voted "92 to nothing" urging the president to "retaliate against Japan for its trade practices." The American people not only were becoming increasingly "hostile" toward Japan, they also had come to believe that the situation was part of a "well-ordered plan." He threatened that if "reasonable solutions" were not found, then "drastic solutions" such as "import surcharges, higher tariffs, maybe quotas" would result. At this point, he presented negative visualizations of America "bleeding," and Japan as "the target, and the big loser." He followed the negative vision with a positive solution in the form of the "level playing field," surely a visual image to which both Japanese and American baseball fans could relate. He equated this playing field with the concept of "fairness," which should be the "goal of any sensible trade policy."

Iacocca blamed both America and Japan for "still living in the mid-nineteenth century" when "Japan was the ultimate protectionist" while "America was just the opposite." He contrasted free trade with managed trade, free trade with protectionism, saints and sinners, and he concluded that all of these concepts were relative rather than absolute. Both sides would need to accept half the blame for the problem—America's currency problems, budget deficit, and "credit card junkies"—Japan's "trade barriers and closed markets." Both governments' acceptance of "piecemeal negotiations" served to "prolong the friction and deepen the resentment."

At this point, Iacocca presented his action request to Japan, phrased in terms of "Japan's best interests." After asserting that Japan was "protecting the wrong market," by protecting its domestic rather than its American market, he claimed that the "best way to protect its American market is to open its Japanese market." This action would benefit Japan by creating a "lobby in Washington made up of people like you in this room who do business in Japan." With this statement, he tied his immediate audience to his broader audience and gave them a reason to work for mutual gain. Before completing the speech, Iacocca presented two further negative visual images, one of pressure building "until it explodes," the other predicting a "revolution budding" among Americans. He then presented the vision of the Chrysler-Mitsubishi partnership as a positive model of "equal investments, equal risks, equal benefits." In his conclusion, he appealed for attitude change among both the American and the Japanese audiences, taking characteristics from both traditions, asking for "a sense of fairness, some old-fashioned, enlightened self-interest, and a good healthy dose of that 'Oriental wisdom'—on both sides of the Pacific."

REMARKS DURING CONGRESSIONAL VISIT

In this speech, Iacocca spoke directly to the forty-two members of Congress who came to Michigan "to hear about our problems," and he took the opportunity to praise Congress and blame the administration for those problems. His statement of purpose given twice in the speech—"to talk about public policy" and "to ask for the order"—clarifies the single question we may focus on to determine his strategies: How can I persuade Congress to change the trade rules with Japan?

Iacocca combined emotional and logical appeals to express the needs of the automotive industry. He presented military images of enemies "massing on our borders" and "not just holding maneuvers." He backed this threat with statistics showing that this enemy had captured "34 percent of our passenger car market" by the end of 1990 but had gained "three full share points" by March 1991, with "every point . . . worth over $2 billion in revenue!" These problems were caused not by our "lazy" workers or "stupid" managers but by Japan's ability to "set the policy for U.S.-Japanese trade." Iacocca then outlined six consequences of following "rules set by Japan."

Iacocca's solution came in the form of a "managed economy," which could only be achieved by the audience members themselves. After reminding them of their "job" of rule setting, he asked for a "single set of rules" that both Japan and America could "live with." He moved next to two negative visual images, one of an athlete dressed for tennis but playing an opponent in "football pads" and "getting clobbered" in the "rough-and-tumble" game of trade, the other of the "best fighter plane in the world" being "targeted" by the enemy. His action step involved eight requests from Congress ranging from the creation and enforcement of rules of trade to regulating "health-care costs." He backed these requests with the image of the "Big Three" selling "the same number of vehicles in Japan in a year that Japan sells here in about forty-eight hours." He concluded by repeating his admonition that Congress must change the rules, which he softened by pleading that "we really need your help."

REMARKS TO THE ECONOMIC CLUB OF DETROIT

Iacocca sought audience attention in the Detroit speech with the visual image of business leaders riding in the "front of the plane" accompanied by "generals and admirals . . . and Foggy Bottom types" from the State Department. He spoke to nearly three thousand members of Detroit's business community, to a live radio audience, and, of course, to the world by virtue of his having just accompanied President Bush to Japan. If, in the face of this vast audience, we could isolate a single compelling question, it would necessarily encompass his frustration, his exhaustion, and his sense that Japan was winning a trade war with the United States. It would ask: How can I persuade Americans that current economic theories on which our policies are based will not solve our trade problems with Japan resulting from unrecognized differences in our two economies?

Iacocca presented the need or problem in war images: "they have this industry targeted, and they're not about to take us out of their gunsights:" "They're winning! They're beating our brains in." The results of this war included "unemployment . . . closed plants . . . lost tax base . . . insidious Japanese economic and political power within the United States." The causes of low sales of American cars in Japan included their failure to accept "our certification," their "inspection" requirements, the "maze of red tape," and "distribution costs." Their trade practices never included either "free trade" or "fair trade" but only "predatory trade." Indeed, it could be called "ugly mercantilism at its worst." We were behaving like a "colony" while they played the role of "mother country."

Iacocca designated three surface problems as "dumping, targeting, and scoffing at our laws," but the "real problem" lay in Japan's "different . . . fundamentally different" economy. He outlined seven differences and concluded that their "managed economy works . . . because they have the giant American market as a dumping ground and a pressure relief valve." He traced the historical development of our recessions and wars and then presented seven repetitions of "what ifs" that would make us more equal with Japan. Included in his list of "things we should have learned by now," we find his denunciation of "Adam Smith's theories" as "totally irrelevant" in a "world of managed trade."

In a reversal of his statements in the 1985 speech in Japan, Iacocca here outlined nine problems with transplants and voluntary restraints. He compared transplant openings with existing plant closings; the deficit shift from $14 billion to $30 billion; new job creation with existing job loss; new dollar contribution to old dollar loss; age, pay rate, minority status, health care, and pension needs of transplant workers and existing workers; and location of transplants in "cornfields" with existing plant locations in "urban America."

He compared the percentage of American jobs represented by imports (1 percent), transplants (48 percent), and Big Three companies (88 percent). He defined "Oriental patience" as a "weapon" and urged the acceptance of "good old-fashioned American impatience" as a similar weapon. He referred to the Japanese and their "Chrysanthemum Club apologists" as "economic pacifists."

In his calls for action, Iacocca had advice for both Americans and Japanese. In order to protect free trade, we would have to "retaliate against those who don't believe in it." We should "make Japan not only understand the rules, but play by them," perhaps even "change some of those rules." Our use of impatience as a weapon would mean "demanding a solution to the problem now. And retaliating now if we don't get it." Japan would have to "open their market . . . back off . . . reform their whole economic structure" and prepare to bear "responsibilities, pain, [and the] dislocation that comes with living in a global economy." Of the Detroit audience, he asked that they "be just as loud" as he was in their protests and that they "pull together."

REACTION OF THE AUDIENCE

For all three speeches, Iacocca received warm receptions from enthusiastic audiences. In Tokyo, he spoke to a "standing-room-only crowd" (Lienert 6B). Favorable responses came from both Republican and Democratic members of the congressional delegation in Highland Park. Representative Joe Barton, Republican of Texas, said, "When Iacocca talks about how desperate the situation is, you've got to pay attention." Representative Marcy Kaptur, Democrat of Ohio, said, "I've heard Iacocca many times. . . . This time he was superb. They ought to put his speech on TV and show it to everybody" (Sedgwick 2A). In Detroit, he "brought a . . . crowd of 3,000 to its feet"; they responded with "thunderous applause": and a radio station carrying the speech "was deluged with callers who . . . liked it so much they wanted the station to re-broadcast it" (Gardner 5A). As one of his critics delighted in pointing out, however, he was "preaching to the choir" in Detroit (Waldmeir 1C).

Press criticism provided a mixed reaction to these speeches. The *Los Angeles Times* carried a highly critical commentary in response to the Tokyo speech which referred to Iacocca as both a "truly great American" and a "villain in disguise" who "[u]nderneath the star-spangled red, white and blue is the sneak thief of free enterprise" (Graham 7). A Detroit reporter called Iacocca "a charmer" in response to the Highland Park speech, which otherwise received little coverage by the press. The Detroit speech, on the other hand, received wide press coverage. One columnist criticized Iacocca's "bellyaching" and his "loud, demanding, and . . . boorish" speaking (Wald-meir 1C).

One auto analyst was quoted as saying, "Getting up and ranting and rav-ing and implying that people are unpatriotic doesn't do it," while a local Michigan resident said, "I don't care what Lee says, I believe in a free market" (Sweeney 6A). A writer for the *Wall Street Journal* claimed that Ia-cocca had "stretch[ed] the truth" (Chandler A10). A *New York Times* edi-torial argued that Iacocca's claims were "worse than wrong. They're reck-less." The writer felt that the speech might "incite chauvinism, even xenophobia" ("The Excuse Maker" A22). A writer for the *Los Angeles Times* referred to Iacocca as a "veteran Japan-basher," whose criticism was "especially harsh" and "heavy with sarcasm and sneering disdain" (Harmon D2). A *New York Times* writer found the speech to be "vintage Iacocca, crammed with hyperbole, statistics, his trademark expletives and folk wisdom" (Feder 33, 44).

The harshest criticism of Iacocca's attacks on Japanese trade practices seems to take the perspective of objective public policy debate rather than corporate advocacy. In these and other remarks about fair trade, Iacocca was serving as an advocate of his company and his industry—an industry where he had spent his entire career and a company he had brought back from near bankruptcy through painful sacrifice. Beyond these immediate constituen-cies, Iacocca was also serving as an advocate of American jobs.

EXAMPLES OF CORPORATE ADVOCACY

Corporate advocacy is "the research, analysis, design, and mass dissemi-nation of arguments contested in the public dialogue in an attempt to create a favorable, reasonable, and informed public opinion which in turn influences institutions' operating environments" (Heath, 371). Such advocacy has been divided into four types: "economic justification, company storytelling, issues management, and crisis management" (Schuetz 276). Advocacy campaigns may consist of the ideological promotion of business values such as free en-terprise, corporate defense or apologia, replies to media charges, positions on public issues, or appeals for public or special interest support (Waltzer 41-55). From an interpretive perspective, these messages generated for external audiences often *become* the organization to those seeking its position on so-cial and political issues (Tompkins, Tompkins, and Cheney).

These three speeches given by Iacocca represent not only corporate advo-cacy, since he is fully identified with Chrysler Corporation, but also industry advocacy, since in each instance he referred often to the auto industry or the domestic car industry. With the exception of the first speech, in which he justified through corporate defense, or apologia, Chrysler's joint venture with Mitsubishi Motors, he used advocacy methods as issue management to marshal support for the industry as a whole as it struggled against competition from Japan. While we might perceive such corporate or industry rhetoric as aiming messages only toward external publics, internal audiences listen in as well. In terms of these speeches, Iacocca sought to unite the Big Three against their common external threat, and to unite the various constituencies within each corporation through the same appeal.

With regard to Iacocca's use of reasoned discourse, all three speeches form a blend of logical and emotional appeals. He certainly packs his presentations with statistical data that are arranged and argued forcefully. He often translates his numbers into jobs or dollar figures or, more compellingly, into visual depictions of consequences. He argues from historical references, from analogy, from comparison; he uses repetition, if-then or problem-solution arrangements. His recurring use of the motivated sequence speech pattern illustrates the complexity of his approach to persuasion.

Iacocca's most common emotional appeals in these three speeches were to threat and to patriotism. His genius may lie in his audacity in utilizing these appeals in the same speeches targeted to both Japanese and American audiences. He sought to strike fear in the hearts of citizens of both nations by pitting them against each other, while reassuring both of his interest in their welfare. He apparently either found no contradiction in this approach or saw it as a method of bringing both groups to his position, that only through cooperation could both sides win. He stressed in each speech that he had no quarrel with the Japanese people. He praised their good qualities and those of some of their leaders. However, he heaped scorn on the Japanese bureaucracy and its policies, as he did on the American bureaucracy and its policies. Considering what he actually said in these speeches, compared with what he is accused of saying, charges that his message is racist seem both exaggerated and inappropriate.

One scheme for evaluating organizational advocacy suggests that we look for inconsistencies, inadequacies, overstatements, unqualified claims, predictions not linked to evidence, irrelevancies, and justifications (Schuetz). Iacocca has been accused by his critics of hyperbole, a charge we might concede. His arguments, however, over the course of these speeches, have remained consistent, have brimmed over with both numerical data and historical analogies to justify his position, and have been backed by detailed evidence supporting his forecasts of damage to or destruction of the American automotive industry. His message has also brought consistent public attention to a very difficult issue.

No rational critique can take into account the force of personality, the power of reputation, or the nebulous links between speaker and historical context. His most criticized speech in Detroit came wrapped in risk taking born of exhaustion and was delivered to an audience immersed in a culture that perceived itself under siege. All his words took on relevance to that audience at that time. His greatest task, perhaps, was to help or to force the rest of the world to comprehend how that audience felt.

Emotional appeals aside, in the Detroit speech, Iacocca sought to explain and win support for the idea that the Japanese economic structure was and would remain so different from the American economy that classical theories would never suffice in the process of creating economic policy toward Japan. A recent *Wall Street Journal* article indicates some movement toward agreement with Iacocca's position on the part of the Clinton administration (Davis A7). Laura Tyson, White House chief economist, is quoted as saying that she became convinced that "Japan really was quite different" and that the United States could not "rely solely on conventional economic forces and liberalized trading rules to restore balance." Lawrence Summers, Treasury undersecretary, is also quoted as saying he had concluded that "Japanese trade barriers were stiffer and more intractable than those in the U.S. and Europe" (Davis A7). Iacocca may yet see his convictions, so convincingly expressed in these three speeches, incorporated into future trade policies with Japan.

CONCLUSIONS

If we reach below the surface of criticism of Iacocca's speeches on Japan, we might put our fingers on an underlying but unspoken assumption that corporate spokespersons should not tamper with public policy issues, especially foreign policy issues. However, if we take the pluralistic systems view of American politics, we recognize that no one group determines policy in a democracy.

Issue management theorists have often argued that "the corporation, as an institution, has every moral and legal right to participate in formation of public policy—not merely to react, or be responsive, to policies designed by government" (Jones and Chase 7). In models of issue management, the "dynamic" option that "anticipates and attempts to shape the direction of public policy decisions" is often presented as an optimum strategy (Jones and Chase 17). In terms of an action program, the corporate spokesperson should attempt to bring together "prior research, analysis, and priority setting to become an effective participant in the public policy debate" (Jones and Chase 18). These three speeches on U.S.-Japanese trade relations provide excellent concrete examples of the use of both the dynamic option in which Iacocca tried to shape trade policies and the action program through which he presented research and analysis to urge Congress and the president to prioritize auto industry jobs in the national economy. They also demonstrate how issue management efforts evolve. A progression may be seen in the speeches, in that the first fairly mild speech was given to a group of people who work closely with Japanese associates; the second and more forceful speech asked members of Congress directly to take steps to relieve the trade pressures from Japan; the third speech condemned practices that presented real consequences to the immediate audience, but were not subject to their control. This suggests that Iacocca adapted his arguments as the issue of trade developed.

Iacocca's support for the North American Free Trade Agreement with Canada and Mexico reveals an answer, perhaps, to a question that has long hampered his efforts to change U.S.-Japan trade policies: Is he a protectionist? His assignment involved using his persuasive powers to counter or neutralize Ross Perot's highly emotional argument that the NAFTA would cost jobs. Iacocca's role was particularly appropriate given his long-standing efforts to address fair trade and protect American jobs. His speech campaign on this issue also served to neutralize the critics who label him a protectionist and either fail to see or ignore his differentiation between free trade and managed trade with Japan.

WORKS CITED

Chandler, Clay. "Iacocca's Claim on Jeep Sales Questioned." *Wall Street Journal* 14 Jan. 1992: A10.

Davis, Bob. "Clinton's Get-Tough Stance with Japan Signals Rise of Revisionist Thought." *Wall Street Journal* 14 June 1993: A7.

"The Excuse Maker." (Editorial) *New York Times* 14 Jan. 1992: A22.

Feder, Barnaby J. "Blunt Talk by Iacocca, Just Back From Japan." *New York Times* 11 Jan. 1992, sec. L: 33, 44.

Gardner, Greg. "Iacocca Declares War, Chrysler's Chief Blasts Japanese." *Detroit News and Free Press* 11 Jan. 1992: 1A and 5A.

Graham, John. "Iacocca's a Good Salesman, but Not for Free Enterprise." *Los Angeles Times* 18 April 1985, sec. II: 7.

Harmon, Amy. "Iacocca Calls for Retaliation Against Japan." *Los Angeles Times* 11 Jan. 1992: D1-2.

Heath, Robert L. "Corporate Advocacy: An Application of Speech Communication Perspectives and Skills—and More." *Communication Education* 29 (Spring 1980): 370-377.

Jones, Barrie L. and W. Howard Chase. "Managing Public Policy Issues." *Public Relations Review* 7 (1979): 3-23.

Lienert, Paul. "Lee Talks Tough in Tokyo." *Detroit Free Press* 18 April 1985: 6B.

Monroe, Alan and Douglas Ehninger. *Principles and Types of Speech.* Glenview, IL: Scott, Foresman, 1935.

Schuetz, Janice. "Corporate Advocacy as Argumentation." *Perspectives on Argumentation.* Prospect Heights, IL: Waveland, 1990.

Sedgwick, David. "'Off-the Cuff' Iacocca Proves He Still Is a Charmer." *Detroit News* 26 April 1991: 2A.

Sweeney, Ann. "'Iacocca Got It Right,' Car Show Visitors Agree." *Detroit News and Free Press* 12 Jan. 1992: 1A and 6A.

Tompkins, Elaine V. B., Philip K. Tompkins and George Cheney. "Organizations as Arguments: Discovering, Expressing, and Analyzing the Premises for Decisions." *Journal of Management Systems* I.2 (1989): 35–48.

Waldmeir, Pete. "Iacocca Preaching to Economic Club Sounds Suspiciously Like Sour Grapes." *Detroit News and Free Press* 12 Jan. 1992: 1C.

Waltzer, H. "Corporate Advocacy Advertising and Political Influence." *Public Relations Review* (Spring 1988): 41–55.

REMARKS TO THE AMERICAN
CHAMBER OF COMMERCE IN JAPAN

Tokyo, Japan, April 17, 1985

The audience was mostly American business people, but the setting was Tokyo. U.S.-Japan trade friction was high, and Iacocca was prescient in saying that it would go even higher unless Japan's trade policies were changed. He warned that protectionist Japan, whose economy depended so heavily on sales in the United States, was protecting the wrong market.

Good afternoon to all of you. I'm told this is a big turnout, but I've also found out that the turnout was influenced by someone putting out a memorandum that I would be available for autographing books in the lobby right after lunch. There's no truth to that. I'm not here to plug my book today, but my Japanese publisher dropped by the hotel last night. He looked overwhelmed. And I didn't know this, but he told me that as of last night they had sold 331,000 of the Japanese edition. I only tell you this because you American businessmen say it's so difficult to sell in Japan. I found that if the product is right, you can do it.

Now if I can only find out how to sell a few more cars here.

I've been here in Japan three days now, and I must confess I don't get to Japan often enough. It's been six years, in fact, since my last visit. I was here in 1979 just a few months after I joined Chrysler. And at that time I expected that I would come back pretty regularly, but a few things got in the way.

They were little things like, as soon as I got home, we had run completely out of cash and we were contemplating declaring bankruptcy. And then we found ourselves trying to dig our way out of three and a half billion dollars of losses in the ensuing thirty months.

Things like that can play hell with your travel schedule, believe me.

But I'm glad to be back. The last time I was here, we were in the middle of the energy crisis. And we were starting an economic downturn in the U.S. that turned into a first-class depression, and that almost killed Chrysler by the way. And people in the States at that time were very worried about all those Japanese cars coming in.

Well, here I am, six years later, and now gas in the U.S. is cheap, and there's a lot of it. It dropped to under a dollar a gallon in New Jersey last week. The economy is booming. Chrysler is healthy again. And people are worried about all those Japanese cars coming in.

So, you see, some things in life change, and some things always stay the same.

Now I'm worried about all those Japanese cars, too. In fact, that's why I'm here.

As you probably know by now, I signed an agreement on Monday of this week with Mr. Tate, president of Mitsubishi Motors (MMC), creating a new joint venture between our two companies. The result, hopefully sometime in 1988, will be a new car plant in the United States directly employing 2,500 people. Additionally, almost 9,000 other jobs will be created for our suppliers —for a total of about 11,300 jobs in the U.S. auto industry.

That new plant will allow Chrysler and Mitsubishi to jointly produce and distribute cars for the American market.

Now I won't bore you with this. I don't know how interested you are in all the details, but this will be a state-of-the-art facility producing about 180,000 cars annually. Each of the partners will hold a 50-percent equity in the venture. MMC, however, will take the lead in the day-to-day operations and in the building of the plant. They'll be the ones dealing with our many state and local governments on site selection. And I have to add here, they'll be dealing directly with the union. It's one of those unique and rare experiences that I wanted to share with my friends and partners!

I'm excited about this venture, because it's one of those "everybody wins" situations. Mitsubishi will become a major participant in the American market. Chrysler will have a new source for small cars. And 11,300 Americans will be put to work.

We also signed another agreement on Monday that will increase Chrysler's ownership in MMC from 15 to 24 percent over a two-year period. And finally, we've asked Mitsubishi and MITI for more imports.

Now, I'm one of the guys who was screaming the loudest a couple of months ago about keeping the Voluntary Restraint Agreement in place. And now here I am, I've just signed an agreement that will help us import more cars from Japan. Maybe some of you are confused. Well, let me try quickly to straighten it out for you.

Nobody fought harder than we did to keep the auto restraints in place. We wanted them in place until the underlying trade problems that give Japanese cars a huge advantage in the American market were worked out. We were right to fight, I'm convinced of that, but we fought the good fight. And guess what? We lost.

We knew we lost on the morning of February 19th when the President's Cabinet Council voted twelve to nothing not to extend the restraints. A lot of things in Washington confuse me, but I can sure as hell read twelve to zip. A couple of weeks later, the president announced his decision.

And it's simple. It's now the policy of the United States government to allow an unrestricted flow of Japanese cars into the U.S. Those are the new rules. And, of course, Chrysler will play by those rules.

We knew the new rules meant a significant increase in Japanese imports. They do have an advantage of about two thousand dollars a car, most of that, by the way, from the out-of-whack dollar, so we knew that a lot more cars would be coming in.

Then I had our people run the numbers for me. The conclusion was crystal clear—we would need a greater reliance on our Mitsubishi partners to compete in the low end of the U.S. market. It's the only way Chrysler can protect the investment and the jobs it now has in the States. And it's the only way we can protect what our people went through six years of absolute hell to build.

When we were going broke—just forty-eight months ago, or whenever it was—our market share got as low as 8 percent. We've fought like tigers to get it up to 12.5 percent today. That's a 50-percent increase in share. We need that share to succeed, and we're going to do whatever it takes to keep it. It's that simple.

So if it's government policy that 25 percent or more of the American car market will be Japanese imports, then we want enough from our Mitsubishi partners to maintain that 12.5-percent share. And we also want a joint manufacturing venture in the United States.

Now Chrysler and Mitsubishi are obviously hoping for a long and productive relationship. We've been partners for almost sixteen years, and that partnership got a lot deeper last Monday at noon.

We've been able to work out an arrangement that is fair to both of our companies, and that will help us compete together as partners. We looked at where we want our companies to be five and ten years into the future and we think that—working together—we know how to get there.

But I gotta tell you, it may be tough because even though Chrysler and Mitsubishi can agree on a long-term relationship, our two countries seem to be moving further apart in *their* trade relationship.

Last week the United States Senate voted ninety-two to nothing on a resolution telling the president to retaliate against Japan for its trade practices. "Retaliate" was the word they used. For the Senate to use that word means that the situation really has become critical. And I gotta tell you, for the vote to be *unanimous*—well, those guys can't even get a *unanimous* vote to go home for Christmas! So you know they felt strong about this.

Now we've all lived with this trade friction for so long now that maybe we're starting to take it for granted. I've been telling people for a long time that it's going to boil over, and I think we're getting very close to that point. I'm not at all surprised, but I must say I am concerned.

The mood of the American people is more hostile now toward the Japanese trade situation than at any time in my memory. And I go to Washington a lot, believe me. At least, that's what I hear when I talk to people, from my mail, and, of course, from what I read in our own press.

And I think it's fairly easy to understand. The American people see a trade relationship that they perceive as being increasingly "one-way."

They see Japanese companies taking more and more of the American market and American jobs, and they see a Japanese market that is virtually closed to American companies.

They believe there's a well-ordered plan in Japan to take as much as possible from America, while putting little back, and to protecting Japan's industries and agriculture from any significant competition.

Those are the *perceptions* that are coloring the mood of America right now. I want to emphasize, by the way, the word *perceptions*. Maybe the facts are different, maybe they're not. I don't know that. It really doesn't matter, because in a democracy—where people's collective will gets translated into policy—*perceptions* are all that count. Especially in this age of thirty-second television.

Personally, I believe that there is at least enough substance to justify a lot of those perceptions. Now, I've gotta pat Japan on the back. I don't think any nation in history has ever come so far so fast. Japan is an example to everybody of what people can accomplish with strong will, hard work, perseverance, and intelligence. Behind all the criticism you hear in America of Japan's trade policies, there is also deep admiration for the Japanese people and what they've accomplished.

But I don't mind patting America on the back, too. I don't believe the Japan we see today would exist without the generosity, the patience, and the friendship of the people of the United States. I take nothing away from the Japanese when I say that—nothing at all. I simply believe, and I think most Americans agree with me, that it's a historical fact.

And that's why so many Americans are frustrated today—so frustrated that they're actually applauding that ninety-two to nothing vote in the Senate.

Every culture has a cornerstone, and America's is *fairness*. It's not a common religion, or a common ethnic heritage—it's simply *play fair with me.* That's about the only thing we worship together in the United States.

In the Japanese trade situation that we have today, the American people believe that sense of fairness is being violated. And that's why they're so angry.

I don't understand the Japanese culture, so I can't explain why Japan has let the situation fester so long. Japan has not been acting in its own best interests, long-term. I only hope that the Japanese understand American culture better than I understand Japan's. I hope they understand that American political swings can, and often do, go to wild extremes.

Public opinion in the United States is clearly for closing some of America's market to Japan until Japan's market is open to American goods.

Ambassador Mansfield is probably the best judge of the problems and the mood in *both* countries. Believe me, both countries are lucky to have his counsel right now during these difficult times. Some of you may not know this but Mr. Mansfield has been through many wars in the Congress of the United States. He was a majority leader in the Senate for seventeen years. I believe that was the longest in the history of the nation. He served thirty illustrious years in both the House and the Senate.

I asked him the other day at the embassy whether he would like to be back there now. He's got a lot of problems in Japan, but would he like to be back as a majority leader trying to cut the $225 billion deficit in half? He said, "No thanks. I prefer to stay here."

But he did say just last month that it's likely that America will close some of its markets to Japan if progress isn't made on opening the market here. And he ought to know. He knows congressional moods, I think, better than anybody. And of course he's right, by the way. I hear a lot of that on my trips to Washington. I hear it in Detroit, I hear it in New York; in fact, all over the country. And I get a lot of mail on the subject because maybe some of you have heard I've made some strong comments of my own on this issue.

I've had a chance in the past few days though, to talk with a number of Japanese colleagues of mine and many government leaders. And I've already concluded just one simple thing: Everybody understands the problem. You don't have to draw anybody any pictures right now!

By the way, my hat is off to Prime Minister Nakasone for the courageous thing he did just last week by going on television. I don't think anyone hearing that can doubt his sincerity or his determination to solve this problem before it gets out of hand. And I sure wish him well . . . I think we *all* do.

But the bureaucracy—they're the same all over the world—it's pretty entrenched here too, just like the one in Washington. You can't just push a button and change things.

Still—mark my word—some changes are coming, believe me, one way or another. There's too much frustration right now in America, Democrat versus Republican, doesn't matter; blue collar, white collar, it doesn't matter. And this frustration has been building too long now.

If *reasonable* solutions for the trade imbalance are not found, then I can almost predict you are going to see some fairly drastic solutions. And I'm talking about short-term fixes like import surcharges, and higher tariffs, maybe quotas, I don't know. If you can't agree on a long-term trade policy that's *fair*, then quick fixes are inevitable just to stop the bleeding.

And make no mistake about it, America is bleeding a little right now. We went from a $40 billion trade surplus in goods to a $123 billion deficit in just forty-eight months when you adjust for inflation, those are the numbers. That's a negative swing of $163 billion. If you disregard oil imports—and they stayed constant, by the way, during those four years—almost 62 percent of our total deficit last year came from trade with just one country—Japan.

So Japan will be the target, and the big loser, if all this frustration should boil over.

Now people have called me a lot of things in my life, and some have called me a protectionist because I wanted to keep the Voluntary Restraint Agreement. But I'm not a protectionist. I don't even consider myself part protectionist. By the way, I am not a die-hard "free trader" either, I might add. All I'd like to see is what we call a "level playing field." We at Chrysler coined this phrase—level playing field. And it seems to have caught on. And the reason we know it caught on is because they love buzz words in Washington. And they call it LPF now. So I know it's being accepted.

But what are we talking about—level playing field? We are just talking about *fairness*, that's all. I don't care how we get there. That should be the goal of any sensible trade policy. It's very simple, and there's nothing too complicated about it.

It only gets complicated when it gets all tied up in ideology, because then you lose sight of the goal, and I have to believe that's a big part of our trade problem right now.

You see, I think both countries are still living in the mid-nineteenth century. Back then, Japan was the ultimate protectionist. It was totally isolated, cut off from the rest of the world. And America was just the opposite. It was *reaching out*. The doors were wide open—to immigration, to new ideas, to *everything*.

Well, things have changed some since then, but really not *enough*. Japan has become a major factor in the world economy, and that's a big switch from one hundred fifty years ago. But it has held on to the idea that it can shelter its markets from foreign competition.

We're the great free traders, on the other hand. Our policy is to throw the doors wide open to anybody and everybody. The administration has made that as clear as a bell. Never mind that Japan and everybody else in the world has gone to some form of "managed trade."

Now I don't know who's right, but we're never going to sit down and hammer out a fair trade policy for the two countries if we've got two different trade philosophies—one free trade and one managed trade.

We don't have to pick one philosophy over the other, by the way. A sensible compromise would do. Just as long as we're on the same track. Let's get ideology off the table. Let's forget where we *came from*, and figure out where we're *going*.

We Americans sometimes get emotional over words we don't even understand. Like "free trade" and "protectionism." We treat them like absolutes. You're either a saint or a sinner—there's no in between.

Well, they aren't *absolutes*; they're all *relative*. Nobody has free trade today, not even the United States. It just pretends it does. And nobody is totally protectionist, either. Not even Japan.

So we're chasing a myth, and we're wasting our time. Every other country in the world manages its trade in its own self-interest, and what's wrong with that? So should the United States.

It's not a sin anymore. Everybody does it. You don't go blind or get warts from it.

And I think when we get rid of the myths and the ideologies, we can start getting at the goal—which is fairness.

That's how we negotiate with our unions. I don't know if any of you have ever had the pleasure, but, believe me, we don't bother much about philosophies. We know going in that both sides have to give. Both sides know they will not "win." They'll have to settle for something unreasonably "unfair" to both of us!

And we never get to a fair settlement without listening to the other side, either.

Japan is right, for example, when it says we have to put our *own* house in order. Well, that's *half* right. We get at least half the blame in my book for our trade imbalance. And Japan gets half. That's fair—half and half. There's plenty of room for compromise if each side accepts half the blame.

The currency problem is mainly *our* fault. Maybe Japan fiddles a little with the yen. I don't know that for sure, but you hear a lot of rumors where I come from. But let's face it, the high dollar is a bastard child of our own scandalous budget deficit in the United States, and only *we* can fix that. We cannot look for scapegoats on that one.

We're living beyond our means with deficits of $220 billion. Those are the roots of all evil, right now. We've become credit card junkies. We're charging everything.

And I get despondent about that deficit because I see us burying our kids under a dung heap of public debt. And I don't know how in hell those kids are going to ever be able to dig themselves out of it.

Well, I don't want to get into that. It's another speech. But the deficit and the high dollar—let's blame ourselves, nobody else. That's our half.

But trade barriers and closed markets—that's Japan's half. It's not fair that Japan has open season on our markets, and we have to crawl through a maze of bureaucratic regulations in order to sell over here. It's especially unfair with a deficit of $37 billion, and it's getting worse every day.

And that "perception" of unfairness by the American people—this is what you have to watch for—could cause a swing back to strict protectionism, just like we had in the '30s.

A new round of protectionism would be disastrous for Japan, of course. Japan is really vulnerable. It exports a lot of goods that people *want* all over the world, but it doesn't sell much that people absolutely *need* and that they can't get somewhere else.

So, here's the message I'd like to get across to you today. By not opening its markets as widely as ours are, Japan is really *letting us off the hook*. The focus right now is on Japan's protectionism, not on our high dollar. So we've got an excuse to retaliate without doing a darn thing about *our* half of the problem.

People don't get excited about the high dollar. Not on Main Street, U.S.A., they don't. That's "economics" . . . the old dismal science. The explanations all get a little fuzzy. People don't really understand it. So nobody's going to get up in arms over the high dollar.

But *unfairness*—now that really winds them up! That they understand. And they see it every day or they read about it in Japan's closed markets. Every day, it seems, in our papers we are reading about metal baseball bats or oranges or cigarettes. Right now it's telecommunications and plywood. I think I saw someplace that walnuts are next. That doesn't get me too excited, but it probably does something for the walnut growers. You can recite a whole litany—tomato puree, potato chips, you name it. Every month there's something.

These piecemeal negotiations—one product at a time, month after month, year after year—they just prolong the friction and deepen the resentment.

It's okay to have all these barriers if you're a Third World country, and it was okay for Japan while it was rebuilding. But look around you. Japan's the success story of the century. No question about it. It's earned a place at the top as one of the economic leaders of the world. And I say, "Congratulations. Welcome to the club. I'm glad you're all here. And oh, by the way, there are some *dues* we all have to pay."

You know, I think if Japan tore down every one of its barriers tomorrow, we'd still have one hell of a big trade deficit. And it would continue to grow.

But then Japan could point the finger at us and say "Okay, we've taken care of *our half* and you guys are still going in the hole, so maybe you'd better do something about *your half.*"

And without protectionist Japan to blame anymore, who knows, maybe we might get serious in the U.S. about the currency problem and the deficit that's causing it. I'm not making any guarantees, mind you, because a lot of people in the U.S. barely admit that it's even a problem. But maybe with a wide open Japan—with the scapegoat gone—we'd have to face up to *our half* of the responsibility for the logjam that we've got ourselves into.

I'm simple-minded. I think that's worth a try. If Japan is protectionist, and, by the way, people say that about me, so I'm not throwing stones here, then I think it's protecting the *wrong market*. It's protecting its market *in Japan*, when it ought to be protecting its market in *America*. That's the market that's really in danger. And that's where it stands to take its biggest loss.

The best way to protect its American market is to open its Japanese market. That means some sacrifice, of course. Some people are gonna get hurt, just like millions of Americans have been hurt by our open market. That's part of the price, part of the *dues*.

But look what Japan would be protecting. The U.S. is by far Japan's largest single market. More than one-third of all its exports go into that one single market. And I think that market is in jeopardy, right now—at least a good part of it.

One thing Japan would gain right off the bat is a lobby in Washington made up of people like you in this room who do business in Japan. That lobby is pretty small at the moment. Do you ever think of that? Oh, there are plenty of lobbyists for *Japanese* companies looking after their *American* business interests. But you don't see many *Americans* looking out for their *Japanese* business interests.

Japan needs a lobby or constituency like that long term.

It also needs another lobby. It needs a lobby made up of Americans who earn their living in America working for Japanese companies. Or joint ventures like our new arrangement with Mitsubishi. I don't usually do this, by the way, not publicly, but I've got to toss bouquets to two of our competitors —Honda and Nissan—because of their very, very big investments in the United States.

Still, Japan has about $60 billion right now invested in the States, but less than a quarter of it is direct investments in brick and mortar projects that create jobs and thus help build a constituency. Three-quarters of that $60 billion is in portfolios and bank deposits. And I got news for you, T-bills do not build a constituency.

So Japan is vulnerable right now because America is vulnerable. And the mood of America is shifting. We just went through a presidential election in which the trade deficit never became an issue. It never even came up once. But I want to tell you how fast things change. It's an issue today—and it's a big one.

It's an issue because the trade imbalance is now getting spread around. It used to just be cars. I went to Washington five years ago—I got there first—I don't know why God was so good to me, but I got there first. The following year the steel guys followed. The year after that, the machine tool people.

This past year, the telecommunications people. And in the last few months, even the farmers have convened in Washington. Everybody's getting into the act.

Even the high-tech people are getting kicked in the head. I can still remember all the editorials in the U.S. newspapers from just a couple of years ago. It said, "It's too bad that old smokestack America can't compete anymore, but don't worry about a thing, boys, because high-tech is gonna save America."

I just keep reading the numbers. I looked at the trade figures. In the past four years, foreign (mainly Japanese) penetration of the U.S. computer market went from 3 to 13 percent. And in semiconductors, it went from 6 to 15 percent.

So I don't think high-tech is going to save us. Until we get the dollar at a sane level, until we write a trade policy for America to compete, and until we get a level playing field, the trade imbalance is going to hurt almost everybody.

And the pressure will build until it explodes.

I'm glad to see my good friend Dr. Kubo with us today. He was chairman of MMC until a few years ago. I have great respect for him and we are very good friends. I'll never forget a conversation we had once. I said something about where we should be as partners with Mitsubishi ten or twenty years out —a long time, whatever it was. And he said to me, "Now you're finally showing some Oriental wisdom, you're finally taking the long view." And I took it as a big compliment coming from Dr. Kubo.

But I think there's such a thing as Occidental wisdom, too. And it probably goes something like this, it's short and snappy: If you don't solve *today's* problems, you might not have a future at all. We sure found that out during our dark days at Chrysler.

I always tell the story of when I came to my senses at Chrysler. It was a night in November of 1980 when I found out from our top financial people that we had a million dollars left in the bank. And that didn't sound like much to me because our payroll and parts bill every Friday every week was $240 million. That focused my attention in a hurry on attacking problems.

I'd like Japan and the United States to sit down and agree on their trade relationship for the year 2000 and beyond. But there are serious problems that we've got to settle *today*.

Like the high dollar, like closed markets, and like a very real $37 billion trade imbalance. I see in the paper this morning that the U.S. is casually saying it will probably go to $45 billion in 1985. So get ready.

The high dollar is *our* problem, and I've made some very specific recommendations to our government about how to deal with it. They didn't listen, but at least they were told what was on my mind.

Restrictive trade policies are Japan's problem, but I'm not going to tell Japan how to handle its part. That would be presumptuous, and I don't think we should do that anyway.

For example, I'm not going to say to the Japanese people, "Buy more American oranges," or "Don't send so many VCRs to the States." To tell you the truth, I don't want to read any more about plywood or tomato puree. I'm not even going to suggest how many *cars* they should ship.

I don't think we should be telling Japan how to handle its internal problems—many of them political. We sure as hell wouldn't stand for it if the shoe were on the other foot. That's the wrong approach.

A better approach would be for the two sides to sit down and agree on a goal to take that $37 billion number down. Agree on a number. Maybe you freeze it for twelve months at $37 billion and then the following year take it down to $30, or some number. The figure is negotiable. Then let the Japanese decide the best way to get there. If it's not possible to open some markets, then offset it with a reduction of exports. But the choice should be *theirs*.

This isn't just a market access issue. This issue is a $37 billion imbalance. So we shouldn't get bogged down trying to dictate how the Japanese should solve their part of that problem. Let them manage their own solution.

The fact is, Japan manages its trade. And there's nothing wrong with that, is there? Japan's a sovereign power and calls its own shots. But I think in its own best interest and ours, its trade surplus with the States should be managed *downward*. I really don't care *how*.

Because if the current hard feelings don't end, I'm afraid the whole U.S.-Japan trade relationship could break down and quickly. The American people simply won't tolerate a one-way transfer of dollars or jobs. It won't work. There'll be some kind of revolution budding.

Trade has to be a win-win situation. If we can't work that out, then what's the sense of having any trade at all? We'll just go backward in time until we all become isolationists again, and that would be pretty stupid.

Trade, you know, is like any other business deal—both sides have to benefit. Chrysler and Mitsubishi have been partners for almost sixteen years. If it had been one-sided, that partnership wouldn't have lasted; believe me, it would have cracked up some place along the line. And it wouldn't have lasted if either of us was just looking at the immediate interests.

The running rules for trade in cars between the two countries just changed. Now, I fought to keep the old rules because until the currency situation and other problems are solved, the playing field remains tilted.

But with the new rules, I've got to be pragmatic. I'm not a philosopher, I'm a businessman. And the day after President Reagan announced the change in quotas, I went on TV and laid out our game plan—Plan B. I changed our whole plan in the company, because I'm a realist.

But—and this is very important—I haven't given up on fairness as our goal. Within the new rules, we're working harder than ever toward that elusive goal of fairness.

And fairness in trade means both sides have to give something up. Both sides have to sacrifice and take some risks. Chrysler and Mitsubishi have just agreed to do that, by the way. The ink is hardly dried on our three agreements of yesterday and the day before.

Think of it a minute. Car quotas went off just two and a half weeks ago. The most profitable way to sell a car in America right now—*by far*—is to ship it in from Japan. You still have that $2,000 advantage.

So ask yourself, why in the world would Mitsubishi, very smart people, by the way, decide to make a huge investment to build cars with us in America? Well, I gotta believe that maybe it's that "Oriental wisdom" Dr. Kubo used to talk about. They're taking the longer view. Big profits on imports in the short run do not buy you a future. They're willing to invest, they're willing to pay the dues, because they want a future in the American car market.

That's a big investment for them, by the way. They won't see a return for several years. And because of that investment, and *ours*, 11,300 more Americans are going to have jobs.

So MMC is doing the fair thing. Because they want a bigger share of the American market, they're willing to invest in America and create some American jobs. They aren't coming in on the cheap just by sending imports for big profits in the short run.

In return, we're making a rather big investment in MMC, too. That's our half of the deal.

Our two investments are about equal. Investment for investment. You could call it a quid pro quo time. Equal investments, equal risks, equal benefits. Everybody looks to the long term. Now that's fairness.

In addition, we're asking MMC for about two hundred thousand more imports. In return MMC will participate with us in building an equal number of about two hundred thousand more cars in America.

Narrow Japanese interests would say build them all in Japan, and narrow American interests would say build them all in America. But our *mutual interests* say half-and-half again. That's fair.

I think Chrysler and Mitsubishi have gotten together and done a very simple thing. We compromised. And we've made, I think, a good start toward that goal of fairness.

Now let me close on this. There are a lot of angry people in the United States right now. And all you hear about are arm-for-an-arm and tit-for-tat *reprisals*. We're not hearing about tit-for-tat *sacrifice*, or tit-for-tat *investment*, or tit-for-tat *commitment*.

When I went to school, that's how trade was supposed to work. It's supposed to bring people together. It's supposed to make them see their common interests.

Chrysler and Mitsubishi have achieved that. And we're pretty good, but we're not geniuses, we don't have some secret here. If we can do it, then why can't our two countries do it?

All it takes, I think, is a sense of fairness, some old-fashioned, enlightened self-interest, and a good healthy dose of that "Oriental wisdom"—on *both* sides of the Pacific.

Thank you very much for having me today.

REMARKS TO THE
CONGRESSIONAL DELEGATION
Highland Park, Michigan, April 25, 1991

After almost ten years of going to Washington to warn about Japan's mercantilistic trade policies, Iacocca had the opportunity to host a number of lawmakers who came to Detroit to see the U.S. auto industry firsthand. And he took the occasion to lobby for a more rational trade arrangement with Japan.

Let me first thank all of you for making this unprecedented trip. To have forty-two members, 10 percent of the House of Representatives, come to hear about our problems and try to better understand them is truly a historic occasion!

Well, you've heard about what we're facing in this economy and this industry, and about what we're trying to do to stay competitive.

We aren't perfect. We make mistakes. But every time I hear critics of this industry say that we haven't invested enough, or that we've gouged the customer with price hikes, or that the Japanese deserve to run away with our market, I write them off as . . . well, let's keep it polite tonight . . . as "uninformed."

So, I appreciate all of you coming to learn more about our industry. There's a lot going on—and a lot of confusing things to sort out.

The euphoria of a big military victory is over. It didn't last long. We're back to recession, and unemployment lines, and now Kurdish refugees.

It's also spring, and people get a little crazy in the spring. I know from reading the papers.

This from the *New York Times*. A *Japanese* typewriter company goes to *our* International Trade Commission and says another company that is 48 percent owned by the *British* is illegally *dumping* in this market. I read that and felt like Alice looking through the looking glass.

And this from the *Washington Post*: "Trade Deficit Down," says the headline. Good news. Then you read the story. Oil prices are low because we won the war and consumer demand for foreign goods declines because we're in a recession and people aren't buying. Then really *deep* in the story: "The value of Japanese car shipments were *up significantly* in February, to $1.85 billion . . . and March auto exports to the United States by Toyota and Nissan *surged*." Somehow the words and music don't match.

191

I also read *Agents of Influence* this spring. The first half made me mad; the second half scared the hell out of me. If it's only 80 percent true, I simply don't know where we're headed in this country.

Just last week, though, I read this little book Paul Tsongas sent me. At last some *sanity*! If you haven't read it, get it. He's got advice for both Democrats and Republicans. To the Democrats he says: "You cannot redistribute wealth that is never created." A lot of Democrats don't understand that. And to the Republicans he says: "American companies need the United States government as a full partner if they are to have any hope of competing internationally." A lot of Republicans don't understand *that*.

I tried to convince the *top* Republican of that a few weeks ago when Bob Stempel, Red Poling, and I went to the White House. The first time in ten years that the three CEOs went together—you know we're in trouble! The first thing I did was remind President Bush of a small dinner he and I were at at the White House in 1983. I said, "Mr. President, remember what we talked about that night? *Rice and cars.* Well, it's eight years later and here we are, still talking about rice and cars."

That was the same week that some of our people were almost thrown in the slammer because they took a ten-pound bag of rice to a trade show in Tokyo. I brought that up. And it was the same week that MITI told Japan's car companies to go easy in Europe because they didn't want to make the Europeans mad and face a backlash. I brought that up, too, and I pointed out that Japan isn't going easy in *this* market. They're not afraid of making *us* mad.

Well, that gets me to my part tonight. I'm going to talk about public policy —*good* policy and *bad* policy—because that will largely decide whether we have an American auto industry in another decade or so. I wish the issue were going to be totally decided here in our design labs and on our plant floors. But that's naive. If we somehow all get smart enough to build the perfect automobile, we still won't make it if we have to compete under bad policy.

We just told you about all the cars they've piled up on the docks and in the parking lots behind their transplant factories. We're cutting back production because the market is lousy, but they're producing to beat the band. Volkswagen is shipping cars *back* from this saturated market, but there are no Japanese cars going back. They'd die first.

They're massing on our borders for *something*. They're not just holding *maneuvers*. Could it be deja vu all over again? Ten years ago this country was in a recession. We were preoccupied with problems in the Middle East. The dollar was getting stronger. And the auto industry was facing a whole new set of regulations. Sound familiar? And while we weren't looking, Japan's share of our car market suddenly went from 14 to 22 percent in three short years.

Another quick market grab like ten years ago will be a disaster, and it's already started, as we showed you. The Japanese finished 1990 with 34 percent of our passenger car market. But in the first three months of this year, while we were all watching the war on CNN and trying to figure out how long the recession would last, they weren't distracted for a minute. When the numbers came in for March, they had 37 percent of our car market—three full share points in one ninety-day period! And in this business, every point of market share is worth over $2 billion in revenue!

Now, there are two schools of thought about what's going on here. The first one is that we deserve it. Our workers are all lazy and our managers are all stupid. The Japanese are smarter and tougher, so naturally they're gonna win. We've been hearing that for fifteen years or more, in one form or another. I don't buy it. And I don't think you do, either.

The other one is that the Japanese are smart, all right. And tough. Smart enough to set the policy for U.S.-Japanese trade, and tough enough to make it stick. The policy, in a nutshell, is simply this: "I will do what I please in *your* market, and you will do what you are *told* in mine."

They set the rules, and let me tell you how those rules work when it comes to cars.

Under those rules Japanese companies can use my own distribution system to beat my head in, but I'm not allowed to use theirs to sell in Japan. We enforce our antitrust laws and they don't. So foreign cars are sold at about twenty-three thousand dealerships in this country, while their dealerships are closed to us, except for a few token stores designed to fool visiting American trade officials. Honda recently agreed to distribute some Cherokees for us. Good, I thought, we should sell fifty thousand a year there because they have nothing like it in Japan. Honda ordered one thousand—one per dealership.

Under those rules a funny thing happens in the middle of the Pacific Ocean. Right at the International Date Line, the price tags on vehicles sailing *that* way go up while the stickers on cars coming *this* way seem to get marked down. My Jeep Cherokee jumps from $25,400 to $38,800 fees and distribution costs, they tell me while the Toyota Previa heading this way *drops* from $22,808 to $19,590. The American consumer can buy most Japanese cars here even *after* the boat ride for less than the Japanese consumer can buy it right off the assembly line. It could be that the Japanese automakers just have a soft spot in their hearts for *American* consumers . . . it could be.

Under those rules Japanese car companies are welcome to manufacture here. There are no foreign car plants in Japan, though. Are they prohibited by law? No. But the so-called structural impediments like no dealers will sell the cars mean that there are no plants there. None. No Germans, or French or Italians or Americans. Even the Koreans right next door can't get in.

Under those rules Japanese car companies pay virtually no American taxes on profits they make on the cars they ship here. They've got transfer pricing down to a science.

Under those rules dumping cars here to keep their people employed and to "buy" a bigger share of our market is tough to prove but everybody knows it's going on. The administration tells us, "Give us a good dumping case and we'll move on it." Why do we, the *victims*, have to take the lead? Why doesn't the government do its own investigation and enforce the law?

Under those rules, Japanese companies have the same open access to you people in Washington as any voting American does, but Japan's government is for Japanese only.

I hate to bring up the MPV decision of two years ago, but nothing—and I mean *nothing*—proved the reach of Japan's power better than that one. In one fell swoop, they got the administration to reduce tariffs on those vehicles from 25 percent to 2.5 percent and transferred about $500 million from the U.S. Treasury to their corporate profits. Now, that's what I call *lobbying*! I know, it was the *administration* that got snookered on this deal, not *Congress*.

Think how hard they laughed at us in Tokyo after that one: The same vehicle to EPA is a *truck* for clean-air laws . . . to NHTSA it's a *truck* for safety regulations . . . to DOT it's a *truck* for CAFE . . . but to *Treasury*, it's suddenly a *car* for tariff purposes. Do you see why we get upset with the rules? Our competition is making them!

As a carmaker, I was stung by the MPV ruling because it hurt me competitively. But as an American, I was embarrassed at seeing my government being led around by the nose. With a bilateral deficit over $50 billion that year, don't you think we could have gotten *something* in return? *Anything*? Hell, we didn't even *ask*! Can't we hire at least a few good poker players as trade negotiators?

Well, in the end the rules are different because the United States and Japan operate under totally different philosophies. We're free traders and Japan is protectionist. We're a consumer-oriented society; Japan is a producer-oriented society. We think everything will work out in the end if we keep our trade doors wide open. They only let into Japan what Japan needs or wants. Anything else stays out. They *manage* their trade. We don't. Their government and their companies have worked hand-in-glove for years to expand exports and restrict imports. But every time I just *mention* "industrial policy" in the White House, the metal detectors go off.

Two philosophies . . . two sets of rules . . . one country builds up a foreign debt of $750 billion in the '80s, and one banks a surplus of more than $400 billion . . . one big *winner* and one big *loser*.

Now, setting the rules is your job in Washington, not mine. And I'll let you in on a little secret. I'm easy to get along with. I don't give a damn which set of rules you decide on down there.

If America is to be a free trader, that's fine with me. If we want to manage our trade like everybody else in the world does, and (God forbid) even *protect* some of the industries that are essential to our economic survival, I'm game for that, too.

I can live with *either* set of rules. But I can't live with *both*. I can't live with a little of each. That's the killer. When I'm told to suit up for a tennis match and the other guys come in football pads, I've got a big problem in the rough-and-tumble game I'm in. And that's why this industry and this country have been getting clobbered in trade.

So before *anything* else, let's decide on the rules, and then enforce them. Free trade would work fine if we enforced it. And to enforce it, you simply have to say to your trade partner: "If you want to sell one thin dime's worth of goods in my market you will fix it so I can sell anything I want in yours." Period. End of discussion. No talk about "cultural differences" or the sacred symbolism of rice, or anything else. If I've got the best fighter plane in the world and you won't buy it, and instead you build your own at twice the price so you can target my aircraft industry in a few years, you've just sold your last VCR, camera, or automobile in my market.

But, on the other hand, if we want to manage our trade, that's fine with me, too. I'm willing to adopt Japan's philosophy if that's the decision. I'd do it a little differently, though. I don't think we should punish our own consumers in order to grab foreign markets, like they have. But every other country manages trade, so maybe we should, too.

Now, I'm almost done because this is supposed to be a dialogue here tonight, not a monologue, and I know you've got lots of questions. But when we did the division of labor for tonight, I pulled the assignment to ask for the order. What do we want from you as policymakers? What's our "wish list"?

First, give us *one* set of rules, not *two*.

Second, whatever set you decide on, enforce them! That's the big one. Look at dumping. Look at the keiretsu. Look at transfer pricing. Look at Japan's closed auto market.

Third, and this is the most immediate problem, Japan is poised to grab another huge hunk of this market while we're mired in a recession. Just to hold their 1990 share of the U.S. car and multi-purpose vehicle market, they'd have to reduce 1991 shipments by five hundred thousand units. Instead, they're building inventories. Our government should tell Mr. Kaifu in the strongest possible terms that we expect to see a half-million *fewer* imports this year. And let's get this straight, because I've been falsely accused of trying to cut auto jobs in Tennessee and Kentucky—I'm talking about cutting back on *imports*, not *transplants*. At least you get a half a loaf on a transplant.

Fourth, maintain competitive exchange rates. Japan had a severely under-valued yen for at least four years, and used it as a big competitive advantage in our market. We deserve a few years of that kind of advantage.

Fifth, do something about health-care costs. For us, they're up to $700 a car. Other countries spread the costs over the whole tax base; in this country the bulk of it is picked up by big employers like us, and that makes us less competitive.

Sixth, start collecting taxes from the imports. A little franchise fee for open access to the most lucrative market in the world is not unreasonable. Do it in a way that helps us *compete*. Dick Schulze's Uniform Business Tax is just the kind of tax we've been pushing at Chrysler for years. I hope it becomes law. It's a way for you people to lay your hands on $50 billion a year. It would help us compete. It's simple and it's not regressive.

Seventh, help get the truth out to the American public about where these heavily advertised "Made in America" transplants really come from. Dick Gephardt has a "Truth in Content" proposal that would do that.

Eighth and last, automobiles are 73 percent of this country's bilateral trade gap with Japan. You can't balance the trade unless you deal with autos. The Japanese have cost advantages we can't touch. Most of those advantages come from *policy* differences between the two countries, not from the way we manufacture or sell automobiles. As long as those policy differences remain, we won't close the trade gap.

Those are eight things you could do that would help us.

Now, before the questions, let me anticipate one of them. I get asked it a lot: "How can you criticize the Japanese and our own government's trade policies when you've got a Japanese partner yourself and you buy so much from Japan?"

Well, the fact is, we are dependent on some Japanese purchases to stay competitive. Under free trade, there's nothing wrong with that as long as the other guy is also dependent on us for some things, too. That's called *inter*dependence. That's good. That's how trade is supposed to work. You sell to me and I sell to you. I rely on you, and you rely on me. But it doesn't work that way between us and Japan.

The issue isn't that Chrysler buys from the Japanese, it's that they don't buy in return. They don't want any *inter*dependence. It scares the hell out of them. They want to go it alone. I know—we've tried!

Five years ago when the currency turned, Chrysler went international again. We've sold over one hundred thousand units in Europe in the past few years, but Japan isn't buying. Last year we sold seven thousand in Taiwan. But in Japan we sold just over two thousand. Chrysler sells more vehicles in *Belgium* than we do in Japan.

America's total auto exports last year amounted to $14.3 billion. But only $1 billion of that was to Japan. It takes the Big Three a whole year to sell the same number of vehicles in Japan that Japan sells here in about forty-eight hours.

If they don't like American cars, at least we must make some *parts* they can use, don't you think? Well, Japan sold America $10.6 billion in parts last year and *bought* from us a grand total of $800 million worth. (13 to 1). Funny thing, though, we sold $22.2 billion in parts to the rest of the world. So it can't all be junk.

The club there is closed to new membership. Trust me on this. It's *closed.* Ask Boone Pickens. You can go over there and *buy into* a company and they still won't let you in the door. So what do I do? I don't make the rules. They're made in Washington and Tokyo—mostly *Tokyo.* But I have to play by them.

Oh, I could get mad and say "I'll show 'em." I could shut the Japanese out of Chrysler. I could go it alone like the Japanese do. But, then I'd put some of my dealers at risk because I'd have no subcompact cars to sell—and I wouldn't have enough V6 engines. So you see, I'm *dependent*, and they're not —like so many other American industries have become.

Well, I'm not going to do that. I've got over one hundred twenty thousand people at Chrysler, plus dealers and suppliers. They're already *victims* of our screwy trade rules. I'm not going to ask them to be *martyrs*, too.

So, I won't do that, but I won't shut up, either.

Nothing I can do will change the rules. That's *your* job in Washington. And we really need your help.

REMARKS AT THE DETROIT
ECONOMIC CLUB

Detroit, Michigan, January 10, 1992

Iacocca and the chairmen of Ford and General Motors had been part of a business delegation that accompanied President George Bush on a controversial trip to Japan intended to open the Japanese market to more American goods. He had gotten off a plane from Tokyo only a few hours earlier. He was tired, and he was angry at some of the press criticism of the trip. Before a packed audience at the Detroit Economic Club, he delivered his most blistering attack ever on Japanese trade practices.

Thank you.

But, I gotta tell you, I think my battery is just about dry. I've had a tough four days: A day to fly over, a day to fly back, and in between a brutal schedule of meetings and dinners designed to kill you just in case the jet lag didn't do the job!

The Japanese are terrific hosts. But they can wear you out. And you can forget what you went for. That didn't happen this time, though.

This was a historic trip, and let me start by saying that President Bush set a very important precedent. He took some heat here and in Japan for dragging along a business delegation. The Japanese didn't know what to make of it, except something had changed.

What's changed is that economics finally made it to the front of the plane along with the generals and admirals and all the Foggy Bottom types. In the past, we weren't even invited to ride coach. The president just tore a page from Japan's book. Their leaders have always taken business people on missions like this because they've always put economics first.

Now we're doing that. The Cold War is over. The Soviet threat is gone. Now we can start taking care of business, like Japan has been doing for the past forty-five years. I think the trip served notice on that. Seeing American government and business arm-in-arm for the first time ever sent the Japanese a message.

And I think they got it.

They got it. They didn't like it. They fought it. Boy, did they fight it! And they made a *start* in dealing with it. But *only* a start. Frankly, from a Detroit perspective, a *weak* start—but a start.

The Big Three told the President that there should be a 20-percent reduction in the bilateral deficit in '92, going down another 20 percent a year for the following five years until things are balanced. For 1992, it would have meant $8 billion off the total deficit. That translates to about one hundred eighty thousand Americans going back to work.

That's pretty much what I told the Japanese in a speech there back in 1985. I said their trade surplus with the U.S. was going to backfire. It was then $37 billion. Now it's $41 billion, so you know how well they took *my advice*.

But this time the President was there, too. And I think they listened better.

Back in '85, I said they could take that deficit down any way they wanted: Sell us less or buy more—their call.

We weren't specific this time, either. But with autos and parts 75 percent of the problem, you'd have to assume that they'd be the major part of the solution.

Hell, I didn't go to Japan to help open the rice market. The last time I looked, we don't grow any rice in Detroit. Correcting the deficit has to be done mainly in auto trade. There's no other way.

The Japanese know that as well as we do. And they're going to fight it every inch of the way, believe me. They have this industry targeted, and they're not about to take us out of their gunsights.

The auto parts commitment looks good on paper, but we can't sort out how much of the increase they promised will come from their keiretsu suppliers here.

And on autos, we got promises to make their dealers available to American imports. Again, a *start*. But they wouldn't touch the bigger issue: the flood of vehicles they're sending into this market. And if they're serious about closing the auto deficit, *that's* where they have to start.

I don't want to get into specifics. It's too soon. I literally saw the auto agreements late Thursday afternoon in Tokyo, and I've been on an airplane most of the time since. I need some time to sort things out, but I'll agree with the quotes I saw from Red Poling and Bob Stempel this morning: *Too little, way too little!*

This trip didn't *resolve* this country's trade problems with Japan. Nobody expected it to. You can't resolve in three days problems that have developed over twenty years. But it did help bring those problems to a head. And frankly, that's been long overdue.

The president applied pressure—lots of pressure. Now Congress will have its crack. Dick Gephardt, John Dingell, the Levin brothers, Lloyd Bentsen, and others have a bill in to force the 20 percent deficit reduction that the Big Three were suggesting. So, stay tuned!

It's important that we use all the leverage we have because without persistent outside pressure the Japanese will not move at all. And why should they? They're winning! They're beating our brains in. So *we'll have to move them.*

We have to because we can't handle the sheer size of the imbalance—$41 billion in one year with one country . . . over $400 billion in a decade.

And the pattern is still the same: We ship them food and chemicals and raw materials—just like a *colony.* And they ship us value-added cars, and machine tools and electronics and all the high-tech stuff where the good, high paying jobs are—just like a *mother country.*

We can't handle the unemployment that deficit causes, or the closed plants and lost tax base, or the insidious Japanese economic and political power within the United States that comes with it.

In this city, of course, we've got a special problem. The Big Three sold less than fifteen thousand vehicles in Japan last year. (Hell, the Japanese *transplants* in this country sold more cars in Japan than that!) By contrast, Japan sold about 3.8 million cars and trucks here.

They say it's because our stuff is junk. I don't think so. I wonder if there's another reason. Like maybe because my Jeep Cherokee costs $12,000 more in Japan than it does here because they won't accept our certification, and everything has to be inspected, and there's a maze of red tape and distribution costs not designed to protect the Japanese consumer but to keep us out!

If they don't like our cars, then you'd think they could take some American parts and help shave the auto trade deficit. They haven't done that, either. America sells less than $2 billion worth of parts a year to Japan, but we sell $22 billion worth to the rest of the world.

It's funny, isn't it? Those parts are good enough for Mercedes and BMW, but not good enough for Isuzu and Daihatsu.

We're getting stiffed. And when Detroit gets stiffed on autos, then America gets stiffed on trade—period. That's because cars are America's rice. Any argument for protecting Japan's rice farmers is an argument for completely shutting Japan out of our auto market.

Now, I don't want to do that. And I don't know anyone who does. I'm called a protectionist, but I'm really a free trader. The thing I want to protect is free trade. And the way you do that is to retaliate against those who don't believe in it.

And if there's anyone here who thinks for a second that Japan practices free trade, I've got some S&L's I'd like to sell you.

Japan has no use for free trade. It certainly has never practiced *fair* trade. No, what Japan practices is *predatory* trade. Let me give you an example of how that works.

We recently got some research from a major American financial institution. You'd know the name, but they asked us not to use it because they do some business in Japan, and they got some of the numbers from their clients there.

According to their study, Japan lost $11.7 billion in North America from 1987 through 1990 in autos. No 1991 numbers yet. That comes as a surprise to the average American who thinks Japan must be making a ton of dough in this market. But no, they *lost* almost $12 billion. How could they stand the pain? No problem. They made $36.4 billion during the same period in their own *protected* home market.

You see, they operate from a *sanctuary*. They have almost no competition at home and they won't allow any foreign competitor to be a factor in their market. In total, all foreign auto makers from all over the world have only 3 percent of the Japanese market. In Europe, foreign companies have 15 percent, and in the United States they have a whopping 35 percent of our car and truck market.

Well, when you operate from a sanctuary—when your market is closed and the other guy's is wide open—that gives you some neat options. You can gouge your own consumers if they'll stand for it, and the Japanese consumers do, keep all your people employed, and use some of the profits to grab big chunks of the other guy's market.

And that's what's happening. They are simply taking about one-third of their enormous profits from their protected sanctuary at home and subsidizing their market share grab here. That's ugly mercantilism at its worst.

It's a good strategy. They get full employment . . . they get huge profits overall . . . and when they control this market they'll call all the shots and will get their investment back—*in spades*!

Sure, American consumers get a break—for a while. But Japanese consumers get an even bigger one: You see, they *all have jobs*. Remember—the most useless consumer is an *unemployed consumer*.

One way they give Americans a break is through "dumping," and we have laws against that. It's obvious that it's going on, but it's hard as hell to prove because their real costs are camouflaged within their keiretsu arrangements. And even when you *can* prove it, why bother?

The Commerce Department found Japan guilty of dumping minivans last month, and Toyota immediately *declared victory* because our government said Toyota wasn't cheating *by much*! They break our laws, but only by *a little*, so that's okay. I'm sure Toyota expects the same slap on the wrist Toshiba got a few years ago for selling submarine technologies to the Soviets. Back when there *were* Soviets.

The case isn't closed, though. Now commerce wants to look at those Japanese books and see if the actual costs they provided are as high as they claim. And if they *are* real, then Japan's reputation for efficient, low-cost production goes right down the toilet.

But, so far, the Japanese would have to be stupid *not* to keep breaking our laws—and the Japanese are not stupid.

And now, the European Community has capped Japan's sales there at 16 percent through the end of the century. Without Japan complaining, by the way. That leaves the U.S. and Canada as the *only* free market for autos on the entire planet . . . the only dumping ground left for Japan's excess auto capacity.

The Japanese have almost 7 million units of excess auto capacity, 75 percent of world overcapacity, and now almost all of it is targeted at us!

But the problem is even deeper than dumping, and targeting and scoffing at our laws.

It's time that we came to understand in this country that Japan's economic structure is as different from ours as ours is from Cuba's. Oh, it has all the trappings of free enterprise, but it is *different . . . fundamentally different.*

Their closed home market . . . business-government collaboration through MITI to penetrate foreign markets . . . an export/import bank set up to fund that market penetration . . . the keiretsu . . . banks holding most of the corporate equity . . . deliberate inefficiencies like distribution and agriculture . . . the second-class status of the consumer . . . and even a form of government which is really more of a bureaucracy than a democracy. All of these not only make Japan *different*, many of them are patently illegal in our country.

They have a *managed* economy in Japan, pure and simple. It may be economically irrational by everything we learned in school, but it works and works well for one simple reason: Because they have the giant American market as a dumping ground and a pressure relief valve.

Among other things, that means they don't have recessions. They're just not allowed there. The only time they've had negative growth since we helped them recover from the war was in 1974, but that was due to the OPEC oil shock not the business cycle. We're in our eighth recession since the war, but Japan has been immune.

Let me ask you: Do you think we'd be in a recession right now if we had a completely open market roughly twice the size of ours to sell into, and if we had an endless web of formal and informal barriers that kept those people out of our market? Do you think we'd be closing plants and laying people off?

Recessions are bad news for America, and *terrible* news for this city. But U.S. recessions have been *terrific* news for Japan. That's when they've grabbed most of our market.

Over the past few years, we Americans have not only had to deal with a recession, but a war, too. They haven't had either of those burdens to worry about in Japan. It's just been business as usual, and that included grabbing another nine share points of our car market while we weren't looking. That's what they've gained since car sales began to soften here in 1988.

It happens every time our economy hits the wall. OPEC One in the early
'70s—four quick points. OPEC Two, 1979-1981 the one that almost killed
Chrysler—eleven points. And now nine more points when we hit our third
recession, plus Desert Storm!

That seems to be the pattern—they gain a point a year in the good
years . . . a point *quarter* in the *bad* ones . . . ten more points every recession. That's a recipe for taking the *whole* U.S. auto market in just a few
more downturns!

And I, for one, am fed up hearing from the Japanese (and some Americans, too) that all our problems in this industry are our own damn fault. We
don't have idiots running General Motors, Ford and Chrysler or our suppliers. Our workers are not lazy and stupid.

I won't do a commercial here, but take a look at the new Dodge Viper . . .
at the new Jeep Grand Cherokee . . . and the new LH cars coming next summer—the Dodge Intrepid and Eagle Vision. I'll put them against anything in
the World!

Sure, the Japanese make good products, too, and they're *the* economic
force to be reckoned with in the world today. But let's not be too impressed.
Any one of the Big Three would be geniuses too if we operated from the same
closed sanctuary . . . if we had a huge, wide-open market like the United
States to sell into . . . if the government ran interference for us . . . if we could
prohibit our dealers from selling foreign cars . . . if we had company unions
and sweetheart deals with our banks and our suppliers . . . and if American
consumers wouldn't squawk about paying six times the world price for rice
and $12,000 more than U.S. sticker price for a Jeep.

And we'd also be heroes if we had the same cost of capital over the years.
The cost of capital in Japan has historically been as little as half of ours. It's
about equal now, but you can bet that's a temporary problem they'll correct.

Chrysler just spent a billion dollars each on a new tech center and a new
inner-city assembly plant. If I were in Japan at the time I contracted for those
facilities, I could have built them *both* for the same billion!

So let's not be so hard on ourselves. The Japanese aren't geniuses, except
when it comes to manipulating our own laws and our own market for their
ends.

I picked up *Forbes* magazine a couple of years ago and saw a quote that
tells it all. It was by Hideo Morita, the son of Akio Morita of Sony. His father, as you know, likes to lecture us poor, dumb Americans on what it takes
to succeed in business these days.

Here's what his son said.

"My father's generation knew that they were playing by different rules
from the West when it came to trade, but they pretended they didn't understand the rules. That's why they won."

By the way, I met Akio Morita this week in Tokyo for the first time, and I think we *liked* each other. One good thing American and Japanese business leaders did this week was *talk* to each other. Maybe we should be doing more of that.

But, ladies and gentlemen, I think it's time to make Japan not only understand the rules, but to play by them. And it might even be time to *change* some of those rules.

That won't be easy. I've been dealing with the Japanese for a long time, and I have immense respect for their ability to win at the negotiating table. One way they do it, of course, is to hire away our negotiators. In recent years, one-third of our top trade negotiators have quit to become foreign lobbyists, most of them for the Japanese. So when we send someone over there to bring home the bacon for us, we don't know if the trip will turn into a job interview.

There are also a few other things we should have learned by now when it comes to dealing with Japan.

First, our problems with Japan are unique. We trade with about two hundred countries all over the world, but two-thirds of our deficit is with one single nation—Japan.

So we have a separate and distinct trade problem between ourselves and Japan. And that probably means we need a separate and distinct set of trade rules for Japan than we have for everybody else.

Second, we have to deal *both* with Japan's closed market and Japan's business practices that affect this country. I'm talking about things like the keiretsu, dumping, and control of key technologies. Focusing *only* on opening up the Japanese market would be a mistake. We can get snookered if we spend all our energy prying it open but by then our companies are too weakened to take advantage of it.

Third—and this comes from bitter experience—be careful what you ask for because you might get it.

We twisted Japan's arm to quit artificially depressing the yen. Beginning with the Plaza Accord in 1985, they finally stopped. The yen doubled in value. That should have promoted an explosion of exports for us and cut down on imports.

We thought the currency swing would even out the trade. Guess what—since then we've run up almost $300 billion in red ink with Japan, and that translates to about 7 million jobs. So something is rotten—and not in *Denmark*—but in *Japan!*

The currency swing would have helped if Adam Smith's theories worked in a world of *managed* trade. But they don't. They're totally irrelevant. We went from zero to forty thousand units in Europe in just a couple of years, but had a helluva time getting to *one* thousand in Japan. In that big market we should be selling at least twenty five thousand!

Honda has sold four hundred Cherokees for us so far. They got generous this week. They promised to *triple* Jeep sales to twelve hundred by 1994. And triple the dealers from one hundred to three hundred. That means by 1994 each of those dealers will sell one Jeep every three months! Wow. How did we get so lucky?

We also told Japan that if it wanted to sell in this market, it should manufacture in this market. That turned out to be a mistake. Our mistake was taking them at their word when they said transplants would replace built-up imports under the so-called voluntary restraints. They reneged, and about 70 percent of the transplant capacity became incremental.

Since those "restraints" in 1981, seven transplant facilities have opened and a net of nine Big Three assembly plants have closed. In those ten years, our auto deficit with Japan has gone from $14 billion to $30 billion . . . every new job created has cost two old ones . . . and every new dollar contributed to America's economy drove out two old ones.

We also find ourselves with a helluva competitive disadvantage because the average transplant worker is twelve years younger and the cost of his labor is twelve dollars an hour less. That's because all the new Japanese plants except Mazda in Flat Rock were built in cornfields. The younger workforce uses less health care, and they're at least twenty years away from collecting pensions.

The location of the plants also allowed the Japanese to duck any of the responsibilities of urban America. The Big Three workforce is 21 percent minority. The transplants have only about 5 percent minorities. When you drive by our new Jefferson North plant in Detroit, keep in mind that no Japanese company would ever consider building that plant.

So the lesson in dealing with Japan is that you have to focus on *results* not on *process*. If you let them decide on the process (and the timetable), you will never see results. At least not the results you were looking for.

And one of the results we must insist on is employment.

The content of every Japanese import represents about 1 percent American jobs. For the transplants, it represents about 48 percent. But for the Big Three it's about 88 percent. It's pretty obvious where our priorities should be if the objective is to get Americans back to work. Ford, General Motors, and Chrysler create American jobs. The Japanese don't.

President Bush said it right when he started his trip: The issue is jobs . . . jobs . . . jobs.

Finally, we have to beware of the ancient art of Oriental patience. They don't *solve* problems in Japan, they *manage* them.

The Japanese are masters at making you peel the onion. You get through one layer and you're looking at another one just like it. One year we negotiated on oranges, the next beef, the next tomato puree, and even ravioli, yet! And in the end we're further and further behind.

I used to believe myself that the Oriental "long view" was a great virtue and something we could learn from the Japanese. I was wrong. It's not a virtue at all, it's a *weapon* and we have to disarm them if we're going to get anywhere at all.

We need to use our own weapon, good old-fashioned American impatience. That means demanding a solution to the problem *now*. And retaliating *now* if we don't get it. We've already shown all the patience anyone could ask —forty-five years of patience. First, we helped them rebuild. Then, we defended them. Then, when they were fully recovered, we continued to allow them open access to our market while they shut us out of theirs. We even had to listen to such crazy and insulting excuses as our skis aren't right for their snow and our construction companies don't understand their dirt.

Japan has a set of standard excuses every time they're called to task.

They say they *create jobs* in this country. Not true. Net-net, they *cost* us jobs by the tens of thousands.

They say Japan is unique and deserves *special treatment*. I say Japan has had a free ride long enough.

They say they're *changing*. They're not. The only changes that will take place in U.S.-Japan trade relations are those that we force them to make.

They say if you criticize Japan you must be a racist. That's just a weak attempt to cut off the criticism.

And finally, they say all the problems are *our fault*. That's like blaming our army and our navy for Pearl Harbor because they weren't ready. Japan targets this market and particularly this industry, especially when our defenses are down (like in a recession), and we deserve what we get—that's the way that argument goes.

No, we don't have to show any more patience toward Japan. None. That's a trap. And we don't have to listen to any more phony excuses from Japan. We've heard them all for too long.

It's also sad to hear Japan's propaganda mouthed over and over by some American editorial writers and columnists, including some in this city, which is hurting so badly right now. And it's ironic because none of them has ever faced even a single minute of foreign competition in their entire lives. (Not even *fair* foreign competition!)

We have local pundits telling the Big Three how to compete in the global automobile market, when they can't even compete with the paper *down the street*. They rail against protectionism while they live under the protection of a Joint Operating Agreement—the ultimate irony!

The standard line is that Japan's protectionism hurts Japan more than us. Tens of thousands of people in this city and this industry just went through a Christmas season wondering if they'd have jobs when they came back. Most of them are *still* wondering. Tell *them* the Japanese are just hurting themselves! (And tell those who've *already* lost their jobs.)

The Japanese and their Chrysanthemum Club apologists in this country (I call them "economic pacifists") are always warning against "quick fixes." As a result, we get no fixes at all. I've got news for them—it's high time for some quick fixes, and they should then be followed by more permanent repairs.

Now, I'm getting into the question time, so let me wrap up.

If I sound a little hot under the collar about what Japanese trade and economic policies are doing to this country and this city, I am. Our argument, of course, is with those Japanese *policies*, not the Japanese *people*. And with our *own* policies that have tolerated those Japanese policies. Both must be changed and changed fast mainly in our own self-interest, but in the long run for the good of the Japanese as well.

I warned them back in 1985. I said, "You guys are protecting the *wrong market*. You're protecting your market in *Japan* when you should be protecting your market in *America*."

They didn't listen. Forty percent of everything Japan ships comes here. When American workers are out of a job, Japan's *customers* are out of a job. They haven't seemed to catch on to that yet.

In their own self-interest, the Japanese have to truly open their market, back off on their penetration of this one, and reform their whole economic structure to align it with ours and that of the rest of the world.

That would mean some severe problems for them. Maybe they would even have to taste recession for the first time . . . deal with unemployment . . . close some plants . . . and accept some of the *responsibilities*, the pain and the dislocation that come with living in a global economy.

I think the real test of the value of the president's trip this week will be whether or not Japan finally accepts some of those realities and responsibilities.

Before the trip, some of the Japanese press was speculating on what "souvenirs" would have to be offered to placate the Americans this time. I resented reading that. I know we've been soft on Japan in the past, but I don't think we're going to keep selling our economic independence for a few beads and trinkets. And I don't think the $400 million Japanese lobby in this country is going to keep American resentment in check much longer.

I'm optimistic after this trip. Naturally, I'll wait to see the results, and I've been disappointed before. But this trip was more than show. I know, some people both here and in Japan said that Stempel, Poling, and I were being used. We were called, among other things, "window dressing," "clowns," and "potted plants."

Well, I can't speak for anybody else, but if I can help convince the Japanese that Americans won't tolerate their predatory, mercantilistic attack on this industry and this market any longer, then I'll be glad to sit around like a potted plant all day long.

But if they keep pretending they don't understand the rules . . . if it turns out that they stiffed the president of the United States and sent him home with only a few "souvenirs," . . . then I will become the loudest *philodendron* you've ever heard!

And I hope every one of you will be just as loud.

Thanks. And I hope you all enjoy the auto show. Pay some attention to the American stuff, will you? It's pretty damn good. If we can all pull together, we're going to start *winning again* in this country.

6. Information, Motivation, and Audience Adaptation in Addressing General Business Problems

Jerry Tarver

Commenting on Lee Iacocca's popularity as speaker, author, and TV ad-man, *Time* magazine pointed out that Iacocca "was not famous simply for being famous: he had done something.... He had managed to whip a sprawling company into shape and saved American autoworkers' jobs by tens of thousands" (Andersen 32–33). As a management genius, whether in saving Chrysler or in choosing a new automobile design, Iacocca excelled in two critical areas: He made difficult decisions that proved to be correct, and he motivated key players both inside and outside the auto industry to accept his vision of what should be done.

In exploring Iacocca's success as a public speaker, it is interesting to consider if any aspect of his decision-making style might be reflected in his approach to motivation, especially in his speeches to the Poor Richard Club, the National Governors Conference, the American Bar Association Convention, and the Naval War College. In these four speeches, Iacocca was not addressing his traditional and familiar Detroit manufacturing-oriented audiences. Did the factors that entered into making decisions have any relation to the process he used in bringing others, particularly those who did not have a direct interest in the auto industry, around to his way of thinking?

Objecting to charges that he sometimes made management decisions on impulse, Iacocca responded, "I may act on my intuition—but only if my hunches are supported by the facts" (Iacocca and Novak 53). He then noted that no decision maker could expect to gather absolutely all of the pertinent data. He believed that after collecting a reasonable amount of "relevant facts and projections," a good manager should be prepared to draw on experience and take a "leap of faith" (Iacocca and Novak 54).

The "relevant facts" useful to Iacocca the decision maker proved equally valuable to Iacocca the motivator when he took on the challenge of making ideas acceptable to listeners with no direct relationship to the automobile business. Moving from the regional theater of audiences related to the auto industry onto the national stage of public policy required careful adjustments and adaptations. In the speeches presented here, in which he addresses governors, lawyers, naval officers, and the members of Philadelphia's Poor Richard Club, Iacocca was careful to rely on facts rather than vague generalities to build his arguments.

In facing these audiences, Iacocca was clearly unwilling to ask to be believed simply because of his reputation in the automobile business. Rather, he grounded his arguments in facts that were relevant to the audience. Three aspects of his use of information in these four speeches will be examined: the appropriateness of information, the symbolic nature of information, and the application of information to prove a point.

APPROPRIATE INFORMATION

Iacocca tailored the information in these speeches so that it fit his audiences' interests, needs, and experiences perfectly. It may appear at first glance that his topics would not have much to do with the automobile industry as he turns to such subjects as the ideas of Benjamin Franklin or the increase of litigation in American society as starting points for a discussion of global business competition.

There is certainly no reason to assume that his audiences expected Iacocca to limit himself to talking about cars. After all, a select handful of corporate leaders have become what John B. McDonald calls "the superstars of business rhetoric." "They are," he states, "the intellectual statesmen of the corporate world. They've earned their spurs by impressive deeds, probably served a stint in government. They've won the right to talk about issues beyond their corporate interests" (205).

McDonald identifies Iacocca as "clearly a leading business superstar of the 1980s" (206). Pointing to the extensive publicity Iacocca has received, McDonald argues: "Whatever people may say, they pay attention to what the corporate superstars are advocating. . . . These CEOs are watched because they chart the forward edge of corporate thought—projecting the business viewpoint into the media/political melting pot of ideas which forges national policy decisions" (205).

In the four speeches under consideration here, Iacocca unquestionably wore the mantle of the corporate statesman as he addressed the need for the United States to be competitive in a global economy. He was not addressing autoworkers, shareholders, or dealers, and his normal opportunity to "ask for the sale" in a way that would aid Chrysler seemed beyond his reach. However, as McDonald points out, there are some occasions in the speeches of the business superstars "when national policy is viewed as the answer to individual corporate or industry problems" (McDonald 205).

This was clearly the case in these four speeches on competition. Although Iacocca was giving his views on a national problem, the solutions he offered obviously would be helpful to Chrysler. As a corporate superstar taking on the special obligation of representing the specific interests of his business in the realm of national policy, Iacocca faced the problem of adapting a corporate message to a noncorporate audience. His skillful selection of information was a major factor in helping him make his case so that his analysis of problems and their remedies was always from the point of view of his audience. As a result, his call for policies beneficial to his company, while honest and open, never appeared gratuitous or self-serving. At the beginning and perhaps at the end of speeches, most corporate speakers bow to rhetorical convention and make a few comments about the audience or the occasion for the speech. Iacocca did not stop there. Information directly relevant to his audience permeates his speeches.

The 1992 address to the Naval War College, for instance, consists of just under four thousand words. In only three places does Iacocca allow himself to say more than two hundred words without including information specifically related to the military in general or the Navy in particular. Iacocca never forces the military references; they fit smoothly and naturally into his message. He easily illustrates America's shrinking industrial base by comparing the large number of jobs available to returning World War II veterans with the lack of opportunities for the "new Cold War veterans." He compares Chrysler work teams organized to cut through red tape to the Navy's dynamic SEAL teams. And he boasts of American know-how, saying, "I have to believe that somebody who can slide a smart bomb though a window in Baghdad can somehow help us build better cars."

Iacocca's conviction that managers could never expect to have every single fact in hand when making a decision appears to be reflected in his use of information in the speeches. He uses selected facts—the facts that fit the interests and experiences of his audience. In his address to the American Bar Association, he called attention to the way in which he chose appropriate data: "[J]ust two weeks ago I talked to all the governors, and I found out what *they* do at their conventions: They run for president. I looked it up—sixteen state governors have gone on to become president. That's a pretty good average, they're batting about 400. So, I told the governors they make good presidents—and they loved it! Then, when I was coming out here, I got curious, so I hit the books again and guess what—I found that twenty-six presidents (of our forty) have been—you guessed it—*lawyers*! You're batting well over 600!"

A careful reading of all these speeches will reveal consistent attention to appropriateness of information. Each audience got a message on national economic policy and its relationship to competition, but Iacocca did not merely dish out data warmed up from previous speeches. The information he chose made each speech uniquely suitable for the audience being addressed.

THE FACT AS SYMBOL

Nowhere is the importance of information more obvious in Iacocca's thinking than in the way he would often emphasize a particular item that he saw as representative of a larger idea. He did this in talking and writing about the Statue of Liberty, a concrete object that to him embodied broad, important principles. In his second book, Iacocca discussed the value of Lady Liberty as a symbol. "We didn't spend millions of dollars just so that the statue wouldn't fall into the harbor and become a hazard to navigation. . . . We did it because we wanted to restore, remember, and renew the basic values that made America great" (Iacocca and Kleinfield). In his address to the American Bar Association, Iacocca reiterated his view of the statue as symbolic of larger values: "Whether you first saw her from the deck of a steamer as my parents did . . . or sailing off to war . . . or as a schoolkid learning about what made this country great, it captures and holds all your feelings about America —whatever they are!"

Throughout history, speakers have made use of a single, powerful example to represent a larger concept they wish to have accepted. The slogans "Remember the Alamo" or "Remember Pearl Harbor" illustrate how a piece of information (the enemy attacked ruthlessly) can be easily translated into a message (we must fight on to victory).

For each of the speeches examined here, Iacocca held up a solitary object, person, or action to represent his central idea. In the Philadelphia speech, Ben Franklin became the personification of Iacocca's message on the need for a new approach to global competition that would be fair to the auto industry. By creating an imaginary scenario in which he sits down to have a drink with Franklin, Iacocca brings into the speech Franklin's hypothetical question "Are you still free?" Using the rest of his speech to answer the question, Iacocca depicts a Franklin who would disapprove of the policies that Iacocca attacks. Franklin becomes, like the Statue of Liberty, a revered symbol—a symbol standing with Iacocca in opposition to those who would turn the United States into a colony again and forfeit the hard-won freedoms of the American Revolution.

We are losing our freedom, Iacocca argued in the Poor Richard Club speech, because "we've got the trade pattern of a colony" in which we export raw material and pay dearly for imported finished goods. Criticizing weak trade negotiations by U.S. representatives, Iacocca summoned Franklin to his aid when he declared, "Boy, how things change. A couple hundred years ago we sent Ben Franklin to France, and he talked them into sending us their whole damn navy. Our guys today can't even get oranges or beef into Japan or straighten out the exchange rates."

Iacocca cited the national debt as a limitation on freedom and pointed out that it took from Franklin's time until 1981 to "accumulate our first trillion dollars in debt." Noting that the second trillion was to be reached in eighteen months, he added, "I sure wouldn't be proud to tell ole Ben Franklin about that. I wouldn't be proud to tell him that we don't have the discipline to handle our bills."

Franklin's image was evoked also in attacking U.S. energy policy and the growing deficit. By the time Iacocca brings Franklin back for the conclusion of the speech, the audience has seen the venerated statesman grow into the very incarnation of all the changes Iacocca supported. To reject Iacocca would be almost the same as rejecting Franklin himself: "We're here tonight to remember Ben Franklin—good, old—simple—pragmatic—common sense Ben—a man who risked it all because he didn't want to live in a colony. Well, I don't either. And I don't think any of you do. So the best tribute we'll ever pay Ben Franklin is to be damn sure that America never becomes a colony—of any kind—again."

In his speech to the governors, Iacocca briefly makes customers into a symbol as he equates the voter to a customer whom the governors must keep happy by good governmental practices. He soon abandons the image, however, and spends the remainder of this particular speech dealing with competition directly.

In the other two speeches considered here, Iacocca once again makes extensive use of powerful symbols that embody his ideas.

The Bar Association address, more than any of the other speeches, presented Iacocca with the possibility of a hostile audience. The case against excessive litigation and its harmful effects on competition would have to be made before a group that included trial lawyers and others who would naturally be skeptical. Iacocca needed a symbol for his argument that would be as well received and as powerful as Ben Franklin had been in Philadelphia two years earlier. Fortunately, an equally powerful and universal symbol was at hand.

213

Iacocca addressed the ABA in 1987, the bicentennial year of the U.S. Constitution, and the Constitution became the central symbol of his talk. It was an especially interesting choice because Iacocca explicitly stated in the speech that, unlike the Statue of Liberty, the Constitution was not a symbol but rather "a tool, and a blueprint, and a process." In making the distinction between tool and symbol, Iacocca was simply stressing the fact that the Constitution had important practical applications. In the sense in which the word symbol is being used in this essay, however, the Constitution served precisely the same function in the ABA speech that Ben Franklin served in the Poor Richard Club address.

If Iacocca could present the Constitution as a practical tool that lawyers were supposed to employ with common sense, he could equate that respected document with his central idea that frivolous and unfair lawsuits limited competition and hurt the country. He partly revealed his strategy when he said that the Constitution did not deal with such modern problems as competition and added, "That's my bag, of course—*competing*. And I want to talk about that for a few minutes this morning. My only problem is, how do I tie it to the Constitution? And I found the answer—a very simple answer—you."

On one hand, Iacocca flattered lawyers as "the right people to lead the rest of us" in celebrating the Constitution's two-hundredth year. But if the Constitution was a symbol of the lawyers' "special *opportunity*," it was also an equally powerful symbol of what Iacocca called "one helluva *responsibility*."

He pointed to case after case in which "unbridled advocacy" punished companies for taking normal risks and thus punished competitiveness and progress. Continuing to build his image of the Constitution as a practical, reasonable document, Iacocca stated, "Nobody wants to give up the rights that the Constitution gave us, but if every one of us pushes every one of those rights as far as we can, then one of these days *none* of us will have any rights." By having the Constitution represent reason and fairness throughout his speech, Iacocca avoids a direct, personal attack on the lawyers and instead plays the role of defender and explainer of America's great charter of rights. The case for allowing risks and enhancing opportunity to compete is argued not by the speaker alone but by the symbol as well. That may account in part for the standing ovation at the end of an address that criticized many in the audience.

As a central symbol in his Naval War College speech, Iacocca made a somewhat unglamorous choice: military planning. Iacocca praised the Navy's "war plans, and battle plans, and strategies, and tactics" in contrast to the country's lack of a comprehensive national economic plan or "industrial policy." "On the world economic sea," he declared, "we have no battle plan."

Although military planning is not mentioned quite as often in this speech as Franklin and the Constitution were in earlier speeches, Iacocca nonetheless periodically calls military planning to mind as a paradigm of intelligent preparation for the future. Military planning becomes the symbol that represents and justifies planning on the economic front. "[A]ll we need is a plan," Iacocca contended. "Just a basic strategy. A national policy that puts the same priority on America's economic competitiveness that we've put on our national security."

One indication of the importance Iacocca attached to the symbols in his speeches can be seen in the way he returns to them in the conclusion of his remarks. For instance, all but three lines of his closing remarks at the Naval War College directly link military planning with the idea he wanted his listeners to accept. His account of "War Plan Orange" associates in dramatic form Admiral King's war game with the economic battle plan Iacocca desired for the country. He made the connection unmistakable when he said, "But for this battle, ladies and gentlemen, the country has no War Plan Orange. And I think it's high time we got one. It's crucial! I hope all of you agree."

Iacocca made extensive use of symbolic information. He would present a concrete fact that the audience knew and respected (Franklin was a wise patriot; the Constitution was practical and enduring; military planning was necessary), and throughout the speech he would equate that symbol to the position he wanted accepted. In this way, he made business issues such as fair trade, industrial policy, and competitiveness familiar and relevant to non-business audiences.

INFORMATION AS PROOF

Just as Iacocca the manager understood how key facts could point the way to the right decision, Iacocca the motivator appreciated the contribution facts made to the believability of ideas in his speeches. Iacocca often made references such as "I did a little homework" or "I looked it up." Actually, he spoke somewhat more precisely when he told the Poor Richard Club, "I asked our research people to give me a hand," but there should be no question that Iacocca was the final author of his speeches and that the information in the speeches reflects his personal approach to motivation.

As a manager, he knew how to draw on the help of a team and then make his own decision; as a speaker, he knew how to use the service of a speech writer to produce his speeches. Those speeches, like his decisions, bore the bold and unique mark of Iacocca himself. Many instances could be cited to show how Iacocca dealt with advice and information. In March 1987, Iacocca's top managers recommended that Chrysler not purchase American Motors. "I heard them out," Iacocca recalled, "and then I overruled them and told them that we were going ahead" (Iacocca and Kleinfield 83). It was time, he felt, to take on another challenge. In explaining his decision, Iacocca revealed that he relied on information rather than the opinions of others. Facts in the form of "three big pluses" supported his conclusion: "worldwide fame of the Jeep name and product; a third dealer organization we could build on; and a brand-new state-of-the-art plant in Canada" (Iacocca and Kleinfield 84).

When Iacocca developed his ideas and arguments about competition in his speeches, he showed his respect for the information and did not merely toss out random facts. He also showed respect for the audience by saying, in effect, "You are intelligent people who want to hear facts and not just opinion." The information he supplied his audience had several important characteristics. It was varied, abundant, interesting, relevant, and personal.

Iacocca never relied on just one type of data. The variety of evidence at the Poor Richard Club typifies his approach. In this and other speeches, his favorite way of supporting an idea is to give punchy, specific examples. For instance, he attacked the trade imbalance with Japan by saying, "We send the Japanese hides, and they send us leather goods." These short and direct examples are characteristic of his no-nonsense speaking style.

At times, he related a brief story, as in his account of the Vietnamese artist who donated a painting in honor of the Statue of Liberty. He occasionally turned to analogy, as when he compared dependence on foreign capital with dependence on drugs. He made sparing use of statistics (on the trade deficit) and quotations (a phrase from a Polish contributor's letter).

Iacocca was never guilty of reciting a string of glittering generalities. He served up volumes of concrete information in the speeches examined here. His audiences had every reason to be impressed with the breadth and depth of Iacocca's knowledge.

His fondness for examples contributed to the ample amount of material in his speeches. Because the examples were brief, he often clustered two or more of them together. When Iacocca wished to stress how important Benjamin Franklin was in American history, he drew on examples from the *Encyclopedia Britannica*. In a relatively short time, he was able to give twenty-four specific citations.

Although he is an engineer by training, with a sound grasp of the accounting data supplied by corporate "bean counters," Iacocca's sales background may have been responsible for the lively and vivid way he presented his facts. While there were many stories he could have used to tell the lawyers that the world is not risk-free, Iacocca chose to regale them with the account of the British soldier who collided with a lone tree in the Sahara.

For the governors, he illustrated Japanese resistance to free trade by citing how U.S. construction companies were not allowed to bid because "Japanese dirt is different from American dirt." At the Naval War College, he said that without better competition supplying more jobs, we cannot find a position for the "technician who can pull a license plate number out of a satellite photo from fifty miles up." With vivid language and a touch of wit, Iacocca made sure his facts were never dull.

No matter how many facts are cited and no matter how interesting they may be, facts serve no real purpose in a speech if they fail to help make a speaker's ideas clear and convincing for the audience. At any point in an Iacocca speech, the relationship between his idea and his evidence is always strong.

That relationship must be considered, it should be noted, in light of Iacocca's previously mentioned conviction that one can't have all the facts in hand before deciding what to believe. When he made speeches, Iacocca was a motivator who naturally emphasized the facts that were most compelling for his case and related most directly to his audience. So long as his information was honest, he was doing what should be expected of any advocate.

Listeners could evaluate Iacocca's evidence for themselves easily because he made explicit the relationship between his point and his data. He told the ABA that merely the risk of litigation can drive companies out of the marketplace and then gave compelling examples. A Virginia company "that made driving aids for the handicapped," "companies making football helmets in this country," and the entire industry of "light aircraft in this country" had determined that business was simply "too risky."

Iacocca's evidence was directly on the point with the governors when he illustrated the problem with tax laws that do not encourage exports, by saying, "I can make $1,100 to $1,200 more per car if I ship them from our plants in Canada and Mexico instead of from Michigan, Illinois, or Missouri." And to his Navy audience, he backed up his boast about the unlimited capability of American manufacturing by noting, "I read that Motorola developed an IFF beacon for the troops in Desert Storm last year in just eight days."

Iacocca has often noted that "Public speaking does not mean impersonal speaking" (Iacocca and Novak 55). He revealed his hands-on experience with the information in his speeches. Speaking of the decline of the nation's manufacturing base, he told his Navy audience, "I grew up almost literally in the shadow of the Bethlehem Steel Company in Pennsylvania, and I've also seen what's happened to that most basic of all industrial sectors."

Iacocca readily used the personal pronoun to show his interest in his facts and his personal relationship to the examples. Unlike many business leaders who hide behind the corporate we, he was not afraid to take responsibility for his beliefs. In the Navy War College speech he pulled no punches when he said of the U.S. refusal to retaliate against unfair trade, "I call that 'economic pacifism.'" The Navy speech also reveals Iacocca's ability to leaven his personal stories with a touch of self-deprecation. For instance, in telling the story of his three-day stay aboard the *Nimitz*, he said, "I have firsthand experience. . . . I really roughed it! I had the admiral's quarters," and at another point referred to himself as "a guy who got a D" in physics at Lehigh University. Even without the self-deprecation, Iacocca's personal touch adds strength, character, and a personal style to his facts. Perhaps it is this personalization of information that most clearly sets Iacocca apart from most other business speakers.

CONCLUSION

The four speeches discussed here show that Iacocca employed information as effectively in making speeches to nonbusiness audiences as he did in making business decisions at Ford and Chrysler. These speeches are models for any speaker who wishes to understand how a fact may become a symbol for an idea, how material can be tailored to fit an audience, and how evidence can be marshaled for proper support of an argument.

Iacocca's use of information also demonstrates how ideas and values from one arena can be applied to another by a speaker who understands an audience. In his first book, Iacocca noted that one of the keys to motivation is talking to people in their own language (Iacocca and Novak 55). In the foreword to this collection of his speeches, he observes that a good speech begins with a "deep sense of obligation to the audience." Because of his sensitivity to the audience, his ability to speak to their needs and in their language, Iacocca was able to solve a central problem facing the corporate superstar: making the corporate message relevant to the needs and interests of the noncorporate audience.

WORKS CITED

Andersen, Kurt. "A Spunky Tycoon Turned Superstar." *Time* 1 April 1985: 30–39.

Iacocca, Lee A. and William Novak. *Iacocca: An Autobiography.* New York: Bantam Books, 1984.

Iacocca, Lee A. and Sonny Kleinfield. *Talking Straight.* New York: Bantam Books, 1988.

McDonald, John B. "Speech Writing Experts in Action." *Inside Public Relations.* Ed. Bill Cantor. New York: Longman Inc., 1984. 204–219.

REMARKS AT THE POOR RICHARD CLUB

Philadelphia, Pennsylvania, January 17, 1985

It was Ben Franklin's birthday, and Iacocca addressed the annual Poor Richard Club dinner in Philadelphia. An actor dressed as Franklin was part of the program. Iacocca took a look at America in 1985 as Franklin himself might have seen it.

Thank you. I didn't know Ben Franklin was going to show up.

It's been a long day—but a memorable one—in spite of the lousy weather here in Philadelphia.

First let me thank all the members of the Poor Richard Club for this award. I'm deeply honored by it, believe me. At lunch I got this medallion. I'll treasure it.

I'm also glad to be back in Philadelphia, so close to my roots. I spent a lot of my early years here, and I actually learned to love this city. The city has changed a lot, but not the people. They're still warm, and very friendly and very happy. We used to call it brotherly love—I think you still do, by the way.

But today I think a lot of you in this room outdid yourselves. Some of you wrote songs about me, and serenaded me with a banjo. Some of you even wrote poems about me. And some of you had the audacity to compare *me* to Ben Franklin.

And a lot of you gave me gifts of all kinds. And then you took me on the pilgrimage, and I really did have a sense that I was visiting some *holy* places. And I just don't mean Christ Church when I say that.

And I guess Ben Franklin does qualify as the patron saint. I've sure heard a lot about old Ben today. I visited his grave (in spite of him showing up tonight), sat in his church pew, saw his office, and visited his memorabilia accumulated at the Franklin Institute.

Everybody in this room knows all about Ben Franklin—or at least you think you do. Well, I knew there would be a lot of talk about him today, and I didn't want to get caught short. So I asked our research people to give me a hand. They've got a computer that taps into all kinds of resources, and one of them is the *Encyclopedia Britannica*.

They came up with an amazing discovery. When you say "Ben Franklin" to the computer, it spits out seventy-three different citations from the *Britannica*.

219

Obviously, his own biography is in there. He's certainly in the section on "U.S. history." And I guess I wasn't too surprised that the section on "electricity" talks about him and his kite.

But what about those seventy other articles? Let me just give you part of the list.

Ben Franklin shows up under "philosophy," under "literature," and under "the history of science." He's also there under "ballooning," "glassmaking," and "chess." (He helped make chess popular in the Colonies.)

If you look up "gulf stream," you learn that he figured out what the gulf stream is.

You run into him under "education" (he started a college) . . . under "library" (he started the first library here) . . . "insurance" (he started the first life insurance company, too) . . . "pharmacy" (he opened the first pharmacy) . . . "postal system" (you guessed it, the first post office).

Well, it just goes on and on. "Biophysics," "the Enlightenment," "hypnosis," "liberalism," "luminescence"—look any of them up and you run into Franklin.

He's even there under "heating, ventilation, and air conditioning." His stove is still a hot seller.

Seventy-three different subjects, and he was important enough in every one of those areas to get mentioned in the encyclopedia.

Oh, by the way, look up "autobiography," and you find out that he gets credit for helping to make autobiography an accepted form of literature. I guess I *really* have to thank him for *that*!

And the amazing thing, after going through that list, is that all of them were really just sidelines. When we think of Ben Franklin, we usually think of the wise old man with the hippie haircut and little glasses who helped found the United States of America.

We saw the room today where he and the others wrote the Constitution. And I couldn't help wondering what he'd say if we could resurrect him after almost two hundred years and ask for a critique.

Of all the people in history, Ben Franklin is the man I'd most like to meet. I'd like to have a drink with him. (I'd have a scotch, and he'd have his glass of port.)

He'd probably start by saying, "Iacocca, that's a hell of a name. I never heard a name like that before." And I'd tell him all about the big waves of immigrants that came over. (I'd probably talk a lot about that because since I got involved with the Statue of Liberty and Ellis Island project, I've become something of an expert.)

I think he'd be pleased, for the most part, with how things have gone. The Constitution is almost intact . . . just a handful of amendments in all that time. I think he'd be impressed at all the progress in this country, of course.

And he'd be pleased that we could go through all that we have, and still hold on to the original ideals.

But of all the men who sat in that room and hammered out the Constitution, he'd probably be the *least surprised* by all the amazing things that have happened since then. I don't think he'd fall off his chair when I told him we'd been to the moon. He was a philosopher and a scientist. He was always looking ahead. He understood what people can do when they pull together. He knew about human potential. He had vision.

I suspect that if Franklin had just *one* question for me after all this time, it would be "Are you still free?"

He and the others dedicated most of their lives and risked everything to gain independence for the Colonies. And that independence is the legacy they left us.

I'd start by assuring him that, yes, we've managed to maintain our political independence. In fact, we're stronger than ever. We may have some enemies in the world, but nobody's thinking of invading the United States.

But there's more to independence than just that kind of security. And maybe we ought to examine just how independent we really are today.

First of all, of course, we're living in a different world. We're living in a world that is interdependent. Countries have to rely on each other for food, raw materials, machines, and markets. No country is self-sufficient today. Nobody can go it alone. Nobody's even trying.

Doctor Franklin once said that "No nation was ever ruined by trade." Well, today, no nation can even *survive* without it. And, ironically, that's why it *is* possible today to be ruined by trade, if that trade isn't *fair* trade.

It can cost you a big part of your independence.

Remember your history books? Remember why England, France, and Holland established colonies? It was to provide the mother countries with two things: raw materials and markets.

The colonies exported raw materials and foodstuffs, and served as markets for the manufactured goods produced in Europe.

In those days, Japan was so isolated that it might as well have been on a different planet. But now it's the best example we have of this new economic interdependence.

And today, America's leading exports to Japan are corn, soybeans, and coal—foodstuffs and raw materials. While Japan's top exports to us are cars, trucks, and video recorders—all high-value manufactured goods.

Is this beginning to sound familiar?

We send the Japanese hides, and they send us leather goods. We send them logs, and they send us stereo cabinets. They take some oranges, but not if we squeeze them—because that's labor. They squeeze them. They take potatoes, but no potato chips—because it takes labor to make potatoes into chips.

What we have then is a classic definition of a colony. All we're missing are the Redcoats.

Right now, our trade deficit with Japan is running a little over $3 billion a month. Our deficit with the rest of the world is only $6 billion a month. In 1984, our total trade deficit with all countries was $120 billion. And that's double the all-time world record deficit of $60 billion the year before.

Part of the reason is the high dollar. But a big part is the fact that we don't play the trade game by the same rules. I'm sure you're as familiar as I am with the pattern. The Japanese have protected their home market while they built a heavy industry based on exports. The government cooperates with industry through tax incentives and other practices.

And I don't want to just pick on the Japanese. It wouldn't be fair. The fact is, almost every country has some kind of plan to succeed in the international marketplace—except us.

We're wedded to a set of nineteenth-century free trade ideals that everybody else in the world ignores. We live in an era of "managed trade." That's a euphemism for the same kind of mercantilism that existed in Franklin's time.

Simply put, every nation devises policies to keep its trade in balance or to gain a surplus. That's because trade means jobs. If you buy more than you sell, you export jobs. Our own Department of Labor estimates that each billion dollars of the trade deficit equals thirty thousand jobs. So with a deficit of $120 billion, we're talking about 3.6 million American jobs.

Meanwhile, with our high dollar, we're a magnet for foreign goods. In fact, do you know what the *real* economic importance of America to the rest of the world is today? It's not our corn or our coal. Other countries can get along without them. It's our *market*. We've become the world's shopping center. More and more, this isn't where things are *produced*, it's where they're *sold*.

Take cars. Japan exports more than half the cars it builds. And half of them come to the United States. Because their competition is so intense, Japanese car companies are just breaking even in their home market. And they barely do the same with their exports to Europe and the rest of the world. The only place that the Japanese car industry makes any real *profit* is here in *America*.

And it's a *big* profit. The Japanese squealed when import limits went on their cars here four years ago. But in the early years of those quotas, the Japanese auto industry made $9 billion in profits in North America, while American companies lost $14 billion.

And things would have been a hell of a lot worse without the quotas. With the yen/dollar equation way out of whack and their government behind them, the Japanese could have gobbled up a lot more of our market, and our jobs.

Those import restraints are due to come off at the end of March, by the way. Our government can't make up its mind whether to ask Tokyo to keep them on or not. Our trade representative says they should come off. The Commerce secretary seems to be saying they should stay put. The president won't commit himself.

Even the American auto industry is divided on the issue. General Motors wants the quotas removed because they've got a strategy to source most of their small cars in the Far East rather than build them here. I don't want you to forget that six months ago they announced their strategy to source 1 million cars over in Japan or Korea.

I want the quotas to stay. After all, the Japanese have quotas on many of our agricultural products. They say it's in their national interest to have a strong agricultural base. Well, I think it's in *our* national interest to have a strong *industrial* base.

If you want to see if those quotas are working, by the way, look at how the Japanese are reacting. Nissan now has a plant in Tennessee. Honda is making cars in Ohio. Toyota is in California. Mazda is going to build a plant in Michigan. None of them would bother unless they felt we were going to get serious someday about protecting *our* national interest.

I don't want the quotas forever. Just until we're competing fairly . . . just until I'm only competing with Mr. Honda and Mr. Toyota, and not competing against the whole Japanese government. And just until Washington and Tokyo get together and do something about the currency situation.

I talked to Mr. Reagan about the yen/dollar gap last year. He agreed that something had to be done. So he sent a team to talk with the Japanese. When I talked to him, to show you how persuasive I am, the yen was at 230 to the dollar. Now it's 10 percent higher—or weaker—at 255. I guess they better stop talking and come home! We're going in the wrong direction.

Boy, how things change. A couple hundred years ago we sent Ben Franklin to France, and he talked them into sending us their whole damn navy. Our guys today can't even get oranges or beef into Japan or straighten out the exchange rates.

Well, that's not entirely fair. It's not *all* their fault. Tight money and high interest rates here have a lot to do with the exchange rates, too, because they are attracting so much foreign investment.

And as a result, we've got the problem of a growing foreign debt as well as a trade deficit.

If you've got a couple billion dollars in loose change these days, the best place to put it is here in America because our interest rates are so high. You could call that a vote of confidence in America, I suppose. And God knows, without all that foreign capital coming in, those interest rates might be even higher.

Last year, we attracted about $100 billion in foreign investment. That's about equal to the interest we paid on the national debt. So one way to look at it is that foreign investment replaced the capital that the government soaked up in order to service the debt.

In the old days (before Mr. Volcker came aboard) we used to *print* money to cover our debts. That was bad enough. Now we *import* it to cover the debts.

Now, that might *look* like a good deal. But I don't know. It means that literally any day now we will become a debtor nation for the first time in sixty-seven years. And at the current pace, we'll pass Brazil next year as the biggest debtor nation in the world. And by 1987, our foreign debt will be bigger than Brazil's, Argentina's, and Mexico's *combined.*

We were a debtor nation during the last century, too. But back then we used capital from Europe to build our railroads and canals and factories. Now we're using it to service our debt.

Right now, there is more than $800 billion of foreign investment in the United States. But damn little of it is direct investment in industry, the kind of investment that creates jobs.

Sixty percent of it is made up of private holdings in American banks or portfolios. The economists call that "hot" money because it could be pulled out overnight. Another 23 percent is money foreign governments have invested here. That could be pulled out, too.

Only about 17 percent of that foreign capital is directly invested in American business or real estate. Less than one-fifth is going into projects like those Japanese car plants that put Americans to work.

We need this money now because we don't save enough ourselves to give the banks what they need to lend. We're great *consumers* in this country, but we're lousy *savers*. I guess nobody reads "Poor Richard's Almanac" anymore —the part about "a penny saved is a penny earned."

So in order to fuel the economy, we need foreign capital. Some people have an idea that all this foreign money is coming here because we're a so-called safe haven. Well, that's becoming a myth. That money is coming here because we're *bidding* for it. Our interest rates are high. We've even changed some of the tax laws to make it easier for foreigners to invest here.

Now, I think we're heading for real big trouble. And I'll tell you why. We've become too *dependent* on foreign money. We have to keep interest rates high to keep that foreign capital coming in, and to be sure that the money already here doesn't go home.

It's like a drug habit. You have to keep taking more and more. You can't cut back or you get sick. Stop altogether, and you'll see the worst case of cold turkey ever. I mean the whole world would go into convulsions.

We aren't doing ourselves any favor by sucking up all the capital in the world. And we aren't doing the rest of the world any favor, either.

We're taking money out of countries that need it for their own development. Here's a shocker, I'll bet you didn't know this. Twenty-two percent of the foreign investment in this country comes from Latin America. That's right, from countries like Brazil and Argentina and Mexico that are strapped by their own foreign debts. More than $182 billion from Latin America is invested here.

We're taking bread off somebody's table. Something's wrong here, it really is. Why is the richest country in the world siphoning off capital from underdeveloped countries to feed its own debt? And what will happen when those countries get wise and call in all their notes?

When you stop and think about it, most of the threats to our independence today stem from one big problem. And that's a federal deficit that is so wildly out of control. The high dollar that's helping to make us a trade colony, and the high interest rates that are making us a debtor nation, can be traced to that deficit.

We're robbing our kids by passing this debt on to them. It's "taxation without representation" again. But this time we're taxing our *own kids*. And when they realize it, they aren't going to dump tea off the dock, they're going to throw *us* in the harbor.

Do you know that it took two hundred six years for us to accumulate our first trillion dollars in debt . . . from Ben Franklin's time all the way to 1981? And that we're going to reach our second trillion in about eighteen months from now?

I sure wouldn't be proud to tell ole Ben Franklin about that. I wouldn't be proud to tell him that we don't have the discipline to handle our bills.

And I don't think he'd be too proud of *us*.

And we're doing something else with this debt. We're *deindustrializing* America. The high deficit causes high interest rates. High interest rates cause the high dollar. The high dollar brings in foreign goods. American industry can't compete on price, so it closes down or moves its plant overseas.

That's what this vicious circle is leading to. We're turning ourselves into a colony again. And it all starts with the deficit.

And here's another one I wouldn't like to explain to Franklin over that drink. *Energy*. I don't know when we felt more like a colony than during the two big oil shocks of the seventies. All of a sudden we found ourselves at the mercy of a foreign oil cartel. And when they turned off the oil, they showed us just how dependent we were.

We got scared ten years ago. And we resolved to do something about it. It got to be patriotic to join a van pool or ride a bike. We passed a law that the auto industry had to increase gas mileage. We passed the 55-mile-per-hour speed limit.

But we didn't do the *one thing* that could have made the biggest difference. We didn't tax gas like the rest of the world does to force consumers to conserve fuel and *demand* the high-mileage cars. We didn't make the same sacrifice others were making.

It was cheap gas more than anything else that made us so dependent on OPEC. And we're still joyriding on cheap gas in this country. We pay about half the price for a gallon of gas here that they do in other countries. In Europe, they pay more *tax* on a gallon than our *total* price. Italy overdoes it. They're over $3 a gallon. Their tax is about $2.12 per gallon.

And because gasoline is so cheap in our country, big cars are selling like hotcakes. At Chrysler, we thought we would have phased out our V-8 Fifth Avenues by now. But we can't. We're working overtime to build enough of them. We're making too much money to drop them.

Now Ford and GM are lobbying to dial back the fuel economy standards. They want the law changed so they can sell more big cars. Because that's where the bigger profits are.

But that leaves the other end of the market for the Japanese. And it keeps us living in a fool's paradise. I hope we don't have another oil shock, because they'll really cream us. We can become an energy *colony* if we don't come up with an energy *policy* that guards our independence.

You know, I really don't know if I'd like to have that drink with Benjamin Franklin, after all. I don't know what I'd say when he asked that big question —"Are you still free?"

I don't feel free when we've got the trade pattern of a colony. I don't feel free with a foreign debt that's going to be the biggest in the world in a matter of months. I don't feel free when we're so dependent on a foreign cartel for oil.

And I don't feel free with budget deficits that are tieing us up so tightly in a knot of debt that neither we nor our kids will ever escape.

I think I'd be a little ashamed to tell Ben Franklin all this.

He and the others left us a tremendous legacy—our *independence*. And they left us a tremendous challenge—to preserve that independence.

Every other generation has met that challenge. And they had to make some huge sacrifices to do it. Is ours going to be the first one to fall short? I honestly don't know.

As you know, I've been involved with the Statue of Liberty and Ellis Island restoration for two and one-half years. And I've learned a lot. Since my parents were among the 17 million people who came through Ellis Island, I thought I understood what that experience was all about.

But in the past two and one-half years, I've come to appreciate more than ever just what those two symbols in New York Harbor stand for.

I've learned from the hundreds of people who've told me their own stories, or those of their parents. And I've learned from the tens of thousands who've sent me letters.

And if you reduce all those experiences into just two words, they would be *hope* and *sacrifice*.

The statue, of course, was the symbol of hope for all those immigrants who passed by it. And Ellis Island was the symbol of sacrifice. It was the reality they met when the adventure was over. It was cold, and hostile, and even frightening.

But they took a ferry over to the Battery, and they picked up the challenge that Ben Franklin and the others left. They broke their backs to build something strong and lasting for themselves and their families.

Last fall I met a Vietnamese artist—one of the boat people who've taken such horrible risks to escape that country.

She settled in Alaska and came all the way down to Seattle to present me with a beautiful painting in honor of the Statue of Liberty. She still had some trouble with the language, but she had no trouble at all communicating how much America meant to her.

And we've heard from people who haven't been as lucky as she was. We got a letter from a man in Poland. He enclosed a couple of silver certificates for the Statue of Liberty—for what he called simply "that beautiful symbol." (It seems that those who don't have freedom understand it the most!)

I guess, in the end, that's all the statue and Ellis Island are—symbols. But I think we need them now more than ever before to remind us of the tremendous legacy—really, the sacred trust—that Franklin and the others left us.

I hope we're not beginning to take that trust too lightly. And I hope we're not forgetting all the sacrifices that so many others have made along the way to keep it alive . . . I hope not.

We're here tonight to remember Ben Franklin—good, old—simple—pragmatic—common sense Ben—a man who risked it all because he didn't want to live in a colony.

Well, I don't either.

And I don't think any of you do.

So the best tribute we'll ever pay Ben Franklin is to be damn sure that America never becomes a colony—of any kind—again.

Thank you.

REMARKS AT THE NATIONAL GOVERNORS ASSOCIATION CONFERENCE
Traverse City, Michigan, July 25, 1987

As chairman of Chrysler, Iacocca never missed an opportunity to remind politicians that the country's competitiveness depended as much on public policies as it did on what happened in the country's factories and board rooms. When the nation's governors came to Michigan, he laid out a seven-point plan for them. And he correctly predicted that someone in the room would someday be president of the United States: Bill Clinton of Arkansas was chairman of the National Governors Conference that year.

Thank you, Jim [Blanchard] . . . and congratulations on hosting this great conference. And thanks for coming up and helping us celebrate one hundred fifty years of statehood.

It's also good to see some other old friends here. Governor Jim Thompson, Governor Celeste, Governor Orr, Governor Castle. Maybe you've noticed, but, wherever I've got a plant . . . I try to know the governor well!

And my good friend Governor Cuomo. I not only have a *plant* in his state —he even once offered me a job as head of his Transit Authority. I won't go into why, except it had something to do with the fact that Mussolini got the trains to run on time!

I'm truly honored that you asked me to be a part of this meeting, even though I seldom work on the Sabbath! But, frankly, it was an offer I couldn't refuse. First of all, there's a good chance that someone in this room may be a future president of the United States, and I wanted a shot at him early.

In fact, the odds are kind of impressive, I looked them up. Did you know that sixteen governors have gone on to be president, seventeen if you count Taft, who was governor of *Cuba* for a while. And that in thirty-five of the fifty presidential elections we've held in this country, at least *one* of the candidates was a governor or former governor? Now, I don't know why you people have such a burning desire to trade in a good job for a lousy one, but that's your business.

I guess the real reason so many governors get to be president is because being governor is a great training job for the country's top CEO position.

You all know what it's like running a big organization . . . meeting a pay-roll . . . trying to keep the *customers* happy . . . and most of all—you know what it takes to balance a budget. Every governor balances his budget. And all but one of you *by law*! It seems Vermont doesn't need a law!

I'll have to say, though, that some governors seem to forget everything they learned while they were governing once they get to Washington—espe-cially the part about balancing budgets! They always blame it on defense, of course . . . or the Congress. I think we're getting used to the idea in this coun-try that defense is something we *need*, but something we don't have to *pay for*. We just sort of put it on the tab. As for Congress, the current fashion in Washington seems to be to pretend it's just not *there*.

Something else that certain governors seem to forget about when they go to Washington is *competing*!

Which is ironic, because it looks like competitiveness is going to be the big issue in next year's presidential election. So I want to talk about *compet-ing* for a few minutes today, and then, and this is a really big announcement, I'm going to tell you who I'm going to vote for in that election, and *why*.

First of all, I know that I'm preaching to the choir here today. You discov-ered "competitiveness" long before it got to be the popular buzzword it is to-day. The states have had programs for a long time designed to attract new in-dustries and support old ones. In fact, four of you covered me for $207 million in loans that helped Chrysler survive a few years ago, and things like that, well—you never forget.

Today, I see fifty states fighting for jobs. But a funny thing: I don't see that same kind of fighting spirit in Washington. I see the fifty subsidiaries doing a decent job, but you aren't getting much help from the home office.

And every state seems to have a foreign trade policy, with missions going all over the world to increase exports and attract new jobs. But I've looked for a long time now, and I can't find an *American* trade policy. I can't find a policy in Washington with the same determination to *compete* in the world.

Maybe it's simply because you people are closer to the problem. You see firsthand the human tragedies that come from an America that seems to be losing its competitive edge. You live, up close, with the realities of a ghetto or a mill town where the mill just closed. You have to, because over and above the human suffering, your *tax base* changes every time one gets shuttered.

I couldn't help notice over the years that there just aren't many ideologues in the state houses. Hell, you've got to get the *damn trains* to run on time!

There are plenty of practicing ideologues in *Washington*; but not in Lan-sing, or Columbus, or Springfield, or the other state capitals. I don't think many of you tuck yourselves in at night reading Adam Smith. Eighteenth-century economic theories don't help you explain to your constituents why the local steel mill is going belly-up.

As governors, you've got to be pragmatic. You've got to *govern*. You've got to solve *problems*—and you have to solve them *today*.

Some of you *really* got pragmatic a couple of years ago when the GM Saturn plant was up for bids, remember? You fought like tigers. You tried to outgun each other with free land, free training programs, free roads, low-cost energy, tax abatements—anything it took.

And I thought to myself, "This is really strange. Nobody in Washington is fighting for American jobs, but we've got the states fighting *among themselves* for jobs."

(By the way, at the same time I saw our own labor unions resisting productivity changes in our *old* plants—but cutting any deal it took to represent employees at any *new* plant financed by foreign capital.)

Well, the sad fact is that *you* may be competing, but without a coherent *national* policy, and without the same commitment in Washington that you people have, you're competing for pieces of a smaller and smaller pie.

And I'm afraid that one of these days you're going to find yourselves fighting over the crumbs.

Let me tell you what we're up against as a nation right now. This is a quote from Wataru Hiraizumi, a prominent member of the Japanese Diet, talking to an American reporter: "Japan is not going to change. We love to work hard and Americans don't. . . . The result is that we'll continue to work hard and amass huge surpluses of money. We'll buy up your land and you'll live there and pay rent. We won't go to war. We won't destroy each other. We're *condemned* to live together."

Gee! That kind of takes your breath away, doesn't it? I learned early in life how to read between the lines, and what I read between *those* lines scares the hell out of me.

Hardworking Japanese against lazy Americans . . . America as a nation of renters, leasing back our country piece by piece from our Japanese landlords . . . the two peoples merely *condemned* to live together, as though something a little higher, like *mutual respect*, isn't possible. Is that the kind of world we're going to hand off to our kids?

I don't think so. Mr. Hiraizumi has a lot to learn about Americans if he thinks that scenario will ever play out. But I can understand why he thinks it's coming. Look at this: This is a full-page ad that a big Japanese conglomerate took out in the *New York Times* a few months ago to brag that it just had "a landmark year" . . . and that it has "awed U.S. industry by snapping up $1.8 billion in real estate in a scant 12 months." Including ARCO Plaza in Los Angeles and the ABC Building in Manhattan, by the way. And here's the kicker line: They say . . . "stay tuned for future developments" . . . *"the best is yet to come."*

They really know how to rub a guy's nose in it—I'll say that for them!

A lot of Japanese made a fortune exporting to the United States when the yen was at 250. And now that the currency has flip-flopped, some of them are taking those windfall profits at 250 and buying American real estate at *150*! I think they got a hell of a bargain—*both ways*!

Well, the Japanese always talk a good line on free trade, of course, but when our construction companies wanted to bid on the new airport in Osaka, the Japanese said: "No—you don't understand the soil conditions here." When our ski manufacturers wanted a piece of the action in Japan, they were told: "No—Japanese snow is different from American snow."

Is that their idea of free trade?

You know, I really hate to pick on the Japanese, but they give us such great material to work with—I just can't help myself!

Well, I think we're spinning our wheels in a bunch of theoretical debates when we really need to cut through all the fog and get down to the business of *competing*. We've run up a cumulative trade deficit since 1980 of almost $700 billion. That's a lot of IOUs!

While we've been debating, we've been losing the economic war. Like anybody who does that, we've now got reparations to pay, and we've only got a few options available to do that.

We could default, but that's unthinkable. Maybe it's an option in South America, but not here.

We could start the printing presses and inflate the currency, and pay back the debt at fifty cents on the dollar. But that cure is worse than the disease. Remember Germany in the '20s.

We could swap all the IOUs for our land and businesses. But there's a limit to that. Geez—they already own most of Hawaii and a good chunk of California!

We could cut our wages and lower our standard of living so we can undersell the competition. My economics department tells me that if we cut our standard of living by roughly ten percent a year for ten years, we could probably do it. How would you like to sell that idea to the voters?

Or we can regroup and get serious about competing through a combination of greater American productivity and smarter American economic policies—so we can export goods and services to pay off the debt.

I don't know about you, but the last is the *only* one of those options that makes any sense to me. And we better figure out how to do it!

Let me bring back Mr. Hiraizumi for a minute; he's that Diet member who's going to rent back America to us one day. He said something else in that same interview that I happen to agree with 100 percent. He said: "Americans have never had an economic or business competitor of this magnitude. This is why you Americans are having a hard time with us. You're *un*naturally scared."

He's absolutely right. We're *un*naturally scared. But what the hell are we afraid of? Have we suddenly forgotten how to *compete*? Have we gone *soft*? The American farmer is still the most productive in the world, isn't he? Come on down to Detroit when you're through here, and I'll take you through some auto plants that are as modern and efficient as anything they've got in Japan or anywhere else.

We've got the natural resources, we've got the technology, and we've got the human talent to compete with anybody. What we seem to be lacking is the *will* to compete. And I'm not just talking about *individual* will here—you know, the guy who wants to featherbed on the job or stay home to sober up on Mondays. I'm talking about the *national* will. I'm talking about national *policies* designed to help America compete, like the national policies in the countries that are cleaning our clocks right now.

And maybe at the bottom of this whole lack of *will* is the fact that we don't want to face up to the *costs* of competing. Getting competitive again is going to be *expensive*. We won't do it with pep rallies and lapel buttons. It's going to take one helluva lot of *sacrifice*.

I've got a plan to make America competitive again. But then, who doesn't? Everybody's got a plan these days. And it doesn't take a genius to put one together. The things we need to do aren't hard to see. They're right before our eyes. But I'm afraid that what we don't *want* to see is the *cost*.

My plan has seven points—all of them *simple*, and all of them *expensive*.

Number one on *my* list, and it better be number one on *everybody's list*, is to cut the federal budget deficit. Any argument on that one? That's the root of all evil, and we've got to dig it out.

Almost a trillion and a half dollars of new federal debt just in this decade, and an annual bill for interest alone that's pushing $190 billion—we've gotta be losing our minds! We went from the biggest creditor nation to biggest debtor nation in just a couple of years because we've had to suck in so much foreign capital to feed this monster.

And when we try to get the Japanese and others to mend their mercantilistic ways, they throw our own debt right in our faces and say "If you didn't have a *budget* deficit, you wouldn't have such a huge *trade* deficit." And, of course, they're absolutely right!

Even on that score, they could help out a little by sharing the burden of the defense budget. At $300 billion a year for our defense (and *theirs*), we don't look so good. The debate raging in Washington is over the last 5 percent (or $15 billion). Why don't we ask the Japanese to help out—has anyone even asked them to kick in?

But how do you *really* fix it? Well, you can dance around the truth all you want, but it won't go away: You have to cut spending, *some* defense, and *some* of those entitlements *and raise taxes*. Politicians have to call them "revenues," but I can get away with calling them "taxes."

That means *sacrifice*, by *everybody*. Even for *you*, because it might mean fewer dollars going from Washington to the states, and you'd have to make it up somehow. Sorry about that. We all have to face the music.

Number two on my list is a competitive *trade* policy. We're playing by different rules than everybody else, and we can't keep it up.

If you really believe in free and fair trade, we should be retaliating right about now. Instead, even though we're the ones getting mugged, we're worried about the guys with the super surpluses retaliating. Do you think they are crazy? This is not only their biggest market, this is where all the profits are!

I went to Washington earlier this year and lobbied for the Gephardt amendment because I thought it was at least a *start*. But it's been labeled "protectionist," and any red-blooded guy down in Washington would rather be called a *pervert* than a protectionist.

Hell, nobody's talking about closing the borders or bringing back Smoot-Hawley. (Which is a red herring the *New York Times* and the *Washington Post* throw up every time you bring up the subject of free trade.) But we can't let the American market be the dumping ground for the world's excess capacity, either. And that's what we're doing.

We need a trade policy with teeth, that says to our friends, "Hey, trade has to be *two-way*, fellas. Don't give me any more crap about soil conditions or the snow being different. It's okay for you to come and *sell* here, but while you're in town, you better do a little *shopping!*"

But, of course, a tough trade policy has *costs*, too. We'll probably all pay a little more at the store for imports. And it might be tougher to control inflation. But there's no free lunch.

Number three: If we're going to compete, we've got to change the tax code. But, wait a minute—we just *did* that last year! The first big change in seventy-four years. *True*, but we screwed up.

A tax code should do three things: It should be *fair* to everybody; it should raise enough money to *pay the bills*; and it should help the country *compete*. Well, we spent a whole year on tax reform and only got one out of the three right.

I'll grant, the new law is *fairer*. But it had to be revenue-neutral, they said, so it didn't raise a dime against the deficit. And it shifted about $120 billion directly onto the backs of American business. So we got less competitive. Hell, Toyota made out better than Chrysler!

Everybody else writes tax laws that encourage exports. Ours do nothing to encourage exports. I want to start exporting a few cars to Europe this fall. But guess what, I can make $1,100 to $1,200 more *per car* if I ship them from our plants in Canada and Mexico instead of from Michigan, Illinois, or Missouri —purely from tax savings! And that's enough to make or break the deal.

So we have to do tax reform again. And this time I have a strong hunch that some of those rate cuts most of us got last time might not be there when it's over. Part of the price of competing!

Point number four: We need an energy policy. We had one for a while, but we dropped it when the OPEC guys started fighting among themselves and oil prices dropped. We're right back in the 1960s—joyriding on cheap gas again. We just won't learn from history.

We've already been clobbered twice, and we're setting ourselves up for a third fall—especially when you look at the headlines from the Persian Gulf. The import share of our oil is higher than it was just before the first oil embargo. The federal fuel economy standards for cars went out the window last year. And I wish I had a lot more big V-8's because I could make a ton of money.

I don't know how we got so blind so fast, after all we went through before. We cannot compete without a secure and independent energy source, but we have been capping our wells, and the oil patch has been bleeding like the rust belt was a few years ago.

To maintain our energy independence, we've *all* got to bleed a little. We need an oil import fee, or, better still, a gas tax, or both, so we don't get hooked again on foreign oil. Another price of competing, I'm afraid.

Number five: We've got to gang up on the corporate raiders and run them out of town. Last year, more money was spent on takeovers in this country than on all the new plants and equipment, and a lot of our best management talent that should have been trying to ward off the Germans and the Japanese was busy warding off the raiders.

My biggest supplier, Goodyear, escaped by the skin of their teeth by taking on $2.6 billion in needless debt, and an Englishman named Goldsmith walked off with a cool $94 million in greenmail profit. All that money moving around, and not a dime of it made either the company or the country one bit more competitive.

We're involved in a big acquisition of our own at Chrysler right now, but it's not a very sexy one because there are no raiders involved . . . no greenmail . . . no proxy fights, poison pills, junk bonds or leveraged buyouts. Our American Motors acquisition is just an old fashioned deal that will, by the way, make everybody involved *more* competitive.

But the big money lately has been made on deals that pull equity out of a company and load up its balance sheet with debt. We need to stop that, and of course there's a *cost*: All the easy money made by the raiders, and the arbs, and the paper pushers on Wall Street will have to be made—as Mr. Houseman says—the old-fashioned way. And that means by *competing*.

The sixth point in my plan is to give our kids an education that equips them to compete.

Here's an irony that I just can't fathom: America still has the best graduate schools in the world. Harvard and Stanford and MIT are meccas for the brightest students from Japan, Korea, and everywhere else. They come over, study hard, then go home and beat our brains out. But across town in our own high schools we have students who can't read, can't write, can't count, and—you can bet on it—can't *compete.*

The Japanese kids go to school longer and they study tougher subjects at an earlier age. They're not only taught math and physics and the other tools of a high-tech future, but they're taught how to *compete!* Geez!—They even take tests to determine what *kindergarten* they go to.

We've got to spend more money on education if we're going to catch up. We've got to do a lot more than *just* throw money at the problem, of course, but we can't duck the costs. (You can debate all day whether the money should come from the feds or the states and cities, but we'd better get our act together.)

Finally, number seven, companies such as mine have to spend whatever it takes to get more productive than the people overseas. And there's some good news on this one: We *are.* Chrysler is spending $12.5 billion over five years on plant and product, and our productivity has gone up 9.1 percent a year every year since 1980.

The whole manufacturing sector has chalked up productivity gains of more than 4 percent a year during the '80s, compared to 2 percent a year during the '70s. Most people don't realize it, but manufacturing productivity in this country has been a raging success.

But do you know what the productivity gains have been in the nonmanufacturing side of the house—the service sector? Zero! That's right, *zero.* And with the shrinkage in manufacturing, 76 percent of our labor force is now in the service sector.

Now, that 76 percent of the workforce doesn't do much about our trade problem, of course, because services are a little tough to export. On the other hand, the service sector is a whole lot *safer* place to be these days because there's virtually no *foreign competition.* Banks being the big exception, and you see what's happening to them. The fact is, there's just not much incentive to improve productivity because nobody from Japan or Korea is breathing down your neck.

We don't send our laundry to the Far East, yet. We can't call up Swiss Air and fly to Chicago. The *New York Times* and the *Wall Street Journal* can write editorials all day long telling people like you and me how to handle foreign competition—but they've never in their lives ever *faced* any foreign competition.

Do we *really* want to become just a *service economy* and maybe *hide* a while longer? Or do we want to encourage the investment needed to make our heavy industry and our country even more competitive? I think the answer is obvious—if we're serious about *competing* in the world.

Well, those are my seven simple points: Cut the deficit, give us a trade policy, take another stab at tax reform, maintain our energy independence, run off the corporate raiders, give our kids a better education, and encourage more investment in our industrial productivity.

They're *simple*, but they're all *expensive*. They all mean *sacrifice*.

Now, I'll be honest, I've lost track of how many people want to be president next year. My hat's off to *anybody* who wants it because that poor soul will pay for all our sins over the past few years. We are either going to end up with another Herbert Hoover or a Franklin Roosevelt—I really don't know which, at the moment.

One thing is sure: Every candidate will have his or her own competitiveness program. Maybe it's a five-point program, or a ten-point program—it doesn't matter. But what *does* matter is that they level with us about the *costs*.

And that's how I'm going to wind up today.

You see, *everybody* is saying that we have to get more competitive, but almost *nobody* is willing to talk about the *costs* of getting competitive.

And as a voter, that's what I'm going to be listening for in the next fifteen months. I'll listen to anybody's campaign promises, as long as the last line of the promise is always "By the way, folks, here's what it will *cost* you."

Promise me anything you want, but then tell me what my *bill* will be.

I will toss off as a phony any candidate who implies that somebody *else* will pay the costs. And if I hear that competitiveness is *free*—well, I'll just stop listening altogether.

I'm going to assume that the candidate with the guts to talk about the *costs* will be the right one to tackle the *problems*.

Now, even though I'm not a politician, I understand how risky it can be to take that kind of message to the voters. But presidential elections are about *leadership*, and this is going to be *my* measure of leadership.

We don't need any more blue-ribbon commissions to study American competitiveness; all we need is a blue-ribbon *commitment* to accept the *costs* of making America competitive again.

And the candidate who *asks* for that commitment is the one who'll get my vote.

My best to all of you, and thanks for having me here.

236

REMARKS AT THE AMERICAN BAR ASSOCIATION NATIONAL CONVENTION
San Francisco, California, August 10, 1987

This was a case of Daniel in the lion's den. Iacocca's mission was to lecture the ABA that the legal profession's inability to deal with the crisis in liability litigation was helping to sap the country's competitiveness. He broke the ice with humor and followed with some solemn words about the Constitution and the Statue of Liberty before letting the lawyers have it with both barrels. Always a master at telling people things they don't like to hear, he got a long standing ovation at the end.

Thank you, very much. And good morning to all of you.

I hear last night they paid $1,000 for a single ticket to see the Bolshoi Ballet perform—right here on this stage. This morning I hear you got in here for nothing—absolutely free. So you, too will get what you paid for!

Let me just say that it's an honor to be asked to be here. And a little bit of a surprise, to tell you the truth. When I got the letter from Mr. Thomas last December, it said, "It is my privilege to invite you . . . " and ended by wishing me "happy new year."

Most of the letters I usually get from lawyers start out, "You are hereby summoned," and wind up with "Ignore at your peril."

So this is a treat. And I'm glad to be here.

I'm also a little curious because I've often wondered just what lawyers do when they have a convention. I know what *car dealers* do!

I noticed, for example, that as soon as I sit down you're scheduled to get into something called "The Statement of the Assembly Resolutions Committee."

Now, that sounds like *serious business*: Last year at *our* convention, my speech was the warmup act for *Willie Nelson*!

Now, I have a feeling that you probably get more accomplished at your conventions than we do. You share ideas . . . learn something . . . and get deep into the major issues of the day.

But I gotta tell you, I have a feeling that we have a helluva lot more *fun*!

So I've got an idea. Maybe we ought to switch agendas some year. It would probably do us *all good*. You could go to Las Vegas, loosen up, and listen to Willie Nelson . . . and we'd get together somewhere and read up on the *odometer law!*

. . . Come to think of it, we should have done that *last year!*

By the way, since you people sometimes take things too seriously, I'd better say for the record, Mr. Meese—that's a *joke*—not an *admission.* And it also makes my Chief Counsel in the audience feel better!

And, speaking of conventions, just two weeks ago I talked to all the governors, and I found out what *they* do at their conventions: they run for president. I looked it up—sixteen state governors have gone on to become president. That's a pretty good average, they're batting about .400.

So, I told the governors they make good presidents—and they loved it!

Then, when I was coming out here, I got curious, so I hit the books again, and guess what—I found that twenty-six presidents (of our forty) have been —you guessed it—*lawyers!* You're batting well over .600!

So, if any of you in the audience have any lofty political ambitions, at least the odds are with you! I guess I'm forced to say lawyers make good presidents.

I don't really want to encourage you that much, by the way.

And that's another reason I like car conventions: *Nobody's* running!

Well, as I said, it's an honor to be here with you to kick off your convention. This is a very *special* one, of course, because this is the bicentennial of the Constitution.

Everybody is *talking* about the Constitution these days, and I'm privileged to be here with a couple of thousand people who actually *read* it from time to time.

But, when you stop and think about it, the Constitution is like the Bible: You really don't have to read it every day to know what's in it. You don't have to memorize every word to know what it stands for. So I hope you don't mind if a layman like me has a few thoughts about the Constitution this morning.

You know, we've been doing a lot of celebrating and remembering in this country lately. Last year it was the Statue of Liberty, and this year the Constitution.

But it's not quite the same, is it?

Last year, we put a new dress on Lady Liberty. We brought in the tall ships. We bathed her in fireworks. We invited the whole world to come and watch us show our devotion to all that this country stands for, and our gratitude for all that it has given us.

It's a little quieter this year, isn't it? Not quite as much emotion. Maybe a little more reflection.

The statue, of course, is really just a *symbol*. Whether you first saw it from the deck of a steamer, as my parents did . . . or sailing off to war . . . or as a schoolkid learning about what made this country great, it captures and holds all your feelings about America—whatever they are.

But the Constitution is *not* a symbol. It doesn't stand in the middle of the harbor with a lighted torch; in fact, it sits in a glass case at the top of the stairs in a dark building in Washington.

It's not a *symbol*, instead it's a *tool*, and a *blueprint*, and a *process*, that we have to use every day to preserve all that the Statue of Liberty stands for.

The words of Emma Lazarus at the base of the statue—"Give me your tired, your poor, your huddled masses yearning to breathe free"—those words bring tears to your eyes. And that's good, because we need to have tears in our eyes once in a while.

But the words of the Constitution don't do that. By contrast, they seem pretty hard, and cold, and distant. There's not much poetry and not much of a ring to them. They're mostly (and please forgive me) lawyers' words. And they were hammered out by a group of men who understood that democracy doesn't happen because of bare-knuckled idealism, but because of tedious and exacting negotiation and compromise.

Their compromise wasn't perfect—we all know that. They gave us a basic law that contained both high ideals, and also some low expediency that had to be cleaned up later. But they gave us the *tool*, the *blueprint*, and the *process* to fix whatever flaws they left in it.

The centerpiece for the celebration this year has been the first three words of the document: "We the People." President Reagan said in his State of the Union Address this year that the whole story is told in just those three words: "We the People."

Well, today, I'd like to focus on the very *next* phrase of that preamble, and three words that I think are even *more important* than those first three: "in order to."

They're pretty basic words, aren't they? They'll never sing to you from a poster, and you won't find them chiseled on a monument in the park. They're *functional* words, because the Constitution is a *functional* document.

It was written "in order to" form a more perfect union . . . "in order to" establish justice . . . "in order to" insure domestic tranquillity . . . and all the rest.

And for two hundred years, it has done those things. It hasn't always done them *perfectly*, perhaps. But it has done them—and better and better the older it got.

Let's face it, we don't hang onto the Constitution as a symbol of anything. We keep it around for one simple reason: because it still *works*! And, of course, that's because for two hundred years men and women have *made* it work.

We have to give a lot of credit to the founding fathers, but when you get right down to it, the Constitution today is a much better document than they ever conceived. And that's because of the sacrifice, and the wisdom, and I think the basic *decency* of the American people, for the past two hundred years.

That's really what we're celebrating, isn't it?

The real genius of the Constitution, it seems to me, is that it has held firm to a few fundamental values that we just can't afford to mess around with, and at the same time given us the freedom to deal with problems that those fifty-five men in Philadelphia never dreamed of.

They were smart enough not to try and tell us—two hundred years later—how to solve our problems. They just gave us the freedom we need to find our own solutions.

You can read the Constitution all day long and you won't find an answer to most of the big problems we face today. There's nothing in it to tell us how to handle terrorism, or nuclear proliferation, or acid rain. Nothing on Third World debt, or even air bags.

And nothing in it to tell us how to *compete* in the world. That's my bag, of course—*competing*. And I want to talk about that for a few minutes this morning. My only problem is, how do I tie it to the Constitution?

And I found the answer—a very simple answer—*you*.

You see, as lawyers, you're a little more equal than the rest of us. You're trained to *use* the freedoms granted by the Constitution. We all *have* them, of course, but you know better than the rest of us how to *use* them. That's your job. And I'm here this morning to ask you to use them to help us *compete*.

Competitiveness is the big new buzzword all over the country these days because we've suddenly realized that America is *not* competing—at least not very effectively. We've run up a cumulative trade deficit since 1980 of almost $700 billion, and we went from being the world's largest creditor to the world's largest debtor in just a couple of years.

There's plenty of blame to go around for that, of course. American industries—including my own—got a little lazy and careless for a while. Then, we've more than doubled our federal debt just in the '80s to well over $2 trillion, and it's awfully tough to compete when you're carrying a piano like that on your back. Geez—the payments for interest alone are over $15 billion per month. And our archaic trade policies have been so far out of sync with the rest of the world that we've been set up as patsies.

Everybody gets part of the blame, and everybody had better pick up part of the solution. That's the message I try to take to everybody I talk to—politicians, businessmen, the unions—*everybody*. And that includes you in this room.

Maybe *one* reason we aren't hooking and jabbing with the guys overseas is that we're spending so much time and energy and money fighting *each other* in this country.

And we're pushing every single one of the rights guaranteed by the Constitution *so far*, that we may be tying ourselves up in tight little knots. Sometimes I think we're losing hold of the art of compromise.

We're the most litigious society on Earth. We sue each other at the drop of a hat. They tell me that 90 percent of all the civil actions tried before juries in the whole world are tried right here in the United States, and that we're spending about $30 billion a year just suing each other.

Our courts are jammed, and it's no wonder, because so many people are looking to the courts these days not just to distribute *justice* anymore, but also to redistribute the *wealth*.

And I don't *think* that's what the framers of the Constitution had in mind, did they?

I know this is the famous "Casino Society" we're living in, but do we really want to let our court system become part of this giant crap shoot?

Last year we had the biggest civil award ever in this country—$10.3 billion! Now, I'm sure some of *you* might take a scholarly look at the merits of that case, but do you know what kind of a signal it sends to everybody else? A very simple one: "Hey how can I get a piece of *that action*?"

And there are enough wacky things going on to make it worthwhile to roll the dice. The burglar falling through the skylight and collecting damages, for example. Anything is possible when you go to court these days.

A big drug company lost a case and $3 million for failing to post a warning label that the FDA had specifically *forbidden* them to post. It's Catch-22 time out there!

Well, don't worry, I'm not going to waste your time and mine going through the standard list of horror stories. Probably some of them are flukes, anyhow. I hope!

I'm more concerned about *trends*. Trends like:

A thousand percent increase in product liability cases in federal courts between 1975 and 1985,

An 835 percent increase in medical malpractice awards,

A 401 percent increase in liability awards in roughly that same period.

Those are trends that you can put numbers to. But the worst trend of all is the one that's hardest to quantify: The drop in America's *competitiveness* that's tied to all these numbers.

You see, the first thing you have to be able to do in order to compete is take a risk. If you can't afford to take a risk, then you can't afford to compete. And what we're doing to ourselves in this country right now is making it more and more difficult to take even a small risk.

241

If you're a drug company, for example, you don't want to mess around with *vaccines*. Too risky. A simple vaccine for diphtheria and whooping cough that cost 12 cents a shot in 1980 costs $12 today, and almost all of that cost increase goes into a liability fund.

We've had some awful new diseases showing up lately that seem to be begging for a vaccine, but I guess if you were in that business you'd be tempted to spend your R&D budget on something safer, like maybe growing hair. But, even then, watch out for the *side effects*! You'd have a helluva case for mental anguish if the hair grew on your feet!

Every business and every product has risks. You can't get around it. My industry sure does. Automobiles are involved in *half* the tort cases in the country, and account for *half* of all compensation paid. Cars get safer every day, and yet the number of lawsuits goes up and up.

This is a true story. For years, there was a tree in the middle of the Sahara Desert. It was a freak of nature—the only tree within hundreds of miles in any direction. During World War II, an Englishman ran into it—in a *tank*! If it were *today*—in *this* country—he'd *sue*! I don't know *who*, but he'd sue.

Somehow, and I don't think you can find it in the Constitution, we've adopted the curious notion in the United States that whenever something *bad* happens to us, somebody is at fault, and somebody has to pay.

The National Cancer Institute says that more cancer deaths come from exposure to the sun than from all the man-made products known to cause cancer. A couple of months ago, everybody laughed at the secretary of the Interior, Mr. Hodel (I did once, too!) for saying that we should all wear hats and sun glasses. Remember that flap? Well, he's not so dumb. If you get sick from the sun, who are you going to sue?

I always tell the young people, "Don't be afraid to take some risks, but don't take the life or death risks. Don't take the risks that can kill you."

Well, for American business today, I'm not sure there are any *small* risks. That $10.3 billion judgment last year qualifies in my book as *capital punishment*. Somebody got the *chair*!

If you happen to be a small company right now, you may not even have to wait to get sued. Just the *risk* of getting sued can be too risky.

A small company in Virginia that made driving aids for handicapped people went out of business because it couldn't afford the liability insurance. Too risky.

There used to be eighteen companies making football helmets in this country, but the liability crisis has pared them down to just two. Nobody makes gymnastics equipment or hockey equipment anymore. Too risky.

We've virtually stopped making light aircraft in this country. The biggest production cost is the liability insurance. Too risky.

One of these days we're going to wake up and say, "The hell with it—*competing* is just too risky!"

Other countries don't spend their time looking for Mr. Deep Pockets. They're too busy beating our brains out in the marketplace. The biggest damage award *ever* in the history of Great Britain was a little over a million bucks. That's practically a nuisance suit here!

The Japanese—our biggest competitors these days—don't waste their time in court. They've got about as many lawyers in Japan as we've got sumo wrestlers in America.

But—great news for American competitiveness, maybe. As of last April 1 —April Fool's Day—American lawyers can now practice in Japan! This could be the opportunity of a lifetime for some of you, and I hope you've got your visas ready.

It's also a chance to serve your country. You see, our government can't seem to slow down the Japanese through trade negotiations, but you could really throw them for a loop. I'll tell you how: Just get them to buy the idea of *punitive damages.* That would slow the hell out of them!

They don't know about them over there. In fact, punitive damages are almost unknown anywhere outside this country, but they're wreaking havoc here.

I'm no lawyer, but I *think* they're supposed to punish gross negligence or reckless disregard for safety. And I can't really argue with that. If somebody is totally irresponsible, he should pay for it.

But I'm afraid that we're beginning to punish more than just gross negligence in this country; I'm afraid that we're beginning to punish some of the normal risks that simply can't be avoided when you produce almost any kind of product.

And when we do that—when we punish *normal* risk—then we're also punishing *competitiveness,* and we're punishing *progress.*

We don't live in a risk-free world, and never will. If we're not willing to accept some of the risks that other countries are, then even if the Constitution lives to three hundred years, I'm not sure there'll be much to celebrate.

I don't want to get into the nuclear power debate, for example, but it seems to me that if a perfectly safe plant is ever going to be designed and built, it probably won't be here because other countries have their *engineers* working on the problem, while we seem to have turned it over to our *lawyers.*

Now don't get me wrong, I'm really not trying to break your rice bowl. Some of these issues need to be debated. And we need strong advocates on both sides in order to find the answers. But if the debate never ends—if compromises are never reached short of the courthouse—then we go nowhere.

Advocacy is your profession, of course. And it's an honorable one. The Constitution might tell us that our rights are sacred, but sometimes they aren't worth a dime unless people like you, skilled in the law, are able to push them and protect them for us.

When we get into trouble, we all want a bulldog sitting next to us, not a *potted plant*!

Advocacy is fine; it's *unbridled* advocacy that's the problem today. And it's getting out of hand. Advocacy may be necessary to settle our legitimate differences, but *unbridled* advocacy seems to be *creating* differences that we didn't know we had, and differences that we probably can't *afford.*

It's sort of like unbridled capitalism. We don't have that in this country anymore. We came close to it around the turn of the century, but then we suddenly discovered that a couple of guys owned all the steel, and a couple more owned all the oil, and a few others had all the railroads. We learned that if you have absolutely unrestrained competition in the marketplace, pretty soon you wind up with no competition at all.

And I think we all may be getting a little carried away again like we did in the robber baron days. Nobody wants to give up the rights that the Constitution gave us, but if every one of us pushes every one of those rights as far as we can, then one of these days *none* of us will have any rights.

Maybe that's why sixteen states and the federal government are all looking at tort reform proposals, right now. And I for one am glad they are. We've been going a little crazy, and we've got to stop it.

It's time to change some of the rules, even if we may have to compromise some of our rights to do it, because America today just can't afford all this unbridled advocacy.

And that's nothing new; it's been our willingness for two hundred years to find sensible compromises that has kept the Constitution alive. It was *born* in compromise; it has *survived* because of compromise; and as soon as we forget how to compromise, I think it's doomed.

So, in closing, let me say that this is the *right place* and the *right time* to put the Constitution on a high pedestal and celebrate everything that it stands for. And you are the *right people* to lead the rest of us in that celebration.

As lawyers, you've got a greater opportunity than the rest of us to see that the Constitution continues to work as well in the future as it has in the past.

In my book, by the way, that special *opportunity* is also one helluva *responsibility*!

But keep this in mind, too: In our democracy, the final judges will always be laymen like me, and all the millions like me, who don't read that Constitution regularly . . . who don't study all the interpretations of it . . . and who may not even understand everything it says.

We'll be the judges of the *effectiveness* of the Constitution . . . and the *wisdom* of the laws written under it . . . and the *integrity* of your profession.

Furthermore, we'll make our judgments against some very simple standards. We'll always ask ourselves simple questions, like:

"Does this make sense and is this fair?"

"Is the Constitution, which was written to *protect* my rights, being used to keep me from *exercising* my rights?"

"Does a law written to prohibit something *bad* keep me from doing something that's *good*?"

"Is that lawyer really trying to get *justice* for his client, or is he trying to do an *in*justice to me?"

Those are the simple questions that will always be asked because, in the end, it all comes down to those *other* three basic words: "in order to."

This isn't the year for tall ships and fireworks. What we're doing this year is too serious for that. As I said, Americans aren't going to get too misty-eyed about the Constitution: They just damn well *expect it to work!*

And you people have the best opportunity of all to engineer the compromises that will keep it working . . . and keep America working, too!

Well, thanks again for inviting me. Have a great week here in beautiful San Francisco. Next week I go back to Las Vegas for another car convention —I'll say hello to Willie Nelson for you.

Good luck to all of you. And thanks again for having me.

REMARKS AT THE U.S. NAVAL WAR COLLEGE

Spruance Memorial Lecture, Newport, Rhode Island,
April 8, 1992

The Cold War was over. The United States won because it had a plan to counter Soviet aggression. Using language and examples they understood, Iacocca told the officers attending the War College that the country needed a similar plan to counter economic aggression.

Thank you, Admiral. And good evening to all of you. It's a real honor for me to be here. Of course, I know this place by reputation. Wow, I'm glad to have a chance to get to know it first hand.

I jumped at the invitation to come for a couple of reasons. First, I tried like hell to get into the service in the days right after Pearl Harbor, but nobody would take me. Not the Air Corps, not the Army, not you guys. Nobody wanted a skinny kid just getting over rheumatic fever. I kept waiting to hear from you. Finally, fifty years late, I get the call.

And after all this time, I guess it's a good thing for all of us that you just want to hear me *talk*—not fight!

Secondly, I know about the contribution that this institution has made to national *security* over the years. You've helped the Navy and the country understand the threats to that security, and how to deal with them.

I just wish there was a place like this to do the same thing for our national *competitiveness*. But believe it or not, there isn't. And that's what I want to talk to you about tonight.

A dozen years ago, when Chrysler was asking the federal government to cosign a few little bank notes for us, I tried to make a case for some kind of broader national economic plan for the United States. What I had in mind was nothing more than a basic strategy for America to compete in the world.

The new term of art for this sort of thinking back then was *national industrial policy*. And it quickly became a dirty word.

Somehow—without anybody ever setting down a comprehensive plan that I know of—it was assumed that any national industrial policy meant central planning of the economy by the government and heavy subsidies for U.S. industries.

It was dismissed almost out of hand. You see, economic planning is somehow un-American. It's the first step on the road to socialism . . . then *communism*, or what's left of it . . . then God knows where.

You know—"Get out there and compete in the global economy, but don't have any sort of comprehensive national strategy to do that or it will lead to ruination!"

Now, the irony was that we actually *did* have industrial policies—hundreds of them—in place. And we still do. The Merchant Marine, farm subsidies, the FHA, the Small Business Administration, Lockheed, loan guarantees to the steel industry—the list goes on and on.

I felt bad about going to Washington for help so Chrysler could live and six hundred thousand Americans could stay employed. It went against my grain to ask them to guarantee the $1.2 billion in loans that we needed. That is, until I found out that there were already $409 billion in loan guarantees of one kind or another already on the books! Then I didn't feel so bad, at all.

We got our loan guarantees, or—as the news media still puts it—the famous Chrysler *bailout*, even while the purists were shouting that helping Chrysler would lead to an industrial policy and create a precedent that would bring a quick end to free enterprise as we know it.

What happened, of course, is that we survived and we paid off the loans three years later and seven years early. What most people still don't know is that the federal government actually made a *profit* of almost $350 million on the deal. *Some bailout!*

Now, if that's an example of industrial policy, I'll take it.

The problem is, we've never folded all these mini-industrial policies into a single, comprehensive national plan.

Japan has always had such a plan. Germany has a plan. The twelve nations of the European Community now have a plan. Chrysler has a plan. Hell, the Boston Red Sox and Notre Dame have plans. But America has no plan.

We got our economic theories of free trade and free enterprise from a book by Adam Smith in 1776, the year America was born.

In 1776 his ideas made sense. They still do—in theory.

But the world changes. And theories give way to reality.

Think about Naval warfare in 1776. A captain was commissioned, usually some big shot's brother-in-law. He went down to the waterfront and hired a crew. Then he sailed around until he found someone to shoot at who happened to be flying the wrong flag.

Since then the Navy has gotten a lot more sophisticated. It now has war plans, and battle plans, and strategies, and tactics. You put to sea with a battle group that has picket ships on the periphery, and air cover overhead, and attack subs below. You work as a team, and you make damn sure that team is *protected*. The reason I know all this—I have firsthand experience. I spent three days at sea on the *Nimitz*. I really roughed it! I had the admiral's quarters and you don't worry about how long you shower!

Economically, however, we're still back in 1776. On the world economic sea, we have no battle plan. American companies are still forced to ship out alone like privateers in the old days, while the competition sails in a well-protected armada.

My exaggeration is for effect, but I'm not overstating by much. Our tradition of entrepreneurship and free enterprise has generally worked well within our borders. But it doesn't work quite as well in the new global economy.

That's because our ideas of fair competition aren't universal. Neither are our antitrust laws. Protectionism is bad in America, but not everywhere else. We don't believe in subsidizing and protecting our basic industries. Other countries do.

We believe in the survival of the fittest. Our competitors—they just believe in survival.

The Japanese Ministry of International Trade and Industry, for instance —the famous MITI—may be the most important agency of the whole Japanese government. Its mission is to help Japanese companies penetrate foreign markets, and to protect those industries it considers essential from foreign competition. We have nothing like that.

As I said, economic planning is just plain *un-American*.

And that's dangerous—maybe fatal—in a world that's changing as rapidly as ours is.

Right now, I'll bet many of you are working on plans for the post-Cold War American Navy. You had a plan for a six hundred-ship Navy. Now you need a new one. The world changed. And you have to change with it.

But I don't see anybody planning for the post-Cold War American *economy*.

I know that here at Newport the whole concept of war gaming has been elevated to a high art. Or maybe *science* is a better word. And I was encouraged to learn that your current Global War Game Series has an important economic component to it. Hell, at least *somebody* is thinking.

But I don't think there's a big maneuvering board and a bank of computers in Washington where people are playing "what if?" with this country's economic future.

What if our federal deficits keep getting bigger and we end up paying so much to service our debt that we can't afford to defend the country or educate our kids? The interest on the deficit just passed $313 billion—more than our total defense budget by about $25 billion.

What if our trade deficits keep mounting and other countries keep using their surpluses to buy up our land and our companies? What if they call in all the notes they've been picking up at our Treasury auctions every Tuesday and decide they don't want anymore of our IOUs?

What if we continue to lose major industries like consumer electronics?

What if the underpinnings of our whole industrial base like autos and steel and even airplanes are the next to go?

You see, before you come up with some kind of national economic battle plan you first have to recognize the *threat*. I'm afraid that—as a nation—we still haven't recognized the threat.

If we did, maybe we'd also see an opportunity right now.

We're all euphoric because our deadly enemy, the Soviet Union, just folded its tent. But now what? How do we demobilize? And I don't just mean the troops!

When peace broke out we had about 3 million defense workers in this country. I've seen conservative reports that three hundred thousand of them will be out of jobs pretty soon. Defense accounts for only about 5 percent of the workforce, but about 25 percent of the jobs lost in the current recession have come from defense.

The Charleston Naval Ship Yard just laid off fifteen hundred people last month. Over in Groton, up to four thousand workers could be let go this year and these aren't exactly unskilled day laborers: They built your nuclear submarines!

We're going to see numbers like this in communities all over the country. Highly skilled technicians. Engineers. Project managers. Where are they going to go?

Not to Chrysler. We're cutting back ourselves. Not to General Motors. They're eliminating seventy four thousand jobs even as we speak. Not to IBM or Dupont. They're slashing their work forces, too.

You hear a lot about America not having enough of the brains and high-tech skills needed to compete in the world. Well, here are people with the brains and the skills but no place to go because America's industrial base is *shrinking.*

The boys came home from World War II to lots of good-paying factory jobs. After Korea, manufacturing still provided well over a third of all jobs in the country. Even after Vietnam, it provided 28 percent. But as the Cold War ends, only about 17 percent of American jobs are now in manufacturing— that's *making* things.

Since I joined Chrysler in 1978, we've cut our U.S. employment by almost half—from more than 142,000 to under 70,000. How's that for a decade of growth? And, sadly, we're *typical*, not *unique*. I grew up almost literally in the shadow of the Bethlehem Steel Company in Pennsylvania, and I've also seen what's happened to that most basic of all industrial sectors.

I remember when Bethlehem employed over three hundred thousand people. I remember when it built 1,121 ships back during World War II—one new ship every single day of the war! How many ships could the United States build today in an emergency—going flat out? It's a scary thought, isn't it? Don't even think about it!

Even in 1960, Bethlehem Steel still employed one hundred fifty thousand Americans.

Do you know what they employ today? Take a guess. Would you believe 26,500! And here's the kicker: Even as it gets smaller and smaller, it may soon pass USX as the country's *largest* steelmaker.

So if we're going to put these new Cold War veterans to work so they can give the American economy the same edge they gave the American military, I don't know *where* the hell we're going to put them. If there's a plan, I haven't heard of it.

Last fall, Deputy Secretary of Defense Donald Atwood led a delegation of U.S. businessmen on a tour of Soviet defense plants. He said the U.S. would be willing to help them convert to civilian production. That makes sense to me. But do we have a plan to convert our *own* defense plants? I don't know of one.

We have a plan to help Russian scientists find work so they don't hire out to the Libyans or Iraqis. Smart move, in my book. But what about the American scientists who've been making *our* sophisticated weapons?

We've spent trillions on defense—most of it "sunk costs" that we'll never get back—but the price, stiff as it was, was worth it.

Still, a lot of that money is investment we should be able to recoup because it was an investment in *people.* We can't turn tanks into taxi cabs or retrofit battleships into oil tankers, but we sure can use some of the skills we've paid for to help America compete as well economically as we have militarily.

The problem is, there are fewer and fewer places to put those skills to work.

Now, I have to believe that somebody who can slide a smart bomb through a window in Baghdad can somehow help us build better cars.

But I don't have a job for him!

I also have to believe that a technician who can pull a license plate number out of a satellite photo from fifty miles up can somehow give us better television.

But the television industry is *gone.* It's all in the Far East! Too late, guys!

It's gone because while we had our eyes on the Kremlin, Japan was targeting Main Street. Not with missiles, but with TVs and VCRs and radios and cameras and cars. And they were doing it mostly with our own technology.

We're living in one of history's true turning points right now. We were at war—both hot and cold—for fifty solid years! It ended so quickly that we still haven't gotten our heads around what it really means. The former Soviet Union is in turmoil. It's still a very dangerous situation. But if it settles down and all our euphoria turns out to be justified, then history will have a lot to say about *you people.*

It will say that America achieved the greatest military victory in the annals of warfare—without firing a shot. In the end, you won it not by dropping bombs or sinking ships, but by being *prepared*—by focusing on a threat and neutralizing it—by putting a strategy in place for the other side to see . . . by having a *credible deterrence* to the Soviet Union. In short, you won by *having a plan* . . . a plan so good that the other guy finally blinked!

Wouldn't it be tragic if we failed to take what we've learned from this great victory we've just won and apply it to the economic battle we're now losing?

But when it comes to dealing with the *economic* threats facing this country, you dare not suggest a *plan.* Creating a national strategy to defend this country's economic interests is too dangerous. Just mention the idea of *deterrence* toward those who are committing economic aggression against this country, and some people will say, "Are you crazy? Do you want to start a *trade* war?"

They haven't learned what you people in the military have known all along and just proved for the whole world to see—that the way to prevent a war of *any* kind is to be prepared to fight one!

One way we've met and defeated military aggression is to *promise* retaliation. But when faced with economic aggression, we promise just the opposite —that we *won't* retaliate.

I call that "economic pacifism."

We'd be a Russian colony today without a defense strategy. We'll be somebody else's colony one day soon without an economic strategy.

You can draw a lot of analogies between the military and industrial sectors right now. Both need to downsize while at the same time getting more efficient. Both need to recognize and adapt to major changes taking place in the world. But the military is flush with victory—victory in the desert last year and victory in the Cold War.

American industry, on the other hand, holds about the same place in the public mind that the military held just after Vietnam. There's a perception of weakness, of incompetence, of lost opportunities, of confusion, of too much fat, and of too little self-confidence—of an overall *lack of will.* People are becoming defeatist. They believe we *can't win*, that we're becoming a nation of *losers!*

Well, that perception was wrong fifteen years ago about America's *military* will. And it's wrong today about America's *industrial* will.

In spite of what you read, American industry hasn't been asleep at the switch. We realized long ago that the world is changing for us . . . that foreign competition has caught us and in some cases passed us . . . that a global market means that we don't have the kind of clout or control we once did . . . that consumers are more demanding . . . and so are shareholders . . . and environmentalists . . . and employees.

We know pretty clearly what we're up against. And we know what we have to do to compete.

At Chrysler, we've redone just about every one of our plants in the past decade. We've invested $25 billion in new plants and products. In just the past year we spent a billion bucks on the most advanced automotive research center in the world and another billion on a new assembly plant and a new Jeep Grand Cherokee.

The company has been completely reorganized from top to bottom to compete.

We used to have too many layers of management and too many walls for our people to climb over. We've cut them out. We used to be organized like an infantry division. Now we're organized into SEAL Teams. But we call them "platform teams"—small, tight teams of designers, engineers, and people from every discipline in the place who take a car from initial concept right to the showroom floor.

It used to take us five years to do that. Now we can do it in three. You'd have to be in the auto business to understand just how big a jump that is. It's sort of like the difference between the turning radius of a battleship and a frigate.

We've got the hottest new sports car on the market today—our Dodge Viper. It was developed in just thirty-six months by a small team of just eighty-five people.

And quality has come along just as fast. The only big difference in quality today between what comes from Detroit and what comes from Japan is a difference in *perception*.

We're proud of what we've done, but we aren't alone in getting more efficient. Companies all over America are doing it. I read that Motorola developed an IFF beacon for the troops in Desert Storm last year in just *eight days*. Stupid, lazy Americans did that! Huh? That's what some people are saying about us!

The two big buzzwords in industry these days are lean production (doing more with less, and doing it better), and agile manufacturing (the flexibility to react fast to change).

The latter term was coined by some researchers at my alma mater, Lehigh University. They work in a specialized unit that focuses solely on American competitiveness, and it's called the Iacocca Institute.

By the way, if you wonder how a guy who got a D there in physics winds up with his name on the building, it's simple. You help them raise $60 million!

What they've come up with is a concept too complicated to lay out here, and yet rooted in something old and simple—teamwork and collaboration. Teamwork among companies, among industries, and between industry and government.

In fact, guess who's funding one of the projects? The Defense Department's Management Technology Program. Somebody down there is thinking ahead. Somebody has figured out that the country's military security and economic security in the twenty-first century are really going to come from the same place—and that's the *factory floor.*

There's another project at Lehigh with DOD. This one with the Air Force. It's to adapt some of the training techniques developed in the military to civilian use.

Nobody's been better at technical training than the military. And there's probably no better example of that anywhere than the Navy's Nuclear Power Program. We want to train our people just as well in our tech schools as you do in yours.

So don't believe all you read about how America's factories and the people in them can't compete anymore. They *can.* And they've spent billions getting in shape to compete. And they're willing to learn.

Now all we need is a plan. Just a basic strategy. A national policy that puts the same priority on America's economic competitiveness that we've put on our national security for the past half-century.

And we don't have to socialize our basic industries to do that, as the guys with the Adam Smith neckties keep warning. We don't have to tear up GATT and our other trade agreements. We don't have to close the borders to keep the competition out and retreat into isolationism. But if the other guys aren't playing by the rules and they're clubbing you, you have to *protect* yourself. Hell, in baseball, you protect the plate; in football, you protect the middle; in basketball you protect the lane. It's a natural instinct, but we don't do it.

But we do need a game plan. A plan that brings government and business and labor and education and Wall Street and all the other players to the same table. A plan that takes a realistic look at the world we live in, and sees . . .

That we cannot remain economically independent if we allow someone else to own all the technologies that will define the twenty-first century, or someone else to own the factories that put those technologies to work.

And sees that if we allow someone else to write the trade rules, someone else will win.

And sees that no nation can be a military power, or a political power, or (for that matter) even a moral power in the world, if it is not first and foremost an *economic* power.

That's the broad preamble to an effective economic strategy. Let me give you a few specifics.

A sensible plan would protect certain technologies, like microchips, without which a modern economy or a modern military simply can't function. It would also preserve a strong industrial base as the most essential creator of wealth.

It would cut the federal budget deficit and even start whacking away at the $3.5-trillion-dollar national debt that is bleeding us white.

It would reform the American education system, starting with keeping our kids in school as long as the kids in Japan and Europe they'll have to compete against—220 or 240 days a year instead of 180.

It would take some of the massive runaway health-care costs off the back of business, and provide investment and research incentives our competitors have but we don't.

It would begin to tax consumption more and savings less to encourage capital formation.

It would rebuild the country's roads, and bridges, and sewer systems.

It would reform our tort system to make innovation and risk-taking acceptable again. Japan produces ten engineers for every lawyer while America graduates ten lawyers for every engineer. Who in the hell do you think is going to win that battle? We used to build the better mousetraps; now, we don't bother. We just *sue* the guy who builds one!

A national industrial strategy would also put some spine into our trade relations. When somebody slams the door on our products, we should slam the door on theirs. Not permanently. We want to *encourage* trade, not cut it off. But we should—or must—do it until they *play fair.*

And when you've got a fighter like the F-16 and somebody wants it, you make them buy the *plane*—and at full retail! You don't sell them the damn *specs* so they can become your *competitor* instead of your *customer*! Hell, that's no way to compete!

All of these things and more need to go into a plan to compete. But before you talk about what goes *into* it you have to decide that you even *need* a plan in the first place.

And we aren't even that far yet. We can't even agree that we need a national economic policy, or strategy or whatever you want to call it. By any name, it's still a dirty word in this country.

And frankly, I just can't understand that.

Let me close by saying that I did a little homework before coming here.

I learned about something called "War Plan Orange." I learned that for almost forty years, people here at the War College helped devise and refine War Plan Orange. And I found out that Admiral Ernest King personally wargamed the entire strategy for victory in the Pacific right here—eight years before Pearl Harbor!

So when war came, there was a plan on file. And the man in charge of the U.S. Navy knew that plan backward and forward. All he had to do was execute it. And the plan was successful.

Well, the country is locked in a different kind of battle today. An *economic* battle. And in the long run, the stakes are just as high.

But for this battle, ladies and gentlemen, the country has no War Plan Orange.

And I think it's high time we got one. It's crucial!

I hope all of you agree.

So, with that, let me say thanks again for inviting me. Good night and good luck to all of you.

Or, as you say around here, I wish you fair winds and following seas.

III

Speeches Concerning
Social Values and Issues

7. Lee Iacocca's Commencement Addresses

Ronald L. Lee

A commencement address is an oration delivered on the occasion of graduation. The term designating the speech conveys the dual dimensions of the rhetorical task. "As graduation," John Brubacher writes, "it faces the past; it is the culmination of a period of academic discipline. As commencement it faces the future; it is the beginning of putting one's recently trained powers to the test of life" (xxv).

The style of enacting this past-future transition has substantially changed with the evolution in American higher education. In earlier times, when college degrees were rare, commencements were small, and each graduate delivered an address to assembled faculty and visitors. The speeches were public evidence of students' knowledge of their chosen fields. Later, when classes got too large, a single distinguished speaker was invited to deliver an address. At first, speakers came from the ranks of the faculty and administration. These addresses were elite in character, often delivered in Greek, Latin, or Hebrew, and treated such esoteric topics as "whether Three Persons in the Godhead are revealed in the Old Testament" or "whether it is lawful to resist the Supreme Magistrate, if the Commonwealth cannot otherwise be preserved" (Brubacher xxxi).

As time passed, the function of higher education changed. Colleges became more secular and were no longer only of interest to a small group of men who wished to enter the guild of scholars. Higher education began to serve broader social purposes as students came to study business, agriculture, and engineering. Even the liberal arts curriculum became populated with courses thought to improve students' vocational opportunities. Not surprisingly, the style and substance of the commencement message reflected this populist expansion of college education. Forsaking the esoteric, commencement speakers drew attention to a world beyond the academy. They shifted the audience's direction of gaze from inside to outside. This new rhetorical function demanded a different kind of speaker. As a result, colleges invited distinguished citizens who had made substantial contributions to commerce, politics, and the professions to deliver the commencement address.

Lee Iacocca is a speaker who directs the graduates' gaze outside to the world of work. He is an icon of American business and personifies the difficulties facing the nation's corporations. In the late 1970s, the Chrysler bankruptcy symbolized what Jimmy Carter called the national "malaise"; but by the early 1980s, the Chrysler recovery was an emblem of what Ronald Reagan hailed as "morning in America." America was, a *Saturday Evening Post* writer observed, "simply, a nation in despair. But then there was this pugnacious Iacocca fellow, briskly striding through Chrysler commercials as if . . . he were on his way to the radiator department to show the workers how to bolt 'em in so they wouldn't rattle" (Stuller 46).

Unlike the pessimistic Carter and the ebullient Reagan, Lee Iacocca was portrayed as a pragmatic man. He was the "old war horse" who was still standing after the tough political and economic battles were over. He fought the good fight as a plainspoken realist who was a tonic to soft-headed liberalism and romantic conservatism. As a result, Iacocca is nearly the perfect representative of the world of hard knocks that lay beyond the ivy-covered walls.

Yet Iacocca's gaze outward was tempered with a long-standing commitment to the importance of what a student could learn inside. For unlike some icons of practical affairs, Iacocca's image was not stained by anti-intellectualism. Although his presence at the podium marks the separation between theory and practice, Iacocca has long been associated with the pursuit of intellectual excellence. In his 1988 book *Talking Straight*, in remarks before the National Education Association, and in a speech at the Running Start Kickoff in 1989, Iacocca discussed the importance of education for the economic health of the nation. It is with this history and public image that Iacocca delivered the two addresses considered here. On May 8, 1987, he spoke to the graduating class at the University of Southern California, and, three years later, on June 9, 1990, he addressed the graduates at Michigan State University.

An abiding custom shaped Iacocca's USC and MSU remarks. In this respect, commencement speeches are akin to inaugural addresses, declarations of war, or State of the Union messages. As presidents must tailor their remarks to meet constitutional requirements, historical precedent, and audience expectations, so, too, was Iacocca hemmed in by the history of the form. Communication scholars refer to speeches of this type—speeches highly regulated by the tradition of a recurring occasion—as specimens of a genre. A genre embodies a discursive tradition "typified by substantive, stylistic, and strategic similarities" (Campbell and Jamieson 6–7). Generic classifications provide a framework for explaining what makes a speech consequential. In the present case, genre is a touchstone for understanding and evaluating Iacocca's commencement address.

Tradition may either stifle or inspire the speaker. In Iacocca's case, the commencement form forced him to present his economic message in an interesting new way. It offered him an opportunity to translate his business image into a rhetorical resource with which to celebrate traditional American values. In what follows, I explore the relationship among generic requirements, Iacocca's rhetorial resources, and Iacocca's economic message.

GENERIC REQUIREMENTS

Speeches fall into both broadly and narrowly defined categories. The USC and MSU remarks are broadly classified as epideictic speeches and narrowly defined as commencement addresses. Understanding the general function of the epideictic genre aids the critic in explaining the more particular speech form.

Since the earliest writings on public communication, rhetorical theorists have recognized a speech form known as epideictic.[1] Frequently delivered on ceremonial occasions, speeches in the epideictic genre include the eulogy, the retirement message, the Fourth of July oration, and the commencement address. Speakers in these circumstances take as their primary task the reinforcement of traditional values. "The speaker," Perelman and Olbrechts-Tyteca write, "tries to establish a sense of communion centered around particular values recognized by the audience, and to this end he uses the whole range of means available to the rhetorician for the purposes of amplification and enhancement" (51).

Despite the audience's prior commitment to these values, the epideictic speech is a formidable rhetorical undertaking. Values considered separately may not be controversial, but values considered in relationship to one another are often contested. The art of the epideictic orator is to make a persuasive case for ordering values in a given circumstance. We all can remember tense situations in recent American history when traditional values competed for ranking in the social hierarchy. The McCarthy period brought loyalty into conflict with the freedoms of speech and association; desegregation legislation required a rethinking of the relative importance of property rights and equality; Vietnam-era discourse contested the relationship between conscience and patriotism; and recent labor-management partnerships have required a discourse that elevates cooperation and devalues competition.

261

Despite this potential for eloquence, epideictic speeches can devolve easily into the mouthing of empty platitudes. I suspect this is the reason so few of us can remember what was said at our own graduations. Francis Horn, a longtime university president, writes: "I graduated from Dartmouth College in 1930. I do not remember who the commencement speaker was, let alone what he had to say. This is the experience of most college graduates, even those of us who have spent our lives in higher education and who, therefore, might be expected to carry a more positive memory of this important academic ceremony." Barnaby Keeney, former president of Brown, "found that among some thirty of his administrative colleagues at the university, only one could name the speaker at his commencement, and no one remembered what the subject was or what the speaker said" (Horn ix).

Although the commencement address is an epideictic address, it has a special function that separates it from other speeches of this type. The commencement speaker is expected to reinforce traditional values in order to advise the graduating class. As Linkugel, Allen, and Johannesen put it, the commencement address "speaks to the values which should be reflected in [the graduates'] future lives." (328). As I examine Iacocca's remarks, keep in mind three requirements: reinforcement of traditional values, reordering those values in light of present circumstances, and the use of this reordering to guide the audience.

IACOCCA'S RHETORICAL RESOURCES

Iacocca surely must have understood that he had to satisfy the ceremonial purposes of the occasion, that he must select values worthy of veneration, and that he must give those values memorable expression.[2] The strategies he chose to accomplish these tasks provide an interesting illustration of the business person taking an economic message to a general audience. Iacocca's speeches demonstrate how economic interests may be furthered by appeal to the nation's civic virtues.

The USC and MSU introductions formally satisfy the requirements of the occasion by recognizing the circumstances and announcing the speaker's purpose. Both addresses do this in nearly identical ways. "My job today," he tells the East Lansing audience, "is to impart the final wisdom you'll get here. I'm here to wrap up . . . everything you've learned from your professors . . . and everything you've figured out all by yourselves." Acknowledging the impossibility of the task, he quips, "And President DiBiaggio told me that I have to do all of that in just fifteen minutes."

Next, Iacocca previews the values that thematize the addresses. At USC in 1987, he exhorts the graduates to live a life filled with challenges. "So, I hope you're all leaving here today with a certain sense of *adventure*. I hope you're all itching, in fact, to climb a couple of mountains." Three years later at MSU, Iacocca tries to instill a sense of national pride and self-confidence. He tells the assembled students to take their pride of graduation and use it to reignite American self-confidence. "And it's okay for you graduates to take that feeling with you when you leave. In fact, that's my main message to you this morning. Walk out of here just a little full of yourselves because right now this country needs that pride as much as it needs the professional skills you've learned at Michigan State."

Having set out the themes, Iacocca's difficult rhetorical work begins. He had to assess the resources at his command. He must use these resources to impress the audience with the importance of the values he has come to honor. Among these resources is Iacocca's image. After all, there is something audacious about assuming the position of adviser, especially an adviser who presumes to counsel an audience about its values. Only speakers who are themselves perceived as virtuous have the moral standing to engage in epideictic discourse. "The character of the speaker," Aristotle writes, "is a cause of persuasion when the speech is so uttered as to make him worthy of belief; for as a rule we trust men of probity more, and more quickly, about things in general, while on points outside the realm of exact knowledge, where opinion is divided, we trust them absolutely" (Cooper 8).

Iacocca connected his public character to the content of these speeches. This we might refer to as a rhetorical enactment of virtue. The audience's trust, Aristotle counsels, "should be created by the speech itself, and not left to depend upon an antecedent impression that the speaker is this or that kind of [person]" (Cooper 8–9).

At USC, the message's theme—competitiveness—is consonant with Iacocca's own life. He celebrates competitiveness as both the personal virtue of facing tough challenges and an economic necessity in the new global economy. Yet, Iacocca introduces this theme with a personal anecdote about the ups and downs of his career. "Dr. Zumberge," Iacocca begins, "was very kind in his introduction, and I appreciate it very much. He said I left Ford after thirty-two years to take on a big challenge at Chrysler. And, by the way, he was nice enough to leave out a few of the *details*. Actually, what happened was . . . I got *fired*." Iacocca's failure at Ford and triumph at Chrysler provide the audience with a way of looking at him that is consistent with the point of the talk. As the USC speech progresses, Iacocca moves from his personal struggle to the corporate challenge. "Chrysler Corporation," he says, "is alive today not because those men and women went *looking* for a challenge (they would have been crazy to do that), but because they had the moxie to *accept* a challenge that all the so-called experts from Wall Street to Washington told them was hopeless."

The MSU speech has fewer speaker self-references. Partly, I suspect, this was because the Chrysler recovery was old news by this time, especially in Michigan. Also, I imagine Iacocca believed that this speech called for a subtler intertwining of his character and his theme. The MSU speech brought a message of renewed pride in America. Iacocca pointed to America's ethnic diversity as a chief source of this pride. He used his own Italian name and his strong public identification with the refurbishing of the Statue of Liberty and Ellis Island to create an authoritative position from which to discuss this issue. "Probably half of you here today," he says, "had parents, grandparents, or great-grandparents who first set foot in America on Ellis Island." Then, effectively adapting to the particular audience, he continues, "You only have to look through the mosaic of names in today's commencement program to see that legacy. Biondo . . . Jaworski . . . O'Reilly . . . Tatigian . . . Lee Valeski . . . and my favorite—Dallapiazza. I don't know where you are, Amy, but that one has a great ring to it! You beat my name—five vowels to four."

Once Iacocca has established his authority to speak, he tells his audience that they are part of a community defined by specific values. To say, in other words, that a person belongs to American society is to identify that person as committed to a set of values. We often take community as a phenomenon—an observable physical presence. We assume that demographics—location, citizenship, language—are synonymous with community. Yet this assuredly is not the case. Communities are distinguishable by the constellation of convictions people share. We share these convictions by giving allegiance to a discursive tradition.

Similarly, speakers frequently assume the audience is a fixed object—a sum of preexisting attitudes and beliefs held by the assembled listeners. Instead, the collective identity of an audience is crafted by the speaker's message.[3] A jury, for instance, is not simply a gathering of individual citizens but a collectivity that remakes itself into the deliberative body described in the judge's instructions. Likewise, the charge of the epideictic speaker is to recraft audience members into a community so that they may act collectively to address current circumstances. At both USC and MSU, Iacocca strived to recreate a sense of American identity and use that identity to argue for an approach to the nation's economic problems. He approaches this task differently in each address.

The USC speech presents Iacocca with a difficult challenge. The speech is filled with bad news. It is, in one sense, a long discourse on the failure of Iacocca's generation to preserve America's economic heritage. "We've suddenly sobered up to find that our trip through the 'feel-good' '80s has been chemically induced by a *dope* called *debt*. And I hate to be the one to bring you bad news, but we've run up that debt on *your* credit cards. *You* get to take care of the bills." He describes the debt as a disgraceful generational legacy. "Now, if I'm starting to stir you a little or even make you mad—that's good. . . . Because I am not *proud* of the kind of debt we're handing you. In fact, I'm truly embarrassed by it. Nobody stuck me with a due bill like this when I was your age."

His generation, Iacocca argues, abandoned the values that created America's prosperity. He, then, impresses on the audience the importance of returning to these older, sounder values. Rather than recalling old glories as a method of building community, he recounts recent mistakes as a rallying cry to return to firmer footing. "[W]e certainly have to blame *ourselves* for this blind consumption binge that we've been on. And we have to blame *ourselves* for worshiping so long at the altar of 'free trade' that we've become blind to how the world really works out there." This backdrop of failure introduces the call "to lead." "It's the job of leaders to set the *rules* . . . and to *enforce* the rules . . . and most important, when the rules don't work anymore, to *change* the rules."

The tenor of Iacocca's MSU remarks is more optimistic. Yet he still uses a variation on his USC strategy. He builds a value consensus—or community—by recounting attacks on American values. "A few years ago," he says, "the prime minister of Japan got in some hot water when he said that America was falling behind because we have so many minorities in our population." He continues, "The popular theory goes like this: Some countries have competitive advantages over the United States today because they are homogeneous societies. Everybody comes from the same racial stock, shares the same culture, and holds the same values. That all adds up to harmony and teamwork. They have common goals, and they work harder, longer, and smarter than we do to achieve them."

In rallying the audience to reaffirm core values Iacocca had a purpose beyond the rehearsal of familiar patriotic themes. He hoped to recraft the audience's definition of American community as a way of advancing an economic agenda. In essence, Iacocca's argument may be restated like this: "Given how you ought to see yourselves, this is the economic course you must insist upon."

ECONOMIC MESSAGE

Typically, epideictic speeches are set apart from policy addresses. The former are about increasing adherence to traditional values, and the latter are about urging action. Even casual reflection, however, reveals that politicians justify action by arguing that it is consistent with social values. Although epideictic speakers are rarely overt in pressing specific policies, they prepare audiences for later partisan appeals.

From this vantage point, Iacocca's commencement addresses are moral justifications for economic policies. This explains, for instance, why trade policy is an important subject in both speeches. At first, given the demands of the occasion, this seems odd. Yet, when reflecting on the virtues of self-confidence, competitiveness, and diversity, it is not surprising that trade would become an important example of these values. Moreover, the public's image of Iacocca is closely linked with the automobile industry's trade disputes with Japan.

In the USC address, the veneration of personal and economic competitiveness leads Iacocca to comment on the nature of leadership. In describing the crippling accumulation of debt, he discusses the failure of leadership in the 1980s. He proceeds to contextualize this failure in the realm of trade. "The largest maker of cars and trucks in the world," Iacocca tells the audience, "is no longer the *United States*—it's *Japan*. But for years now, the Japanese have taken 100 percent of their total worldwide automotive profits from just one, single market—ours." He continues, "We haven't had the same access to foreign markets, of course. We didn't even *ask* for it for a long time because we wanted to give our friends a chance to develop. But when they were up and running . . . we asked very politely for equal treatment, and their doors still stay *closed*." This, Iacocca argues, is a failure of leadership: "We should have pushed those doors open, but we didn't. That was also a failure of *leadership* . . . because leaders don't let themselves get pushed around." The consequences are that "we've shipped millions of American jobs overseas, and buried ourselves under a dung heap of public debt."

Iacocca's prescription is the triad of personal challenge, national competitiveness, and tough leadership. Given a recommitment to the proper values, America's political leadership can insist on open markets. "Today," Iacocca says, "the importance of the American market gives us all the muscle we need to forge a trading system that's fair to *us* and fair to our friends around the world. And it's that market that still makes us leaders in world trade—at least for a while longer." Our rapidly diminishing advantage makes leadership urgent. "But with leadership," he says, "you either *use* it or *lose* it. That's the great danger that America faces in our trade relations *today*, and that's the great danger we all face in the *years ahead.*"

At MSU, trade policy is again a central theme. Here, however, Iacocca weaves trade into a speech focusing on American self-confidence and diversity. Using the imagery of the Statue of Liberty and Ellis Island, Iacocca reminds audience members of their ancestors' courage in leaving their homeland to come to a country where they had to start over. "And man, they had it tough. They absorbed a new culture, learned a new language, and pledged their allegiance to a new flag." But more than merely inhabiting a place, these immigrants created a nation with the moral resolve to right what was wrong.

"Then," Iacocca continues, "they took a look around and found that this new world wasn't perfect. There was discrimination. Sometimes they weren't getting a fair shake, no matter how hard they worked. So they got together and helped to change some of the rules."

Iacocca portrays the immigrants' circumstances—as analogous to the graduates' situation. They are moving into a new economic world, a world of global competition. Moreover, they also are entering a new world where the rules are not fair, and no matter how hard they work they can not get a fair shake. "Like the other immigrants before you, you're walking into a game that is, in many ways, rigged against you. In this global economy of ours, we don't have much say anymore about the rules. And that's our own darn fault. We have used our strength as a nation to help see that other people around the world are treated fairly, but we haven't used it to demand fairness for ourselves in return."

As the story spins out, Iacocca adds another dimensions to the immigrant parallel. Xenophobic attitudes, expressed as ethnic and racial slurs, made blacks, Hispanics, Italians, Irish, Poles, and many others feel that they were inferior. They were led to believe that their economic condition was the result of a lack of natural ability. The same kind of charges have been leveled against America because of its ethnic diversity. "But never fall," Iacocca counsels, "for the phony idea that you aren't up to the job. If we've lost some of our competitiveness in this country, it's because we've made some mistakes, not because the people we're competing against are just naturally smarter and tougher than we are. And it's not because we don't all look alike, talk alike, act alike, think alike, salute the same ideas, and march to work in the morning singing the company song." The reason is the failure of leadership. "It's simply because some of our policies have been wrong."

At the conclusion of these two speeches, the audience is crafted into a people committed to a set of values that justify a change in American trade policy. The audience, moreover, is presented a tough, blunt, and plainspoken image of Iacocca. Thus, the speaker is consubstantial with the message. Finally, these images are starkly placed against a backdrop of failed American leadership. In this sense, Iacocca, Iacocca's policies, and Iacocca's America are embodiments of traditional national values.

CONCLUSION

Iacocca's performances bring an overarching impression to the commencement occasion. We might think of two kinds of judgment: first, the judgment made by the impartial spectator who looks down on the flow of events from a lofty perch and makes an evaluation; and, second, the judgment made by the person in the arena who makes an evaluation based on the practical lessons of experience.[4] The first form characterizes the academic life. The second form characterizes the world of business and politics.

Iacocca has been portrayed as America's "foremost symbol for 'hanging tough,' for 'toughing it out' under high-pressure nerve-wearing situations" (Furlong 72).[5] Everything about the USC and MSU commencement addresses creates credibility based on what the Greeks called *phronesis*, or practical wisdom. Iacocca speaks in the language of action—the words of tough leadership—to listeners who have just emerged from years of tutoring in the great ideas. His language is informal—contractions, colloquialisms, mild profanity—and his economic themes press immediate problems on the audience. Thus, these speeches mark the students' return to the world of practical affairs. By celebrating higher education as an important stage in the preparation for the world of hard knocks, Iacocca is able to make the transition appear a natural one.

Iacocca's efforts might be criticized on realist grounds. His recitation of American history is romanticized; his diagnosis of economic difficulties is nationalistic (Japan-bashing); and his leadership prescription is largely mythic (John Wayne as trade negotiator). Yet the epideictic speech invariably appeals to romance, nationalism, and myth. Every rhetorical enactment of collective identity, regardless of its appeal to the facts, emphasizes and deemphasizes, spins out one story and debunks another, and uses the results to further a cause. If the epideictic genre and its social purpose are properly understood, then I may safely conclude that Iacocca effectively negotiated the constraints of the occasion, the expectations of the audience, and the requirements of his economic purpose.

A critic can never know—for such knowledge is the province of the pollster—the effect of a given address on a particular audience. Yet, in these two cases, the fit among situation, speaker, and message was so snug that on the occasion of the USC and MSU graduates' twenty-year reunions, they will remember who spoke and, if not recalling precisely what was said, they will recollect the emotional texture of Iacocca's remarks.

NOTES

1. Rhetorical theorists continue to disagree about the defining qualities of the epideictic genre. See, for example, Kenneth Burke's *A Rhetoric of Motives* (71), Chaim Perelman and L. Olbrechts-Tyteca's *The New Rhetoric* (47–51), and Richard Weaver's *The Ethics of Rhetoric* (172). Also see more recent articles by Beale and Duffy.

2. Linkugel, Allen, and Johannesen list these as the three criteria for evaluating speeches to intensify social cohesion (329–31).
3. This notion is similiar to Michael McGee's concept of "The People."
4. This distinction is the subject of Ronald Beiner's *Political Judgment*.
5. For an interesting analysis of Iacocca as mythic hero, see Dionisopoulos.

WORKS CITED

Beiner, Richard. *Political Judgement*. Chicago: U of Chicago P, 1983.

Brubacher, John S. "Introduction: The Traditions of Commencement." *Go Forth, Be Strong: Advice and Reflections from Commencement Speakers*. Ed. Francis S. Horn. Carbondale, IL: Southern Illinois UP, 1978. xxv–xxxiii.

Burke, Kenneth. *A Rhetoric of Motives*. Berkeley: U of Calif P, 1969.

Campbell, Karlyn Kohrs and Kathleen Hall Jamieson. *Deeds Done in Words: Presidential Rhetoric and the Genres of Governance*. Chicago: U of Chicago P, 1990.

Cooper, Lane. *The Rhetoric of Aristotle*. Englewood Cliffs, NJ: Prentice-Hall, 1960.

Dionisopoulos, George N. "A Case Study in Print Media and Heroic Myth: Lee Iacocca 1978–1985." *Southern Speech Communication Journal* 53 (1988): 227–43.

Furlong, W. B. "Chrysler's Lee Iacocca." *Saturday Evening Post* March 1982: 72–75, 88, 91, 116.

Horn, Francis H., Ed. Preface. *Go Forth, Be Strong: Advice and Reflections from Commencement Speakers*. Carbondale, IL: Southern Illinois UP, 1978. ix–xxiv.

Linkugel, Wil A., R. R. Allen, and Richard L. Johannesen. *Contemporary American Speeches: A Sourcebook of Speech Forms and Principles*. 5th ed. Dubuque, IA: Kendall/Hunt, 1982.

McGee, Michael Calvin. "In Search of 'The People': A Rhetorical Alternative." *Quarterly Journal of Speech* 61 (1975): 235–49.

Perelman, Chaim and L. Olbrechts-Tyteca. *The New Rhetoric: A Treatise on Argumentation*. Trans. John Wilkinson and Purcell Weaver. Notre Dame, IN: U of Notre Dame P, 1969.

Stuller, J. "Lee Iacocca and an America that's Back on Its Feet." *Saturday Evening Post* Oct. 1984: 46–47, 104, 106, 110.

Weaver, Richard. *The Ethics of Rhetoric*. South Bend, IN: Gateway, 1953.

REMARKS AT THE UNIVERSITY OF SOUTHERN CALIFORNIA

Los Angeles, California, May 8, 1987

Iacocca gave a commencement speech nearly every year during the 1980s, and brought graduates the bad news that the country had been mortgaging their futures with ever-increasing federal budget deficits and weakening their ability ever to pay off that debt with poor fiscal and trade policies. When he spoke at USC, the country was riding high, but Iacocca warned that there was more illusion than reality to the good times. Six months later, the country had the worst stock market crash in its history.

Thank you, thank you very much.

President Zumberge, fellow honorees, members of the board of trustees, faculty members, distinguished guests, parents, and members of the Class of 1987 . . . I want to thank all of you for asking me to share this very *special* day with you.

As Dr. Zumberge said, my association with USC goes back almost seventeen years. So, it's good to be back on campus, and I am proud to be part of the "Trojan Family."

First, let me congratulate all of you graduates. This is *your* day, and I'm fully aware that one of the few things still standing between you and your degrees is *me*.

And I am smart enough not to stand in the way very long, *believe me*.

But I've got a duty here today, and I have to do it. Otherwise I won't get *my* degree. I haven't *earned it*, like you have, but I would like to *keep it*.

Now, that duty as your commencement speaker is to impart the final wisdom you'll get here at USC before the champagne gets warm!

But this is your day to pop a cork and *relax*. But don't overdue it, okay? Relax, but don't go to *sleep*, because tomorrow the *real* final exams start. And they'll go on for the rest of your lives. I'm going to try to give you a little peek at the exam, but I won't be able to help you with the answers. They are going to have to come from you.

Dr. Zumberge was very kind in his introduction, and I appreciate it very much. He said I left Ford after thirty-two years to take on a big challenge at Chrysler. And, by the way, he was nice enough to leave out a few of the

270

details. Actually, what happened was . . . I got *fired.* And I went to Chrysler because the auto industry happened to be my *life,* and because Chrysler was the *only game in town* at that moment, by the way, with an open seat.

I was not *looking* for a challenge, and neither were the thousands of men and women who surprised the world by bringing Chrysler back from the dead. We were all just trying to survive, that's all. No more—no less.

Chrysler Corporation is alive today not because those men and women went *looking* for a challenge (they would have had to be crazy to do that) but because they had the moxie to *accept* a challenge that all the so-called experts from Wall Street to Washington told them was hopeless.

You see, the *easiest* challenges are the ones you dream up for yourself; the *tough ones,* the really lousy ones, are those that just get dropped in your lap.

So, I hope you're all leaving here today with a certain sense of *adventure.* I hope you're all itching, in fact, to climb a couple of mountains. But here's my first piece of advice for you today: Don't go looking for *new* mountains to climb until you get to the top of the one *you're on.*

And the one you're on right now—the slope on which *my* generation has left *your* generation—is *steep,* and it's *strenuous,* and, I hate to tell you, a little *slippery.*

You're coming of age in a country that has begun to ask itself an awful, awful question . . . and one that it has never asked itself before—and I mean *never!* And the question is simple: Can we *compete? Competitiveness* has become the big buzzword all over the country, now. Especially in Washington, D.C., where, by the way, they don't really understand it. The question is: Can we keep going up that mountain that Americans have been climbing for two hundred years? Or have we reached the limit of our endurance? And will yours be the first generation not to go higher?

We're asking those questions all of a sudden because in the four short years that you graduating seniors have been in school here, there have been a few big changes off-campus.

When you came in as freshmen, the United States was the largest creditor nation in the world . . . American banks were the largest in the world . . . and Wall Street was the undisputed center of the financial universe.

As you graduate today, our country is the world's largest debtor with more debt spread around the globe than Mexico and Brazil *combined* . . . four of the five largest banks in the world today are in *Japan* . . . and so, as of two months ago, is the world's largest *stock exchange.*

When you were freshmen, America was still the breadbasket of the world, but today as you leave, more farmers are losing their land than at any time since the dustbowl days of the Great Depression.

And I'm sure you must have been told as freshmen, especially here in California, that America's world leadership in science and high-tech was insur-

271

mountable, and that it virtually *guaranteed* your future prosperity. Well, now we've got a trade *deficit* in high-tech. And we've just slapped some tough tariffs on the Japanese to try to deny them a worldwide monopoly in the most crucial technology of the day.

So, a lot's been happening while you've been in school. But you might say, "Hey wait a minute! Things don't *look* all that bad, do they?" Maybe you don't know it, but you are one of those rare classes that have gone all the way through school from your first day as freshmen to today, without even a hint of a recession—that's seventeen straight quarters of economic growth! The stock market has gone up since you arrived on campus that first day—it's gone up 1,100 points while you've been here. It went from 1,300 to 2,400 in the Dow Jones. Income is way *up* in those four years. Taxes are way *down.* These have really been the "feel good times," right?

Well, that's what we thought. But we've suddenly sobered up to find that our trip through the "feel-good" '80s has been chemically induced by a *dope* called *debt.* And I hate to be the one to bring you the bad news, but we've run up that debt on *your* credit cards. *You* get to take care of the bills.

While you've had your noses in the books, we've quietly been *doubling* the national debt. It took us two centuries to book our first trillion dollars of debt, and by the way, that included eight wars, a couple of depressions, the opening of the west, the Square Deal, the Fair Deal, the New Deal, the Great Society, and the terms of thirty-nine presidents!

But while you weren't looking, we just made it *2 trillion*—and we did that in just a little over five years—and those were five years of peace and prosperity.

Now, if I'm starting to stir you a little or even make you mad—that's good. That's what I'm supposed to do here today. Because I am not *proud* of the kind of debt we're handing you. In fact, I'm truly *embarrassed* by it. Nobody stuck *me* with a due-bill like this when I was your age. And nobody wondered out loud back then whether America could *compete*, because we had taught the whole world what *competing* was all about in the first place.

I sat in your place in those happy days at the end of World War II when America was flush with victory, and we were the new leaders of the whole world.

Believe it or not, back in those innocent days, a lot of people really thought we had a chance to build a *perfect* world, but a few things went wrong. There were a couple more wars (Vietnam) . . . there were eight recessions . . . there was Watergate . . . and a dozen other man-made disasters along the way.

However, in spite of all that, we did manage to wipe out a few diseases. We put a man on the moon. We produced more technological change than all of those who came before us, and I mean *combined.* And we made America, I think, a little bit more *just*, a little more *fair*, and maybe, just maybe, a little bit more *humane*.

To be honest with you, we're handing you more than anybody has ever passed on to their kids. Generations ahead of you were lucky if they inherited a little shack on the back forty. You're getting a big, beautiful mansion on a hill. That's what we're leaving you.

But just one thing before you get all choked up with gratitude—we haven't bothered to pay for all this yet. We're leaving you the *mansion*, all right, but it's got a little *mortgage* on it.

You've got a right to be mad about that mortgage, and if you're as smart as your degrees say you are, you're going to do something about it.

You've had a *theme* here at USC for the past couple of years. It's the theme for your half-billion-dollar fund-raising program. And I think it captures what this university has tried to *give* you, and also what it *expects* from you. That theme, of course, is *"Leadership for the Twenty-first Century."*

It's going to take a different kind of leadership to shoulder all this debt and keep moving up that mountain, because the twenty-first century is going to be different for America.

It's not going to be the *"American century"* again, for one thing. We're not going to *dominate* the twenty-first century like we have the twentieth. Hopefully, *nobody* will, by the way—it's better that way. We're going to have to *compete* for most of what we now *take for granted*, including our standard of living. And it takes stronger and wiser leadership to *compete* than it does to *dominate*.

Our domination and our leadership came by default, when you think about it—not because we *sought* it. We happened to be there to pick up the pieces after World War II, but no nation, and remember this, has ever exercised its domination more *generously*, or its leadership more *responsibly*, than we have. That's the legacy of the American century that we are going to leave to history, and it's a proud one. But that proud *legacy* may also turn out to be our *epitaph* if we don't learn to *compete* effectively in the world that we have so generously and so responsibly helped to create.

And today, we are *not* competing effectively. The red ink is up to our knees, and still *rising*. Of our twenty largest trading partners, we're in deficit with seventeen of them, now. Oh, we have small surpluses, very small, with Holland and Belgium and Australia, but after those countries, we have to rely on such lush and lucrative markets as Paraguay, Greenland, and, are you ready for this, the Falkland Islands! We even had surpluses with Russia, Vietnam, and Libya, believe it or not. But we've had trouble selling much of anything to our friends. There's a moral there someplace, but I won't get into it today.

273

In the four years that you seniors have been at USC, our cumulative trade deficit worldwide has totaled more than a half a trillion dollars. And that's why, as you graduate today, the headlines almost every day are warning of a *trade war*!

And there's plenty of blame for that. We can blame our friends overseas who have repaid our generosity with policies calculated to enrich themselves at our expense. We can blame them for flooding our open market while they shut us out of theirs.

But we certainly have to blame *ourselves* for this blind consumption binge that we've been on.

And we have to blame *ourselves* for worshiping so long at the altar of "free trade" that we've become blind to how the world really works out there. We've got this silly notion that it's a mortal sin to play by the rules everybody else is using—even to protect ourselves.

I always like to say we're like those few crazy hockey players who still refuse to wear helmets. And we're getting our brains beat out.

So there's lots of blame out there, but it's not the job of leaders just to *find blame*: It's the job of leaders *to lead*!

It's the job of leaders to set the *rules* . . . and to *enforce* the rules . . . and most important, when the rules don't work anymore, to *change* the rules.

I'm not bothered for a minute by the thought that America may not *dominate* the twenty-first century, but it scares the hell out of me to think that we might also give up our *leadership*.

I know for sure that we'll give it up if we don't get rid of this brutal debt load that we're carrying as a nation. *Debtors* aren't *leaders*. It's the guy *holding* the IOUs who calls the shots. I hope you people in business administration understand that. But our record of borrow and spend, borrow and spend —with the bills passed on to you, our *kids*—that's not the kind of record that makes you a world *leader*.

We're already seeing some of the dangers of that debt burden in the current trade debate, by the way. We're being warned now, literally warned, that we can't defend ourselves against some clearly unfair practices of our trading partners . . . because if we do, those countries will cut off the financing that we've become hooked on to cover the debt. Now, it's bad enough that we got hooked on their VCRs and their TV sets . . . now we're hooked on their *money*.

So we're becoming *hostages* to our own debt, and it doesn't take a degree from USC to figure out that *hostages* can't be *leaders*, either.

But we don't have to let ourselves be held hostage—to *anybody*—because even though the rest of the world can get along, and they can, without our steel, and our cars, and our grain, and even our high-tech now, we've got a hole card that tops anything the others can lay out on the table.

And it's called the *American market*. That's our ace of spades, don't forget it. None of the major trading nations of the world today can survive without the American market. More than 40 percent of Japan's exports come to this market. We take 48 percent of Taiwan's; and 40 percent of South Korea's; and we take 32 percent of the exports of the entire Third World as a whole.

And the profit numbers get even higher. The largest maker of cars and trucks in the world is no longer the *United States*—it's *Japan*. But for years now, the Japanese have taken 100 percent of their total worldwide automotive profits from just one, single market—*ours*.

We haven't had the same access to foreign markets, of course. We didn't even *ask* for it for a long time because we wanted to give our friends a chance to develop. But when they were up and running and in many ways, were even *more competitive* than we were, we asked very politely for equal treatment, and their doors still stayed *closed*.

We should have pushed those doors open, but we didn't. That was also a failure of *leadership*, by the way, because *leaders* don't let themselves get pushed around.

By not having the leadership to insist on fair and equal treatment, we've encouraged our friends to become overdependent on the American market. And I might add, in the process, we've shipped millions of American jobs overseas, and buried, ourselves under a dung heap of public debt.

We simply can't afford it any longer. Why am I saying we? *You* can't afford it any longer, because *you people* will have to pay off that debt—and you make no mistake about it!

But our friends overseas can't afford it, either. Remember, you never do anybody a favor in the long run by letting them become too *dependent* on you.

So, we're unfair to *ourselves*, and we're unfair to *them*, by allowing the United States to become the world's shopping mall—a giant bazaar where everybody comes to pitch a tent and peddle their wares—and there are no questions ever asked!

It's really time to start charging *admission* to the American market . . . and the price of a ticket has to be a little *fairness*, and a little *reciprocity*. If we're *leaders*, truly leaders, then it's our responsibility to set some rules, for a change.

By they way, I don't want to alarm you, there's not going to be a trade war. Maybe a little *skirmishing* for a while—but no war. Nobody *wants* one. Nobody will *win* one. It makes no sense, and it's absolutely unnecessary. But if we *do* have one, it will result not from a failure of *reason*, but again from a failure of *leadership*.

Today, the importance of the American market gives us all the muscle we need to forge a trading system that's fair to *us* and fair to our friends around

275

the world. And it's that market that still makes us leaders in world trade—at least for a while longer.

But with leadership, you either *use* it or *lose* it. That's the great danger that America faces in our trade relations *today*, and that's the great danger we all face in the *years ahead*.

Remember that as you prepare for leadership in the twenty-first century. *Use it or lose it!*

You are a long way from the top of that mountain I mentioned a couple of minutes ago. In fact, the top isn't even in sight. The end of the American century doesn't mean the decline of America. It simply means that millions of people around the world have looked at what we have here, and said, "Hey, we'd like a little of that, too."

That's part of the legacy of the American century. We can all be proud that the tide of human expectations throughout the world is rising because of our *example*, but it doesn't mean that it has to rise at our *expense*, does it?

You can go farther up that mountain, but only if you use your leadership. Don't believe all those who say that *your* generation will be the *first* generation of Americans that will have to settle for *less*. I don't believe that for a minute, so don't *you* believe it. When anybody says that to you, just tell 'em to get the hell out of your way!

Let me warn you, there are no road maps. Unfortunately, I can't leave you a road map today. You see, I don't know what kind of leadership it's going to take for America to compete in the twenty-first century. You're going to have to figure that out all by yourselves. You'll have to take a look at the problems, and you'll have to come up with your own solutions. And don't be scared—every generation has to do that.

This year, the country is celebrating the bicentennial of the Constitution. It may be, and probably is, the most brilliant document ever devised by the mind of man, but you can read it all day long and you won't find a single answer to the big problems that you face today.

There's nothing, absolutely nothing, in it that will tell you what kind of *leaders* to be for the twenty-first century. There's nothing in it to tell you how to protect the environment . . . or what to do about terrorists . . . or how to reduce the threat of nuclear war . . . or how to *compete* in the world. Nothing.

The founding fathers were too smart to tell you (or me)—two hundred years later—how to solve your problems. You see, they left us a little framework to protect our freedom, but they didn't tell you anything about how to *use* it.

So, I'm sorry, but I'm not going to tell you how to use it either, but I will leave you with a few hints on how *not* to use it. This is the lesson:

Don't look for all the answers neatly tucked away in one ideology or another, because you're never going to find them.

Don't let the people with the pat answers ever take over. The extremists (from *either* direction) will *always* screw things up if you put them in charge.

Don't be afraid to compromise when you *can't* win, and don't be afraid to dig in your heels and fight like hell when you think you *can*.

Don't be so idealistic that you can't see what's going on in the world around you, but don't be so pragmatic that you don't ever stand for anything.

Don't be afraid (you've heard this many times) to make mistakes, but for starters try to practice with the small ones, okay? And oh, don't make the same big mistake twice.

And finally, don't let anybody tell you that you can't keep going up that mountain . . . because with the brains you got from God and a little help from USC—you'll do just fine!

So, good luck to every one of you.

And fight on for Old SC—go get 'em, *Trojans!*

REMARKS AT MICHIGAN STATE UNIVERSITY

East Lansing, Michigan, June 9, 1990

Diversity was the topic. It was timely. Much was being written about the advantages that Japan and some other countries had over the United States because they had homogeneous populations. Iacocca reminded the graduates that America's diversity was a strength, not a weakness.

President DiBiaggio . . . members of the Board of Trustees . . . members of the faculty . . . parents . . . and the Michigan State University Class of 1990. Congratulations to all of you on a job well done, but especially to you graduates. This is your day, and I am profoundly grateful that you asked me to share it with you.

I'm a year late, however. I was invited to speak to the Class of 1989 here in the Breslin Center, but a funny thing happened on the way to graduation last year—the roof fell in! But now the place is up, and it stands as a living testimonial to one of the greatest Spartans of them all—Jack Breslin. Who, I'm proud to say, began his career at Chrysler.

Well, my job today is to impart the final wisdom you'll get here. I'm here to wrap up everything you've learned from your parents . . . everything you've learned from your professors . . . and everything you've figured out all by yourselves. And President DiBiaggio told me that I have to do all of that in just fifteen minutes.

But if he got his timekeeper from the NCAA, I guess I've got a little extra time!

Now, if there is one emotion that should fill this day for all of you, it is pride. You parents should be proud of the sacrifices you've made. You teachers should be proud of the direction you've given. And you graduates should be proud of what you've accomplished here and the degrees you'll be awarded today. This is the day to pop champagne corks and pat yourselves on the back.

And it's okay for you graduates to take that feeling with you when you leave. In fact, that's my main message to you this morning. Walk out of here just a little full of yourselves because right now this country needs that pride as much as it needs the professional skills you've learned here at Michigan State.

You see, you're taking your place in a society that is developing a fundamental problem: For the first time in over two hundred years, it's beginning to lose its self-confidence. And that's a danger bigger than any external threat we've ever faced as a nation.

There seems to be a national inferiority complex building in this country. And you see it clearly in the misconceptions some people have. Today America's economy is still the biggest in the world—double Japan's. But over half of all Americans actually believe that Japan's economy is bigger than ours.

And you see this inferiority complex especially in young people. Somebody interviewed a sampling of American high school kids, and I couldn't believe this. Our seventeen-year-olds are so intimidated by foreign competition, they think America has reached its peak . . . that we're now on our way down . . . destined to be second-class citizens of this world. Another interviewer talked to college kids. By the way, they're supposed to be smarter than high school kids. Right? Well, less than one-third say the United States will still be the world economic leader by the year 2000.

And of course, I see it in my business every day. Many Americans believe that any car built here in Lansing, or in Flint, or in Detroit is automatically inferior to anything that's shipped in from overseas—even before they kick the tires, take it for a ride, or look under the hood. If it's not foreign, they won't buy it.

If it's not Godiva chocolate, they won't eat it. If it's not a Gucci, they won't wear it. If it's not a Cuisinart, they won't cook with it. If it's not Perrier, they won't drink it.

Status today wears a trademark from Europe or the Far East. And you've heard all the reasons why: We don't care about quality anymore. Our workers are lazy. Our managers are all greedy and consumed by short-term thinking. We've lost the edge in technology. Our schools are lousy. We just don't have that fire in the belly anymore.

And then there's the one that really jolts me whenever I hear it—and that is that we're doomed because of our diversity. Now, if we ever start believing that, we are dead!

A few years ago the prime minister of Japan got in some hot water when he said that America was falling behind because we have so many minorities in our population. But what's worse is that I'm afraid too many Americans are beginning to believe that.

The popular theory goes like this: Some countries have competitive advantages over the United States today because they are homogeneous societies. Everybody comes from the same racial stock, shares the same culture, and holds the same values. That all adds up to harmony and teamwork. They have common goals, and they work harder, longer, and smarter than we do to achieve them.

Americans, on the other hand, are a motley group, a mixture of dozens of races and a hundred different cultures, with values that continually clash. We're in constant conflict. We can't team up to work toward common goals. And that's why we can't compete in this new, global economy we live in.

Now, if you've learned anything in the past four years, I hope you've learned that every generalization has enough truth to make it seductive, and enough hokum to make it dangerous.

The truth is, uniformity is an advantage ... but it's also an anchor on creativity ... a stifling sameness that most of you wouldn't tolerate for long.

And the truth is, diversity is a problem. We do fight each other too much. But that diversity is also our country's greatest strength. And that is something that we must never, ever forget.

We will always spend too much of our time arguing among ourselves or suing each other. That's what happens in a pluralistic society. Don't look for harmony, you won't find much of it. All those shanties that sprang up in protest here on campus this spring were symbols of competing ideas and competing interests. They sure wreck the landscape, but be thankful that nobody was allowed to go in and smash them down.

So, diversity—it isn't something we have to put up with ... it's something we have to be proud of.

Let me tell you a little story. It sounds like a parable, but it actually happened.

In 1984, an Indian politician visited New York and saw the Statue of Liberty standing in the harbor. He decided that he wanted to provide a symbol like it for his home state in India. He spent five years and $3 million carving a giant Buddha out of a mountainside. He had the roads widened to transport it. He built a platform in the middle of a lake on which to place it. And he hired a barge to get it there.

Then came the big day—March 10 of this year. The Buddha was placed on the barge. It was 50 feet tall ... 440 tons of solid granite—probably the largest monolithic statue anywhere in the world.

A hundred feet from shore, with thousands of people staring in horror, the giant figure toppled of its own weight and sank forever to the bottom of the lake.

What went wrong?

Well, back in '84, the man should have taken a closer look at Lady Liberty. He would have seen that she is not a monolith ... that she could not be a monolith and stand that straight and that tall ... that she was created piece by piece ... transported piece by piece ... and assembled piece by piece.

That's her strength. And it's our strength as a nation, as well. A beautiful mosaic, put together piece by piece over a two hundred-year period.

Next September—just a few hundred yards from the Statue of Liberty—I'll have the honor to participate in the reopening and the dedication of Ellis Island. It will be a museum honoring the 17 million immigrants who passed through it on their way to building a new life in America. Probably half of you here today had parents, grandparents, or great-grandparents who first set foot in America on Ellis Island.

You only have to look through the mosaic of names in today's commencement program to see that legacy.

Biondo . . . Jaworski . . . O'Reilly . . . Tatigian . . . Lee . . . Ehrnstrom . . . Vandenbrink . . . Obermiller . . . Valeski . . . and my favorite—Dallapiazza. I don't know where you are, Amy, but that one has a great ring to it! You beat my name—five vowels to four.

Now, I picked those names at random. I don't know any of you. But I know that every one of those names has a story attached to it. More than likely, it's a story that began in sheer desperation.

Think of this a minute—maybe your story started when the potato crop failed in Ireland. Or maybe when a young German got sick and tired of Europe's endless wars. Or when a Russian Jew had seen the cossacks tear up his village once too often. Or when a Mexican couldn't feed his family and came north to pick fruit for a few cents an hour.

Maybe it began in Africa three hundred years ago when a young woman was slapped in chains and brought here against her will in the smelly hold of a slave ship. Or maybe it happened only fifteen years ago when a Vietnamese family set out in a leaky boat hoping like hell that somebody would pick them up . . . that somebody would take them in.

A thousand different names . . . a thousand different stories. But stitch them all together and you have one huge saga. And it's our saga . . . our common heritage as Americans. All of us different. All of us forced to live together and accommodate those differences. And out of that came a nation that remains today, in spite of all our problems, a model for every other country in the world.

We are all the sons and daughters of people who found within themselves the guts to gouge out a whole new life in a strange new world. We are—and should be proud to be—a nation of immigrants.

And it's not over.

You see, you, the class of 1990, are immigrants again. You are being thrown into a strange new world that's going to be very different from the one your parents knew. This time, however, there's no long boat ride. This time that new world is coming to you.

And like the immigrants before you, you have to do two things: You have to adapt to this new world, and then you have to help change it—to help steer it on a straight and sensible course. That's what those 17 million brave people who came through Ellis Island did.

And man, they had it tough. They absorbed a new culture, learned a new language, and pledged their allegiance to a new flag. They learned first to tolerate, the Irish and the Italians were always fighting, then to accept, and finally to embrace people who were different from themselves.

Then they took a look around and found that this new world wasn't perfect. There was discrimination. Sometimes they weren't getting a fair shake, no matter how hard they worked. So they got together and helped to change some of the rules.

Like the other immigrants before you, you're walking into a game that is, in many ways, rigged against you. In this global economy of ours, we don't have much say anymore about the rules. And that's our own darn fault. We have used our strength as a nation to help see that other people around the world are treated fairly, but we haven't used it to demand fairness for ourselves in return.

We've thrown our market wide open to anyone who wants to play in it, and it's still the most lucrative market in the world, but we've stood by and let the same people who are getting rich in our market keep theirs virtually closed to us.

We're operating under antitrust and tax laws that don't apply to the competition. We have no economic game plan in this country to bring government, industry, and labor together to help America compete . . . while foreign governments and companies work hand in glove.

And here's perhaps the biggest problem of all. My generation has buried yours under a dung heap of debt—$3 trillion that you'll carry on your backs like a piano for a long time to come. And that's a burden that you simply shouldn't have to bear—because it's just not fair.

These are real problems. Everybody my age owes everybody your age an apology for leaving these problems to you. We created them. Now you have to help fix them.

But never fall for the phony idea that you aren't up to the job. If we've lost some of our competitiveness in this country, it's because we've made some mistakes, not because the people we're competing against are just naturally smarter and tougher than we are. And it's not because we don't all look alike, talk alike, act alike, think alike, salute the same ideas, and march to work in the morning singing the company song.

It's simply because some of our policies have been wrong. When your country's economic and trade policies are weak . . . you're bound to lose. That is a simple fact of life in the world we live in today. You will lose no matter how good or bad your schools are, how good or bad your technology is, how good or bad your workers are. When you let somebody else write the rules—you will lose. (Just trust me on this one!)

And yet every time we set a new record for our trade deficit, or another American industry starts to disappear, we hear somebody—thinking he's being original—quote from, of all people, Pogo. How many times have you heard it? You know, the tired old line about "We have met the enemy and he is us." Well, graduates, here's one last item to write down in your notebooks: Pogo was full of crap!

Self-criticism has always been one of our strengths in this country, but lately it has gone too far. Healthy self-criticism has turned into irrational self-doubt. We've been blindly blaming ourselves for every one of our problems. And that's just as dumb as never accepting any blame.

This self-doubt is even more irrational when you take a look at what's been happening in Eastern Europe just since last fall. One after another, East Germany, Hungary, Czechoslovakia, Poland, and Rumania are ending up with democratic governments almost overnight . . . and Gorbachev has old Mr. Lenin spinning in his tomb.

And where did the inspiration for all this come from? Why is it that Lech Walesa has read the American Bill of Rights over and over so often that he practically has it memorized? Or think of Vaclav Havel. Just last October 27, he was tossed into the slammer in Czechoslovakia. Two months later he was elected president of his country. And two months after that he was in Washington quoting Thomas Jefferson to the U.S. Congress.

The biggest irony of all is that Americans are beginning to doubt themselves just when so much of the rest of the world is turning to our example, and saying, "Yeah, that's the kind of country I want to live in." Nobody seems to have noticed that we appear to have won the Cold War. We should be patting ourselves on the back: We stood up to totalitarianism for forty-five years . . . spent billions to defend the free world, think about it—that's a term that may even be going out of style . . . we fought two bloody wars . . . gave billions in aid to old friends and old enemies alike . . . and accepted the awesome responsibility of world leadership.

But leadership is like any other responsibility you're given in life—you either use it or you lose it. We used it to protect our vital political interests around the world, and the Berlin Wall is now sold in small chunks as souvenirs of our success. We did not use that leadership to protect our vital economic interests, however, and we wind up the biggest debtor nation in the history of the world.

Now, my generation hasn't been completely asleep at the switch. The world really is a lot better off than we found it. But we left a big challenge for you, too.

They say that you are graduating at the end of the American century. You'll be hearing that term a lot in the '90's—the end of the American century. Don't be afraid, that doesn't mean the United States is washed up. It simply means that from now on America must compete in a world that it no longer dominates. It means that you don't have a head start like I did.

It means that you are all immigrants in a new world, again. You're going to have to adapt to it, and you're also going to have to help change it. That's the simple challenge we've left you.

But you're up to it, I know that. People before you have done it, and so will you. With the heritage you got from your families, and the brains you got from God, and the education you got from Michigan State, you'll do just fine. As long as you understand where you've come from . . . don't listen to all the doom-and-gloom guys around you . . . never regard your diversity as anything but your greatest strength . . . and never, but never believe that the end of the American century means the end of the American Dream.

Good luck and Godspeed to all of you.

8. Lee Iacocca's Addresses Concerning Education

Gustav W. Friedrich

As this book testifies, Lee Iacocca was a frequent and successful public speaker. In the foreword to this book, he tells us that "I don't know how many speeches I gave in my forty-six years in the auto industry, but it was easily more than a thousand. By actual count, I gave 663 during my fourteen years at Chrysler." That translates to an average of about fifty speeches a year. In choosing opportunities to speak, Iacocca was forced to be selective. Kurt Andersen, writing a cover story on Iacocca for the April 1, 1985, issue of *Time*, tells us that "Of the more than 3,000 speaking engagements he was offered last year, he accepted only 46" (33). "During January and February alone, Iacocca was asked by 1,270 different groups to give speeches" (30).

Whether the audience was an internal one (Chrysler employees, dealers) or an external one (governors, newspaper editors), the focuses for most of Iacocca's speeches were themes directly related to the auto industry—perfectly natural for a business communicator. The three major exceptions are the speeches on broader social themes contained in this section—commencement addresses, addresses concerning education, and addresses about the Statue of Liberty renovation. In these speeches, instead of serving primarily as a business communicator, Iacocca championed what he perceived to be significant causes for the preservation of democracy and the American experience. He spoke as a business statesman. The issue to be explored in the next few pages is Iacocca's selection of education (from a vast array of potential topics) as an issue to be addressed publicly. The most obvious explanation of Iacocca's choice of education as a speech topic is a self-centered one—education and educated workers are good for business. It is this theme, in fact, that he highlights in both his speeches on the topic and in his discussion of the "school crisis" in Chapter 13 of *Talking Straight*: "I'm a hard-nosed businessman, and mostly I worry about how the hell we are going to compete in this new world."

Had "education is good for business" been Iacocca's only motivation for speaking on an important social issue, however, it is unlikely that Dionisopoulos would have been able to locate a large quantity of media statements proclaiming Iacocca as a "national folk hero" and one of the country's most admired figures. It is also true that in Iacocca's message, education is necessary to the maintenance of democracy and the American Dream. In exploring these speeches, then, we can learn something about how Iacocca viewed the relationship among education, business, and democracy. Before exploring an additional (and more personal) answer to the question of motivation for speaking on education, it is useful to explore Iacocca's development of "his education and educated workers are essential" thesis. It is developed in three parts.

A COUNTRY'S ABILITY TO COMPETE IN THE GLOBAL ECONOMY DEPENDS ON ITS EDUCATION SYSTEM

The first theme is a common one in the reports of the 1980s on the status of education. Starting with the National Commission on Education's well-publicized report, *A Nation at Risk*, educational reformers have focused on the implications of the changing nature of the world economy for our educational system. The heart of the argument is that our current system of education evolved in the context of an economy based on mass production. Thus, the goal of education was to inculcate routine skills and to facilitate the acquisition of a stock of facts. People with these skills can use machines to produce goods that lead to a good standard of living for all. Now, however, the basis of a nation's economic strength has shifted to become knowledge-based. Thus, the focus of schooling must shift from teaching to learning, from the passive acquisition of facts and routines to the active application of ideas to problems. This is a theme that Iacocca addresses both in his speeches and in his autobiography. In Chapter 13 of *Talking Straight*, for example, he writes: "A country's competitiveness starts not on the factory floor or in the engineering lab. It starts in the classroom. We've got to get cracking on education —at all levels—or we'll get run over by the Far East" (Iacocca and Kleinfield 232). "To me, education is the price of admission into our democracy. Having a strong long-term educational program is the core of a good strong nation" (233).

Iacocca's first theme, then, is that having citizens who are well educated is the only way that the nation will be able to compete with countries like Japan and Germany. In short, without an educated workforce, according to Iacocca, it is impossible for America to maintain its current level of economic opportunity and standard of living. This economic opportunity is central to the larger notion of the American experience of sacrifice, hard work, and a better life he addressed so eloquently in the Statue of Liberty speeches.

THE EDUCATION SYSTEM IS NOT CURRENTLY PREPARING STUDENTS TO COMPETE

Iacocca's second theme is that the educational system is failing to produce individuals who can compete in the global economy. In developing this theme, he argues that education is doing less well today than it did when he went to school. "We're not progressing; in fact, we're going backwards. I have to wonder about a country in which two out of three high school juniors don't know in which century the Civil War was fought. I have to wonder about a country in which one out of five high school kids believes the telephone was invented after 1950. I really have to wonder about a country in which 700,000 kids who graduated from high school in 1986 couldn't read their diplomas!" (Iacocca and Kleinfield 232).

Iacocca argues that the failure of the educational system is especially severe in the inner city—a part of our society of special concern to Iacocca. In a speech to the National Education Association, he illustrates his concern by describing Chrysler's gamble in choosing to build a new plant in inner city Detroit next to the Jefferson Avenue Assembly Plant—one of Chrysler's oldest plants (1907) and one employing three thousand people: "we'll be drawing our work force from a city where the daily school attendance rate is below 75 percent . . . and where barely half the students who enter high school ever graduate. We'll get them from a school system that is almost bankrupt, run by a board that once voted themselves personal chauffeurs and paid those drivers more than they paid the teachers in the schools. We'll get those workers from a school system that spends less than 30 percent of its budget on basic education."

Because the educational system is failing, Iacocca argues, American business has been forced to assume an additional burden: "Things are so bad that three out of four U.S. corporations—Chrysler is one of them—are forced to train new workers in basic reading, writing, and arithmetic. It's reckoned that the lost productivity is tacking on a whopping $25 billion a year in costs to American industry" (Iacocca and Kleinfield 233).

287

PREPARING STUDENTS TO COMPLETE IN THE GLOBAL ECONOMY REQUIRES THAT GOVERNMENT, INDUSTRY, PARENTS, AND TEACHERS COOPERATE TO IMPROVE THE EDUCATION SYSTEM

The solution to the crisis in education is found in cooperation among the principle parties, reminiscent of the same cooperative efforts that proved so powerful when Chrysler faced down its own crisis. Iacocca's proposed remedy has four subthemes: first, the government must provide adequate funding; second, American business should follow Chrysler's example and provide guidance and support; third, parents must become actively involved in the educational enterprise; and fourth, the major portion of educational funding should go to teachers who teach kids the basics—how to read, write, speak, and count.

The government must provide adequate funding. In his autobiography, Iacocca differentiates between other government-sponsored programs, "a farm program that goes up and down year to year, a defense program that is also as adjustable as a yo-yo," and education. Education is a program "that no government should tamper with—except to improve them" (Iacocca and Kleinfield 233). Iacocca also points out the danger of limiting funding. "In 1986 the administration proposed cutting $5 billion out of education at the same time that the president told all of us that America had to get more competitive. Who's he kidding? As Derek Bok the head of Harvard, put it: 'If you think education is expensive, try ignorance'" (233). Iacocca's first point, then, is that government must provide education with adequate, dependable, and stable funding.

Industry should provide guidance and support. For his second point, Iacocca describes what Chrysler has done to help education and suggests that other companies ought to be similarly involved. Chrysler, Iacocca reports, made 1989 the "year of education" by (1) spending more than $3½ million to sponsor a five-part PBS series entitled "Learning in America," (2) making a half-million-dollar grant to the National Board for Professional Teaching Standards, and (3) contributing $2.1 million to a Reading Is Fundamental Project called "Running Start." In Chapter 13 of *Talking Straight*, Iacocca tells us that "A few years ago, Bob McNamara's wife, Margie, got me involved with Reading Is Fundamental, an organization committed to teaching kids to read. There are few things I feel more strongly about" (241).

In Iacocca's view, then, industry has an important stake in the production of an educated citizenry—industry can only be globally competitive with an educated workforce. Because industry stands to benefit, it has a unique obligation to provide leadership and economic support. Thus, it is imperative that industry provide both guidance (e.g., Chrysler made a choice to emphasize teaching and reading) and support for the educational enterprise.

Iacocca's third point is that parents must be actively involved in the education of their children: "I picked up the paper on the plane just a week ago today and saw Mrs. Futrell being quoted 'that only 25 percent of parents ever visit their children's schools.' That's unbelievable! I saw that and thought to myself, 'How the hell could I control my product quality if I never even got to talk to 75 percent of my suppliers?' I have to get my suppliers involved in my business or I can't fit those twelve thousand parts together and make a car. I'd build a lousy product that couldn't compete. If you can't get the parents involved, I don't know how you fit all the parts together into that complex mosaic called a human being!"

Iacocca's final point is that the educational system needs to focus its resources on important things—decent salaries for teachers who teach the basic skills. In Iacocca's message, the teacher is the heart of the educational experience. Scarce resources should not be wasted on additional administrators, counselors, or athletic coaches. In addition, Iacocca suggests, the focus needs to be on the early years of schooling. "My feeling is that the quality of an education depends more on how you introduce kids to the basics than on how many days you keep them at it. To me, the ten-year span from kindergarten through the ninth grade is the crucial period in the educational cycle. . . . Because I believe it's the ages from five to fifteen that really shape a person, I think this country puts too much emphasis on secondary schools" (Iacocca and Kleinfield 234–235).

AN ALTERNATIVE RATIONALE

While Iacocca's status as a hard-nosed businessman is no doubt sufficient rationale for his decision to speak out on education, an equally compelling rationale is contained in his personal history. As he tells us in *Iacocca: An Autobiography*, Iacocca attributes much of his career success to education—and especially to that portion of his education he received in the public schools of Allentown, Pennsylvania. After high school, Iacocca went to Lehigh University. At Lehigh, he switched from mechanical to industrial engineering, took business and psychology courses, and worked on the school paper. Upon graduation, he went to Princeton for a master's degree. What, then, are the features of his education that Iacocca wishes to see available to students today? They are basically three: parental involvement and concern, teachers who know how to motivate students, and an early mastery of educational basics.

An important source of Iacocca's motivation for achieving success in school, according to him, was his father. As he describes it: "When I was a kid, being a good student was very important to me. And in case I ever forgot just how important it was, I always had my father around to remind me" (Iacocca and Kleinfield 231). "With all my extracurricular activities, I still managed to graduate twelfth in a class of over nine hundred. To show you the kind of expectations I grew up with, my father's reaction was: 'Why weren't you first?' To hear him describe it, you'd think I flunked!" (Iacocca and Novak 17).

In addition to his father, Iacocca attributes his motivation to succeed to the use of competition by teachers: "When I was in school, the teachers motivated us by turning drudgery into a competition. In my junior-high English class, for instance, we had to write a five-hundred-word essay that was due every Monday. We would get a gold star for an outstanding paper. During the course of that year, those students who received three gold stars hit the jackpot: They didn't have to write any more essays. You'd better believe everyone worked on those papers until their eyes were blurry and their fingers ached. I know I did more drafts than I do today on my speeches and columns" (Iacocca and Novak 243).

In addition to parental involvement and motivating teachers, Iacocca saw an early focus on mastering educational basics as central to his later success in both education and business. Among the most important basics was an ability to communicate effectively: "By the time I was ready for college, I had a solid background in the fundamentals: reading, writing, and public speaking. With good teachers and the ability to concentrate, you can go pretty far with these skills" (Iacocca and Novak 18). By recognizing the influence of his teachers, Iacocca set the teaching profession apart: "I still remember the teachers who molded me in elementary and high school" (16).

Iacocca has often distinguished his own education on the basis of lessons about communication: "The most important thing I learned in school was how to communicate." This included writing weekly essays and enriching his vocabulary with the "Word Power Game from *Reader's Digest*. Without any advance warning [the teacher would] rip it out of the magazine and make us take the vocabulary test. It became a powerful habit with me—to this day I still look for the list of words in every issue of the *Digest*" (Iacocca and Novak 16).

The written word and vocabulary power were combined when "Miss Raber started us on extemporaneous speaking. I was good at it, and as a result I joined the debating team, which was sponsored by Mr. Virgil Parks, our Latin teacher. That's where I developed my speaking skills and learned to think on my feet" (16). This is where Iacocca learned perhaps his most important lesson: "You can have brilliant ideas, but if you can't get them across, your brains won't get you anywhere" (16). The ability to communicate, instilled by a high school teacher and debate coach, was a basic skill upon which much of his subsequent career as executive, corporate leader, and business statesman was built.

CONCLUSION

Iacocca's messages about education in many ways tell more about his worldview than any other set of speeches in this volume. In these addresses, Iacocca speaks to all the critical constituencies including teachers, parents, government, business, and the students themselves. He urges cooperation and responsiblility in finding solutions. Business, as a primary beneficiary of an educated workforce, has a special obligation. Business is part of the larger social structure and must take steps to ensure quality in education much as it must be involved with suppliers to ensure the quality of parts.

But education is not just part of business, economic gain, and the creation of wealth in Iacocca's worldview. It is part of the larger democratic and social system unique to America. It is essential not only to economic success, prosperity, and competitiveness but to personal freedom, liberty, and independence. Even in his remarks to first-graders about the importance of reading, the fundamental value of education in self-discovery and personal growth is evident: "The most important things you'll own are your books, so treat them like they're your treasures, because they are."

In summary, then, it is likely that Iacocca chose to make speeches on educational issues for both professional and very personal reasons. As a hard-nosed business person, he knew that educated workers are a necessary foundation for global economic competition. Equally compelling, however, was the fact that Iacocca attributes his career success to participation in an educational system that helped him develop important basic skills. Based on both sources of motivation, education is central to Iacocca's view of America—a land of great opportunity where one can work hard, sacrifice, become educated, and, as a consequence, become successful. Whatever his true motivation for speaking on education, it is the case that Iacocca's involvement with and advocacy for an important social issue is both unique and important for a business communicator. It may even partially explain why Iacocca is in very select company with few peers—an individual identified with big business who is widely liked and admired rather than respected or feared.

WORKS CITED

Andersen, Kurt. "A Spunky Tycoon Turned Superstar." *Time* 1 April 1985: 30–39.

Dionisopoulos, George N. "A Case Study in Print Media and Heroic Myth: Lee Iacocca 1978–1985." *Southern Speech Communication Journal* 53 (1988): 227–243.

Iacocca, Lee A. and William Novak. *Iacocca: An Autobiography.* New York: Bantam, 1984.

Iacocca, Lee A. and Sonny Kleinfield. *Talking Straight.* New York: Bantam, 1988.

REMARKS TO THE NATIONAL EDUCATION ASSOCIATION

San Diego, California, March 3, 1989

The decline of America's schools was an issue that frequently got Iacocca's blood pressure to rise. Just as he did with lawyers in San Francisco, he told teachers in San Diego the blunt truth about what was expected of them.

Thank you, and good evening, ladies and gentlemen. It's a real pleasure for me to be here to kick off your conference. I accepted your invitation with enthusiasm because I decided to make 1989 the year of education for both myself and for my company. We're going to get deeply involved—I hope for the good of all of us, and our children. Tonight I first want to congratulate you on your theme—"Education and the New Economy." By "new" economy I assume you mean the "global" economy we live in today. We're still trying to come to grips in this country with the uncomfortable idea that we really *do* live in a single, worldwide economy that we don't have a lot to say about. At least, not as much as we used to.

We're being forced to realize that two oceans, and a huge military, and a wealth of natural resources, and a strong, stable political system don't give us the kind of protection they once did.

What we're finding out—the hard way—is that the United States of America is dangerously vulnerable like we've never been vulnerable before.

And one place we seem to be most vulnerable is in our education system. We all know our schools have problems, but different people probably see those problems in different ways.

You as educators, for example, must hemorrhage a little inside whenever you think of the wasted human potential in functional illiteracy rates that run 30 percent in this country.

If you're a sociologist, you have to be scared about the future of a democracy in which one in five adults believes the sun revolves around the Earth, can't name even a single country in Europe, and doesn't have the foggiest idea where the Pacific Ocean is!

If you're an economist, you have to wring your hands about ever getting this country's fiscal house in order when 75 percent of U.S. high school students don't know what inflation is . . . 66 percent don't know what profits are

293

. . . and 55 percent don't have a clue as to what a government budget deficit is.

Well, I worry about wasted minds, too . . . and about economic illiteracy. But first of all I'm a hard-nosed businessman, and mostly I worry about how the hell we are going to compete in this new world.

And my first worry is schools—schools that equip our kids to compete—that's my main concern.

Let me tell you why I'm concerned by telling you about Chrysler's Jefferson Avenue Assembly Plant. It's the oldest plant we have, going all the way back to 1907. It's not productive enough anymore. The technology and the structure itself are out of date. So it has to go.

But it happens to be one of the few plants of its size left in the Detroit inner city. Almost three thousand people work there. If the plant goes, so do those jobs, and so does the economic base of a whole section of Detroit. It would accelerate the industrial flight from the inner city which has been going on for more than twenty years.

So we made a tough decision a couple of years ago to build a brand-new plant right next to the old one. If you follow our industry, you know that new auto plants these days are built in rural areas of Ohio, Tennessee, Kentucky or Illinois. You just don't put them in the inner city. But we are. I don't know if that's the smart thing to do, but for a lot of reasons, we think it's the right thing to do.

We're taking a helluva risk, though. That plant will come on line in a few years and will immediately have to compete with the most productive plants in Japan, Korea, and Europe. That'll take skilled workers equal to those overseas. And we'll be drawing our workforce from a city where the daily school attendance rate is below 75 percent . . . and where barely half the students who enter high school ever graduate.

We'll get them from a school system that is almost bankrupt, run by a board that once voted themselves personal chauffeurs and paid those drivers more than they paid the teachers in the schools.

We'll get those workers from a school system that spends less than 30 percent of its budget on basic education. Can you believe that? Seventy percent of the budget goes for various support services and less than one-third goes to teach kids how to read, write, and count.

Now, we had an election recently and a group of reformers got on the school board promising to get the schools turned around in Detroit. I hope they do, because I'll let you in on a little secret. Our new Jefferson Avenue plant—after we invest approximately a billion dollars in it—won't be able to compete if they don't.

We're already spending $117 million a year on training at Chrysler. But it doesn't all go to train workers how to run computers, or robots, or stamping presses. A big part of it goes to teach our people the three R's they didn't learn in school. In some of our plants we have about 25 percent of our people reading at grade 6 or below, many of them functionally illiterate.

We're not unique at Chrysler, by the way. Nationally, I'll bet you didn't know this, American industry spends more money each year teaching remedial math to its employees than all the grade schools, high schools and colleges spend on math education—combined!

Now, the worst part is that these people are competing against a Japanese workforce that has no illiteracy problem functional or otherwise, and whose math and science skills are way beyond ours.

It's enough to really get you down. I keep looking for some good news, but there isn't any. Well, I take that back. Last June I picked up the *New York Times* and right below the box that says "All The News That's Fit to Print" was a glowing story that told me "the back-to-basics movement in education has succeeded in assuring that almost every American high school graduate can now handle basic arithmetic."

That's news? "Man bites dog"—that used to be news. Now if our kids can make change for a dollar by the time they graduate from high school—that's supposed to be news!

Now, we all know that the schools are just a reflection of society itself, and fixing the problem is going to take government, and parents, and industry, and everybody else accepting part of the responsibility.

We're trying to do our part at my company. Like most companies our size, we've got a scholarship program for employee children . . . and a matching program for employee contributions to education . . . and we've had cooperative programs with local schools to keep potential dropouts in school.

But these things are just part of being a good corporate citizen. As I said at the beginning, this year we made up our minds to make education our number one extracurricular activity. Let me mention a few of the things we're doing.

First, beginning on March 27, we're sponsoring a five-part PBS series entitled "Learning in America." It's being produced by the McNeil-Lehrer people, with Roger Mudd as the host. It may not match "Lonesome Dove" in the ratings, but it could be the most important TV series of the year, and I hope all of you will try to make it mandatory viewing.

The opening segment will focus on my special concern—educating our kids to be able to compete. Another will discuss equality in education—does every kid get an equal chance? Another will be on you, the American teacher. Another will look at the curricula—are we teaching the right things and teaching them well enough? And the last hour will discuss accountability— are we getting our money's worth?

We're spending a bundle—over three and a half million dollars—on "Learning in America" because we think improving American education starts with everybody understanding the problem, and everybody understanding what will happen to this country if our schools are not world class.

Secondly, we've just made a half-million-dollar grant to the National Board for Professional Teaching Standards. This is a new organization, just over a year old. Mary Hatwood Futrell is on the board. The aim is to create for the first time a set of national standards and an accreditation process for teachers. They won't replace the state requirements already in place, but they will help give your profession the stature it deserves.

Then—and this may be the most lasting contribution we can make—we just provided the largest grant in history, $2.1 million, to Reading Is Fundamental. That's a program I've been involved in since it began.

The money will support a project we're calling "Running Start." It will focus on nine communities where we have plants, and provide books to first graders along with a structured program to motivate these youngsters to read.

These first-graders next fall will be the first high school class to graduate in the twenty-first century. They'd better be equipped to compete in that century. And I can't think of a better way to prepare them than to make sure they can read.

I've learned that the average primary school student in this country only spends seven or eight minutes a day actually reading. Maybe that's our whole problem, or at least the root of it.

Reading really is fundamental to everything else. And it has to start young. A child who falls behind in reading falls behind in everything. That's why I think for at least the first six years, every class should be a reading class and every teacher a reading teacher. I don't care what the subject—geography, science, arithmetic—every class has to push reading skills.

That's because an American kid who can't compete in the classroom with a foreign kid when he's twelve almost certainly won't be able to compete in the marketplace when he's thirty. Especially if he can't read. What happens at Harvard doesn't matter so much as what happens in the grade school down the street.

And that's our focus at Chrysler. We're trying to create some awareness by sponsoring "Learning in America." We're supporting new standards to elevate the stature of the teaching profession. And we're doing what we can to give kids a running start through Reading Is Fundamental.

We're not kidding ourselves, though. These programs, and others like them, won't get our schools' and our kids' performance up to where we want it. In the end, that's going to be up to you. We're doing these things because we want to help. We've got a huge stake in our schools, and it's frustrating to sit on the sidelines and see our kids fall behind students in other countries.

Remember, we're already handing them a $2.6 trillion national debt load to carry for the rest of their lives because of our selfish and irresponsible fiscal policies in recent years. Now, it seems, we're also denying them the educational tools they'll need to compete in the world, so they can pay off that debt, and maybe even enjoy the same standard of living we've had during our lives.

Now, I'm fully aware that simply comparing our test scores to those in Japan and Europe and other countries can be misleading. You can say our social values are different. We don't just concentrate on our brightest kids, we try to educate everybody. We're a multiculture country, and that puts different demands on the schools.

Nobody is suggesting that our values are wrong, but make no mistake about it, if we lose the ability to *compete*, we'll lose all those values, too.

Like it or not, that means competing in an increasingly high-tech world. Right now, 60 percent of the engineering Ph.D.'s granted from American colleges and universities go to foreign students—students who take that knowledge back home and then beat our brains out in the marketplace. Japan graduates ten engineers for every lawyer each year, and we graduate ten lawyers for every engineer. Doesn't that alone tell you something?

That's why we at Chrysler are doing what little we can. And I know how little it is. I tell my people all the time that we compete on the factory floor. The rest of us are just there for support. Same thing with the schools. The job has to be done in the classroom. The rest of us can only provide some support.

Money is a big part of that support, of course. We'll spend $328 billion on education this year, more than for any other public service, including national defense. And we spend a lot more of our GNP on education than any of our overseas competitors—including Japan and Germany.

How we spend those billions, however, is something else. I already told you about the school board chauffeurs in Detroit making more than the teachers. Does anybody in their right mind want to try and defend that one?

There are slightly more administrative and support personnel in education today than there are classroom teachers, and the gap is growing. Some of us can remember when the only support personnel were a couple of custodians and the ladies who ran the lunch room.

At Chrysler, 90 percent of our employees are directly involved in designing, engineering, building, and selling cars and trucks. If I had half of my people doing administrative or support work, I'd be out of business in a couple of months.

I know about overhead better than anybody. When I came to Chrysler it was killing us. I cut our white-collar force in half—from forty thousand to twenty thousand. And we went from building ten cars per employee per year in our plants to twenty, now it's twenty-three. It's called productivity, making the best of your investment. That's how you compete. And it can't be a lot different in your business.

Some schools—parochial schools—seem to do just fine without all the extra help. In Chicago, there is one "administrator" for every 133 students in the public schools and one for every 6,250 in the parochial schools. In New York City, it's one for every 147 kids in public schools and one for every 4,200 in the parochial schools.

I hate to tell you, but before the schools get a lot of sympathy from the voters for more money, they have to show they know what to do with the money they have. And spending only 30 percent of the school budget on basic education, I hope Detroit is not typical, gets you no sympathy at all.

At Chrysler Motors, nine out of every ten dollars in our budget go to produce cars and trucks. Why? Because that's what we're in business to do.

Well, the schools are in business to teach. And I think somebody had better take a close look at every dime that isn't spent to teach.

The most important employee in the school is the teacher. Somehow, I don't think I'm going to get a big argument about that here. But when I say "teacher," I'm talking about that man or woman who's actually standing up in front of the class trying to dilate a mind or two. I'm not talking about guidance counselors or football coaches or curriculum supervisors. They are the rear-echelon support troops, in my book.

That's one bias of mine that you won't ever shake, by the way. And maybe nothing says more about the decline of American education than what's happened to the prestige of classroom teaching in this country. The biggest difference between the American and Japanese schools may not be the test scores, but the fact that teachers in Japan are revered and honored, while teachers in this country are usually regarded, I hate to say it, but it's true, as just another public employee group. By the way, do you know who else the Japanese put on a pedestal? Well-educated factory workers!

We're really upside down. In a completely rational society, teachers would be at the very tip of the pyramid, just above "king," not near the bottom. In that society, the best of us would aspire to be teachers, and the rest of us would have to settle for something less. Passing civilization along from one generation to the next ought to be the highest responsibility and the highest honor anyone could have.

Too bad we don't live in that perfect world. In pay and prestige, teaching in the United States has to rank pretty close to the bottom of all professions for which a college education is required. Teachers today are usually coming from the bottom 20 percent of our college classes, not the top.

You can do better financially working in one of our plants, without the time and money you invested going to college. But without tenure, of course, or the summers off.

Too many of you start out dedicated to this noblest of professions and wind up selling real estate or stocks and bonds by your mid-thirties because you're burned out, or disillusioned, or need more money, or you're just plain tired of being at the bottom of the pyramid.

What the hell happened? I remember the great teachers I had as a kid back in Allentown, Pennsylvania, in the '30s and '40s. I remember how respected they were. Everybody in town looked up to them, not just the kids. And I remember a few of them who had more influence on my life than anybody outside my own family. And, by the way, I've hung around with some pretty important people over the years.

I remember all that, and I look around today, and I read the headlines, and I ask myself, "What the hell happened?"

Has the quality of education gone down because teachers today aren't as good as I remember? Or are the people running the schools less competent? Are the social problems the schools are asked to deal with overloading the system? Are we spending too little money on the schools—or maybe too much? Are we demanding enough of our schools—or maybe too much?

In many ways, I think we are asking too much of you. We're asking you to be cops, and social workers, and surrogate parents, and drug counselors, and psychiatrists. Just being a good teacher is tough enough. You shouldn't have to do any more than that.

Believe it or not, four years ago they actually started putting metal detectors in the schools in Detroit to keep out the guns, and the ACLU got hot about it and said it was violating somebody's rights. The schools wanted to ban the guns, and the ACLU wanted to ban the detectors! Fortunately, the schools won and the detectors stayed.

I think every kid has a right to go to school in this country, but only until the first day he shows up with a gun, a knife, or a little white bag of coke. Then you write him off. We have to take crime out of the schools and get it back into the gutter where it belongs. That might mean we have to resort to a kind of educational triage; there are some kids who'll make it no matter what you do or don't do . . . then, there's the large majority who need a lot of help from you to make it . . . and there are some who just can't be helped and shouldn't take resources and attention away from those who deserve it.

That principal with the ball bat in New Jersey, Joe Clark, got his picture on the cover of *Time* and they just made a movie about him because, frankly, most Americans agree with him. They're just plain tired of spending money on schools that put up with a bunch of bums who keep other kids from learning.

I know we've asked you people to do too much. You're not responsible for whether somebody winds up in the gutter or the White House. You're just responsible to try to give him or her the basic intellectual skills to survive . . .

299

and maybe a little sense of history . . . a respect for the scientific method . . . and maybe a love of language and the ideas it can store. It seems to me that's enough. When they try to make you godparents to every kid in your class, that's asking too much.

I think we've lost something else in many of our schools besides discipline. We've lost the value of failure. The first thing some youngsters flunk these days is life itself. That's because they've been passed from one grade to another, and eventually graduated, even though they've been failing at every step. The only problem is, nobody's told them. In attempting to shield these kids from failure, we've guaranteed it. Who are you really helping this way? Nobody!

Well, there's a word for that in my book, and it's called malpractice. I think a teacher who passes a kid who can't do the work is no different than the surgeon who sews you up with a sponge still inside. Kids can handle flunking fifth grade, but finding out 10 years later that they don't have the basic skills to earn a living is a shock they never get over. That's the real killer.

Our drop-out rate is a tragedy, but a bigger tragedy is the number of high school graduates who can barely read their diplomas—six hundred thousand people like that graduated last year.

I gotta confess I couldn't read my diploma, either. But mine was in Latin. Theirs was in English!

That's not funny, by the way, when those kids try to go to work. It's tragic, but the joke's on them because they're competing against high school graduates overseas who can read their diplomas—some even in Latin or any one of four or five different languages!

But it's the ability to compete—that's what we're cheating them out of.

I started out tonight by telling you about our Jefferson Avenue Assembly Plant in Detroit. And that's how I'm going to wind up. Jefferson Avenue is a billion dollar gamble for us. And take my word for it, there won't be many more Jeffersons in this country if somebody like me is standing here before you ten years from now giving this same speech. Factories will go overseas, not to seek cheaper labor, but to find better-educated labor.

As you consider what the new global economy means for education, I'd like you to keep one thing in mind. That new world out there is absolutely unforgiving. You as teachers will be judged coldly, objectively, and purely by the product you turn out. If that product is defective, nobody will listen to any explanations or alibis.

The problem, of course, is that the product that you put out depends so much on the raw material you get in.

You know, at Chrysler we have to make ten thousand cars a day, each of them with twelve thousand parts, and 70 percent of what goes into each of those cars comes in the back door, from our four thousand suppliers. And if a part is defective and my customer complains, I can't tell him, "Hey, that's what they shipped me. I just put it together. What do you expect from me?." No, I have to work with my suppliers and try to fix the problem.

And believe me, we work closely with them. They know our problems and we know theirs. We help each other. We work as a team. We have the same goal, after all—and that's to turn out the best possible product.

Well, your product is a helluva lot more complicated than mine—and profoundly more important. Yet you don't have much control over the material you get in your back door. That's the real breakdown, and the real tragedy in our education system.

I picked up the paper on the plane just a week ago today and saw Mrs. Futrell being quoted "that only 25 percent of parents ever visit their children's schools." That's unbelievable! I saw that and thought to myself, "How the hell could I control my product quality if I never even got to talk to 75 percent of my suppliers?"

I have to get my suppliers involved in my business or I can't fit those twelve thousand parts together and make a car. I'd build a lousy product that couldn't compete. If you can't get the parents involved, I don't know how you fit all the parts together into that complex mosaic called a human being!

I know . . . the sad fact is sometimes today there aren't parents at all . . . or there's only one parent, and she's lost control. I don't know the answer, but I hope you all get together and raise hell in your communities if you're not getting the support you deserve.

You have to do that because here's the brutal reality: Just like me, you're judged by the product that comes off your assembly line, no matter what kind of raw materials you get coming in your back door. That may not be fair, but that's the way it is.

I know the feeling, by the way, but you can't wait for fairness. There were a lot of reasons why Chrysler almost went broke that were completely beyond our control, ranging from fuel embargoes to stupid trade and antitrust rules to sky-high interest rates. But the American people blamed nobody but us. They told us loud and clear, "We don't want alibis. We want the same quality and value we can get from Japan." And they're still telling us that.

If I build a lemon at Jefferson Avenue, the marketplace won't listen for a second to my sad story about the 50 percent dropout rate of the school down the street. It simply doesn't matter.

Well, you're in the same boat we are. Education has a PR problem. Every new headline about how far our kids are falling behind adds to it. And I've got news for you—nobody wants to listen to the reasons why. You'll take almost all the blame for our educational failures. Sorry, but you can't duck it.

When the Korean eighth graders whip your eighth graders in math, you flunk. Don't bother talking about pluralism, or humanism, or one-parent families. Don't say it's society's fault, or that you're underpaid, or that the tests aren't fair. Don't talk about union-management problems. None of them means a damn thing. There are no excuses. If your students can't cut it, then you flunk right along with them.

You're judged only by your end product. That's the lesson of the new global economy we've had to learn at Chrysler. And it's no different for you —there is just no place to hide.

But remember this. When you turn your product around, just about every other problem you have goes out the window. All the people who are throwing rotten tomatoes suddenly start throwing orchids. That happened with us.

Remember Chrysler of ten years ago? Our bankers had cut us off . . . we were the brunt of Johnny Carson's monologue almost every night . . . and I was in Washington with my hat in my hand looking for help. The image of American education is nowhere near the depths we'd sunk to.

But with three or four years of sacrifice and hard work we started turning out top-quality products again, and we were heroes.

One thing we found is that most of our critics were actually rooting for us all along. They wanted us to succeed. And they applauded the loudest when we did.

So, don't get discouraged by your bad press or your critics. Everybody in this country is on your side. We're not against you. We're with you all the way.

All of us understand that we share the responsibility for quality education . . . but, I don't know how else to say this, in the end it's your job.

And with that, let me say thanks for inviting me, and thanks for listening.

And something you probably don't hear often enough these days—thanks for the thankless job you all do every day!

REMARKS AT THE
"RUNNING START" KICKOFF
Highland Park, Michigan, September 5, 1989

Iacocca believed that the biggest contribution that Chrysler could make to education was to encourage young children to read. Reading made everything else possible. At an elementary school a few blocks from Chrysler's headquarters, he spoke to first-graders and their parents about the importance of reading.

Thank you very much, and good afternoon, parents . . . principals . . . teachers . . . and especially you first-graders.

Now, I don't know if you kids know who I am. I hope at least some of you have seen me on TV before. I go on every now and then to sell cars.

Do me a favor, first-graders: Raise your hand if you've ever seen me on TV before.

I bet there's something else about me you don't know. I don't just read books, I've actually *written* books before. Two, in fact. Did any of you know that? Raise your hand if you knew that I had written a book.

Well, to tell you the truth, I don't really *like* writing books. It's hard work. But I do love *reading* books. If I had my choice, I'd rather *read* a book any day.

And do you know, I can't ever remember a day passing when I haven't read at least something. Every morning, the first thing I do is read the newspaper. Then I go to work and read all about cars. Then I go home and read my mail and letters and sometimes a book before I call it a night.

The reason I read so much is because I want to learn more. If I don't read anything, I can't learn anything, right? If you don't read, you won't learn.

In a couple of weeks, you're going to start learning how to read. You already know the alphabet—that's what Miss Lewis and all the other teachers told me. Pretty soon you'll be putting all the letters together, and you're going to start reading.

Your moms can't wait until that happens. Even your brothers and sisters can't wait, because you'll be able to read to them! Your teachers can't wait—and I know *you* can't wait, either. I'll never forget how much I loved it when I first learned to read.

You kids are lucky, by the way. I looked at some of the books, and they have real interesting names . . . *Whistle for Willie* . . . *Harold and the Crayon* . . . *Cloudy with a Chance of Meatballs.* When I grew up, guess what I had to read—something called McGuffey Readers, and it wasn't too exciting.

So in just a few minutes, we're going to let you pick out a book. But the book doesn't come free. We're going to give you this book, but you have to promise you'll do something in return.

I want you to promise that you're going to take the book home and have your mom read it to you. Maybe she can read it just before you go to sleep. By the way, your teachers told me you're supposed to be in bed by 8:30. Okay?

And every day I want your mom to read you the book, until you know it . . . and understand it . . . and can talk about it . . . and until you can read it *yourself.*

So that's what I wanted to tell you first-graders. Learn to read. And after this book, you'll get a lot more. The most important thing you'll own are your books. You treat them like they're your treasures, because they are.

But I want to talk to your moms for a minute, too.

We want to help you teach these beautiful kids. So Chrysler is putting a lot of money into this program—$2 million. It's not just here in Highland Park. It will be in nine other cities where we have facilities.

We'll give you the resources. We'll give you books, but you're the ones who will have to be resourceful. You'll have to be the ones who read to your kids every day.

Your kids won't appreciate what you're doing for them. Not now. They won't have the foggiest idea how much you're helping them.

But believe me, when they grow up, they'll remember. Then they'll appreciate you. And they'll never forget how much you helped them.

You want the best for your kids. It's the American dream. Every parent does. I want the best for them, too. We need good kids. In twenty years, I won't be around running Chrysler. But some of your kids may be. Some of them may be helping run the place.

So Chrysler's going to give every kid today a running start in life. We're not going to see a quick payoff from this, believe me. It'll be the twenty-first century before any of them are working.

But when they do work, they'll be better off . . . Chrysler will be better off . . . and America will be better off.

So thank you for coming. And if you teachers can do me one last favor— next spring, after everyone has read twenty-one books, will you have each of the kids write me a letter. I want to know what books they liked best.

You see, I have a granddaughter. She was born, in fact, the day before my book was published, so I inscribed the first copy to her. Now, she's 15 months. And I need to know what's on the kids' best-seller list, so I can read the right stuff to her.

Thanks again, and have a good school year.

9. The Statue of Liberty–Ellis Island Speeches: An Analysis of Lee Iacocca's Value Appeals

John J. Makay

No other word better describes the rhetoric of Lee Iacocca than *values*. His speeches and his books are reflections of American values easily mirrored in the words and actions of this powerful spokesperson who has often been identified as a contemporary American cultural hero.

Other authors in this volume turned their analytical lens on a number of key addresses by Iacocca; this chapter continues by turning the interpretive eye to focus on meanings and the message of two speeches Iacocca delivered while he was chair of the Statue of Liberty-Ellis Island Centennial Commission: (1) the speech delivered at the Ethnic Heritage Council of the Pacific Northwest in Seattle, Washington, on October 20, 1984, and (2) the speech delivered at the "Year of Liberty" Gala Concert, in Washington, D.C., October 28, 1985. These speeches are particularly appropriate for study because they represent Iacocca's feelings about core values centered in the nation's renovation and celebration of the Statue of Liberty and her home on Ellis Island.

The interpretive function for the student of rhetoric is illumination. Andrews points out that "a prime function of rhetoric is to interpret and make meaningful what is in the process of happening. The reality of one's world at any given moment is the reality as it is perceived" (6). Iacocca's perception of his world is revealed in his public rhetoric, and his love for what makes America a great country is reflected in this language and value appeals. The words expressed by Iacocca to his audiences underlie essential values grounded in the substance of his thoughts and feelings.

We can assume that his value appeals had great success in exciting various audiences. At the time Iacocca delivered these speeches, he was a highly visible national public figure with widespread popularity. The dramatic Chrysler turnaround, the extensive reach of his television commercials, and the tremendous success of his first book created a public persona of a dynamic yet personable, intelligent, courageous, and extremely successful business chief executive who possessed the skills to communicate with just about everyone (Iacocca and Novak 32). In the 1980s, the country was searching for new heroes, and millions of people were drawn to the Iacocca persona and the message he delivered. His selection to chair the commission extended his opportunities to express love for America and afforded Iacocca the opportunities to appeal to the essential values symbolized by the Statue of Liberty and Ellis Island (Iacocca and Novak 32).

The speeches were rhetorical instruments used by Iacocca to announce and promote national values deeply ground into his personal life as well as his actions as a public figure. In considering these speeches, we must remember that they were part of an overall dialogue he found himself engaged in as he moved to the center of the public arena during the 1980s. Iacocca's success in leading the Chrysler Corporation out of a financial abyss that could have had a devastating impact on the American economy and the labor force in the automobile industry had moved him up front in the attention of the media. His success at personally selling Chrysler products through appearances in Chrysler commercials placed him in almost everyone's home. He possessed a sort of charisma that attracted fans from all walks of American life. Iacocca's name was even placed on presidential campaign buttons by thousands who viewed him as presidential material, but he appeared to have no serious interest in political life, even in the role of president of the United States.

WE WANT YOU TO RAISE MONEY, BUT WE DON'T WANT YOU TO HELP SPEND IT

While Iacocca did not have a serious interest in the presidency, his popular persona seems to appeal to presidents. Ronald Reagan was the first president to ask Iacocca for help. Iacocca's task was to help restore the American Dream through a restoration of one of the nation's most precious monuments. Iacocca did not need more work to occupy his time and energy when he agreed to chair the Statue of Liberty-Ellis Island Centennial Commission. When the president of the United States asks someone to help out, however, he or she is likely to discover that turning the president down is very difficult.

Iacocca was compelled to accept the invitation for personal reasons even more persuasive than a presidential request. Iacocca described the task as "a labor of love for my mother and my father." He recalled that his parents had told him of their immigrant experiences: "The island was part of my being—not the place itself, but what it stood for and how tough an experience it was" (Iacocca and Novak 339).

The task Iacocca faced was huge, and the amount of money the commission raised under his leadership exceeded its initial goal. He met publicly and privately with groups and individuals as he traveled around the country as chair of the commission, and when the money was counted the final figured totaled $305 million (Iacocca and Kleinfield 339). His success, however, was eventually met with a firing as the White House, perhaps sensing a potential rival, copied the earlier action of Henry Ford II by publicly letting Iacocca go. According to Iacocca's account, he was informed by telegram: "In classic Washington double talk, the wire praised me for my past efforts and then, in the best 'we regret to inform you' style, told me there was the 'potential of future conflict or the appearance thereof' between my roles of both the Statue of Liberty-Ellis Island Foundation, which had to raise the money, and the Centennial Commission, which recommends how to spend" (Iacocca and Kleinfield 3).

Iacocca, however, did not buy the argument and, as a matter of fact, labeled the explanation "mumbo jumbo" and declared that the "concept of 'conflict' was hogwash" (Iacocca and Kleinfield 3). But even the "mumbo jumbo" used to terminate Iacocca's work on the State of Liberty-Ellis Island project did not distract him from his view of the meaning of America and the nation's symbols which embrace and embody this meaning. Perhaps his earlier termination at Ford and subsequent efforts at Chrysler had instilled the belief that commitment and hard work should continue even after an unwarranted discharge. Beyond this belief, the Statue of Liberty and Ellis Island project had its own value for Iacocca: "[It] got me thinking about where the country is today and where it might be headed tomorrow. Symbols mean nothing if the values aren't there. We didn't spend millions of dollars just so that the statue wouldn't fall into the harbor and become a hazard to navigation. We didn't fix up Ellis Island so that people would have a nice place to go on a Sunday afternoon. We did it because we wanted to restore, remember, and renew the basic values that made America great" (Iacocca and Kleinfield 10). Iacocca's attention to the "Grand Lady" promoted deeper reflection within his audience concerning the contemporary relevance of traditional American values and symbols and how those values and symbols might guide the country's future course.

A SYMBOL OF VALUES PERSONIFIED AS A GREAT AMERICAN LADY

The Statue of Liberty and Ellis Island are not only geographical spots with historical significance on the American landscape in Iacocca's thinking and rhetorical expressions. They are, his speeches underscore, national treasures to inspire citizens to remain aware of values that brought the nation to world leadership as a democracy of unlimited opportunities. Iacocca told his audience at the Ethnic Heritage Council that considering Liberty as a historical monument to the past was misleading: "She has never stood for the past. Every immigrant, every returning GI and doughboy who sailed by her, was escaping the past and entering the future." The idea that traditional American values and symbols have contemporary relevance is a central notion in Iacocca's scheme.

While the speech to the Ethnic Heritage Council and the speech at the gala concert were delivered on occasions one year apart, together they contain the essence of the Iacocca message delivered many times during the four years he chaired the commission. The structure of his messages was consistent with speeches for special occasions. He made a strong effort to see that his speeches met the expectations of his audiences; he tailored his speeches with attractive and personal references to the audiences; and he relied greatly on personal anecdotes mixed with appropriate humor and thoughtful points that reflected core values to be shared with his listeners (Makay). But the essence of the speeches is found not in structure but rather in the value appeals and the language in which they were expressed.

To convey the image of the Statue of Liberty and the values it symbolized, Iacocca used a strategy of personification. He portrayed the towering monument as a real person, a living being, a "very special lady." For the Ethnic Heritage Council, for example, he announced "her bones are breaking apart." At the gala concert he described the statue as "a lady who has stood tall and strong at the doorstep of our country for nearly a hundred years." The Statue of Liberty needed to be portrayed as more than concrete, steel, copper sheets, and other structural materials and instead became a breathing, spiritual figure whose life could be found in the ongoing lives of those who where inspired, motivated, and guided by her values. "She has stood," Iacocca told his audience at the gala concert, "with a beacon raised to guide the lost . . . with an arm outstretched to welcome the homeless . . . with a tablet proclaiming her promise of liberty." The effort to renovate her honored not only the statue itself but symbolically "the millions who saw her beacon and reached out for her welcome . . . because they believed her promise."

As a spokesperson Iacocca's task was not to persuade listeners to believe what he believed about the country but to reflect about the shared beliefs and values symbolized in the Statue of Liberty and its home on Ellis Island. While these speeches were expressed in the language and form commonly used to inspire audiences on special occasions, they echo values and themes uniquely associated with Iacocca.

VALUE APPEALS TO INSPIRE THE AUDIENCE

Value appeals most often "reveal the nature of the man in quest of public office" (Scheele 51). Value appeals may reveal the politics, philosophy, and ideology of a public figure. While Iacocca was not in pursuit of public office, his name was brought up by important figures as a potential presidential candidate. Moreover, Iacocca was clearly serving the role of statesman when he agreed to head the commission. To identify the value appeals made by Iacocca, I carefully examined his statements and studied, in particular, the very rich language he used. In Iacocca's view, the Statue of Liberty and Ellis Island symbolize what individuals can achieve as part of the American experience. His major appeals can be named by four pairs of interrelated terms: (1) hard work/better life; (2) liberty/opportunity; (3) sacrifice/suffering; (4) competition/success. In Iacocca's worldview, America's atmosphere, guided by people who support a democratic constitution, provides everyone with liberty and opportunity to develop their potential and thus achieve considerable satisfaction in their lives. Personal and professional satisfaction, however, is always achieved by working hard to pursue expectations that a better life is enjoyed by those who work harder than those who avoid such work. Hard work to achieve the good life, however, requires having to make sacrifices and endure, as well, some amount of suffering. This value of sacrifice and suffering is often viewed as a gateway to pleasure, accomplishment, and valuable rewards.

Sacrifice and suffering are, in Iacocca's view, interrelated with competition and success, so much so that whether in the political process, the field of athletics, or the automobile business, no person, team, or organization is likely to achieve success without being highly competitive; and competition always includes the sacrifice and suffering that can lead to success in American society.

The speeches Iacocca delivered as commission chair provided him with a public forum to affirm these values and reinforce his position as a heroic figure in American life. To the two thousand people attending the Ethnic Heritage Council gathering in Seattle, he spoke about liberty and the opportunity that comes with this freedom through a vivid reference to children and other people who contributed to the initial cost of the statue because they were inspired by the American struggle for liberty. He recalled that the value of liberty had proven powerful as the country survived a war between the states, so much so that citizens of France, even schoolchildren, contributed money to build Miss Liberty: "They were thankful because in this American experiment they saw an example for the rest of the world. It was an example of hope and they built the statue as a symbol of that hope." The symbol of the American Dream was portrayed as a Lady of Liberty and as an opportunity to those gathered for the gala concert. Once again, Iacocca relied on a richness of imagery as he personified the statue to inspire his audience to think about and feel the timeless value of liberty. He described the statue as a "young symbol of an old dream—the dream of liberty." While the idea of liberty may be labeled simple the construction of liberty as a crucial standard for political, governmental, and citizenry power is often considerably complex. Iacocca's words avoided complexities by constructing rich images of immigrants bound for freedom in "ships slipping into the harbor with the first immigrants she would welcome to America." The Statue of Liberty was again personified: "Tonight she remembers those ships coming from Bremen and Liverpool and Naples."

In Iacocca's portrayal, however, those seeking refuge and opportunity did not find the nation's streets, as he explained, "paved with gold." They found instead a path to travel through hard work and sacrifice. Iacocca's parents were immigrants committed to hard work and sacrifice. The value that was standard for his parents was one centered in the meaning of the Statue of Liberty as he constituted it for both himself and the audiences he addressed. His achievement through hard work and sacrifice at Chrysler to revitalize a dying corporation was in the minds of those groups who invited him to speak. With the use of repetition, he turned his audience's attention to the immigrants as the initial visionaries of an American Dream rather than looking, for example, at westbound pioneers frequently identified as key citizens directed by a dream featuring freedom, opportunity, work, sacrifice, and reward.

To explain his ideas and the values they relied on, Iacocca frequently used anaphora, repetition of similar phrases, clauses and sentences in terms rich with imagery: "They found the streets were not paved with gold. They were on their own. The adventure was over. Now they had to go to work. Now they had to build something—with brains, and strong backs, and sheer guts. They went to work in factories, and in the mines, and on the railroad generally at the lowest jobs!" And as a speaker, he usually kept his sentences short but packed with the force of ideas and rich imagry that had become characteristic of the Iacocca message. For example, at the Ethnic Heritage Council he remarked: "She kept her promise of liberty, but it wasn't the liberty of streets paved with gold. It was the liberty of the shovel, the freedom of the pushcart, and the dignity of the plow. It was the freedom to work hard, and to keep what that hard work built. They were hardworking in a time when hard work was not something to be avoided. They were builders. They built a country. And what they built was an America we have today."

The hard work for a better way of life that became in the eyes of millions the American Dream in Iacocca's view was one that included suffering accompanied by sacrifice leading to great reward. This value appeal was certainly one he and the employees of Chrysler had portrayed publicly through their combined efforts to keep the company alive. In fact, Chrysler became a metaphor as evidence of the contemporary relevance of the American Dream, and Iacocca was a reflection of the ideology he articulated. In this context, he placed, for example, the immigrant experience equal with that of the pioneer. To the Ethnic Heritage Council, he pictured the immigrants on a voyage to America: "But what a wrenching thing it must have been! And then seventeen or eighteen days on the ocean . . . down below in steerage . . . where everybody was seasick. (My mother got typhoid fever.) They had two to three crowded, smelly weeks to think about what they'd left, and wonder if just half the stories about America were really true."

The dream of opportunity through hard work in a land governed in a national spirit of liberty in Iacocca's public discourse was, then, grounded in the hopes of America's immigrants and mirrored in the renewal of Chrysler. The Statue of Liberty centered on Ellis Island symbolized for Iacocca the realization of these values and hopes.

As a sales spokesperson as well as chief executive for Chrysler with a goal of producing and selling automobiles of the highest quality, Iacocca's public messages placed people acting on deep-seated values as America's greatest resource. These were the forces acting to save the Chrysler Corporation. The aspirations to rewards and a higher standard of living fuel the economy through competition and by people willing to suffer and sacrifice. As an illustration of his perspective on America's resourcefulness, Iacocca, again using repetition to sound his ideology about immigrants and hard work, told those gathered at the gala concert: "America isn't great because of miles of open prairies. It's great because people broke their backs to bust the sod and grow food." It was not the "few industrial geniuses" who made America great. "It's great because of the thousands of others who fired the furnaces and forged the metal."

America is a nation that has proven successful through national competitiveness. Within its borders, competition is valued everywhere: in schools, on athletic fields, in industry, and even within families. At the time of Iacocca's efforts to raise money for the State of Liberty and Ellis Island, nowhere in the blood of the American industrial life was competition to achieve and maintain economic success challenged more greatly than in the production and sale of American cars. And, of course, Iacocca and Chrysler clearly and dramatically proved they could be tremendously competitive and, according to the formula, highly successful. With Chrysler as the overarching metaphor of success in a land of liberty, Iacocca sounded another theme reflected in other speeches, that the dream must not be diminished by a lessening of commitment to traditional values. He addressed the-all-too common notion that these traditional American values no longer operated and that "our kids will be the first generation of Americans that will have to settle for less than their parents had." While Iacocca rejected this notion, he indicated he understood where it had come from. "Look at the size of the public debt we're saddling them with. We're paying our way today by mortgaging their futures. And look at all the whining they're starting to hear about how America can't compete anymore. That's what everybody told us at Chrysler five years ago, remember."

Competition and success along with the other appeals made by Iacocca in his speeches as chair of the Statue of Liberty-Ellis Island Centennial Commission point to core values that provide the substance for these speeches. While symbols are essential in the public messages of Iacocca, he also warned his audience in Seattle, "The symbols mean nothing if the values aren't there." And about the Statue of Liberty, he concluded his speech at the gala concert through personification and tribute: "She is a special lady to all of us, and we honor her tonight . . . because she remembers, and because she helps all of us remember . . . just what kind of people we are."

CONCLUSION

The speeches Iacocca delivered while he was Chair of Statue of Liberty-Ellis Island Centennial Commission provided him with a public forum to tell his audiences just what kind of people the majority of Americans have been and still can be from his view. Iacocca is the personification of the values he articulated, and his experience at Chrysler is evidence that the values and symbols of the American Dream have contemporary relevance. One may understand the instrumental goal of Iacocca and the Statue of Liberty-Ellis Island Commission as simply one of raising money for material reconstruction—replacing rusted bolts, buffing dulled sheets of copper, reinforcing old foundations. On a symbolic level, however, one may understand Iacocca's rhetorical goal as refurbishing traditional American values and symbols to make clear their contemporary relevance. This regular refurbishing and renovation of values and symbols is necessary to maintain the power of the American Dream.

When we examine Iacocca's image and background in American culture, we can easily draw the conclusion that when he was appointed by President Reagan to lead the efforts to raise funds to restore the Stature of Liberty and Ellis Islands, there was no one better suited for the task. Rising from a modest middle-class background in Pennsylvania to achieve both a solid education and a prominent place in the American industrial world is by itself a considerable accomplishment. Iacocca's outlook as mirrored in these speeches was shaped from his experiences as the son of immigrants, the visible leader of a renewed Chrysler Corporation, and a public figure whose success was heroic as measured through the success of his leadership, the sales of his books, and the demand for his voice on professional and public platforms throughout the country. But to be extremely innovative in the automobile world, to rise above a highly public professional setback at Ford Motor Company, and to lead Chrysler out of the graveyard is remarkable. Continued commitment to the Statue of Liberty-Ellis Island rennovation effort even after a public firing was similarly remarkable. Iacocca, grounded in the strong roots of American values and experience and guided by his interpretation of the American Dream was willing to go forward.

WORKS CITED

Andrews, James R. *The Practice of Rhetorical Criticism* 2nd ed. New York: Longman, 1990.

Dionisopoulos, George N. "A Case Study in Print Media and Heroic Myth: Lee Iacocca 1978–1985." *The Southern Speech Communication Journal* 53 (1988): 227–243.

Iacocca, Lee A. and William Novak. *Iacocca: An Autobiography*. New York: Bantam, 1984.

Makay, John J. "Speeches for Special Occasions." *Public Speaking: Theory into Practice*. Fort Worth: Harcourt Brace, 1992. 361–364,

Scheele, Henry Z. "Ronald Reagan's 1980 Acceptance Address: A Focus on American Values." *Western Journal of Communication* 48 (1984): 51–61.

REMARKS TO THE ETHNIC HERITAGE
COUNCIL OF THE PACIFIC NORTHWEST

Seattle, Washington, October 20, 1984

Time and again, he called it his "labor of love." When Iacocca agreed to lead the effort to restore the Statue of Liberty and Ellis Island, he did it as a special tribute to his parents, both of whom first set foot in America at the old immigration station. It was an emotional experience for everyone involved. In Seattle, he spoke to about a thousand members of ethnic clubs from all over the Pacific Northwest. They came in costume. The cocktail hour was long. His speech, full of rich imagery of the immigration experience, left few dry eyes in the house.

Thank you. Good evening ladies and gentleman.

It's always a real pleasure to come to the great Pacific Northwest. Thank you for inviting me. Originally, I was going to say "Washington." But I'm so tired of going to the other Washington, I couldn't muster the strength to say it.

I first want to thank all of you for your support of the Statue of Liberty–Ellis Island project.

I also want to congratulate you on forming this Ethnic Heritage Council four years ago. I think it's important for all of us to hold on to our own heritage . . . whatever it is. But we ought to share it, too. And learn more about other people's heritage. You're helping each other do that.

We started doing that in Detroit a few years ago. During the summer we have a series of ethnic festivals on the riverfront. One week the Germans take over, the next the Polish, and then the Italians, and the Greeks, and so on. And everybody's welcome. You get a sense of diversity and unity at the same time, and I guess that's what America is all about.

I know that's true of this group. You're coming together tonight to pay tribute to a most important symbol of our unity as a nation—the Statue of Liberty. And yet the diversity is just as evident. When I was invited, they sent me some background material on your organization. It had the names of board members and committee heads. There's a Filipino named Koslosky . . . a Norwegian named Morrison . . . and a Japanese named Sanchez. And then there's Carin Jacroux. That sounds awfully *French* to me, but she says she's *German*, she works at the *Austrian* Consulate, and she's here representing an *Italian* club!

316

Now, come on. That's carrying things a little too far! Maybe she just likes going to lots of parties. If she lived in Detroit, she'd have to spend the whole summer camped out at the ethnic festivals on the riverfront!

Well, it's fun to dress up in the old costumes . . . to dance to the old music . . . to eat the food and listen to stories about the old country. That's important, and I hope we never lose it.

But when a bunch of us got together a couple of years ago to do something about the Statue of Liberty and Ellis Island, the mood was pretty serious. The Statue looks the same from a distance, but inside her bones are breaking apart. Pieces have actually fallen off and washed up in New Jersey.

Ellis Island is only a half a mile away, and it's a mess. It's been shut down for thirty years now. I don't know how many of you have been there, but to me the place is haunted with 17 million ghosts. That's how many people came through there between 1892 and 1954. Every time I walk into the Great Hall, I feel like I'm in church.

When President Reagan asked me to be chairman of a committee to restore both the Statue and Ellis Island, I was honored. Believe me, I had my hands full at Chrysler, and I wasn't looking for any hobbies. But this is something I had to do. It's a labor of love for me.

Both my parents came through Ellis Island . . . my dad twice. The first time was in 1902. He was twelve years old and scared to death. The second time was in 1921, after he'd returned to Italy to bring back a bride . . . my mother.

So, my roots run deep—and my attachment is great—as I'm sure it is with so many of you in this room.

Well, the restoration is a big job. The statue—for those of you who haven't been in it—is basically a copper skin about as thick as a half-dollar, connected to a structural framework by iron straps. When you put iron next to copper and add a little moisture, you have a battery. That causes galvanic corrosion. The copper skin is in pretty good shape, but the iron straps have just about been eaten away. We're replacing two thousand of them, this time with an alloy that won't react with the copper.

We also have to strengthen the right arm . . . the one that holds the torch. It was damaged during World War I when a munitions plant blew up a few miles away in New Jersey. If the plant was sabotaged—as many people believe—then she was one of the casualties of that war.

The torch itself has been removed, and it will have to be replaced. The new one will be identical, of course, and the old one will be displayed somewhere—I don't know where yet—maybe it will move around the country. By the way, you Huskie fans will be able to see it on New Year's Day in the Rose Bowl Parade.

Ellis Island is an empty shell now. But in two years the Great Hall will be rehabilitated and some of the first exhibits will be in place. By 1992, when the project is completed, Ellis Island will be not just a museum but a living monument to the whole immigration experience in America. You'll enjoy visiting it. It will freeze a moment in time. You'll see it as they saw it. You'll experience their music and literature, and their food and arts and crafts. It will be sort of an ethnic Williamsburg—but not commercial.

Coincidentally, 1992 will be the five hundredth anniversary of Christopher Columbus's first voyage to the New World. That will be a big day for *all* Americans, but especially for Italians, because he was Italian. And I guess for the Spanish, too, because they put up all the dough. See, cooperation started early in this country.

The whole project—the statue and Ellis Island—will cost about $230 million. That sounds like a lot, but it's only a buck for each American . . . the price of a pack of cigarettes. None of that will come from public funds. All of it will be from private individuals, groups like yours, and companies, big and small. We're already over a $120 million in cash and pledges.

Your participation out here has been tremendous. You just saw me get a check for a quarter of a million from the employees at Boeing.

I want to thank all the employees at Boeing for that.

And you may not know this, but the biggest single corporate sponsor in the country is the Chateau St. Michelle winery here in Washington . . . and get this—they've already pledged five million bucks! So my thanks to all the people at St. Michelle.

We're looking for a million and a half from people in Washington, not counting corporate contributions. And a million from Oregon.

So far, we've got about 50 million committed from companies around the country, and a little more than that from individuals and groups—the grass roots effort!

We've got almost 2 million bucks from school kids sending us their nickels and dimes. I opened my mail last Monday and there was a letter from a kid. He said: "Dear Mr. Iacocca, here's my allowance for this week." And there were two $1 bills attached. He said, "Spend it wisely!"

The kids are fantastic. You know, kids are always raising money for something . . . a new school bus, football uniforms, a class trip. But this project has really caught on. They're washing cars, and having bake sales. You name it.

But that's the magic—and the fun of it. Everybody is getting into the act. Right here in Seattle, the Bellevue Terrace Nursing Center is sponsoring Wheel-a-thons, and they've raised thousands of dollars.

One guy rode a motorized surfboard over three thousand miles to raise money.

How about this—we even got $2,000 from the Hell's Angels! Leather jackets, motorcycles, and all—would you believe underneath those guys are patriots?

And when people send in money, they always seem to write a letter. I wish you could read them. People who are immigrants say, "America has been good to me, and I just want to pay a little of it back." The second-generation people say, "Here's something for my mom and dad . . . for all they went through for me." And you can almost see the tearstains on the letters.

One day a guy came into my office and gave me a million dollars. Right out of the blue. He told me about how his family had come here poor, like everybody else. And obviously they did well . . . they got rich. And the man felt a big debt to this country. All he asked was that I never reveal his name. So, if anybody here has a million—I promise to keep you anonymous, too.

Maybe the most touching letter of all came from a man in Poland. He sent some silver certificates worth about $2 for the Statue, and asked for a picture of what he called "This beautiful symbol."

And what a beautiful symbol she is! To us, and to the rest of the world.

I think it's important to remember that we didn't build her. It wasn't our idea. A hundred years ago, French schoolkids collected pennies to build Miss Liberty, just like our kids are doing today. The idea began right after the Civil War. Some people in France were as thankful as we were that this country . . . this experiment in liberty . . . had held together through its darkest hours. They were thankful because in this American experiment they saw an example for the rest of the world. It was an example of hope, and they built the statue as a symbol of that hope.

The greatest gift, as Robert Burns said, is to see ourselves as others see us. It took the French to provide us with this "beautiful symbol." But I wonder if any of us here tonight can see what the Statue of Liberty stands for quite as clearly as that man in Poland. It seems freedom means more if you don't have it. If you do, you just take it for granted.

Americans a hundred years ago didn't really appreciate the importance of that symbol. After the French sent the statue over, our government refused to put up the money for a base to put it on. Some people started a fund drive, but it didn't work . . . until Joseph Pulitzer got involved. He was an immigrant from Hungary, and he owned a newspaper in New York. He made the Statue a major cause. He especially went after the silk stocking crowd in New York, and embarrassed them into contributing.

So even from the beginning, Americans didn't really appreciate what they had . . . what the Lady in the Harbor stood for.

To really understand, you may have to look through somebody else's eyes. Think back with me for a minute what it must have meant to my parents, or yours, or your grandparents . . . to all those 17 million people who came during the big immigration wave.

First, they left their families and their homes. Most knew they'd never get back to see them again. What makes people do that? Courage . . . desperation . . . determination to be free . . . wanting to give their kids a decent life? All of those, I guess. But what a wrenching thing it must have been!

And then seventeen or eighteen days on the ocean . . . down below in steerage . . . where almost everybody was seasick. My mother got typhoid fever. They had two to three crowded, smelly weeks to think about what they'd left, and wonder if just half the stories about America were really true.

None of them remembered that boat ride very fondly. But they remembered the day they got to New York. They all came up on deck, dressed up in their best clothes because this was the biggest day of their lives. They stood on the deck with just those clothes on their back, and maybe a suitcase with a rope around it. And the first thing they saw was the Statue of Liberty.

It was shiny then, because the copper hadn't turned green yet. And they could see it gleaming in the harbor from miles out.

I don't care how sick they were, or how scared, or how lonely, the sight of the Lady saying "welcome" made the whole thing worth it. They never forgot that . . . or what happened next.

If the statue was a symbol of hope, Ellis Island was the reality. They called it "The Island of Tears," and for good reason.

They were herded off the boat into this gigantic building . . . thousands in a single day. It looked like a cathedral, but inside it was a cattle barn. Everybody was jammed in long lines, hanging onto each other, and to the kids, and to the suitcase with the rope around it.

The sheer numbers meant nothing was personal. There were quick medical exams, and some of them were humiliating. They had tags hung around their necks, and they didn't know what they meant. An immigration agent asked them thirty questions in two minutes . . . in a language they didn't understand.

Twenty percent of them were detained on the island for medical or legal reasons, sometimes for days, sometimes for weeks. One in fifty was put back on the boat for Europe. For them the dream was over!

Ellis Island, was reality, all right . . . an almost brutal counterpoint to that hope they were feeling just a few hours before. Earlier this year, a man wrote a letter to the *New York Times*. He called Ellis Island a "charnal house" and said we shouldn't try to restore it we should tear it down. He said it was a symbol "best forgotten."

Well, he's wrong. We need that symbol as much as we do the statue. Because that's where the story really began. That's where they were really introduced to America. They took a ferry across to the Battery and—guess what—they found the streets were *not* paved with gold. They were on their own. The adventure was over. Now they had to go to work. Now they had to build something—with brains, and strong backs, and sheer guts.

They went to work in factories, and in the mines, and on the railroad . . . generally at the lowest jobs those always went to the new arrivals. But in just a couple of decades they built an Industrial America that was the wonder of the world!

They also built homes and neighborhoods and churches. Their kids went to college, fought in our wars, and became leaders in their communities.

So both the statue and Ellis Island are important symbols. One of the shining hope for freedom and a better life. And one of the sacrifice, and the suffering, and the plain hard work that turned that hope into reality.

We need them both.

Almost half of the people in America today are direct descendants of those 17 million whose first glimpses of America were those two symbols.

But they are equally important to *every* American, whether his forebears came three hundred years ago to find religious freedom;

Whether they came from Ireland during the potato famine;

Or from Germany and Eastern Europe to escape their endless wars;

Or from Scandinavia to farm the prairies, or to cut the timber here in the Northwest;

Or from China and Japan to *this* coast . . . or north from Mexico . . . or south from Canada.

The Statue of Liberty stands for the same thing for all of us . . . even those whose ancestors were brought here in chains . . . as slaves. Maybe she is especially important for them.

And the process goes on and on, doesn't it? Let me say again how much I appreciate this beautiful painting that was given to me tonight. Ms. Houng and thousands of other Vietnamese who've risked so much to get here are telling us that everything Miss Liberty has stood for is still alive today. And I think we need them to remind us.

We've let some of our symbols decay, but now we're repairing them. But in the last twenty years or so, we've seen America jerked in a dozen confusing directions, so that some believe that even the basic values behind those symbols are decaying as well.

We've seen our leaders shot down . . . our cities burn in racial violence . . . a president thrown out in disgrace . . . and a war that forced us—painfully—to confront our own limitations.

We've also seen the economic order in the world change. And for the first time in our memory, we are no longer clearly in command of it.

Our own economic base is changing, too. Our heavy industry is shrinking. The jobs that for so long were filled by the newest Americans are moving out of America to the Far East and the Third World.

Some people are even beginning to say that America can't compete anymore—that we can't cut the mustard.

Well, I've spent a lot of time on the Statue of Liberty and Ellis Island. And other people are working *full*-time on it. Millions of people have sent in money. This thing has caught on because these symbols still stand for something beautiful.

We aren't spending $230 million just so the Statue won't fall into the harbor and become a hazard to navigation. We aren't fixing up Ellis Island so people will have a nice place to go on Sunday afternoon. We're doing it because we want to remember, and to honor, and to save the basic values that made America great.

Values like hard work, dignified by decent pay. Like the courage to risk everything and start over. Like the wisdom to adapt to change. And maybe most of all—self-confidence. To believe in ourselves. Nothing is more important than that.

The symbols mean nothing if the values aren't there.

I've heard it said—and so have you—that our kids will be the first generation of Americans that will have to settle for less than their parents had.

I pray to God our kids don't believe that. But I can see how they might. Look at the size of the public debt we're saddling them with. We're paying our way today by mortgaging their futures. Our parents didn't do that to us. And they'd be ashamed of *us* for doing it to *our* kids.

And look at all the whining they're starting to hear about how America can't compete anymore. That's what everybody told us at Chrysler five years ago, remember? How many of you remember the *Wall Street Journal* telling Chrysler to quit fighting—and to "die with dignity"?

Well, we didn't see a hell of a lot of dignity in six hundred thousand people losing their jobs. So we did what we had to do—including a lot of painful things. We practically had to start over. But we survived. We got out of debt. We got rid of the government as our business partner. This year we made a billion and a half dollars just in the first six months. And I just approved a five-year business plan that'll mean investing over $10 billion in technology and jobs right here in America.

Hell, if we could do it, anybody can. Because we had less going for us than just about anybody, believe me.

The country is going through some big changes today. I don't know what to call it . . . "the information age" . . . "the hightech era" . . . "the postindustrial society." And people are scared. They wonder if there'll be a place for them.

Well, hell, what are they scared about? There was a revolution going on eighty years ago, too, when those millions of people were being pushed through the chutes at Ellis Island. It was called the industrial revolution. They came out of the sulphur pits in Sicily and the coal mines in Silesia, and then jumped right into the middle of it. And they didn't even speak the language!

So what's so tough about today? And why can't our kids look forward to even *more* than we have, not *less*?

We make a mistake if we think the Statue of Liberty is just a *historical* monument. We're missing the boat if we think she stands for the *past*. She has *never* stood for the past. Every immigrant, every returning GI and dough-boy who sailed by her, was *escaping* the past and entering the *future*.

She may be almost one hundred years old, but the values she stands for better *not* be as weathered as she is. And I don't think they are. Maybe when we get her polished up, more people will see that.

We're not just preserving a statue here, we're preserving all that she stands for.

And if that's not worth remembering, and honoring, and saving . . . if that's not worth passing on to our kids . . . then let me ask you, ladies and gentlemen—what the hell is?

Thank you.

REMARKS AT THE "YEAR OF LIBERTY" GALA CONCERT

Washington, D.C., October 28, 1985

Iacocca repeated some of the imagery he used a year earlier in Seattle at Washington's Kennedy Center at the premiere of Richard Adler's "The Lady Remembers."

Good evening to all of you.

I've been privileged for the past three and a half years to be involved in restoring two of our nation's most valuable treasures—the Statue of Liberty and Ellis Island. And it's been a labor of love, believe me.

A year from today, the Lady with the Torch will be rededicated on her hundredth birthday, and tonight we begin the celebration of her centennial year.

All this is possible because millions of Americans have contributed more than $170 million so far to keep the torch lit. You've been invited tonight so we could thank you for your generous support.

And we're going to thank you with the world premiere of Richard Adler's "The Lady Remembers," performed by the Detroit Symphony Orchestra, under the direction of Gunther Herbig, with soloist Julia Migenes Johnson.

You know, the last couple of years lots of schoolkids have been sending me their nickels and dimes for the Lady. Some even send me their lunch money, or a few bucks from selling cupcakes or washing cars. And a man once dropped into my office and gave me a million dollars to help shine her up. (As he said "just a simple tribute to my immigrant mother.") It seems like everybody feels they *owe* the Lady something.

And Richard Adler is one of those people.

Richard Adler wasn't *commissioned* to write this piece. He wasn't *asked* to do it. He simply called one day and said: "I *want* to do it. I *need* to do it. Just *let* me do it."

So we let him do it.

It's quite a gift he's giving us, and giving America, tonight. So, please join me in expressing our thanks to Richard Adler.

And now we are about to honor a very, very special lady.

She's a lady who has stood tall and strong at the doorstep of our country for nearly a hundred years. She has stood with a beacon raised to guide the lost . . . with an arm outstretched to welcome the homeless . . . and with a tablet proclaiming her promise of liberty.

We not only honor that lady tonight, but also the millions who saw her beacon and reached out for her welcome . . . because they believed her promise.

And we honor what *they* did to keep her promise alive, and to pass it along to all of us.

Exactly ninety-nine years ago today, a beautiful lady dressed in two hundred tons of copper and iron stood staring through the mist in New York Harbor, a little like a blushing bride. Quite a fuss was made over her that day. Cannons roared, brass bands played, all the ships in the harbor blew their whistles and rang their bells.

She was that day a young symbol of an old but elusive dream—the simple ideal of liberty. Tonight, ninety-nine years later but forever young, she stands not only for that original ideal itself, but also as a symbol of what free people, guided and protected by that ideal, can achieve.

For as soon as the cannons and the bands were silent, she began to see the ships slipping into the harbor with the first of the millions of immigrants she would welcome to America.

Tonight she remembers those ships coming from Bremen and Liverpool and Naples . . . and the cargo they brought. Human beings seeking refuge and opportunity beneath her torch.

They all stood on deck in their best clothes . . . clutching the kids, and maybe an old cardboard suitcase with a rope around it. It was the biggest day of their lives.

And as the ships went by her on their way to Ellis Island, a lot of backs, bent by oppression, began to straighten. And a lot of faces, scarred by tyranny, were suddenly smiling. And a lot of eyes, dimmed by despair, began to glow with hope.

She saw all that, and she remembers it well tonight.

She remembers, too, what happened to them after they passed beyond her gaze.

She *kept* her promise of liberty, but it wasn't the liberty of streets paved with gold. It was the liberty of the shovel, the freedom of the pushcart, and the dignity of the plow.

It was the freedom to work hard, and to keep what that hard work built.

They were ambitious in a time when *ambition* was not a dirty word.

They were hardworking in a time when hard work was not something to be avoided.

They were builders.

They built a country.

And what they built was the America we have today—imperfect, but better by far than anything anybody else has ever built, anywhere.

The Lady remembers how they did it, and so should we.

They did it with pain, and sweat and tears.

You know, America isn't great because of its natural resources, It's great because those people dug into the ground, often under terrible conditions, and took the resources out.

America isn't great because of miles of open prairies. It's great because people broke their backs to bust the sod and grow food.

America isn't great because of a few industrial geniuses. It's great because of the thousands of others who fired the furnaces and forged the metal.

And America isn't great because of a piece of paper called a Constitution. It's great because people fought, and bled, and sometimes died to fulfill its promise of a just and humane society.

So, the Lady remembers, if sometimes we forget. She remembers who we are and where we came from.

We're all her children . . . whether she saw our people arrive on those ships from Europe . . . or whether they came on the Mayflower . . . or from Africa in chains . . . or from the Far East or Latin America.

She is a special lady to all of us, and we honor her tonight . . . because she remembers, and because she helps all of us remember . . . just what kind of people we are.

Thank you.

Contributors

MATTHEW W. SEEGER holds a Ph.D. from Indiana University and is currently associate professor and director of graduate studies in the department of communication at Wayne State University in Detroit. He has authored several articles about Lee Iacocca's public communication. He has research interests in crisis communication and communication ethics and has published in the *Journal of Business Ethics, Central States Speech Journal, Southern Journal of Speech Communication*, and the *International Management Journal*.

CARL BOTAN received his Ph.D. from Wayne State University in organizational communication and has taught at Western Illinois University and at Rutgers University. Today he teaches at Purdue University. Before receiving his Ph.D., he worked on the Chrysler assembly line. He has written extensively about public relations, organizational communication, and research methods. He is coeditor of the book *Public Relations Theory* and coauthor of *Investigating Communication: An Introduction to Research Methods*.

GAUT RAGSDALE is an associate professor in the communications department at Northern Kentucky University, where he serves as coordinator of the speech unit. He has a long-standing interest in business communication and has studied and written about issues related to corporate shareholder meetings and corporate governance. He is also a practicing and certified parliamentarian.

327

Contributors

TIMOTHY L. SELLNOW, Ph.D., is an associate professor of communication at North Dakota State University. His teaching and research focuses on the rhetorical aspects of political communication and organizational communication with an emphasis on communication during crisis situations.

JACK KAY is professor and chair of the department of communication at Wayne State University. His research interests are eclectic, including work on political communication, rhetoric and race, extremists groups, and political debate. He is coauthor of *Argumentation, Inquiry and Advocacy*.

JUDITH HOOVER received her Ph.D. from Indiana University in 1983 and currently is an associate professor at Western Kentucky University. She has published articles on rhetorical theory and criticism in the *Southern Quarterly*, the *Journal of Popular Film and Television*, and *Southern Speech Communication Journal*, and has recently published a chapter in *Martin Luther King, Jr., and the Sermonic Power of Public Discourse*.

JERRY TARVER is professor of speech communication at the University of Richmond in Virginia. He is author of *The Corporate Speech Writer's Handbook* and frequently conducts workshops for corporate and government writers in the United States and abroad.

RONALD L. LEE is an associate professor of communication studies at the University of Nebraska-Lincoln. His work has appeared in the *Quarterly Journal of Speech*, *Western Journal of Communication*, *Southern Communication Journal*, and *Communication Studies*. He is coauthoring a book on the rhetorical construction of presidential legacies.

GUSTAV W. FRIEDRICH is professor of communication at the University of Oklahoma. His research and teaching interests include communication education and communication training and development. He is former president of the Speech Communication Association. He is coauthor of the text *Strategic Communication in Business and the Professions*.

JOHN J. MAKAY is professor and chair of the department of interpersonal and public communication at Bowling Green State University. His research interests include the rhetorical construction of the American Dream, history of public address, and speeches of special occasions. He is the author or coauthor of several books, including *Public Speaking Theory into Practice*.

Index